LOOKING BACK ON THE REAGAN PRESIDENCY

Looking Back on the Reagan Presidency

EDITED BY LARRY BERMAN

The Johns Hopkins University Press
Baltimore and London

© 1990 The Johns Hopkins University Press
All rights reserved
Printed in the United States of America

The Johns Hopkins University Press
701 West 40th Street, Baltimore, Maryland 21211
The Johns Hopkins Press Ltd., London

The paper used in this publication meets the minimum requirements
of American National Standard for Information Sciences—Permanence
of Paper for Printed Library Materials, ANSI Z39.48-1984.

Library of Congress Cataloging-in-Publication Data
Looking back on the Reagan presidency / edited by Larry Berman.
     p.   cm.
   Papers of a conference held at the Intitute of Governmental Affairs at the
University of California, Davis, in May 1988.
   Includes bibliographical references.
   ISBN 0-8018-3921-1 (alk. paper). — ISBN 0-8018-3922-X (pbk. : alk. paper)
   1. United States—Politics and government—1981–1989—Congresses.
   2. United States—Foreign relations—1981–1989—Congresses.   3. United
States—Economic policy—1981– —Congresses. 4. Reagan, Ronald—
Congresses. I. Berman, Larry. II. University of California, Davis.
Institute of Governmental Affairs.
E876.L66 1990
  973.927—dc20   **89-39972 CIP**

FOR FRED I. GREENSTEIN

Contents

Preface

Looking back on the legacy or impact of an incumbent American president can be hazardous to one's mental health. Legacies tend to be malleable and changeable; impacts vary in their depth and focus. History has a way of redefining the contribution of a presidency as well as the skill with which a president exercised his leadership. Moreover, a president's final consequence is frequently shaped by factors well beyond his control—the decisions made by the next occupant of the Oval Office can do much to institutionalize or neutralize change.

The debate on the lasting impact of Ronald Wilson Reagan's administration is well under way. In May 1988, the Institute of Governmental Affairs at the University of California, Davis, hosted a three-day conference on the legacy of the Reagan presidency. The meeting brought together scholars, journalists, a former president, and administration officials. As Thomas E. Mann, director of the governmental studies program at The Brookings Institution, noted when convening the conference, the characteristics of the Reagan impact include a detachment from policy; an ideologically derived commitment to specific policy priorities; and the captivating, disarming personality of the man himself. These characteristics are borne out by this volume's contributors. These nineteen scholars review the Reagan administration's impact in four areas: foreign policy, economic and fiscal policy, institutional changes, and electoral and congressional relations.

Foreign Policy

Robert A. Pastor focuses on Reagan's paradoxical legacy in Latin America: increasing American militancy in areas of trade, debt, Nicaragua, and the war on drugs stands juxtaposed to regional democratization. Robert J. Lieber gives President Reagan mixed marks for his Middle East policies, but the policy debacle in Lebanon and the sale of arms to Iran decrease Reagan's influence and policy success. Condoleezza Rice evaluates U.S.-Soviet relations and argues that contrary to conventional wisdom, the Reagan administration was consistent in its dealings with Moscow. In fact, the agenda Reagan identified in 1981 when he first took office—human rights, cultural and scientific exchange, regional conflicts, and arms control—still dominates the political discussion after he has left office.

Economic and Fiscal Policy

Steven M. Sheffrin reviews the modification of monetary and fiscal policies during the Reagan years. He notes especially two conclusions: the Gramm-Rudman bill and monetary targeting responded to the economic crisis inherited in the early 1980s; and the Reagan administration limited discretionary economic choice by using constitutional rules to solve economic problems. M. Stephen Weatherford and Lorraine M. McDonnell demonstrate that Reagan's economic policy combined ideology with a successful leadership style. Favorable political circumstances—Jimmy Carter's unpopularity, a lack of cohesion within the Democratic party, a strengthened dollar, and sizable foreign investment—created opportunities for Reagan in the economic and fiscal realm. Reagan changed public philosophy regarding government's role in redistributing income and equalizing economic opportunity. Charles E. McLure Jr. analyzes President Reagan's tax policy, considered to be his most important legacy. Yet, as McLure observes, given the burgeoning budget deficit, "it would be ironic indeed if part of the Reagan legacy were the economic and political forces that would lead to introduction of a national sales tax."

Institutional Change

Joel D. Aberbach, Bert A. Rockman, and Robert M. Copeland offer a comparative analysis of the federal bureaucracy under Presidents Nixon and Reagan. They find an ideological move to the right since Nixon, but policy rifts between the president and careerists still remain. Reagan's systematic selection methods, his six years of governance with a Republican Senate, and his large electoral victories minimized strong clashes over policy implementation. Richard P. Nathan analyzes the institutional powers of the presidency under Reagan and differs with those who believe that the presidency as a branch of government is in need of fundamental change. Walter F. Murphy discusses Reagan's judicial appointments and finds that although there may be no immediate judicial revolution, Reagan's Supreme Court appointments portend major changes in governmental authority and individual rights.

Electoral and Congressional Relations

Benjamin Ginsberg and Martin Shefter study the deadlock within the electoral arena. No electoral realignment took place under Reagan's stewardship. Each party attempted to strengthen the institution to which it was allied: the Democrats to Congress, the Republicans to the presidency. Each party sought to dominate the other in the institutional arena. Gary C. Jacobson argues that election results mirror the mutually exclusive policy preferences that voters express to government: presidents pursue broad national interests; members of Congress are more particularistic. The result is sophisticated split-party voting in which voters are acutely aware of the criteria used in selecting a Democratic Congress and a Republican president. Reagan's conflicts with Congress reflected the rational, interest-oriented rift played out in the institutions of government. David Brady and Morris P. Fiorina ask why Reagan did not build an enduring political legacy. They show that although Reagan made a difference in defense spending, the tax system, and the federal deficit, he had little impact upon long-term Republican support for these issues.

Postscript

In evaluating the Reagan administration as a whole, Richard E. Neustadt reminds us that Reagan served neither during war nor depression. Therefore, Reagan may have to be judged by criteria different from those for presidents serving in times of national crisis. Indeed, future circumstances such as the continuing deficit, Gorbachev's Soviet Union, the Iran-contra legal proceedings, and other high-profile issues will all have an impact on how we understand the Reagan impact upon American government.

Acknowledgments

Funding for the conference, The Legacy of the Reagan Presidency, was made possible by the Lynde and Harry Bradley Foundation, the John M. Olin Foundation, and the Smith Richardson Foundation.

Alan Olmstead, Director of the Institute of Governmental Affairs at the University of California, Davis, provided his advice, resources, and energy. I was assisted by two exceptional graduate research assistants, Linda Norman and Scott Hill.

I am grateful to Henry Tom for his initial interest and subsequent commitment to this volume. Marge Nelson did an outstanding job as copyeditor.

The book is dedicated to Professor Fred I. Greenstein. In 1973 I entered Princeton's graduate program where Fred helped formulate my ideas for studying the modern American presidency. The student-mentor relationship later matured into collaborators and friends. I've treasured our relationship, and I'm very pleased to dedicate this volume to a scholar, teacher, and friend.

Contributors

JOEL D. ABERBACH is professor of political science at the University of California, Los Angeles. His publications include *Bureaucrats and Politicians in Western Democracies* (with Robert D. Putnam and Bert A. Rockman).

LARRY BERMAN is professor and chair of political science at the University of California, Davis. His publications include *The New American Presidency; Planning A Tragedy: The Americanization of the War in Vietnam,* and *Lyndon Johnson's War.*

DAVID BRADY is professor of political science, Graduate School of Business and Political Science, Stanford University. His publications include *Critical Elections and Congressional Policy Making* and *American Public Policy in the 1980s* (with J. Anderson and C. Bullock).

MORRIS P. FIORINA is professor of government at Harvard University. His publications include *The Personal Vote: Constituency Service and Electoral Independence* (with John Cain and John Ferejohn) and *Congress: Keystone of the Washington Establishment.*

BENJAMIN GINSBERG is professor of government at Cornell University. His publications include *Politics By Other Means* (with Martin Shefter) and *The Captive Public: How Mass Opinion Promotes State Power.*

GARY C. JACOBSON is professor of political science at the University of California, San Diego. His publications include *The Politics of Congressional Elections* and *Money in Congressional Elections.*

ROBERT J. LIEBER is professor of government at Georgetown University. His recent publications include *No Common Power: Understand-*

ing International Relations. He is also coeditor (with Kenneth Oye and Donald Rothchild) of *Eagle Resurgent?: The Reagan Era in American Foreign Policy.*

THOMAS E. MANN is the director of the Governmental Studies Program at the Brookings Institution. His publications include *Unsafe At Any Margin: Interpreting Congressional Elections* and *The American Elections of 1982* (with Norman Ornstein).

LORRAINE M. MCDONNELL is a senior political scientist at the RAND Corporation. She is coauthor (with M. Stephen Weatherford) of the forthcoming book *The Presidency and Macroeconomic Policy.*

CHARLES E. MCLURE JR. is a senior fellow at the Hoover Institution at Stanford University. Professor McLure served as Deputy Assistant Secretary of the Treasury for Tax Analysis from 1983 to 1985. In that capacity, he had primary responsibility for development of "tax reform for fairness, simplicity, and economic growth," the tax reform proposals that became the basis of the Tax Reform Act of 1986.

WALTER F. MURPHY is McCormick Professor of Jurisprudence at Princeton University and Vice President of the American Political Science Association. His publications include *Elements of Judicial Strategy* and *The Study of Public Law* (with Joseph Tannenhaus) as well as three novels.

RICHARD P. NATHAN is provost of the Rockefeller College of Public Affairs and Policy and Director of the Rockefeller Institute of Government. His publications include *Reagan and the States* and *The Administrative Presidency.*

RICHARD E. NEUSTADT is Douglas Dillon Professor of Government, John F. Kennedy School of Government, Harvard University. His publications include *Presidential Power* and *Thinking in Time* (with Ernest May).

ROBERT A. PASTOR is professor of political science at Emory University. He served as director of Latin American and Caribbean affairs on the National Security Council from 1977 to 1981. His publications include *Condemned to Repetition: The United States and Nicaragua* and *Congress and the Politics of U.S. Foreign Economic Policy.*

CONDOLEEZZA RICE was associate professor of political science at Stanford University when this article was written. She is now director for Soviet and East German affairs for the National Security Council staff. The views here are solely her own.

BERT A. ROCKMAN is senior research scholar at the Brookings Institution and professor of political science and research, University Center for International Studies, University of Pittsburgh. His publications include *The Leadership Question: The Presidency and the American System.*

STEVEN M. SHEFFRIN is professor and chair of the economics department at the University of California, Davis. He is the author of *Rational Expectations* and coauthor of *Macroeconomic Theory and Policy.*

MARTIN SHEFTER is professor of government at Cornell University. His publications include *Politics By Other Means* (with Benjamin Ginsberg) and *Political Crisis / Fiscal Crisis: The Collapse and Revival of New York City.*

M. STEPHEN WEATHERFORD is professor of political science at the University of California, Santa Barbara. He is coauthor (with Lorraine M. McDonnell) of the forthcoming book *The Presidency and Macroeconomic Policy.*

PART ONE

The Legacy of the Reagan Years

Looking Back on the Reagan Presidency

LARRY BERMAN

I begin from the premise that no president since Franklin D. Roosevelt had a greater impact on the American political system than did Ronald Reagan. When President Reagan left office in January 1989, 68 percent of the American people approved of his overall job performance, 71 percent approved of his handling of foreign relations, and 62 percent gave approval to his handling of the economy.[1] After eight years in office, Ronald Reagan had succeeded in redefining the parameters and the vocabulary of political discourse in America. However diffuse Reaganism may have been philosophically, eight years of Reagan rhetoric and budgetary decisions took from the Democratic party its Rooseveltian rationale for expanding the scope of government services. The Democrats of 1989 and 1990 sound a bit more Republican than they did in 1980 or 1984.

That there was any Reagan impact within a political context of divided party control of government attests to the President's leadership skill, particularly in the first two years of the first term. The political opposition controlled at least one house of Congress for the duration of his presidency. Moreover, in completing two terms, Reagan demonstrated that the demands of the presidency need not engulf the occupant of 1600 Pennsylvania Avenue. He was, above all else, psychologically suited for the job—which raises some rather ironic issues with respect to the presidential job description.

Reducing marginal tax rates to 33 percent (28 percent at the top of the income scale) and altering the corporate income scale from 46 percent to 34 percent, the abatement of inflation, the reduction of unemployment, and tax simplification constitute significant changes. The nation's fortieth president presided over the longest peacetime economic expansion in history. Yet, the Reagan tax cuts and defense spending transformed the United States into the world's biggest debtor. A conservative Republican president submitted a 1.15 trillion dollar federal budget to Congress for fiscal year 1990. The fundamental paradox of the Reagan years appears to have been the ways in which actions belied words—and so few American citizens seemed to care.

In foreign affairs, the Intermediate Nuclear Forces (INF) treaty, the Moscow summit, and the Reagan-Gorbachev relationship placed Ronald Reagan in the role of "peacemaker"—a man who once described his Soviet adversaries as an "evil empire." The Strategic Defense Initiative (SDI), Star Wars, engendered great debate, and by 1988 over 12 billion dollars had been committed to the SDI program. Reagan did not get all he wanted, but the program was on the table as a potential bargaining chip. The Reagan doctrine of aiding anticommunist freedom fighters and replacing communist regimes with democratic ones found success and failure. Reagan's tough-line policy, which included selling Stinger missiles to the rebels, hastened the Soviet retreat from Afghanistan. The Reagan legacy in Central America is mixed, and the Iran-contra initiative should bring only an inheritance of chagrin, if not shame. Reagan's fixation on the contras as freedom fighters left unresolved such issues as the serious international debt crisis. From Nicaragua to El Salvador to Panama, the Reagan bequest remains tenuous and in the case of Manuel Antonio Noriega and the administration's antidrug crusade, embarrassing.

A Legacy of Paradoxes: Ideology Confronts Pragmatism

In an imperfect world, where the constraints on U.S. presidents are manifest, Ronald Reagan navigated fairly well. There is a puzzle to Reagan's leadership which is not easily resolved. In one sense, Reagan left an invaluable blueprint to his successors: a president with a carefully defined policy agenda could achieve success by using the persuasive and command powers of the presidency. In his assessment of the Reagan legacy, columnist George Will noted that Reagan understood "the economy of leadership—the husbandry of the perishable hold any president has on the attention of his complacent, inattentive nation. He knows it is necessary to have a few priorities, a few themes. He knows how often—again, the peculiar patience of politics—you must repeat them when building a following. He knows what Dr. Johnson knew—that people more often need to be reminded than informed."[2]

On the other hand, Ronald Reagan left behind a shattered blueprint for managing and organizing the presidency. The Reagan style was one of detachment from White House staff operations, a disinclination to sustain the cerebral combat of press conferences, verbal gaffes, inattentiveness to facts, and more than a casual interest in astrology. Several former staff assistants later drew devastating portraits of life inside the White House.

When it comes to the Reagan legacy, the President was and was not there. His lax management style and detachment from details were hardly the fodder for emulation in transition paper recommendations to President Bush. According to former Budget Director David Stockman, "Ronald Reagan seemed as far above the detail work of supply side as a ceremonial monarch is above politics."[3] The President's lack of intellectual curiosity created an impression of leadership by allegory and anecdote. He often joked, "It's true hard work never killed anybody, but I figure, why take the chance?" The mangling of facts was often a cause for embarrassment but of no consequence. Reagan identified President Samuel Doe of Liberia as "Chairman Moe." He introduced Sugar Ray Leonard and his wife as "Sugar Ray and Mrs. Ray." He failed to recognize his secretary of Housing and Urban Development, Samuel Pierce, and called him "Mayor."

Indeed, the most perplexing aspect of the Reagan presidency are the paradoxes under which Reagan governed, survived politically, and maintained a sustainable base of public support. For a president who made such a discernible impact, Ronald Reagan never articulated a sense of national purpose, no New Deal, no Fair Deal, no twenty-one-point plan for America. Instead, "Dr. Feelgood"[4] left a majority of Americans feeling better off in 1988 than they had felt eight years earlier. In his farewell address to the American people, Reagan described this legacy as a national rediscovery. "They called it the Reagan Revolution, and I'll accept that, but for me it always seemed more like the Great Rediscovery: a rediscovery of our values and our common sense."

Reagan left behind neither a permanent Republican majority nor a stronger Republican party nationally and no apparatus to extend the so-called "Reagan Revolution." There was no Rooseveltian-like electoral realignment. On inauguration day 1981, Republicans numbered 53 in the Senate and 192 in the House. The 1984 election brought a massive 49 state reelection victory for Ronald Reagan and a resounding defeat of the liberal Democratic ticket of Mondale and Ferraro. By 1988, however, Republicans numbered only 46 in the Senate (where the Democrats held a 54 majority); and in the House of Representatives, Republican strength plummeted to 178.

Ronald Reagan did not leave behind a legacy of conservatism as a philosophy of government as distinct from "Dr. Feelgood," the President. The most conservative ideologue ever elected to the presidency left behind ambiguities on the meaning of conservatism whose litmus test traditionally included adherence to (1) balanced budgets; (2) smaller government; (3) respect for law; (4) strong defense; and (5) tough standards toward the Soviet Union and international terrorism. To coin a popular campaign phrase, "Where was Ronald Reagan?" The essence of this ambiguity was captured by conservative spokesman William Buckley, Jr. "The historical record is more ambiguous. Here is what conservatives will need to reflect upon in the next year or two. The most important posthumous event of the Reagan administration is the apparent baptism of the Gorbachev regime. The 'evil empire' about which King Ron told us was quite another empire."[5] Conservative columnist Jeffrey Hart wrote, "nor has Reagan accomplished many of the things conservatives expected of him in 1980. He has not laid a finger on farm subsidies, or on utterly wasteful programs such as Amtrak subsidies, the Small Business Administration, and the Economic Development Administration—just to name a few."[6]

Few political leaders could have escaped as unscathed from the Iran-contra imbroglio. Americans asked "Where was George [Bush]?" during the key decisions of trading arms to international terrorists [Murder Inc.] for the release of hostages and then diverting profits to the contras. Few seemed to care "Where was Reagan?" The President's detachment provided a satisfactory explanation.

Ronald Reagan left behind an expanded rather than a diminished public appetite for government programs. The Reagan Revolution leaves behind a Department of Energy, Veterans Affairs, and Education. In his 1981 inaugural address, the new President declared that "Government is not the solution to our problem; government is the problem." Yet, even though domestic discretionary government was most definitely seen as the problem, Ronald Reagan signed the social security trust fund bailout of 1983—a tax increase on the working income of the middle class. It was also Ronald Reagan who signed the drought-relief bill of 1988 and added catastrophic health insurance to Medicare.

Finally, there is a limited legacy in the government's role in new problems of child care, AIDS research, and the homeless—all of which have become items on the Republican as well as Democratic agenda. As Newt Gingrich, Republican representative from Georgia, explained, "Just saying no wasn't enough. To truly govern America, you have to post a model of how to govern America."[7]

The federal budget during the Reagan years offers a picture of contradiction. Under the Reagan watch, the size of the federal deficit soared, the civilian work force increased, and government spending rose to over a trillion dollars (an increase of $321 billion). Cuts in discretionary domestic spending from 5.7 percent of the gross national product in 1981 to 3.7 percent in 1987 focused heavily on the poor. Education and training, community development, welfare, nutrition, housing assistance, and antipoverty programs were cut the most. According to Rudolph Penner, former director of the Congressional Budget Office, "I'm struck by the paradoxes. It's a record of both incredible accomplishment and colossal failure." Harvard economist, Professor Lawrence Summers, believes that "the Reagan budgets will influence the government for the rest of this century. Just as the Great Society left an imprint of Federal commitment to help the indigent and equality of opportunity, the Reagan budget deficits will leave an imprint of non-involvement."[8]

A Choreographed Presidency

How can we explain these paradoxes as a source of political survival? Ronald Reagan personifies the prominence of public relations symbols as a tool of presidential governing. In many respects, Ronald Reagan's chosen profession as an actor was perfectly suited for the task of governing with symbols. Reagan was at his best and people perceived him at his best when he was performing—delivering a rousing speech or providing the right words of sympathy as he did at the funeral for the Challenger crew. Reagan as performer in the job of presidential chief of state had no equal. No one enjoyed playing the part more than Reagan. Following the 1980 San Francisco debate with Jimmy Carter, for example, Reagan was asked, "Governor, weren't you intimidated by being up there on stage with the President of the United States?" "No," responded Reagan, "I've been on the same stage with John Wayne."[9]

I do not want to be misunderstood. Reagan is a performer with *beliefs*—intense convictions on issues that are presented as *USA Today* or *Reader's Digest* headlines. He was truly the "Great Communicator" because what he had to communicate were bumper sticker slogans with resonance for the general public: taxes are bad, communists are bad, bureaucrats are bad, liberals are bad, abortion is bad, individualism is good, prayer is good, the flag is good, God is good, morality is good, the family is good, balanced budgets are good. Reagan echoed this theme in his farewell message, noting that he was proudest of the resurgence in national pride and the new patriotism in America. "All great change in America begins at the dinner table," explained President Reagan. "So tomorrow night in the kitchen I hope the talking begins. And children, if your parents haven't been teaching you what it means to be an American—let 'em know and nail 'em on it. That would be a very American thing to do."

Reagan's media strategists understood that they could sell this message because their messenger was perfect. Governing was to involve the presentation of image—not of the self but a projection. The Reagan team possessed a sophisticated understanding of the power of *images* in a television age. Their pictures were better than the real thing. When the first clips for Reagan's 1984 reelection campaign were ready to be previewed, a surprise visitor stopped by. "I understand you're all here selling soap," said Ronald Reagan, "so I thought you'd like to see the bar." Reagan actually cried when he previewed the masterpiece effort—an eighteen-minute film that would later be used to introduce him at the convention. "I don't think I'm supposed to cry," said Reagan as he watched himself eulogizing the men who fell on D-Day.[10]

Ronald Reagan's skill at communicating enabled him to accomplish two goals of political leadership: dispense a message, and disarm critics. Ronald Reagan was regularly referred to as "the Gipper," and President Reagan frequently referred to himself that way, as the Gipper was his most memorable movie role. At the 1988 Republican National Convention, Reagan exhorted George Bush to "go out there and win one more for the Gipper." Richard Neustadt reports that the quotation marks that surround "Gipper" were removed from stories on Reagan. *He became the Gipper.* Anthony Dolan, White House director of speechwriting and deputy assistant to President Reagan, writing in the *New York Times* under the title, "Don't Count the Gipper Out," explained that "Mr. Reagan is again moving with the steady self-assurance that is more often the stuff of literature than politics: in, for example, the inescapable Jay Gatsby, F. Scott Fitzgerald's symbol of American optimism, 'alive to the heightened sensitivies of life,' capable of 'an unbroken series of graceful gestures.' Ronald Reagan is at it again and may once again leave all of us—staff geniuses, media gurus, Capitol Hill seers—gasping, reminded once again that we have always been Nick Caraways to his Gatsby, left to marvel with Fitzgerald's narrator: 'He had an extraordinary gift for hope, a romantic readiness such as I have never found in any other person—and which is not likely I will ever find again.' "[11]

The result of this choreography has been a restoration of the presidency to its place of preeminence in the hearts and minds of most Americans. Reagan drew on his tremendous communicative skills for popular support, using television as a component of his leadership style, to arouse the emotions of the people. Polls showed that Reagan made it possible for Americans to hold up their President and to feel good about basic American values. Citizens admired Ronald Reagan, in part, for surviving an assassination attempt and for his courageous battle against colon cancer but even more because they viewed him as he had been choreographed—chopping wood, riding horses, "gipperizing" the landscape. Ronald Reagan personified the American dream. David Gergen, communications director for Ronald Reagan from 1981 until 1984, observed, "over time, he [Reagan] converted much of the country to his own views and values. . . . His more important legacy is in how much he changed our minds."[12] What Ronald Reagan really changed were our images. In Reagan's own words, "I've always thought of myself as a citizen politician, speaking up for the ideas and values and common sense of everyday Americans. That's what I've always tried to do, and maybe that's what it is they like."[13]

The Economy: The Image Starts Early and Lasts Long

Choreography and imagery can go only so far; Ronald Reagan needed policies that worked. Flash back in time to 1980. In a three-man race among Jimmy Carter, Ronald Reagan, and John Anderson, the former California governor carried 44 states, 489 electoral votes, and 51 percent of the popular vote. For the first time since 1953–55, the Republicans held the majority of Senate seats. Several liberal Senators were defeated in the Reagan tide. Thirty-three new Republican House members (the greatest increase since 1920) arrived on Reagan's coattails, but the Democrats retained control of the House.

Did the Reagan victory constitute a vote of no confidence in Jimmy Carter? A repudiation of liberal policies since FDR? A national injunction for a new conservative majority? The election looked like a landslide, and Reagan defined his victory as a national mandate. However, looks were deceiving: Reagan's 51 percent of the three-way vote was a mere 2 percent increase over Gerald Ford's 1976 total.

Reagan strategists were keenly aware that they were outsiders who had run against Washington. Reagan believed that once in Washington, it no longer paid to overemphasize this outsider status. Now, after all, he *was* Washington. For all his partisan rhetoric, Ronald Reagan proved himself remarkably accommodating when necessary. Reagan included House leader Tip O'Neill in a variety of functions, most notably White

House dinners and an invitation to the President's seventieth-birthday party.

Reagan strategists also realized that getting off on the right foot was absolutely crucial. Here Reagan's strategic legacy will be valuable to his successors. "How we begin will significantly determine how we govern" became the organizing theme. Reagan had been elected because a majority of Americans was disenchanted with the direction of the country. Reagan was expected to restructure and redirect public policy.

Beginning with his January 20, 1981, inaugural address, President Reagan made economic recovery the focus of his presidency. Double-digit interest rates, inflation, and high unemployment characterized the economic situation of the day. Reagan won the election with support from conservative Democrats and Republicans for a social agenda that included opposition to abortion and to school busing for desegregation and support for school prayer and anticrime legislation. Yet Reagan decided not to push the social agenda, focusing instead on economic recovery.

Reagan's economic program required Congress to make choices dramatically different from those of the past thirty years. The new President recognized that he needed the support of a group of conservative House Democrats known as the boll weevils. Reagan catered to the boll weevils with trips to Camp David, presidential cuff links, tickets to the Washington Redskins football games, or the presidential box at the Kennedy Center. In a bold step he promised members of this group that if they supported his economic package, the White House and conservative Political Action Committees (PACs) would not target them in the 1982 midterm elections.[14]

At the center of Reagan's economic package were $700 billion in program cuts, $50 billion in tax cuts, and a three-year, 27 percent increase in defense spending. The premise of the administration's supply-side economics was that reducing federal spending and cutting taxes would stimulate the economy. The supply-side theory argued that added tax savings would be invested by upper-income people, who benefited most from the tax act. This investment would trigger productivity, increase employment, decrease welfare, and lead to an increased income base for taxation and somewhere down the road, a balanced budget with reduced interest and inflation rates. David Stockman, director of the Office of Management and Budget (OMB) and point man for the economic program, later admitted that this tax cut was a Trojan horse to help the rich: "None of us really understand what's going on with these numbers."[15]

President Reagan's legislative success was linked to this early strategic control of the agenda. Recognizing that Congress would be willing to vote for significant policy shifts only if a popular mandate appeared to exist, Reagan declared he had a public directive to cut federal spending and thus bring down the tax rate. The use of reconciliation was a brilliant strategy by Reagan and David Stockman, who understood how the procedural requirements could be utilized. The 1974 Budget Act had created reconciliation procedures that allowed House and Senate committees to change legislation to conform with the second concurrent resolution. In 1981, reconciliation was used for the first concurrent resolution. The respective House and Senate budget committees could package every proposed budget cut made by the authorizing committee into a single bill. Congress was asked to choose from a relatively few number of items. Each house cast an up or down vote on the whole package.

Ronald Reagan presided over a fundamental alteration of domestic priorities and political dialogue in America. Domestic discretionary spending was no longer the *modus operandi*. Reagan's policies changed the basic context of debate over government's role in solving domestic problems. "Not since 1932," observed John Palmer and Isabel Sawhill, "has there been such a redirection of public purpose."[16] Democrats insisted that the tax burden for the average citizen had increased as a result of the supply-side tax cut. As inflation pushed people into higher brackets and devalued fixed deductions, taxpayers were really not better off. A 1985 Brookings Institution study found that only for the most affluent fifth of the nation did the portion of family income going to federal income tax between 1980 and 1985 shrink. For middle- and lower-income taxpayers it increased.[17]

Perhaps the most embarrassing legacy for a conservative administration is the size of the federal deficit and its effect on future generations. The supply-siders were dead wrong. Tax cuts did not pay for themselves. Presidential supporter and conservative columnist George Will bemoaned this situation. "In domestic affairs, meaning primarily economic management, Reagan is not recognizably conservative . . . and he has presided over a debilitating feast as the nation has eaten much of its seed corn. . . . The middle six budgets tell Reagan's story. Those budgets produced deficits totalling $1.1 trillion. The budgets Reagan sent to Congress *proposed* 13/14ths of that total. Congress added a piddling of $90 billion, just $15 billion a year."[18]

Tactics of Governing

Ronald Reagan utilized the prerogative powers of the presidency. In August 1981, Reagan fired 11,500 air traffic controllers and decertified their union on the ground that strikes by federal employees were illegal. Later he kept a campaign promise to end the grain embargo with the Soviets (imposed by Carter as a sanction after the Soviet invasion of Afghanistan) and, to the consternation of conservatives, began subsidized trade with the Soviets. Reagan's dramatic appeal for popular and congressional support on the sale of AWAC airplanes to the Saudi Arabians was absolutely critical in the final tally on that measure.

The administration utilized executive office units to enforce a fixed and limited policy agenda. Reagan conceived of governance in political terms. The problem in governing was to achieve a political objective that could be described generically as "retrenchment in government."[19] The Reagan administration's tactics were fairly successful in controlling operations of the federal bureaucracy. The key to "Reaganizing" the bureaucracy rested in the subcabinet political officials who oversaw the day-to-day activities of their departments and agencies and reported to a politically responsive White House.

Learning from Carter's failures, Reagan did not allow Cabinet secretaries to choose their own staffs (although later he did authorize Secretary of Defense Weinberger and Secretary of State Shultz to do so). Prospective officials were screened to identify those who would be most partisan and loyal to the President's ideological goals. "With heavy emphasis on ideology and loyalty," observed Terry Moe, "the appointment power has been put to systematic use in infiltrating the bureaucracy as a means of promoting political responsiveness [and] changing bureaucratic decision criteria from within."[20]

In facing a hostile Congress, Reagan found the threat of using his veto most useful. "Make my day" was his answer to a Congress that was moving toward recommending tax increases: "Let them be forewarned, no matter how well intentioned they might be, no matter what their illusions may be, I have my veto pen drawn and ready for any tax increase that Congress might think of sending up. And I have only one thing to say to the tax increasers: Go ahead and make my day." Yet, in another contradiction, Ronald Reagan actually used his veto power quite sparingly and was very timid about playing this trump card.

Reagan appointed almost half of the federal judiciary, primarily with younger, solidly conservative judges who would most likely serve well beyond the 12-year average length of term for federal judges prior to

1980. In an era in which judges play an active role in many of the major controversies of American politics, this is not an insignificant achievement. Moreover, the appointment of conservative judges, including three associate justices' and the chief justice of the Supreme Court, may allow the conservative domestic policy agenda that was thwarted in Congress to be implemented by the federal judiciary over the next several decades. Key social agenda items involving abortion, affirmative action, church-state issues, and the death penalty have involved 5–4 votes. The Reagan legacy may very well extend into the next century, but that legacy is also dependent on George Bush. Three of the court's most liberal members— William Brennan Jr., Thurgood Marshall, and Harry Blackmun—are over eighty.

Iran-Contra

A private network of skilled operators set out to redirect American foreign policy on a course that contradicted the laws of the United States. The entire enterprise was an exercise in extraconstitutional activity accompanied by the familiar *mea culpa*, "our hearts were in the right place—even if laws were broken."

The inquiry revealed little accountability for covert operations, deception of Congress and the American people, a disregard for checks and balances as well as the rule of law, a reliance on private citizens to execute secret policy, and White House staffing arrangements that isolated the President while protecting him with a cloak of deniability. While the Congress may not have sent clear messages on amounts and conditions of support for the contras, this cannot justify keeping the "freedom fighters" afloat with the Ayatollah's money. Everyone knew where President Reagan stood on the question of Sandinista rule, but that hardly justified the Secord-North-McFarlane-Hakim-Poindexter axis. Witnesses before the congressional inquiry explained that the ends—the Reagan doctrine of supporting anticommunist insurgencies in which, by definition, United States national security was involved—justified the means —in this case, covert White House operations, lying to Congress, and even withholding information from the President by Admiral Poindexter in order to guarantee the President's deniability.

The diversion of funds was premised on the belief that the President—not Congress and certainly not the State Department bureaucracy—has responsibility for the national security. Robert McFarlane's note to Oliver North epitomized this mind set: "Roger Ollie. Well done— if the world only knew how many times you have kept a semblance of integrity and gumption to U.S. policy, they would make you Secretary of State. But they can't know and would complain if they did—such is the state of democracy in the late 20th century." The President should have confronted the Congress on the constitutional question of who controls foreign policy. For reasons that puzzle his staunchest supporters, the President failed to bring his case to a national debate on how Sandinista rule in Nicaragua posed a serious long-term threat to the security of the United States. The two major parties of this country might have then battled politically about what constitutes and defines national security.[21]

Iran-contra also helped reject the clean-desk management style for a president.[22] There were inherent risks in Reagan's operating style. Yet prior to 1985, the hands-off, aloof, disinterested in detail style "seemed" to produce an effective mode for governing. Iran-contra demonstrated once again that detached styles have consequences; adopt them at your own risk. What possessed Reagan to believe that government by staff, interchangeable at presidential discretion or chief of staff initiative, could serve the President's interests? It is very unlikely that Chief of Staff James Baker would have approved selling arms to the Ayatollah. Yet President Reagan gave almost no thought to the idea of switching Baker and Treasury Secretary Don Regan.

Consequences

Ronald Reagan's massive election victory in 1984 was a product of the President's own popularity as well as a state-of-the-art media campaign. With a budget of $1.8 million, Reagan strategists devised a film aimed at "slightly upscale" voters which emphasized the new pride in America. Doug Watts, the media director, wrote the voice-over for the film footage campaign ads: "Just about every place you look, things are looking up. Life is better—America's back—and people have a sense of pride they never thought they'd feel again. And so it's not surprising that just about everyone in town is thinking the same thing—now that our country is turning around, why would we ever turn back?" The television screen showed such images as black and white neighbors washing their common fence, a family carrying a new rug into their home, a tractor tilling a field.

The presentation was remarkably effective in creating a feelgood impression. This strategy possessed adverse political consequences for Reagan's second term. Ronald Reagan wanted everyone, even his political adversaries, to feel good about the economic recovery of the first term. The president's 1984 reelection package shied away from divisive foreign policy or social issues that might have detracted from a possible fifty-state electoral sweep in 1984. Unlike FDR, Ronald Reagan did not seek the anger of his political adversaries; Reagan avoided legislative confrontations. Reagan's "Morning in America" theme provided a rationale for hating no one—even Democrats. Although Reagan's achievements were real, he lost a second-term opportunity to revamp the political landscape.

Nevertheless, the imprint of Reagan's tenure runs quite deep. Among young people in particular, Ronald Reagan constitutes the litmus test for perceptions of presidential leadership. In a word-association test, Jimmy Carter is still linked with the hostages in Iran, the expansion of Soviet tyranny, high interest rates, and national malaise. Reagan is associated with curbing inflation, slashing interest rates, rebuilding America's defenses, and restoring a sense of pride and patriotism for Americans.[23]

The final public opinion polls show that President Reagan received his strongest ratings in the area of reducing the chance of nuclear war with the Soviets. This stands in striking contrast to the greatest fear about Ronald Reagan in 1981: the likelihood of precipitating a nuclear confrontation with the Soviets. The images of Ronald Reagan and Mikhail Gorbachev strolling together through Red Square in May 1988 in the bliss of *glasnost* and *perestroika* had a profound impact on the public. On the flip side, the American public faulted Reagan for his lack of success and effort in reducing poverty, for the size of budget deficits, for few environmental concerns, for a failed drug policy, and the declining quality of education in America.[24]

Looking back on the Reagan years, we see that Ronald Reagan showed that the system can still respond to directed leadership. "What had been written off only eight years ago as an impossible job," observed Stuart Eizenstadt, Jimmy Carter's domestic policy assistant, "destined to crush any mortal, has been turned around. It now appears that a mortal can handle the job and be successful."[25] A mortal who knows how to use symbols and choreograph the political landscape possibly can. Looking back and ahead, the Reagan presidency appears all the more impressive with respect to accomplishments but rather disturbing in its implications for political leadership in our republic.

NOTES

1. See "Reagan's Rating Is Best Since 40's for a President," *New York Times,* 18 January 1989.

2. George Will, "How Reagan Changed America," *Newsweek,* 9 January 1987, 15.

3. David Stockman, *The Triumph of Politics: Why the Reagan Revolution Failed* (New York: Harper and Row, 1986), and William Greider, "The Education of David Stockman," *Atlantic Monthly,* December 1981, 221.

4. See F. Stephen Larrabee, "Is There Life after Dr. Feelgood?" *New York Times,* 10 January 1988.

5. William Buckley, Jr., "The Historical Record Is More Ambiguous" (Copyright 1988, Universal Press Syndicate).

6. Jeffrey Hart, "Reagan Accomplished a Great Deal" (Copyright 1989, King Features Syndicate, Inc.).

7. Quoted in *U.S. News and World Report,* 27 August 1988.

8. Mary Cooper, "Reagan's Economic Legacy," *Editorial Research Reports* 2, no. 6 (1988). See Martin Tochin, "Paradox of Reagan Budgets Hints Contradiction in Legacy," *New York Times,* 16 February 1988; "Deficit Limits Reagan's Options in 1989 Budget," *Congressional Quarterly,* 20 February 1988.

9. I am indebted to Professor James David Barber for this anecdote and the analogy. See also "The Untold Story of Campaign '84," *Newsweek,* November/December 1984.

10. See William Henry III, *Visions of America: How We Saw the 1984 Election* (Boston: Atlantic Monthly Press, 1985).

11. Anthony Dolan, "Don't Count The Gipper Out," *New York Times,* 10 July 1987. See also Mark Hertsgaard, "How Ronald Reagan Turned News Hounds into Lap Dogs," *Washington Post National Weekly Edition,* 29 August–4 September 1988, 25.

12. David Gergen, "Ronald Reagan's Most Important Legacy," *U.S. News and World Report,* 9 January 1989, 28.

13. "Reagan's Final Rating Is Best of Any President since World War II," *New York Times,* 18 January 1989, 8.

14. James Pfiffner, "The Carter-Reagan Transition: Hitting the Ground Running," *Presidential Studies Quarterly,* Fall 1983, 628.

15. See Stockman, *The Triumph of Politics;* Greider, "The Education of David Stockman"; Michael J. Baskin, *Reagan and the Economy: The Successes, Failures, and Unfinished Agenda* (San Francisco: ICS Press, 1987); and Murray Weidenbaum, *Rendezvous With Reality: The American Economy after Reagan* (New York: Basic Books, 1988).

16. John Palmer and Isabel Sawhill, *The Reagan Experiment* (Washington, D.C.: Urban Institute Press, 1982).

17. See "Taxing Facts," *The New Republic,* 26 September 1988, 7–8.

18. Will, "How Reagan Changed America," 15.

19. See Hugh Heclo and Rudolph Penner, "Fiscal and Political Strategy in the Reagan Administration," in Fred Greenstein, ed., *The Reagan Presidency* (Baltimore: Johns Hopkins University Press, 1983), 21–47.

20. Terry Moe, "The Politicized Presidency," in John Chubb and Paul Peterson, eds., *The New Direction in American Politics* (Washington, D.C.: Brookings Institution, 1985), 235–71. See also Laurence Lynn, Jr., "The Reagan Administration and the Reticent Bureaucracy," in Lester Salamon and Michael Lund, eds., *The Reagan Presi-*

dency and the Governing of America (Washington, D.C.: Urban Institute Press, 1984), 339–80.

21. See Douglas Jeffrey, "The Iran-contra Affair and the Real Crisis of American Government," *Claremont Review of Books,* Spring 1987, 3–8.

22. I am indebted to Professor Richard Neustadt for the phrasing.

23. Susan Ayala, "First Time Voters Prefer Bush, Surveys Show, Influenced by Stamp of Reagan's Personality," *Wall Street Journal,* 23 August 1988.

24. See David Broder, "Assessing Reagan," *Washington Post,* 30 June 1988; Dom Bonafede, "Spoiled Legacy," *National Journal,* 7 March 1987; Charles Jones, *The Reagan Legacy* (Washington, D.C.: Chatham House, 1988); Sydney Blumenthal and Robert Edsall, *The Reagan Legacy* (New York: Pantheon, 1989); Sydney Blumenthal, *Our Long National Daydream: A Political Pageant of the Reagan Era* (New York: Harper and Row, 1988); David Boaz, ed., *Assessing the Reagan Years* (Washington, D.C.: CATO Institute, 1989); B. B. Kymlicka and Jean Mathews, *The Reagan Revolution?* (Homewood, Ill.: Dorsey Press, 1988); John Palmer, *Perspectives on the Reagan Years* (Washington, D.C.: Urban Institute Press, 1987); William Hyland, ed., *The Reagan Foreign Policy* (New York: New American Library, 1987).

25. David Broder, "After Reagan, the Presidency No Longer Seems an Impossible Job," *Washington Post Weekly Edition* 16–22 January 1989, 8.

2

Thinking about the Reagan Years

THOMAS E. MANN

I recall three significant events that occurred in the early days of the Reagan administration. The first began inauguration day, January 1981. Jimmy Carter and Michael Deaver have both written about these incredible circumstances under which President Jimmy Carter tried unsuccessfully to reach President-elect Ronald Reagan on the morning of the inauguration to tell him about the progress in the negotiations for the release of the hostages from Iran. As it happened, Carter had been working day and night for the seventy-two hours prior to the inauguration, keeping in touch with the complex negotiations. He was frazzled but nonetheless exuberant because he had learned that the hostages were going to be freed. Inauguration morning he placed a call to Mr. Reagan and was informed by the staff that the Governor did not wish to be disturbed. Jimmy Carter called back again and asked to speak to a ranking member of the staff; once again he received word that the Governor had left explicit instructions that under no circumstances was he to be awakened. Apparently Carter called several more times but still failed to reach Governor Reagan. The report coming from Michael Deaver and other staff was that the President-elect simply was not interested, at that stage, in the status of those negotiations. By all accounts, it was during the ride to the inauguration that Carter was finally able to tell Reagan that the hostages were about to be released. Soon thereafter, the American public was treated to the first success of the Reagan administration.

Event number two happened later that day when Reagan gave his inaugural address, in which he left no doubt what his administration would be about. "These United States," he said, "are confronted with an economic affliction of great proportions. We suffer from the longest and one of the worst sustained inflations in our national history. It distorts our economic decisions, penalizes thrift, crushes the struggling young and the fixed-income elderly alike. It threatens to shadow the lives of millions of Americans." He went on: "In this present crisis, government is not the solution to our problem; government *is* the problem. It is my intention to curb the size and influence of the federal establishment and to demand recognition of the distinction between the powers granted to the federal government and those reserved to the states or to the people."

Event number three was in the spring of 1981, shortly before the attempted assassination. President Reagan had made it clear that he intended to relax and enjoy himself in office and that he would keep to a schedule more like Dwight Eisenhower's than like Jimmy Carter's. As part of that schedule, he would reserve one morning a week for horseback riding. There was a big buildup, of course, and much promotion of his first time out to go horseback riding. It was an event that was astonishingly well choreographed. In the full view of a bank of television cameras, Reagan strode from the White House in full riding regalia. After moving through the bank of television cameras, almost as an afterthought, he glanced up at the Truman balcony from which Nancy, in a flowing white gown, waved affectionately to her Ronnie. The Reagans then proceeded to blow kisses at each other and exchange "Bye-bye dears." It was a scene repeated to millions of viewers on that evening's television news programs and to readers of the next morning's newspapers. Only a hardened cynic could avoid smiling and feeling good about the new occupants of the White House. At this early point, the Reagans demonstrated a sophisticated understanding of the power of images in the television age and an extraordinary ability to disarm critics.

The lack of interest and engagement of the private Reagan, the force and clarity of the Reagan agenda, and the storybook romanticism of the public Reagan all proved to be distinctive features of the Reagan years. We can remember countless examples of similar events illustrating the same qualities of the Reagan years. Just recently, Donald Regan revealed that as treasury secretary he never once had a substantive discussion with President Reagan on economic affairs—a disclosure that certainly speaks to the first point. We have numerous examples of President Reagan sticking to his positions on taxes, on the Strategic Defense Initiative (SDI), and on the contras. There was never a doubt during his administration of the direction and the major goals of his government. As far as the public persona is concerned, I am reminded of how in 1987 in the midst of the Iran-contra affair, President Reagan appeared before the Gridiron

Club and disarmed his critics with the following quip: "Do you remember the flap when I said the bombing begins in five minutes? Remember when I fell asleep during my audience with the Pope? Remember Bitburg? Boy, those were the good old days!"

The Reagan presidency, in many important respects, involved a detached president, a committed ideological presidency, and a captivating and disarming public persona.

The many analyses of the impact of the Reagan presidency implicitly acknowledge that it was an unusually significant presidency, bold in its ambitions and far-reaching in its effects on the lives of American citizens. The bull market in Reagan retrospectives is itself an indicator of the mark Reagan left and of the controversial nature of his tenure in Washington. However, in this analysis a few cautions are in order. First, more than with other modern presidents, where one stands on the Reagan legacy often depends on where one sits ideologically. Although this is not surprising given the unapologetic designs of the Reagan administration to advance a conservative agenda, it is nonetheless sobering to note that many of the President's harshest academic critics are liberals and many of his most ardent scholarly supporters are conservatives. Understandable? Yes. Desirable or acceptable? No.

A related point is the well-known contempt of many intellectuals for Ronald Reagan. This phenomenon is in part a function of Reagan's ideology but is also in part a function of his presidential style—his tenuous hold on facts, his detachment, his lack of curiosity, his tendency to rely again and again on simplistic anecdotes. This contempt is so pervasive that otherwise fair-minded intelligent people can find nothing of redeeming value in the man or his presidency. The distinguished economist James Tobin of Yale argued, "It was only Reagan's smooth performances on television which explain how this simplistic ideologue could have put over on the American people such fraudulent economic programs." A more measured statement came from Arthur Schlesinger, Jr.: "The administration was incoherent, incompetent, duplicitous, and dedicated to rash, mindless policy." We'll call him neutral.

Another caution: when evaluating a president there is a tendency to give him too much credit and to assess him with too much blame. Each president obviously operates within a particular context that presents him with a set of opportunities and constraints. It is more appropriate to ask how he played what was dealt him, not just what cards ended up in his hand. Reagan was dealt a strong hand. His predecessor's tenure was widely perceived as a failure. The U.S. economy suffered no external shocks during Reagan's presidency. A major leadership shift in the Soviet

Union opened new possibilities in superpower relations. What one must ask is whether Reagan took full advantage of these opportunities.

In other respects Reagan faced enormous obstacles that were not unusual in the American political system. With a permanent Democratic majority in the House, he was never in a dominant position on Capitol Hill. The well-known American system of separated institutions sharing power places enormous constraints on central direction and control. Given those constraints, how did he do?

One final caution: in the search for change there is also a tendency to miss important threads of continuity. It is easy to overlook the fact that Jimmy Carter started both the defense buildup and the domestic build-down and that the advance toward democracy in Latin America began under his watch.

Thinking about the Reagan years, one is inevitably struck by a paradox. Daniel Patrick Moynihan, political scientist and senator, has formulated a law of opposites which goes something like this: once in office, presidents are seen to do things least expected of them, often things they have explicitly promised not to do. Previous commitments or perceived inclinations act as a kind of insurance to protect against any great loss if a president acts contrary to expectations. He is given the benefit of the doubt. He cannot have *wanted* to do this, he must have *had* to do it. President Eisenhower made peace, President Kennedy went to war, President Nixon went to China. Even by these past standards, President Reagan seems to have more than mastered Moynihan's law. The prime example is, of course, the huge budget deficit that has become a permanent feature of American fiscal policy. Per the Reagan inaugural address: "But great as our tax burden is, it has not kept pace with public spending. For decades we have piled deficit upon deficit, mortgaging our future and our children's future for the temporary convenience of the present. To continue this long trend is to guarantee tremendous social, cultural, political, and economic upheavals." How can a conservative Republican president be responsible for tripling the national debt? The devil or the Congress must have done it.

The deficits are not the only irony of the Reagan presidency. Ronald Reagan, a fervent anticommunist and the man who labeled the Soviet Union the "evil empire," commended the Soviets for their progress on human rights, successfully negotiated an Intermediate Nuclear Forces (INF) agreement, and remained optimistic about completing a strategic arms agreement in the near future. Then of course there is Ronald Reagan, the man who raised his voice against terrorists and then approved the plan to trade arms for hostages. The leader whose unifying theme was "less government is better government" presided over a restoration of public confidence in government, a growing public demand for a larger governmental role in social policy, and a new social and economic policy activism in the states. Reagan might be said to have reaffirmed the Welfare State.

In spite of these departures of reality from rhetoric, it would be a serious mistake to dismiss or denigrate the rhetorical aspects of the Reagan presidency. In fact, the most distinctive features of the Reagan presidency were the clarity and durability of its broad objectives. There was no doubt what this presidency was about; and therein lies the secret of its political successes.

What of the impact of the Reagan years on policy and politics? We need to look at aspects of economic performance, of the nature and size of government, and of domestic policy, then turn our attention to national security and foreign policy, and finally consider the political impacts of the Reagan presidency and its effect on national political institutions, on public opinion, and on the party system.

Economics

With economic performance, on balance, one has a set of mixed reviews. There are some obvious successes. First, inflation was conquered during the Reagan years. One may want to give credit to Paul Volcker and the Fed, but to do so alone is inappropriate because there is no question that Volcker could not have done it without the support of President Reagan. Breaking the back of inflation was a major success. Although there was substantial pain associated with the biggest economic downturn since the Great Depression, we have had since then over six years of sustained economic recovery. Second, the reduction in marginal tax rates from 70 to 28 percent (or 33 percent, depending on how you count) was a major achievement. It was an important goal of the Reagan presidency, and it was an accomplishment that came in two doses: the initial tax cuts in 1981 and the subsequent tax reform of 1986. These cuts in the marginal tax rates are perhaps the most important and lasting legacy of this administration. Finally, the Reagan administration achieved some renewed respect for markets, for the private sector both here and abroad, and that is reflected in a host of specific initiatives but more importantly in a broad public philosophy.

There are many areas in which things are not that much different than they were in the 1970s. A prime example is real economic growth. In spite of the long recovery since the recession ended in 1983, economic growth during the 1980s is no better than it was in the 1970s, and our national savings have fallen in spite of the supply-side philosophy of the Reagan economic program. On these grounds, frankly, our economy today looks very much like it looked before.

On the debit side, there were failures, of which the budget deficits are the most striking. The deficits were a failure economically, however, they were obviously a political success if one views deficits as an instrument of government. There is no question that the deficits hurt in the long run even though not necessarily in the short run. They lead us to eat our seed corn, they put debts on our children instead of ourselves, they increase the interest burden of government which makes it impossible to do more, and indeed, forces us to do less. The budget deficits are largely responsible for the trade deficits that have moved this country from a creditor to a debtor nation.

Another failure in the Reagan era of unlimited opportunity was the condition of the underclass. The poverty rate is no lower and by some measures is actually higher than before. There are some people in this country who have been left behind. Income distribution tends to shift very very slowly over time, and to the extent that it moved at all during the Reagan years, it moved in the direction of those in the highest end of the income scale. All in all, there were some successes, some failures, and much business as usual on the grounds of economic performance.

Government

What about the size and the scope of government? Certainly that was the centerpiece of the Reagan agenda. The most important success of the Reagan years in this respect was that Reagan's government halted the growth in discretionary domestic spending. One's political preferences may be contrary to this objective, but judging Reagan on his own terms and on his desire to slow the growth of particular government programs, there is no question that the built-in bias for more programs and more spending was broken. In the early days, some programs in the social safety net were cut, but on balance most of the domestic spending reductions were made in programs controlled by iron triangles; Reagan exploded some of the classic triangles that had led to increases in government spending. He also enjoyed some modest success in moving toward further reduction in government regulations; the initial effort had begun during the Carter presidency, but it was accelerated under Reagan. There were some modest initiatives in privatization though nothing worth touting. He reduced funds to state and local governments, which is part of the halt in discretionary domestic programs, and instituted some important cost cutting and modernization of management systems in Washington, unnoticed by most people outside the beltway.

On the debit side of this dimension, Reagan's biggest failure was that government overall became bigger, not smaller, than it was when he came to office. That was obviously a function of the growth in defense spending, in interest payments, and continued growth in entitlement programs. The modest curbing of discretionary programs could not possibly balance the expansion in other parts of the federal budget. This administration failed to curb middle-class entitlement programs, and in so failing, it lost the battle to reduce the size of government.

Reagan talked about dividing responsibilities between the national government and state and local governments and about an appropriate trading of responsibilities and resources; that effort to swap was largely a failure. Reagan, by most accounts, was not as interested in swapping as much as he was in having government just get out of social and economic policy. On that score, the tremendous activism that we see now in the states on economic and social policies in education, health, and economic development is quite extraordinary. There is a renaissance of American government occurring in the states. Whether that was a failure or a success of the Reagan administration depends on whether he was serious about having the states assume an active role or whether indeed he wanted to shrink all of government. Perhaps the largest failure in terms of the size and the scope of government was that there is clearly a host of major new initiatives by the federal government in the offing. More on this later.

Domestic Policy

Reagan deserves credit for the social security reform of 1983. He may not have played an active role, but his administration worked with Congress to salvage the system and put it on a firm financial basis. Also give him credit for the Tax Reform Act of 1986, an extraordinary achievement for a so-called lame duck administration.

On the debit side of domestic policy: the social issue agenda on which Reagan campaigned was not legislated. The administration had serious setbacks in civil rights and in environmental policy. It made some early missteps, achieving little good and doing itself some political harm.

There is of course the additional matter of ethics in government. This was not the first administration to have had officials leave under a cloud, but the Reagan years saw more than a hundred of them. Ronald Reagan was probably too tolerant, too amiable, too willing to let friends get away with things and too reluctant to set a high enough standard under which his people should work.

National Security and Foreign Policy

The irony here is that Reagan was least knowledgeable and least sophisticated in the area of foreign policy, yet perhaps this will be remembered as the area of his greatest success. He achieved the defense buildup that he wanted: a $300 billion defense budget. That buildup occurred from 1981 to 1985; then it basically stopped. Nonetheless, it was a tremendous increase in defense spending, and it had been the highest priority for him.

Ronald Reagan got arms control, and he got it his way. He had to stare down his critics for six years. He faced the nuclear freeze movement. He called for a zero option in Europe and was laughed at. Under pressure here and abroad, he successfully deployed the Pershing missiles, and in the face of political opposition and ridicule, he championed SDI. One may say that those factors really did not have any part in the INF agreement and that instead changes occurring within the Soviet Union were paramount. Some may even argue that the treaty was achieved in spite of the above obstacles put up by the President: the defense buildup, the deployment of Pershing missiles, the clinging to the SDI, and the zero option. However, I believe one is hard pressed to make that case, and the President deserves substantial credit for an agreement that even though modest in quantitative terms was nonetheless very significant.

On the success side, Reagan must be credited for an extraordinary improvement in U.S.-Soviet relations. The very fact that he was criticized so severely by the political right suggests the progress he made; for example, a conservative delegation went to the White House to *protest* the withdrawal of Soviet troops from Afghanistan. Will history see this as a failure? In any number of regional conflicts—most prominently Afghanistan—in the areas of human rights and cultural exchanges, improvements with the Soviet Union have been notable and certainly not predictable during the Reagan years. Reagan would argue that all were made possible by the actions taken during the first five or six years of his administration.

Another success was the limited use of American force during the Reagan presidency. There was something attractive about the Grenada invasion. It was the American citizen's kind of war: it was in the same area code—a soldier could call home without paying too big a long distance bill—it was over within 48 hours, and the United States was able to declare victory. Given our low tolerance for sustained military activity, that was about all we Americans could take. Nonetheless, it was a selective use of force, and by many accounts—including those of many Democratic candidates for the presidential nomination—it was a success. In the same light, one might also consider the bombing of Libya.

Finally, another success of the Reagan administration was the process of democratization—the march toward free governments around the world. Cases in point are the Philippines—with a nudge from Senator Lugar of Indiana—South Korea, Argentina, El Salvador, and Guatemala. Major success: maybe; significant and noteworthy: I think so.

There were failures, of course. The biggest failure is that we are today probably more vulnerable economically than we have been at any time in our recent history. Trade deficits, our Achilles' heel over the next decade, have led to domestic political pressures that could be harmful. Arms to Iran was an abysmal fiasco. The defense bust following the boom and the incredible inefficiencies in the Defense Department are defeats. In Nicaragua, one would have to say that the contra strategy was largely a failure. Marines in Lebanon were a mistake—a mistake the President cut short, but not until lives had been lost. There was little progress in the Middle East. Is America standing taller in the world as the President had hoped? On balance, we probably are militarily, but economically, we are more vulnerable than ever before.

Politics

Our national political institutions are not operating in the same way as they were when Ronald Reagan became president. We had within the parlance of political science and the commentaries from the Committee on the Constitutional System the model of the failed presidency. Presidents go up in the public opinion ratings, they go down, and they go out. Under Reagan we saw a very different pattern of fluctuating fortunes in public opinion and a model of governance which did not require constant success. Reagan's initial victories in 1981—a story that has been told and will be analyzed again and again—established the policy and political context for the entire Reagan presidency. Subsequent legislative defeats were not major substantive and political setbacks for the President. He was ornery, he was confrontational, there were deadlocks, he lost, he had vetoes overridden, but he governed and continued to govern because his was a protective rather than an expansive domestic agenda after the first six months of his administration. All along, of course, he had continuing opportunities for foreign policy leadership.

There are many interesting trends occurring in our national political institutions. First, the centralization and politicization of the executive branch of the government were quite noteworthy beginning with the ideologically coherent personnel system. There were people assigned to critical posts throughout the government who really believed in the Reagan agenda. The Office of Management and Budget was used in a way that allowed budgetary control, regulatory review, and paperwork clearance. This gave the office of the President an opportunity to gain some control over the sprawling executive branch. Also noteworthy were the use of Cabinet councils and the adoption of the clear and polarizing agenda that let everyone in government know what the broad objectives of the Reagan administration were.

Second, a deficit-constrained Congress operated with an extraordinary number of centralizing mechanisms in an era of decentralization and fragmentation as well as with an increased partisanship in an era of weak political parties. These were remarkable developments on Capitol Hill.

Finally, of course, there was the conservative judiciary. Reagan appointed nearly half of all federal judges in this country and three Supreme Court justices in addition to naming the Chief Justice. He instituted a process of judicial selection which relied on a new, centralized process in the White House, an intensive ideological screening of judicial candidates, and a system that challenged the norms of senatorial patronage. There is no question that the Reagan cohort will be different from past cohorts on the bench. There is no judicial revolution in the making at this stage but instead a reinforcement of the trend toward judicial conservatism with the possibility of enormous change over the long term.

The major question one wants to ask about these innovations in national political institutions is this: will the conditions of the next presidency encourage the same institutional trends? I doubt it. First, we have a different set of problems; we are cleaning up some of the mess rather than reshaping the agenda. Second, we are guaranteed to have a less ideological president than the one we have had for the last eight years. How do you populate the executive branch with Bushites? I do not know what they look like.

Public Opinion

Reagan sought to change not only what the government does domestically and internationally but also to change how people think about the role of government and the mission of the United States in the world. On this score, there is good news and bad news for the Reagan presidency. Reagan reaffirmed traditional values: family, work, freedom, strength, patriotism, individual initiative, and local community. These are now routinely embraced by politicians of all stripes. Remember the flag waving at the Democratic convention? Conservative positions on such matters as welfare dependency and the preference for markets now have more credibility among elites. There is a renewed pride in this country and an optimism about the future, although both of these elements have been sullied a bit by the Iran-contra affair and the stock market crash. There is also a general feeling that more is not necessarily better when it comes to government.

At the same time, the American public is looking increasingly to the federal government to provide improved health, education, child care, and protection from nefarious business practices. Politicians in both parties are responding accordingly. In addition, the public has come to view economic challenges as a more serious threat to our national security than the Soviet Union. Support for increased defense spending has collapsed.

Finally, if a new public philosophy emerges, it is likely to be based not on Ronald Reagan's idiom but, if you will, on Pat Moynihan's—that an elected government can be the instrument, the common purpose of a free people, that government can embrace great causes and do great things. That is to say, the public philosophy of the next era will be less individualistic and more communitarian. Therefore, if the Reagan legacy rested on shifts of public opinion, it would be a fragile one. It is the budget deficits and low marginal tax rates that will provide the more enduring inheritance.

The Party System

The final aspect of the Reagan years is the party system. The greatest disappointment of the Reagan administration was the failure to achieve a realignment with the Republicans as the new majority party in this country. After the dramatic change of party control of the Senate in 1980 and the landslide election of 1984, there seemed a possibility the Republicans were on the move toward a majority, but Reagan's political success proved to be top-heavy. Two landslide presidential elections and six years of control of the Senate do not a realignment make. The Republicans remain a minority party in the House of Representatives. Divided government is the rule, not the exception, in American politics.

The fundamental structures underneath the achievements of the Reagan years were not altered.

Perhaps this standard is too demanding. Reagan did improve Republican fortunes. He helped level the playing field against the Democrats. There were measurable gains in party identification. The Republicans are seen as being more competent today than they were before Reagan came to office. The national party apparatus has improved. The Republicans are more competitive in the Senate. There are more Republican governors and state legislators. The image and posture of the Republican party have indeed changed: they do not wear green eyeshades anymore and worry about deficits; they are progrowth, optimistic, and conservative. You know what a Republican is nowadays. Importantly, there have been gains among the youngest voters which, if durable, will prove to be a critically important part of the Reagan legacy. Additionally of course there was accelerated movement of the traditional Southern Democrats toward the Republican party. However, there were clear limits to these gains. There have been some recent setbacks, and Democrats are more bullish than before.

Although Ronald Reagan dominated the 1980s and decisively shaped the policy and political struggles of the next decade, those battles are best fought by others. Subsequent presidents and Congresses cannot escape the Reagan legacy, but they may be able to manage better without him.

PART TWO

Foreign Policy

3

The Centrality of Central America

ROBERT A. PASTOR

If anyone expects just a proud recitation of the accomplishments of my administration, I say let's leave that to history.—Ronald Reagan, 1988

For the eight years of Ronald Reagan's administration, three small, poor nations in Central America—Nicaragua, El Salvador, and Panama—were at the center of U.S. policy toward Latin America. The debt crisis, the drug plague, the fragility of newly emerging democracies, the structural economic problems of the Caribbean, the opportunity of forging new relationships with the region's largest powers—these and other issues demanded the attention of the United States in the 1980s, but the administration was never diverted from its priority: to roll back communism in Nicaragua and defeat insurgency in Central America.

The administration's stiff rhetoric troubled its domestic critics and frightened Latin American friends and foes, but the results of its policies, even in Central America, were meager. Short of applying direct military force, which it did only once in the Caribbean, the administration found that threats did not overturn the Nicaraguan regime, end the Salvadoran insurgency, or expel General Manuel Antonio Noriega from Panama. Outside Central America, the administration discovered that its own debt crisis, which exceeded Latin America's in magnitude if not severity, precluded its leading an effort to find long-term solutions to the debt or drug problems.

The 1980s saw an unprecedented wave of democratization in the region, but instead of taking advantage of the opportunities that this offered the United States, the Reagan administration embarked on a unilateral and interventionist course that engendered resentment. Tragically, there was more democracy and less cooperation between the governments in the region during the Reagan era than ever before.

A Different Pivot

Central America loomed large in President Reagan's policy, but other developments were more important in bringing him to power. Hostages in Iran, the Soviet invasion of Afghanistan, the perception of a Soviet military buildup in the world, inflation, and skyrocketing oil prices—together, these events left Americans feeling that they were losing control, that they were retreating from the assaults of hostile forces and powers. No one articulated American frustration and impatience better than Ronald Reagan. His campaign for the presidency in 1980 was a continuous refrain that the United States could—and if he were elected, would—take charge of its destiny and the world's.

This sea change in American public opinion was incomprehensible in Latin America where no one questioned the power and will of the United States. Nonetheless, most in the region expected the new administration to change alliances with groups in the region. On the right, Latin American leaders were delighted with the change from Carter to Reagan; in the middle, they were fearful; and on the left, they were both anxious and relieved that their preconceptions of U.S. imperialism had come true.

The policy fulcrum of Reagan's predecessor was human rights. Jimmy Carter sought coalitions with Democrats and democratic governments and remained cool, cold, or aloof from military governments. The fulcrum of Reagan's policy was anticommunism. He sought coalitions with military governments against Marxists and initially either ignored or undermined democratic governments unwilling to support this effort.

The differences between the two administrations were most stark at the beginning of Reagan's presidency as he acted quickly to warm the chilly relationship between his predecessor and military dictators. President Reagan invited Argentine General Roberto Viola as his first Latin American visitor to the White House. When asked about the arrest by the Argentine government of three human rights activists just before the visit, State Department spokesman William Dyess criticized Carter's policy rather than Argentine repression: "We want good relations with Argentina. Any abnormality in relations is due to a large extent to the public position this country took regarding human rights practices in the country." A second reason for the new relationship was that the Argentine military agreed to work with the United States against the Sandinista government.[1]

On March 1, 1981, the administration announced its intention to improve relations with Chile by restoring normal export-import bank financing and inviting the government to participate in joint naval exercises. The United States then stopped opposing loans by the international development banks to the military governments of Argentina, Chile, Uruguay, and Paraguay. U.S. Ambassador to the United Nations Jeane Kirkpatrick visited Chile in August 1981, and at a press conference, she said that the United States would "normalize completely its relations with Chile in order to work together in a pleasant way." She refused to meet with several human rights activists, and they were arrested after her departure.[2]

Other meetings with military leaders in Guatemala, Honduras, and Panama by leading officials of the new administration were aimed at underscoring the point first made by Secretary of State Alexander Haig: "International terrorism will take the place of human rights in our concern." Haig's strategy was to repair U.S. relationships with Latin America's military governments so as to maximize pressure on Marxists and leftist governments.[3]

If the ideological pivot of the Reagan administration's policy was anticommunism, then the geographical center was Central America and the Caribbean, the region perceived as most threatened. In February 1981, the State Department released a white paper describing evidence of Soviet bloc support for the rebels in El Salvador. The administration drew a line and warned the Soviets not to cross it. "It is our view," Secretary of State Alexander Haig said about the war, "that this is an externally managed and orchestrated interventionism, and we are going to deal with it at the source." Haig wanted to impose a military blockade against Cuba, but the President rejected his plan.

CIA Director William J. Casey proposed that instead of fighting the Cubans, the United States should borrow their strategy and organize and support insurgents against the Sandinistas. In December 1981, President Reagan signed National Security Decision Directive 17 authorizing $19 million to set up a 500-man force aimed largely at the "Cuban infrastructure" in Nicaragua which was allegedly training and supplying arms to the Salvadoran guerrillas.[4] Three months later, this group—named "contras" for counterrevolutionaries—destroyed two bridges in Nicaragua. The Sandinista government responded by condemning the United States and declaring a state of emergency. Thus begun a downward spiral in which the political space in Nicaragua was systematically reduced, and the government grew more militarized and dependent on the Soviet Union and Cuba.

The Reagan administration interpreted each repressive step by the Sandinistas and each shipment of Soviet arms to them as an additional reason to support the contras. Any proposal to reduce aid to the contras was interpreted as a sign of weakness and thus opposed. Most Democrats in Congress, however, saw the problem differently. They were prepared to support a guerrilla group that interdicted arms shipments to Salvadoran rebels, but they opposed an effort that they viewed as futile to overthrow the Sandinista government. Despite massive efforts by the President to persuade Americans to support the contras, public opinion consistently opposed funding them by 2 : 1; this reinforced Congress's opposition.

President Reagan would neither defer to Congress nor alter his commitment to the contras, and thus he was compelled to devote an increasing share of his time, energy, and political capital to persuading legislators to vote for aid to the contras. This diversion of resources skewed all the policies of the administration, particularly those relating to Latin America.

In his second inaugural address, Ronald Reagan rationalized and elaborated his campaign for the contras into a universal "Reagan Doctrine." "We must not break faith," he said, placing the project on a moral plane where compromise was practically sacrilegious, "with those who are risking their lives on every continent from Afghanistan to Nicaragua to defy Soviet-supported aggression and secure rights which have been ours from birth. . . . Support for freedom fighters is self-defense." In fact, Congress and the American people distinguished between Afghan rebels, most of whom were fighting against Soviet troops and for an Islamic theocracy, and the Nicaraguan contras, who were fighting against other Nicaraguans. The United States had a fundamental interest in raising the cost of intervention to the Soviets, but few Americans felt comfortable about making war on a small country. Congress therefore pressed the administration to provide more aid to the Afghans and less to the contras.

However, once the project was consecrated a "doctrine"—indeed, his only one—Reagan could not abandon the contras even though they embarrassed the administration almost as much as they harmed Nicaragua. The CIA's program to mine Nicaragua's harbors, bomb its oil refineries, and write assassination manuals provoked widespread criticism in the United States and the condemnation of the World Court. The self-destructive aspect of the program is perhaps most crisply evoked by the CIA advising the contras on the destruction of bridges and dams that the Army Corps of Engineers had helped build in Nicaragua.[5]

The administration showed as little regard for U.S. law as for international law. In October 1984 after Congress ended aid to the contras, Oliver North of the National Security Council staff assumed control of the operation and sustained it until October 5, 1986. On that date, a C-123 cargo plane was shot down by the Nicaraguan government, and one of its crew members, Eugene Hasenfus, parachuted to safety. Assistant Secretary of State Elliott Abrams denied any government involvement, but his story and North's operation soon unraveled, revealing extensive government involvement at the highest levels.

After congressional hearings, a grand jury indicted North as well as Robert McFarlane, and John Poindexter, who were two of Reagan's former national security advisors, and two other individuals who had managed the covert "enterprise" that sustained the contras despite congressional prohibitions. The pursuit of North's "neat idea" to use funds generated from the sale of arms to Iran to help the contras led to the administration's worst scandal. Tomas Borge, Nicaragua's minister of interior, once said: "Reagan has become an obsession for us, and we've become an obsession for him."[6] The Iran-contra scandal was the bitter fruit of Reagan's obsession.

Compelled to Compensate

Much else resulted from Reagan's policy toward Central America, but all was not bad. The U.S. style of foreign policy has been to react to crises and then react to criticism that the U.S. only reacts to crises. To prove the criticism inaccurate, American foreign policymakers reflexively propose long-term development strategies to accompany more urgent security initiatives. Thus, the Marshall Plan accompanied the Truman Doctrine, the Alliance for Progress followed the Bay of Pigs, and Reagan's Caribbean Basin Initiative (CBI) arrived with the contras. To secure the region from communism, the administration knew it had to promote reforms and stimulate development.

The CBI was an innovative proposal for allowing one-way free trade for certain products from countries in the Caribbean basin. By opening the U.S. market wider for Caribbean basin countries than for others, the administration was hoping to promote investment and economic development in its strategic "backyard." The concept was sound but only for those countries that did not face an insurgency. For El Salvador, aid—not trade or investment—was essential to keep it solvent. After Congress appropriated aid, the administration's interest in the trade elements of the CBI diminished, and the bill that passed in August 1983 was not as effective as the one first proposed. Nonetheless, it remained a net economic benefit to the region.

If the CBI was designed to win support in the region for the administration's policy, its new policy on democracy and human rights was aimed to secure credibility on Capitol Hill. On the eve of the U.S. presidential election in 1980, Romulo Betancourt, the father of Venezuelan democracy, said: "There is a difference between Carter and Reagan which we Latin Americans readily appreciate. Whenever the Republican party has governed the United States, the White House and the department of state have favored dictatorial regimes."[7] During its first term, the Reagan administration's policy was consistent with Betancourt's point, but after proclaiming the Reagan Doctrine, the administration was compelled to find ways to persuade Congress that its goal in Nicaragua was democracy.

U.S. relationships with the military dictatorships therefore returned to the freezer where they had been in 1980. The administration paired its policies on Nicaragua with its approach to right-wing dictatorships. Whenever Congress voted on aid to the contras, the administration took a tough position against another dictatorship. Before too long, these human rights policies achieved their own momentum, and the administration began to take credit for the spread of democracy in Latin America—an assertion that would have evoked guffaws a few years before.

Democracy had begun to spread across Latin America in the mid-1970s, starting with announcements by the military regimes in Ecuador, Peru, Brazil, Panama, and Honduras of intentions to turn power over to civilians. The economic crisis in the early 1980s hastened the transition as the generals lost their credibility as development engineers.

Reagan's enthusiasm for democracy grew in proportion to his need to obtain approval from Congress of aid for El Salvador and the contras. He vigorously promoted elections in Central America and established the National Endowment for Democracy to institutionalize the pursuit of U.S. interests in democracy. More importantly, the administration sent clear messages to the military that overthrowing civilian governments would mean a cutoff in aid. This represented a significant and positive change in direction. Unfortunately, U.S. leverage was not used to help presidents like Napoleon Duarte of El Salvador widen their political space. Despite the emphasis on democracy in Central America, the military continued to govern in every country except Costa Rica.

The only democratic transition in Latin America for which the Reagan administration could take some credit was that in Argentina. The

Argentine generals had interpreted Reagan's early embrace and his grati-
tude for their helping the contras as a quid they could trade for U.S.
support of an invasion of the Malvinas/Falklands Islands. Their invasion
in the spring of 1982 proved a tragic miscalculation. The only good that
resulted from it was democracy, but the United States paid a heavy price.
The Argentine military and many Latin American governments believed
that the United States had betrayed the region and the Monroe Doctrine
by its support of the British during the war. The Venezuelan government,
which had a territorial dispute with Guyana, a former British colony,
took the lead in condemning U.S. policy and announcing the demise of
the Organization of American States (OAS) for its failure to prevent a
European attack against a hemispheric nation.

Power Disconnected from Diplomacy

Diplomacy without the occasional exercise of power risks being
irrelevant, but power without a diplomatic strategy is nihilistic and
breeds hostility. The threat or use of force by the United States in Latin
America is especially costly because of the region's sensitivity due to the
history of U.S. intervention. Therefore, more care needs to be taken in
using threats or force in the hemisphere than elsewhere. The Reagan
administration used direct force only once—in Grenada in October
1983—but it held provocative military exercises in Honduras and
around Nicaragua since 1983. The threats, covert actions, and the support of the contras were other signs of pressure.

Since the fall of 1981, however, the Reagan administration lacked a
clearly defined diplomatic strategy to translate that pressure to advantage. This was because doctrinaire conservatives, who believed that
negotiating with the Sandinistas was a futile exercise, constantly prevailed in bureaucratic debates within the executive branch over pragmatic conservatives, who were prepared to negotiate. According to one
ambassador, the people "who shoot down negotiations [won] rather
than people who negotiate." John Carbaugh, an aide to Senator Jesse
Helms and an advisor to the Reagan administration, explained that the
reason that a negotiating strategy was never approved was that the
secretary of state "had to throw a bone to the right-wingers. They [the
right-wingers] can't have the Soviet Union or the Middle East or Western
Europe. All are too important. So they're given Central America."[8]

Thus, even when the administration became more flexible in its arms
control negotiations with the Soviet Union, it was compelled to be less
flexible toward Nicaragua, lest the right wing of his party jump from

Reagan's ship of state. Moreover, negotiations were perceived as a sign of weakness or naiveté by the administration. Having committed itself to the contras, the Reagan administration could neither retreat nor change direction. In response to a congressional inquiry about whether he had ever contemplated proposing an alternative approach to the President on Nicaragua or telling him the policy was wrong, Robert McFarlane confessed: "To tell you the truth, probably the reason I didn't is because if I'd done that, Bill Casey, Jeane Kirkpatrick, and Cap Weinberger would have said I was some kind of commie."[9] Inhibited by the fear of looking soft or pink, the administration became tied to a strategy that could not succeed in Nicaragua or be sustained in the United States; all it could do was hurt Nicaragua and diminish the President.

It is worth recalling that the last round of negotiations between the United States and Nicaragua began in June 1984 during President Reagan's campaign for reelection and ended in January 1985 on the eve of his inauguration. The national security adviser visited the region then and announced the cessation of talks to demonstrate the administration's unswerving commitment to the contras. The administration was deadlocked internally as to whether any objective short of overthrowing the Sandinistas was worth pursuing. Therefore, no other goal was pursued, and the contras—with interests very different from those of the United States—were the sole means and end of U.S. policy.

The administration did not negotiate with the Grenadian revolutionary regime for a similar reason. Washington's strategy was to pressure Grenada with threats, military exercises ("Amber and the Amberdines"), constant propaganda barrages from the highest to lower levels, but not diplomacy. In the spring of 1982, President Reagan displayed satellite photographs of Grenada on television to dramatize that Cubans and Soviets were building an airfield. He neglected to mention that Canada and Venezuela were also helping build the airport. (The United States later recognized its importance to the island's development and completed it.)

The U.S. government had numerous opportunities to negotiate limits to the Soviet-Cuban use of the airport, but it never pursued this interest; and when the New Jewel movement self-destructed in October 1983, the administration also failed to explore opportunities to test whether the coup leaders were serious about giving up power and permitting a free election. Instead, the administration resorted to military force as a first choice rather than a last resort.[10]

The human costs of the invasion were high. Eighteen Americans were killed, and 116 were wounded; 45 Grenadians died, 337 were wounded; and 24 Cubans were killed and 59 wounded. There were also serious international political costs as the U.S. action was strongly condemned in both the United Nations and the OAS, but the invasion also generated indisputable benefits. It permitted Grenada to restore democracy, end the militarism of the previous regime, and secure the region. Those, in my view, represented a net gain; the only question is whether the benefits could have been obtained at less cost. As alternatives were not explored, we do not know the answer to that question.

The invasion of Grenada had an immediate effect on the Sandinista government that thought it would be next. The minister of interior called in the U.S. ambassador and showed him a plan for evacuating all Americans in case of emergency, the purported reason for the Grenadian intervention. Reagan administration officials chuckled at the Nicaraguans' fears but did not transform its leverage into results.[11] The reason, as explained by John Horton, a retired senior CIA official, was the same one for why it did not negotiate in Grenada:

> This [Reagan] administration considers agreements with Marxist-Leninists to be risky—as indeed they are—but it also finds them too distasteful and inconsistent with its own tough posturing to be a serious option. The administration did not simply fail to give sufficient hearing to a diplomatic strategy; it ideologically shackled its imagination and so was not free to use the informed pragmatism that enables a skilled diplomat to probe for solutions.[12]

The Unilateralist Temptation

Soon after taking office in 1981, President Reagan and his team faced a pivotal choice as to how to respond to the conclusive evidence of Sandinista material support for the Salvadoran rebels. The administration could choose from two options: (1) encourage and support the government of El Salvador as it used the evidence at the OAS to persuade other governments to condemn Nicaragua and threaten sanctions unless the arms shipments were stopped; or (2) release the evidence itself in the form of a white paper that described the insurgency in terms of the U.S. struggle against world communism. Secretary of State Haig chose the second route, opting for an East-West definition of the problem and a unilateral approach.

The administration never looked back. It tried to recruit governments to its cause, but it was not willing to compromise its policy or support friendly governments that were pursuing alternative initiatives. Indeed, the administration viewed all independent efforts to achieve peace in Central America as threats to the contra program. This explained its reaction to the Contadora Initiative (led by Venezuela, Mexico, Panama, and Colombia from 1983 to 1986), Esquipulas (initiated by Guatemalan President Cerezo in May 1986), Costa Rica President Oscar Arias's plan (accepted by the five Central American governments on August 7, 1987), and finally the Sapoa Accord (signed by the Nicaraguan government and the contras on March 23, 1988). Each time, the administration publicly welcomed the initiative but privately voiced skepticism. In no instance did the administration work to make the peace process succeed; in most cases, it deliberately tried to undermine the peace effort.

The Reagan administration's allergy to any combination of Latin American governments extended into the economic area. Instead of negotiating the CBI with all the countries of the region together, the administration negotiated the program with each country, one at a time. The Treasury Department's approach to the debt crisis was also case-by-case. Even the decision to join with six other Caribbean nations to invade Grenada in October 1983 was intended partly to preempt a decision that was made by the larger thirteen-nation Caribbean community to pursue a diplomatic rather than a military approach to Grenada.

The administration's policy-making style was illustrated by the succession crisis in Panama. The crisis was precipitated by a senior Panamanian military official who quit the armed forces in June 1987 and described the corruption, drug trafficking, and repression practiced by General Manuel Antonio Noriega, chief of Panama's armed forces. The Reagan administration was reported to have previously overlooked Noriega's excesses because he helped the contras, but the disclosures provoked Noriega's political opposition, and the United States was compelled to respond.

Washington then applied economic and military pressure to try to force Noriega to step down. It did not consult or try to coordinate a strategy with Latin America's democratic governments. As a result, on March 29, 1988, twenty-two Latin American governments—representing the political spectrum from Chile to Cuba but led by the democracies—discussed the issue of Panama, but condemned U.S. policy rather than Noriega.

The administration's unilateralism was not a product of inattention or incompetence; it was a core element of its ideology. Assistant Secretary Elliott Abrams explained: "We can't abdicate our responsibility to protect our interests to a committee of Latin American countries . . . the notion that if we have interests at stake we should ask Latin Americans what to do about it is wrong. . . . They want to know what we are going to do. They want to know if we have the guts to protect our interests, and if we don't, then they are going to walk away, and that is the way it should be."[13] He acknowledged in the same interview that the United States and Latin America share some interests, such as in democracy and development, but nonetheless, he thought that Latin America would prefer to follow us rather than to consult on a joint approach.

Muddling through Debt and Drugs

For most of Latin America and the Caribbean, the struggle in Nicaragua has been of peripheral concern. Of central importance has been the economic depression that by 1988 had reduced the per capita income 6.6 percent below what it was in 1980. Latin Americans not only failed to gain in the decade of the 1980s, they were in jeopardy of losing the gains achieved in the 1970s. The major cause of the decline in living standards, the rise in pessimism, and the lack of investment was the debt crisis.

Since the crisis began in 1982, the major Latin American countries have been transformed into capital exporters. From 25 to 50 percent of their foreign exchange earnings has been exported to service their expanding debt. From 1982 to 1988, the net transfer of capital *from* Latin America was $178.7 billion. If one adds to that the State Department's estimate of capital flight for the first four years—$100 billion—then Latin America exported twenty-eight times the Alliance for Progress and sixteen times the Marshall Plan in current dollars.[14]

The Reagan administration reacted quickly to the first symptom of the debt crisis because it occurred in Mexico, and Reagan was correctly very sensitive to the stability of that country. The administration discarded its free-market rhetoric and assembled a package of loans and credits to permit Mexico to remain current on its debt. Subsequently, the Reagan debt policy relied on the International Monetary Fund (IMF) as the broker that negotiated austerity plans in exchange for new loans from the multilateral development banks and the private banks.

By September 1985, this strategy was exhausted, and the leading Latin American debtors—the Cartagena group—were moving toward a unified and more demanding position. To preempt that, then-Secretary of Treasury James A. Baker III adeptly offered a plan that would increase loans from both the World Bank and the private banks. In essence, the plan would pile new unpayable debt on the old unpayable debt. It proved successful in precluding Latin American unity and preventing imminent defaults, but it failed in restoring growth, and it contributed to a further increase in the region's debt from $318 billion in 1982 to $401 billion in 1988.[15] Moreover, as a result of the burden of paying for past loans, Latin America has been unable to invest in its future.

One reason that the United States did not assume the lead in developing a long-term solution was because its own debt crisis made Latin America's seem trivial in comparison. Under Reagan, the U.S. national debt tripled in size, and the combined budget and trade deficits exceeded the national income of all but twelve countries in the world. A long-term solution need not have involved *much* capital from the U.S. government, but it was not in a position to offer *any*.

Because of its fiscal crisis, the United States has had to shorten its reach abroad. For example, despite the importance the administration attached to its relationships with Latin militaries, in 1988, it ended military aid programs to all of Latin America except three countries in Central America. By 1988, there were fewer U.S. military advisors in Latin America—ninety-two plus fifty-five trainers in El Salvador—than at any time in the previous three decades. This represented about 10 percent of the total number of Cuban and Soviet military advisors just in Nicaragua.[16]

Because there were fewer military advisors in the Andean countries, opportunities for curbing the drug problem were reduced. The Reagan administration presided over an explosion of drug imports from Latin America. The Drug Enforcement Administration estimated that the amount of cocaine imported into the country increased nearly twenty times between 1981 and 1987. The drug problem became a source of additional tension in inter-American relations rather than an opportunity for cooperation.

There were other symptoms of a subtle fiscal weakness. Whereas the CBI was moderately positive in helping several of the economies in the region, the U.S. sugar program was absolutely devastating. The region was more dependent on its sugar exports to the United States than on any other crop, and yet the United States reduced the region's quotas in 1988 to the lowest in a century, amounting to 10 percent of their quotas in 1981.[17] Instead of helping the region adjust to a price shock worse than that of oil in the 1970s, the United States precipitated a sugar shock.

Image and Reality

Faced with similar crises in Central America in the first decade of this century, President Theodore Roosevelt consulted with the Mexican president, and the two of them invited the five Central American presidents to a conference in Washington to negotiate peace treaties. The contrast with today is striking. Instead of promoting international law, President Reagan violated it. Instead of seeking negotiations, he avoided them. Instead of consulting with friends in the region to develop a common approach, he tried to avoid or undermine their efforts.

A fundamental change occurred, however; the Latin Americans took the initiative themselves. The four governments of the Contadora group, supported by the new democracies of Argentina, Peru, Uruguay, and Brazil, drafted a treaty that addressed the global and the regional security dimensions of the Central American conflict. Their proposals were further developed by the Central Americans, who contributed provisions on democratization and internal reconciliation. The Central American Accord, signed in Guatemala in August 1987, made a single request of the United States: suspend military aid to the contras. President Reagan ignored the request, arguing that the Sandinistas would negotiate seriously only if Congress provided military aid. At significant political risk, Congress rejected the President's request and responded favorably to Central America's. Congress's decision provided the Sandinistas the face-saving space that contributed to the cease-fire agreement reached in Sapoa in March 1988.

Despite its campaign, the Reagan administration produced little that was positive in Central America and much that was negative. The war in Nicaragua since 1982 claimed over 50,000 casualties, the economy collapsed, and the nation was much more militarized and dependent on the Soviet Union than it had been eight years earlier. (The argument that this trend would have occurred regardless of U.S. policy is an acknowledgment that U.S. policy failed or was irrelevant.) In El Salvador, the right remained strong enough to block serious reforms or negotiations with the left; the military continued to constrain Napoleon Duarte's ability to act as a genuine president.

Aside from Central America, the Reagan administration failed to address either the debt or drug crises effectively. Democracy expanded but remained a fragile flower, and the United States was uncharacteristically reticent in dealing with the one issue that could probably have the most positive effect on democracy's prospects—debt.

There is a curious paradox in contemplating the administration's impact on Latin America. Juxtaposed to the most militant and forceful gestures by the United States in the postwar period was a steadily contracting capacity to achieve its goals. Juxtaposed to the most magnificent spread of democracy in Latin America's history was a widening chasm in inter-American relations and an inability to forge solutions to the hemisphere's double plagues—debt and drugs.

Reagan's fierce bellow of anticommunism and his focus on turning the tide in Nicaragua so transfixed people that few noticed that the United States became weaker in the 1980s. From 1914 until 1985, the United States was the world's largest creditor nation; in just a few years, it sank to become the world's largest debtor. The administration concentrated on Central America because it had few resources to confront other challenges; but even in Central America, it was unable to translate its policies into results.

The U.S. debt crisis precluded helping Latin America resolve its debt crisis or nurturing the roots of the new democracies. The burgeoning budget deficit swallowed the money needed to fight the drug war overseas or to modernize a relationship with Latin America's military. Because the United States was unresponsive to South America's concerns and because of its heavy-handedness and disinterest in consultations, the administration failed to develop a relationship with Latin American democracies which could have permitted an effective solution to the region's problems.

In the end, Reagan's bequest to the region will come in three distinct packages from which different groups can choose. The first bequest is polarization—in Central America and in the United States. The administration's perception of a moral struggle in Central America virtually precluded compromise—already a rare commodity in the region but an essential ingredient to democracy. The contra strategy polarized Nicaragua by encouraging moderate leaders to leave.

Within the United States, the interpretation of Reagan's legacy will be almost as polarized as it will be in the region. Some will look back at President Reagan as a leader who made America strong again and compelled Latin Americans to recognize and deal with the highest U.S. priority in the region—limiting Soviet influence. Others will recall Reagan as an ideologue who wreaked havoc in the small countries of Central America, soiled America's reputation, and refused to deal with Latin America or its problems on its own terms.

The second bequest is more generous. The most positive initiatives that have emerged from the region—the Contadora group and its support group, the Cartagena consensus on debt, Esquipulas and the idea of the Central American parliament, the Arias Plan, and finally the Sapoa Accord—might someday be viewed as consequences of the pressure of the Reagan administration. Without pressure and the fear of U.S. intervention, much of Latin America would have ignored Central America; because of the absence of U.S. leadership, Latin America's debtors came forward with their own plans; without U.S. belligerence, Central Americans would never have united, and Nicaraguans would never have negotiated directly with one another.

As Reagan reacted negatively to these various initiatives, it is hard to argue that he intended to stimulate them. Nonetheless, history might interpret Latin American assertiveness as a result of U.S. pressure; and Latin Americans might have achieved a level of self-confidence and unity which would permit them to develop a new approach to inter-American issues with a new administration readier to listen and compromise.

The third bequest is the most likely in the near future because it is more of the same. Individual governments in Latin America will continue to be preoccupied with their own problems. Latin America will be divided internally and from the Caribbean and the United States. The arrogance of the Reagan years will reap anti-Americanism in much of Latin America, as it did in Honduras when a mob attacked the U.S. embassy in April 1988. The prospect of regionwide solutions will remain low.

The United States will grow more frustrated with its inability to influence developments in Latin America and with its own fiscal crisis. Americans will be tempted to replace the unpopular interventionism of the Reagan era with a political and economic withdrawal from the region's gargantuan problems. Other problems will loom as more important or simpler to address.

The implication of the fiscal crisis—that U.S. debts have made the nation poorer—will compel a reassessment of President Reagan as a man who stood tall but emptied America's pockets. His presidency will be remembered for postponing the major problems at home and in Latin America rather than addressing them. In Latin America, the Reagan era will be remembered for its heavy hand rather than for an attempt to join hands with new democracies. This third bequest is a chasm in inter-American relations.

The administration will be judged primarily by its approach to the region, Central America, where it invested the most, both in resources and prestige. The judgment will be harsh—and not just by critics. In an interview assessing his tenure, Secretary of State George Shultz gave the administration its worst grade in Central America. He admitted that it was "one of the most difficult issues for the administration and for me. It's been a tortured experience." A different approach, he confessed, might very well have yielded better results.[18]

NOTES

I am grateful to Charles Lipson, Michael Desch, and others in the program on international politics, economics, and security at the University of Chicago for comments on an earlier draft.

The epigraph is taken from "Text of Reagan's Address to Nation on the State of the Union," *New York Times,* 26 January 1988, 10.

1. See the following three articles in the *Washington Post:* Terri Shaw, "Argentine Police Raid Human Rights Office, Seize Leading Activists," 1 March 1981, A16; Jackson Diehl, "State Department Official Sees Role for Argentina in Central America," 10 March 1982, A18; and "Ex-Envoy to El Salvador Says Views Caused Ouster," 12 March 1981, A16.

2. John Dinges, "Kirkpatrick Trip Upsets Opposition in Chile," *Washington Post,* 13 August 1981, A25; and Raymond Bonner, "Chilean Exiles Appeal to Mrs. Kirkpatrick for Help," *New York Times,* 22 September 1981, A16.

3. Haig's statement was at a press conference on January 28, 1981, reprinted in the *New York Times* the next day. For his views, see Alexander M. Haig, Jr., *Caveat: Realism, Reagan, and Foreign Policy* (New York: Macmillan, 1984). For a more elaborate description and analysis of the Reagan administration's policy toward Latin America, see Robert A. Pastor, "The Reagan Administration and Latin America: Eagle Insurgent," in *Eagle Resurgent: The Reagan Era in American Foreign Policy,* ed. Kenneth A. Oye, Robert J. Lieber, and Donald Rothchild (Boston: Little, Brown, 1987), 359–92.

4. For an authoritative chronology of the Reagan administration's covert decisions to establish and support a paramilitary group against the Nicaraguan government, see U.S. Senate Select Committees on Secret Military Assistance to Iran and the Nicaraguan Opposition, and the U.S. House of Representatives Select Committee to Investigate Covert Arms Transactions with Iran, *Iran-Contra Affair: Report of the Congressional Committees* (Washington, D.C.: Government Printing Office, November 17, 1987).

5. Joel Brinkley, "CIA Gives Contras Detailed Profiles of Civil Targets," *New York Times,* 19 March 1987, 1, 8.

6. "Interview," *Playboy,* September 1983, 67.

7. Cited in *Colossus Challenged: The Struggle for Caribbean Influence,* ed. H. Michael Erisman and John D. Martz (Boulder, Colo.: Westview Press, 1982), 144.

8. The two quotes are from Roy Gutman, *Banana Diplomacy: The Making of American Policy in Nicaragua, 1981–87* (New York: Simon and Schuster, 1988), 44, 61. Also for a description and analysis of Reagan's policy toward Nicaragua, see Robert Pastor, *Condemned to Repetition: The United States and Nicaragua* (Princeton: Princeton University Press, 1988), chap. 12, 13, and 17.

9. Cited in *Newsweek,* 25 May 1987, 19.

10. See Robert Pastor, "The Invasion of Grenada: A Pre- and Post-Mortem," in

The Caribbean after Grenada: Revolution, Conflict, and Democracy, ed. Scott Mac-Donald, Harald Sandstrom, and Paul Goodwin (New York: Praeger, 1988), 92–100.

11. Pastor, *Condemned to Repetition,* 246; Roger Fontaine, "Choices on Nicaragua," *Global Affairs* 1 (Summer 1986): 113.

12. John Horton, "The Real Intelligence Failure," *Foreign Service Journal* Vol. 62, No. 2 (February 1985): 24.

13. An interview with Elliott Abrams, "Big Sticks and Good Neighbors," *The Detroit News,* 12 September 1985. For the underlying intellectual rationale of the Reagan administration's unilateralism, see Charles Krauthammer, "The Multilateral Fallacy," *The New Republic,* 9 December 1985, 17–20.

14. See Robert Pastor, ed., *Latin America's Debt Crisis: Adjusting to the Past or Planning for the Future?* (Boulder, Colo.: Lynne Rienner Publishers, 1987). For the most recent statistics, see Naciones Unidas, Comision Economica Para America Latina y El Caribe, *Balance Preliminar de la Economia Latinoamericana, 1988* (Santiago, Chile), 18, 24.

15. Ibid., 24.

16. Richard Halloran, "U.S.-Latin Military Contact Withers," *New York Times,* 3 April 1988, 8; and "U.S. Cuts Military Aid; Most Latin Grants End," *New York Times,* 30 January 1988, 2.

17. "1980s U.S. Sugar Imports from Latin America and the Caribbean," *The Times of the Americas,* 10 February 1988, 10.

18. Elaine Sciolino, "Wrapping It Up: George Shultz Looks at His Tenure at State," *New York Times,* 18 December 1988, 13.

4

The Middle East

ROBERT J. LIEBER

The impact of Reagan administration Middle East policy must be assessed in terms of America's exercise of power and foreign policy in the post-World War II world. When the new administration took office in January 1981, it did so against a backdrop of both regional shocks to American positions in the Middle East and a global picture that suggested waning power and influence ("hegemonic decline") for the United States.

Although the outgoing Carter administration had achieved one major success in the region (Camp David and the Egyptian-Israeli Peace Treaty), it had been badly shaken by four major Middle East events: the Iranian Revolution, with the fall of the Shah and the rise of Ayatollah Khomeini in January-February 1979; the subsequent oil shock and surge in oil prices; the Iranian hostage crisis following the seizure of the U.S. embassy in November 1979; and the Soviet invasion of Afghanistan in December 1979.

More broadly, a series of events throughout the 1970s seemed to signal a global recession of American power from its postwar peak. Among these events were the first oil shock (1973–74); the collapse of South Vietnam and the final American withdrawal in April 1975; developing regional struggles in places as diverse as Angola, Ethiopia, and Nicaragua; and the increasing importance of "North-South" issues on international agendas.

The Reagan administration assumed office bent on reversing what it saw as more than a decade of American decline. It proposed a set of policies aimed at reasserting U.S. power and influence. However, its disposition ran counter to strategies of adaptation employed by its Republican and Democratic predecessors. The Nixon and Ford administrations had sought to adjust to the winding-down in Vietnam and a growing diffusion of global power resources by placing more reliance on détente with the Soviet Union, a *modus vivendi* with China, and arrangements with regional powers who could act as surrogates to protect U.S. and Western interests (the Nixon Doctrine). In turn, the Carter administration initially placed more emphasis on multilateral approaches to international problems, increased attention to human rights and the developing countries, and put less reliance on the application of military power and unilateral strategies.[1]

The analysis that follows begins by assessing America's overall global role in the post-World War II era. It then turns to specific consideration of Reagan administration Middle East policy. This region provides an especially useful test for policies that involve a significant component of power or of military force. The reason for this is that the conditions of international "anarchy"[2] (i.e. of the absence of formal authority above the state), and of the resulting imperatives of "self-help," and of the "security dilemma"[3] are especially acute in the Middle East.

This chapter evaluates Reagan policy based on four fundamental American interests in the region: security of oil supplies; regional stability; maintaining close relations with friendly states; and minimizing Soviet influence.[4] Judging by these criteria, the actual performance of the Reagan administration suggests that there has been somewhat greater latitude for the use of military power and for unilateral actions than appeared to be the case in the late 1970s. Nonetheless, constraints on the use and effectiveness of power in the region have been significantly greater than the Reagan administration itself initially assumed. This has meant that the *effective* application of power has been limited to very specific circumstances. At other times and places, the use of this power has proved counterproductive or has had to give way to more traditional forms of policy and diplomacy.

The Debate over America's Global Power Position

In the more than four decades since the onset of the cold war, the world has changed substantially. However, the implications of these changes require more careful analysis. To begin, consider the following contrasts. In 1948, the United States held a nuclear monopoly. The Soviet Union, despite having seized control over Eastern Europe, was economically prostrate and only slowly recovering from the immense physical devastation inflicted during World War II. America's West European allies had also been grievously affected by the war and were gradually beginning the laborious process of rebuilding with generous Marshall Plan aid from the United States. The former Axis powers, Germany and Japan, were under military occupation, and Germany was divided. Both countries had seen widespread destruction of their industries and cities as well as the discrediting of political and social systems that had led to both fascism and a horrendous war.

Outside Europe, the "Third World" did not yet exist as an expression, let alone a reality, and the process of decolonization was just beginning. Above all, America remained unrivaled in most walks of life. It was not only the political and military leader of the free world, but its industrial production amounted to nearly half of the global total. Moreover, American science, technology, industrial organization, culture, and society were widely regarded as models for the rest of the world to emulate.

Over the ensuing four decades, much changed. The Soviets acquired nuclear weaponry and by the late 1960s had attained strategic parity. While recovering from the war, the Soviet Union built a massive industrial economy—albeit one with a gross national product (GNP) roughly half that of the United States. Meanwhile, the countries of Western Europe achieved a level of prosperity unimagined before the war, and their living standard came to rival that of the United States. The growth of the European Community, although much more an economic than a political reality, also gave the Europeans a renewed influence internationally. Among the industrial democracies, the recovery and burgeoning economic strength of Germany and Japan embodied a postwar miracle.

In Asia, Africa, and Latin America, the developing countries became relevant in ways that had never before been the case. Despite enormous internal problems, they grew increasingly autonomous. That is, outside powers would find greater difficulty in determining outcomes in these regions—as the conflicts in Indochina and Afghanistan would ultimately demonstrate to the United States and the Soviet Union. While many of the smaller actors remained quite weak, a series of regional powers emerged. Countries such as Brazil, India, Indonesia, Iran, and Nigeria developed as regional hegemons in their own right. Moreover, the newly industrializing countries (NICs) such as Taiwan, South Korea, and Singapore rapidly became significant participants in the international economy.

Reactions of Western strategists and scholars to these events have been diverse. Some argue that the United States has been entering a period of secular decline. Its military power is seen to have peaked in

February 1965 with the dispatch of combat troops to Vietnam by President Lyndon Johnson. The ensuing entanglement in Indochina and ultimate withdrawal were subsequently described as marking a form of imperial overextension. Together with the decline in America's share of world industrial production and a series of global challenges in trade, finance, and technology, it appeared as though the United States might be recapitulating a cycle of rise and decline, which Imperial Rome, seventeenth-century Spain, and the British Empire had experienced previously.[5]

However, the reality of the contemporary American world role is not adequately captured either in accounts that depict overextension and subsequent decline[6] or by opposing views that effectively deny that any basic change has occurred which cannot be reversed simply by acts of will plus copious amounts of military spending.[7]

Indeed, even some of the more widely cited analyses themselves are more nuanced than often described. Paul Kennedy's book *The Rise and Fall of the Great Powers* describes a problem of "imperial overstretch." Yet, although his approach has been depicted as tying economic and military strength directly together, Kennedy actually sets out three interacting forms of causality. In the author's words, these encompass "first, . . . changes in the military-industrial productive base, as certain states become militarily more (or less) powerful; second, the geopolitical, strategical [sic], and sociocultural factors which influenced the responses of each individual state to these broader shifts in the world balances; and third, the diplomatic and political changes which also affected chances of success or failure in the great coalition wars of the early twentieth century."[8]

Although the United States has experienced a *relative* decline in its power position—the indicators of which include its percentage of world production and trade and proportion of world conventional military power—America's *absolute* standing still leaves it in a position decidedly more powerful than any other major state. As evidence of this standing, the United States can best be described as the only player that is both a military superpower and an economic one. Moreover, characterizations of American military overextension are sometimes exaggerated. For example, even after the large increase in military spending carried out by the Reagan administration, the proportion of America's GNP devoted to defense has been under 7 percent, a level higher than during the previous decade but markedly lower than during the 1950s and 1960s, which were decades of U.S. economic and military leadership. To be sure, the proportionate defense burden is far greater than that of

America's major economic competitors (roughly twice that of the Federal Republic of Germany and as much as six times that of Japan, and this has proved a considerable handicap in economic competition). Yet other countries have flourished economically despite far greater defense burdens (South Korea, Israel), and the overall relationship between economic and military strength remains complex.

In contrast to the United States, the Soviet Union, although undoubtedly possessing military strength that makes it a military superpower and a formidable rival, cannot lay claim to anything like a comparable status in the economic realm. Indeed, Gorbachev's own words portray the Soviet Union as requiring drastic restructuring in order to cope with grave systemic economic and technological problems.

Conversely, although Japan and Western Europe have become economic superpowers, they do not possess comparable weight in the military realm. Japan's armed forces remain modest, and the nonnuclear status of Japan and Germany keeps these states from acquiring a military importance in any way comparable to their economic influence. More broadly, even the Western European countries as a bloc are nowhere near acquiring superpower military status. Although the French and British nuclear arsenals are significant, neither is close to achieving a rank comparable to that of the United States or the Soviet Union, and the lack of effective political unity in Western Europe has the effect of minimizing the military or global power potential that 320 million Western Europeans would otherwise exercise.

In short, whatever may come to pass over the longer term, for example in China or Japan, the contemporary scene is one in which American power remains distinctly greater than that of any other major player on the world stage.

Case 1: The Security of Oil Supplies

The security of oil supplies has long been regarded as a matter of vital American national interest in the Middle East. The position was explicitly enunciated by Presidents Carter and Reagan. Moreover, not only the supply but the price of oil has often been seen as a matter of great concern.[9]

The Reagan administration came to office with a view that—as Benjamin Cohen has observed of its economic policies—held it inconceivable that the United States could not reclaim its accustomed influence and autonomy over events.[10] In approaching oil as well as energy more broadly, it possessed not so much a comprehensive policy as a set of premises.[11] These included, first, an emphasis on the Soviet threat; second, allowing energy decisions to be made by the free market; and third, preference for reducing the role of governmental regulation in the energy realm.

Within a year of taking office, the administration began to benefit from a rapidly easing oil and energy picture. The effect of two oil shocks during the 1970s and a run up in world oil prices from $1.39 to $32.00 per barrel during the decade of the 1970s caused significant structural changes in the world oil balance. Specifically, both supply and demand patterns had begun to alter. Stimulated by higher prices and driven by security concerns, large increases in supplies of oil from nations other than those of the Organization of Petroleum Exporting Countries (OPEC), and of non-oil forms of energy came on stream in the 1980s. In the early part of the decade alone, these included more than six million barrels per day (mbd)—or more than 10 percent of world demand—from Alaska, the North Sea, and Mexico. Elsewhere, increases in the supply of natural gas, coal, and nuclear power (itself accounting for the equivalent of an additional five mbd of oil demand in the countries of the Organization for Economic Cooperation and Development [OECD]) also helped to reduce the demand for OPEC oil and to soften world oil prices.

At the same time, world oil consumption pressures also eased as a function of both market pressures (i.e. higher prices) and government-encouraged conservation programs (for example, the American auto fuel efficiency standards). As a result, world demand for OPEC oil plummeted from 30.9 mbd in 1979 to 22.6 mbd in 1981 and to a low of 16.2 mbd in 1985.[12] In the case of the United States, the resultant drop in net oil imports was dramatic. These declined from a 1977 peak of 8.8 mbd to a low of 5.1 mbd in 1982[13] before turning upward again in 1986–88.[14]

The consequence of these trends was to drive down the price for OPEC—and world—oil from a high point of $34 per barrel in October 1981 to a low of under $10 by mid-1986. To be sure, the 1986 collapse in oil prices was a consequence of deliberate Saudi actions: raising oil production in order to flood the market, reclaim market share, and restore production discipline over members of OPEC as well as non-OPEC countries. Even after prices edged upward, however, they remained in a range of $15 to $19 per barrel, well below their 1981 peak although still far above what they had been on the eve of the 1973 oil shock.

In essence, the Reagan administration thus obtained considerable relief from the effects of high oil prices although essentially as a result of global factors rather than deliberate policy actions.

Concern for security of the oil supply involved the administration in a series of actions, some consistent with its initial premises, others representing a distinct break. First, the *laissez-faire* approach of the Reagan administration gave way to pragmatic accommodation over emergency measures. On the domestic scene and under strong pressure from Congress, the administration grudgingly proceeded with major additions to the Strategic Petroleum Reserve. This government-controlled stock of crude oil stored underground in Louisiana and Texas slowly grew from a figure of just over 100 million barrels at the time the administration came to office to more than 550 million barrels eight years later.[15] Thus, the United States acquired a reserve equivalent to more than 90 days of net oil imports and which could be drawn down in the event of a future crisis.

On the international side, relations with the other members of the International Energy Agency (IEA) (essentially the OECD countries) required the administration to maintain participation in the agency's emergency oil allocation system. This represented a continuation of commitments made by the Nixon, Ford, and Carter administrations after creation of the IEA in 1974, although it ran against the premises of those who saw it as an unwieldy and interventionist measure. Indeed, the administration ultimately consented to an IEA decision on the use of emergency supplies. Member states agreed, in principle, to begin releasing oil stocks if and when global oil markets began to become disorderly rather than awaiting a full-fledged crisis in which global supplies fell by the 7 percent figures stipulated under IEA rules.

Acceptance of government intervention, both through stockpiling and agreements on emergency measures, was undramatic. Far more attention-getting was the administration's decision to intervene militarily in the Persian Gulf by providing naval escorts for reflagged Kuwaiti tankers beginning in July 1987. At one level, the decision appeared straightforward: the government of Kuwait, in response to Iranian attacks on its oil tankers, asked to transfer ownership of eleven ships to American holding companies and thereby to obtain U.S. flag registration. The Reagan administration consented to this arrangement and agreed to provide armed naval escorts in the gulf in order to protect the ships.

In its willingness to project and use force in defense of American national interests, the decision thus seemed consistent with the Reagan administration's overall outlook. However, other dimensions of this case present a far more tangled picture. First, the security of oil supplies had not been threatened in anything like the grave manner suggested by the Reagan response. In reality, the tanker war had been initiated four years earlier and not by Iran but by Iraq. Moreover, only 1 to 2 percent of tanker traffic had been affected. Indeed, the chief result of the sporadic attacks on shipping had been to drive up insurance rates and take the lives of several dozen unfortunate sailors each year. A series of changes in oil supply over the previous decade had diminished the immediate vulnerability of oil-importing countries. These factors included the global decline in demand for Middle East oil, a glut in available world supplies, and in the gulf area itself the construction of a network of overland pipelines through Saudi Arabia, Iraq, Jordan, and Turkey. Thus, regardless of whatever were the other considerations shaping the U.S. action, it is doubtful that Western oil supplies had been gravely at risk.

Indeed, the decision to reflag and escort Kuwaiti tankers may have owed more to other, more controversial reasons. One factor was the need to overcome the damage caused by the Iran-contra affair in which personnel of the National Security Council managed—against the opposition of Secretary of State Shultz and Secretary of Defense Weinberger—to arrange for covert sales of American arms to Iran and then used a portion of the profits to supply weapons for the guerrilla war against the Sandinista government of Nicaragua. Not only did the action contravene Operation Staunch (the official U.S. policy of preventing arms sales to the Ayatollah's Iran), but it proved a major embarrassment to the United States among moderate Arab states of the gulf region.

Naval deployments in the gulf had yet another important rationale. A decisive American action at this point (and the United States did prevail in a number of clashes with Iranian forces) may have appeared as a way of demonstrating resolve to friendly and unfriendly countries alike and of stiffening the gulf sheikdoms against the threat from Iran and radical Islamic fundamentalism. Moreover, inasmuch as the Kuwaitis had also approached the Soviets for protection, the U.S. action could be understood as an effort to forestall increased Soviet presence in the region.

Although other allied countries (Britain, France, Italy, the Netherlands) did provide an additional naval presence, American protection was not initially intended to extend beyond protection of American flag vessels—including the reflagged Kuwaiti tankers. Not until the end of April 1988 did the Reagan administration opt to extend protection to American-owned ships sailing under flags of convenience and to neutral shipping calling at the ports of moderate Arab gulf states.

Despite this presence, both Iraq and Iran continued to carry out sporadic attacks on gulf shipping. Nonetheless, the American policy had the effect of tilting toward Iraq. Neutral shipping calling at ports in

Kuwait and Saudi Arabia and protected by the U.S. naval forces carried cargo bound overland for Iraq. Almost from the time of its September 1980 attack on Iran and the resultant closure of its access through the Shatt-al-Arab, Iraq had been unable to use gulf ports. For the export of oil, Iraq turned to an improvised series of truck and pipeline routes via Saudi Arabia, Jordan, and Turkey. Conversely, Iran's only significant export route remained via the gulf. Yet American policy did not extend to protection of neutral shipping calling at Iranian ports (technically, such ships were entering a war zone). Apart from brief diplomatically inspired pauses, Iraq's attack on these ships and on Iran's port facilities continued largely unabated. Thus, over and above its own periodically extreme actions (religious fanaticism, terrorism, threats to the governments of neighboring states), Iran could view the American presence as unfriendly.

Case 2: Regional Stability and Terrorism

The Reagan administration undertook specific actions in relation to Lebanon, Iran, and Libya. Each of these had the purpose of either enhancing regional stability directly or doing so indirectly through discouraging terrorism.

LEBANON

Of these efforts, the involvement in Lebanon proved the most costly militarily and the most frustrating politically. Following the June 1982 Israeli intervention in Lebanon and the subsequent siege of Beirut, the Reagan administration sought to facilitate withdrawal of the Palestine Liberation Organization (PLO) and the stabilization of Lebanon by deploying a contingent of U.S. Marines in Beirut. The 1,400 troops were withdrawn after the PLO's departure. However, following the massacres carried out by Christian militiamen at the Sabra and Shatila refugee camps on the night of September 14, the marines returned. As Barry Rubin comments, the troops now were introduced on behalf of much more ambitious goals: achieving the departure of all other foreign troops from Lebanon, aiding in the effort to end the civil war, and encouraging a new political arrangement around the recently elected Lebanese president, Amin Gemayel.[16]

The American goals proved unattainable. Lebanon had been in a state of civil war since 1976, and this had caused some 100,000 casualties prior to the Israeli intervention of June 1982. Given the complexity of events, the savagery of the conflict, and the magnitude of the perceived stakes for the local players, the marine force was far too small to impose a solution. The American diplomatic role proved equally inadequate for the bitter local conflict, and U.S. efforts to facilitate a peace treaty between Israel and Lebanon became problematic.

As for the Arab-Israeli conflict itself, the Reagan Plan of September 1, 1982 offered an American initiative for seeking peace. However, here too there existed intractable obstacles. Beyond the pros and cons of the plan itself, the Reagan initiative faced Israeli reservations, opposition by the PLO, and rejection by Jordan's King Hussein in April 1983. Although a peace treaty between Lebanon and Israel was finally concluded on May 17, 1983, the laboriously constructed agreement soon collapsed. Contrary to State Department beliefs, agreement to secure Israeli military withdrawal was the key neither to Hussein's acceptance of the Reagan Plan nor to Syrian troop withdrawal. Moreover, at a time when a badly weakened Syria might have been pressured to withdraw, the Reagan administration focused instead on negotiations over the Israeli-Lebanon Treaty. This provided Syria valuable time to rebuild its forces and for President Assad to regain the initiative.[17]

Meanwhile, the marines found themselves increasingly drawn into the conflict around Beirut; yet they did so with an unclear mission and with their capability to influence outcomes greatly constrained. After a terrorist truck bomb attack on the American embassy in Beirut, a more deadly sequel followed. In the early morning of October 23, 1983, a truck bomb driven by an Islamic Shi'ite terrorist destroyed the marine barracks, killing 241 men inside.

In the end, the American efforts proved fruitless: no progress occurred in the Arab-Israeli peace process, and the role of Syria in Lebanon was strengthened. Although administration leaders had denounced any notion of a pullout, the Marines were suddenly "redeployed" to U.S. ships offshore. The troop presence thus came to an end in early February 1984.

IRAN

Insofar as U.S. interests in regional stability involved Iran, these encompassed ensuring that the Shi'ite fundamentalism of Iran's revolution not spread further in the region as a destabilizing and anti-Western force, and keeping open the possibility of more constructive relations with a future post-Khomeini regime. The first of these interests was to some degree served inasmuch as no other Middle Eastern state underwent a revolution comparable to Iran's. However, a major expansion of Shi'ite fundamentalist activity did take place in Lebanon, particularly involving the actions of the Iranian-supported Hezbollah group in both the Bekka Valley and in southern Lebanon.

The moderate Arab gulf states managed to retain their stability against a series of pressures, in part through their own activities and the efforts of the Gulf Cooperation Council (GCC). American military support provided some backing here, as in the case of equipping the Saudi air force, which in turn shot down an intruding Iranian plane and appeared to have discouraged further inroads. Moreover, the American regional posture made it clear that overt Iranian acts versus Saudi Arabia or its immediate neighbors would be opposed, although the means of this were left ambiguous. The American presence in gulf waters may have served to make the Iranians more cautious, and the outcome of a number of brief but sharp clashes was certainly not lost on the Ayatollah's Iran.

More to the point, however, Iran was fully occupied in its grinding, bloody conflict with Iraq. In the years between 1982 and the end of 1987, despite having turned the tide of battle on land, the Iranians continued to suffer from an imbalance in the air war, in missile exchanges, and in modern battlefield weaponry. They thus were not in a position to bring the war to a victorious conclusion—let alone take effective measures to spread their revolution by force. In any case, by the spring of 1988, the Iranians again found themselves on the defensive as Iraq recaptured the Fao peninsula and dramatically regained the initiative in the fighting.

Stalemate in the war with Iraq did not mean that the Iranian regime was idle, however. The actions of Iranian pilgrims rioting at Mecca in the spring of 1987 were clearly aimed at the Saudi regime. In addition, Iran continued to be implicated in terrorist activity throughout the region, especially through the activities of a number of shadowy Islamic fundamentalist groups that were implicated not only in operations within the gulf area but also more widely in the Middle East and Western Europe.

Although the American military presence in the gulf may have stiffened the resistance of Iran's neighbors and had some deterrent effect, the affair of Iran-contra and arms to the Ayatollah had the opposite result. Not only were the weapons funneled directly into Iran's war effort, but they left widespread cynicism about American credibility and judgment in the region. The notion of strengthening Iranian moderates through the weapons sales was simply not credible. Instead, the Reagan administration policies left an impression of U.S. willingness to trade weapons for hostages—despite a loudly proclaimed policy to the contrary—as well as of broader ineptitude. Nor was it surprising that U.S. efforts to cut off weapons supplies from other countries to Iran were unsuccessful.

The weapons-for-hostages episode undercut a policy of not giving in to terrorists, which American officials had been advocating in Europe and the Middle East. Ironically, the April 1988 hijacking of a Kuwaiti airliner provided an embarrassing contrast to the actual (rather than proclaimed) American stance. In this case, the government of Kuwait, a tiny and vulnerable gulf sheikhdom, refused to release seventeen terrorists of the Al-Dawa group whom it had sentenced for murderous attacks on the American and French embassies in its capital. Yet, Iran-contra investigations indicated that personnel of the Reagan National Security Council (NSC) had previously authorized a private individual to deal with Iran and to prod Kuwait on the possible release of the same terrorists.[18]

As for efforts to end the Iran-Iraq War at the United Nations, U.N. Security Council Resolution 598—passed on July 20, 1987—calling on the parties to halt the war or face further sanctions at first had little effect. The United States lacked effective leverage over the warring states, and the Soviets and Chinese[19] (not to mention other players such as the North Koreans) were unwilling to jeopardize their own influence and arms sales relationships with Teheran. Britain and France—as well as the U.S.S.R.—also continued to pursue their own arms trade with Iraq. Nor were other countries willing to give the effort the priority for which the Reagan administration had hoped.

During the following year, however, the fortunes of war took yet another turn. In March 1988, Iraq stepped up its missile attacks on Iran's cities. It also intensified its use of chemical weapons both against Iran and its own Kurdish population (of whom it killed thousands of civilians at the northern Iraqi town of Halabja[20]). Iran faced an increasingly grim picture that included battlefield reversals, disadvantages in advanced weaponry, economic privation, worsening civilian morale, and growing international isolation.

In this process, although the American role may not have been decisive, it did play a significant part. The elements here included a more assertive presence in the gulf during the spring of 1988, a series of small-scale clashes between U.S. and Iranian forces in the gulf, and the accidental shooting down of Iran Air flight 655 by the cruiser Vincennes during a naval clash on July 30. These developments increased Iran's sense of isolation, the belief that it no longer had the possibility of prevailing militarily, and the perception that the awesome power of the United States was now firmly committed against it. To be sure, there is much here that lies within the realm of "perception" and "belief." Yet although the impact of various contributory causes is open to debate,[21] the extraordinary weight of the United States in the political mythology of Iran (up to and including its characterization as "The Great Satan") suggests that American actions—even including the tragedy of the Iran Air shootdown—had significant consequences.

LIBYA

In the case of Libya, direct American use of force did seem to have an immediate and obvious effect. From the start, the Reagan administration made clear its intent to act forcefully against the erratic regime of Colonel Qaddafi. In retaliation for the regime's overt support of terrorist activity against American interests and allies, the administration tightened economic sanctions against Libya. Subsequently, in August 1981, U.S. carrier-based planes shot down two Libyan MIGS in a dogfight over the Gulf of Sidra. Ultimately, when Libyan complicity in the terrorist bombing of a Berlin discotheque resulted in the deaths of American military personnel, the administration launched a retaliatory bombing raid on April 15, 1986. U.S. Navy planes flying from aircraft carriers in the Mediterranean along with Air Force F-111s dispatched from bases in Britain bombed Libyan military facilities as well as Qaddafi's own headquarters.

Despite (largely *pro forma*) outcries in the Arab world and (predictably) apocalyptic warnings from a number of Middle East experts, the administration's action achieved its objective. The Libyan leader appeared shaken by the raid, and Libya seemed to opt for a more cautious set of policies. Even so, the attack was not without its costs. In addition to the loss of one plane and its crew, the Reagan administration found itself widely criticized abroad. In particular, the raid received a cool response in Europe, where only British Prime Minister Thatcher provided overt support, and where other NATO allies refused to allow U.S. planes to overfly their airspace en route to the raid. The administration had, however, acted prudently in selecting the target country. Despite evidence of active Syrian[22] and Iranian complicity in other terrorist operations including the bombing of American facilities in Lebanon, the administration made the prudential judgment that an attack on Libya could prove effective without excessive cost. By contrast, it was unlikely that the same kind of overt measures against the other two much larger and more powerful states could have been effective without the risk of embroiling the United States in a more dangerous and open-ended confrontation.

Case 3: Relations with Friends

The Reagan administration initially approached the Middle East with the hope that nonradical states could make common cause on the basis of a shared antipathy to the Soviet Union. However, this concept of an anti-Soviet alliance was eclipsed by often intractable local and regional issues. Nonetheless, there did exist a complementarity of interests among diverse countries opposed to various kinds of radical challenges, whether in the form of extreme Islamic fundamentalism (particularly in its pro-Iranian Shi'ite pattern), secular radicalism, terrorism (at least within their own borders), and idiosyncratic threats (such as those from Libya).

Paradoxically, closer U.S. relations with Israel, which the Reagan administration fostered in security and economic realms, did not preclude practical working relationships with most Arab countries. Whereas the war in Lebanon, lack of further progress in the Arab-Israeli peace process, and the unresolved Palestinian problem remained sources of friction in the region, the intimate set of relations between the United States and Israel also enhanced American leverage because only the United States could be effective as an intermediary in the Arab-Israeli conflict. Moreover, America's status as the major external actor in the Middle East made it imperative for Jordan and the gulf states to maintain a *modus vivendi* with the Western superpower. Such a relationship provided them with insurance against spillover effects from the Iran-Iraq War, threats from Iran and Syria, and challenges from other regional elements supported by the Soviets. As one indication of this relationship, the expanded American naval presence in the gulf led to (frequently unpublicized) measures of extensive logistic cooperation between U.S. forces and the moderate Arab states. At the same time, U.S. relations with Egypt remained close, even extending to the holding of joint military maneuvers.

To be sure, there did exist periodic tensions or disputes. Relations with Israel proved abrasive during and after the June 1982 invasion of Lebanon and the siege of Beirut, and relations were also periodically strained after 1985, when Yitzhak Shamir became prime minister in the national unity government. Even so, a substantial elaboration of American-Israeli military cooperation occurred during these years.

During the last year of the Reagan administration, the outbreak of the Palestinian *intifada* in the West Bank and Gaza gave rise to new strains between Washington and Jerusalem. These were exacerbated when, in December 1988, PLO leader Yasir Arafat finally gave verbal endorsement to the long-standing U.S. preconditions (acceptance of U.N. Resolutions 242 and 338, recognition of Israel's right to exist, disavowal of terrorism[23]), and Washington agreed to begin direct contacts with the PLO. However, the obstacles to significant progress in the peace process remained enormous. Yasir Arafat did not possess the character and strength of an Anwar Sadat, and it was unclear whether he would be able to commit the PLO, unambiguously, to the path of peaceful negotiations. In these circumstances, Israeli leaders remained wary, and the problem was one that the outgoing Reagan administration left for the incoming Bush presidency to face.

Controversies over proposed sales of American weapons to countries that had not made peace with Israel (i.e. to Arab states other than Egypt) proved a contentious issue as well. Although American relations with Jordan, the gulf states and the Saudis remained close, this did not preclude the Saudi purchase of Chinese DF-3 missiles (surface-to-surface weapons with a range of 3,000 kilometers) nor the concluding of a major Saudi aircraft purchase from Britain, estimated at anywhere from $12 to $25 billion in value.[24] Nonetheless, most of the bilateral relationships between the United States and the more moderate states of the Middle East were maintained or even expanded during the period.

Case 4: Containing Soviet Influence

As in other regions, Soviet foreign policy under Gorbachev gradually became far more adroit than had been the case under his predecessors. More sophisticated Soviet diplomacy thus complicated the regional picture for the United States. Soviet initiatives during this period included expanded diplomatic contacts with gulf states; a continuing and more flexible role *vis-à-vis* the PLO and Syria; and effective access to both sides in the Iran-Iraq War (which gave the Soviets advantages analogous to U.S. leverage in the Israel-Arab conflict). Moreover, extrication from the Afghan quagmire and the beginnings of an approach to Israel were likely to reduce the impediments to a more effective Soviet presence in the Middle East.

Despite these Soviet measures, the United States still possessed major advantages. These included substantially greater force projection capabilities in the gulf, limits to the Soviet role in the Arab-Israeli conflict unless the U.S.S.R. were to recognize Israel and increase Soviet Jewish emigration, and the fact that moderate states continued to remain wary of the U.S.S.R.

Although initial administration anxieties about Soviet inroads were not borne out, the situation remained fluid. An important reason for this was that many of the factors ultimately conducive to increased Soviet influence were outside immediate U.S. control. These included Soviet policy toward Israel, Soviet influence on Syria and the PLO in relation to the Arab-Israeli peace process, and Soviet policy toward the Iran-Iraq War.

Conclusion

Amid the volatility, drama—and brutality—of events in the region, the Reagan administration appears to have had more latitude for unilateral actions, including the exercise of military power when it judged that American or Western interests were at stake, than prevalent views in the late 1970s might have suggested. Much of this latitude was due to the Hobbesian realities of Middle East geopolitics, in a region where power and force are everyday attributes of interstate relations, and often of domestic politics as well.

Yet if the Middle East is one of the most unstable regions on earth and is an area where power and its use have an unusually conspicuous role, regional realities also impose constraints on the exercise of power. First, existing conflicts often have deep and almost intractable sources that are not readily susceptible to externally imposed solutions, either military or diplomatic. Some of these conflicts are rooted in a process of political, social, and economic modernization which has compressed into a brief period of decades a transformation that took several centuries in Europe. Others involve deep-seated confrontations over rival nationalisms or ferocious struggles over domestic political power in which the stakes are perceived as total by the contending parties.

Next, there are some tasks for which power is not an effective tool or in which the force possessed by indigenous actors is itself of great weight, thus making regional behavior often highly autonomous. Cases in point are Iraq, Iran, Israel, and Syria (of which country the Soviets have commented: they take everything from us except advice). Not surprisingly, small or maladroit efforts to use force can be counterproductive. Moreover, even larger scale and more effective uses of force, as in the case of the American reflagging and naval presence in the gulf, can pose additional dangers. Although the American naval intervention did not give rise to the results most feared by its critics, the potential for serious trouble was very real. Prior to the Iran-Iraq cease-fire, the American action risked ceding the initiative to other actors (Iran or Iraq), carried the possibility of embroiling the United States in war, and at first left unclear how and when the United States would ultimately extricate itself while preserving those interests that the use of force was meant to protect.

There is one other powerfully relevant factor that has shaped and constrained Reagan administration policies in the Middle East. It concerns American domestic politics and the bases of support for commitments of American power abroad. The prevailing realities are best summed up by William Schneider, who has identified a public and congressional mood that desires both peace and strength but whose view of interventionism is best described as: Win quickly or get out.[25] The experience of President Lyndon Johnson epitomizes this problem: his administration ultimately lost domestic support for the Vietnam War because it could neither win nor get out of the conflict. By contrast, the Reagan administration was able to maintain domestic support for its applications of force abroad. Either it could "win" quickly (as in Grenada; the bombing of Libya; the seizure of the Achille Lauro hijackers; and its short, sharp retaliations against Iran in the Persian Gulf) or, in other cases where U.S. purposes could not be readily achieved, the administration chose to withdraw (as in the sudden departure of marines) from Lebanon. Hence, where it could not win quickly, the Reagan administration at least met the criterion of "getting out."

Although domestic support for maintaining American naval force in the gulf was substantial, this could not have been assured indefinitely, particularly if the human costs of the deployment had mounted without a clear end in sight. The accidental downing of the Iran Air passenger plane, with the loss of 290 lives, suggested one kind of peril. However, American commanders also faced risks from being too cautious in their readiness to fire (as evidenced in the May 17, 1987 Iraqi air attack on the USS Stark, which took the lives of thirty-seven American sailors) as well as from other forms of hostile action (for example, the April 1988 mining of the frigate Samuel B. Roberts, which came close to sinking the ship). The July 1988 cease-fire in the Iran-Iraq War allowed the United States gradually to begin reducing its forces in the gulf; but without the opportunity posed by the winding down of the war, the win-or-get-out problem could eventually have posed difficulties for the Reagan administration or its successor.

Against this background, the actual record of the Reagan administration in the Middle East is a mixed bag. Of the four American interests, oil remains at least temporarily secure, even though this appears to be due more to changes in world supply and demand patterns than to the application of force.[26]

As for the second interest, regional stability, although little progress has been made on restoring order in Lebanon, the much more dangerous conflict between Iran and Iraq has come to at least a temporary halt. Relations between Israel and the Palestinians have become more unstable following the uprising in the West Bank and Gaza; and despite the initiation of a U.S.-PLO dialogue, major progress beyond the 1979 American-mediated Egyptian-Israeli Peace Treaty has yet to occur. On the other hand, the immediate likelihood of another Arab-Israeli war is low as long as Egypt remains at peace with Israel. In addition, despite earlier fears, the rise in Islamic fundamentalism has not caused the overthrow of other regimes beyond Iran. In some part, these results have been due to American projection of power as a counterweight to Iran. The U.S. military presence in the gulf region probably did strengthen the moderate states against challenges to their stability. However, diplomatic activity has also been important, as have the choices and policies of the local actors. In addition, the U.S. presence (along with other factors such as diplomatic isolation, declining oil revenues, and the course of the Iran-Iraq War) put pressure on the Iranian regime to moderate its threats to other governments in the region.

In the case of the third criterion, relations with friends, there is, yet again, a mixed picture. The administration has maintained effective working relationships with key countries even though it has sometimes been taken by surprise.

As for the fourth case, restraining Soviet influence, the verdict remains incomplete. Certainly the Soviet withdrawal of troops from Afghanistan has been the result both of American policies (arms to the resistance[27]) and—especially—of a tenacious battle by the Afghans themselves. In any case, dire concerns of pessimists concerning the spread of Soviet influence certainly have not been borne out.

In the end, Reagan administration policy in the Middle East has seen some reversion to more traditional courses of American action. A number of early, ambitious military and ideological aspirations have been scaled back in the face of regional imperatives. Military interventions have occurred, and although these have been more ambitious than actions the Carter administration was willing to undertake, they can be seen as differences more of degree than of kind compared with what other postwar administrations have been prepared to do. Other significant military-related activities have included closer and more effective working relationships with Israel and to a more limited (and less publicized) extent with Egypt and the gulf states. Against this greater ability to act, there have been a number of failures, some of them costly in human or political terms: the marine deployment in Lebanon; a bungled daylight air strike against Syrian artillery emplacements in Lebanon; the fiasco of arms to the Ayatollah[28]; the inability to negotiate an effective peace and Syrian withdrawal from Lebanon; loss of life in the Stark and Iran Air incidents; and the lack of American-mediated progress toward Arab-Israeli peace beyond the previous administration's achievements at Camp David.

The overall picture is thus sobering. On the one hand, there have been times and places in which the presence of U.S. power or the forceful application of military means has been timely and appropriate. In others, this has not been the case. Diplomacy and economic influence have continued to be of great importance as have the intrinsic interests of the local actors who have reasons that often (although by no means always) lead them in directions consonant with American national interests. In the end, the administration's tendency to revert toward a more traditional pattern recapitulates the experience of previous American presidencies. Administrations often come to office with ambitious, sometimes ideologically framed agendas, which are then modified either through the pressing realities of the outside world or by domestic constraints of politics or resources. The preceding administration, that of Jimmy Carter, underwent such an evolution—albeit from the other side of the political landscape—and the experience suggests a lesson for future administrations as they confront the problem of protecting American interests in the environment of a volatile and often dangerous Middle East.

NOTES

1. This interpretation of Carter and Reagan foreign policies is developed in Kenneth Oye, Donald Rothchild, and Robert J. Lieber, eds., *Eagle Entangled: U.S. Foreign Policy in a Complex World* (New York: Longman, 1979); in Oye, Lieber and Rothchild, eds., *Eagle Defiant: U.S. Foreign Policy in the 1980s* (Boston: Little, Brown, 1983); and in idem, *Eagle Resurgent? The Reagan Era in American Foreign Policy* (Boston: Little, Brown, 1987). See in particular Oye's essays, "International Systems Structure and American Foreign Policy," in idem, *Eagle Defiant*, 3–32; and "Constrained Confidence and the Evolution of Reagan Foreign Policy," in idem, *Eagle Resurgent?*, 3–39.

2. For a treatment of this classic problem, which sets international relations apart from domestic politics, see Robert J. Lieber, *No Common Power: Understanding International Relations* (Glenview, Ill.: Scott, Foresman, 1988), 5–6. Antecedents can be found in Thucydides, Machiavelli, Hobbes, and in the work of more contemporary authors such as Hans Morgenthau and Kenneth Waltz.

3. The use of the concept originates with John H. Herz in *Political Realism and Political Idealism* (Chicago: University of Chicago Press, 1951). See also idem, *International Politics in the Nuclear Age* (New York: Columbia University Press, 1959); Glenn H. Snyder, "The Security Dilemma in Alliance Politics," *World Politics*

36, no. 4 (1984): 461; and Robert Jervis, "Cooperation under the Security Dilemma," *World Politics* 30, no. 2 (1978): 167–214, at 169.

4. These are among the most important American interests in the Middle East commonly cited by governmental leaders and scholars. For one such useful listing, see Barry Rubin, "The Reagan Administration and the Middle East," in Oye et al., *Eagle Resurgent?*, 433.

5. See, in particular, Paul Kennedy, *The Rise and Fall of the Great Powers* (New York: Random House, 1987). The theory of hegemonic stability holds that "order in world politics is typically created by a single dominant power," and that "the maintenance of order requires continued hegemony." Robert Keohane, *After Hegemony: Cooperation and Discord in the World Political Economy* (Princeton: Princeton University Press, 1984), 31. See also Robert Gilpin, *War and Change in World Politics* (New York: Cambridge University Press, 1981), 144–45; Charles P. Kindleberger, *The World in Depression, 1929–1939* (Berkeley and Los Angeles: University of California Press, 1973), 305; and Keohane, "The Theory of Hegemonic Stability and Changes in International Economic Regimes," in *Change in the International System*, ed. Ole Holsti, Randolph Siverson, and Alexander George (Boulder, Colo.: Westview Press, 1980), 131–62.

6. See, e.g., Seyom Brown, *New Forces in World Politics* (Washington, D.C.: Brookings Institution, 1974). For a useful critique of these approaches as well as the relevant theoretical literature, see Joseph S. Nye, Jr., "Neorealism and Neoliberalism," *World Politics* 40, no. 2 (1988): 234–51.

7. Bruce W. Jentleson critiques "global commitments theory." He challenges the assumption that commitments to Third World states necessarily contribute to the defense of U.S. interests and that these commitments enhance the credibility of American power or help to deter threats to other U.S. allies. Contrary to those who interpret American setbacks in Vietnam, Iran, and Lebanon as due to a failure to make good on commitments, Jentleson argues that these commitments were abandoned as consequences, not causes, of U.S. defeats. See Jentleson, "American Commitments in the Third World: Theory vs. Practice," *International Organization* 41, no. 4 (1987): 667–704, at 667–68.

8. Kennedy, *Rise and Fall*, 197–98.

9. For analysis of the impact of the two oil shocks of the 1970s on U.S. and European interests, see Robert J. Lieber, *The Oil Decade: Conflict and Cooperation in the West* (Lanham MD: University Press of America, 1986).

10. See Benjamin J. Cohen, "An Explosion in the Kitchen? Economic Relations with Other Advanced Industrial States," in Oye et al., *Eagle Resurgent?*

11. For elaboration of these points, see Robert J. Lieber, "International Energy Policy and the Reagan Administration: Avoiding the Next Oil Shock?," in Oye et al., *Eagle Resurgent?*, 175ff.

12. U.S. Department of Energy, Energy Information Administration, *Monthly Energy Review* (December 1987, published March 1988): 119.

13. Ibid., 51.

14. Average U.S. oil imports for 1987 were 6.5 mbd. Ibid.

15. *Monthly Energy Review* (January 1989, published April 1989): 41.

16. Oye et al., *Eagle Resurgent?*, 444. For an insightful treatment of this period,

including the diplomatic and strategic aspects involving Syria and Israel, see Avner Yaniv, *Dilemmas of Security: Politics, Strategy, and the Israeli Experience in Lebanon* (New York: Oxford University Press, 1987), 137–47, 159–71.

17. Rubin, "The Reagan Administration," 443–45; and Yaniv, *Dilemmas of Security,* chap. 4.

18. For accounts of the Iran-contra investigation, see *Report of the Congressional Committees Investigating the Iran-Contra Affair* (New York: Times Books, 1988). See also *The Tower Commission Report* (New York: Bantam Books, 1987).

19. China's arms exports to the Middle East accounted for more than two-thirds of that country's global total.

20. See, e.g. *New York Times,* 24 March 1988. Later in the year, a Senate Foreign Relations subcommittee staff report found "overwhelming evidence" that Iraq had used chemical weapons against Kurdish guerrillas and civilians in northeastern Iraq. *New York Times,* 22 September 1988.

21. Cf. Janice Gross Stein, "The Wrong Strategy in the Right Place: The United States in the Gulf," *International Security* 13, no. 3 (1988/89): 142–67. Stein's analysis of deterrence is more critical of the American role and places more weight on "factors . . . largely independent of the American naval presence," ibid., 166.

22. Syria's role in a plot to blow up an El Al 747 in London led to the temporary withdrawal of the American ambassador to Damascus.

23. The first two conditions were set out in 1975. In 1985, these plus the third condition became part of U.S. law.

24. Estimates from British sources, cited in the *Washington Post,* 10 July 1988. The higher figure includes the value of a wide range of potential contracts for arms and facilities extending over the next decade.

25. "'Rambo' and Reality: Having it Both Ways," in Oye et al., *Eagle Resurgent?,* 58–63.

26. As of April 1988, noncommunist oil consumption was approximately 49 mbd, of which only 6.5 mbd was exported through the Straits of Hormuz at the mouth of the Persian Gulf. (Of the latter amount, 1.5 mbd could be rerouted through pipelines.) *New York Times,* 20 April 1988, 16.

27. The spring 1986 decision to supply Stinger antiaircraft missiles to the guerrillas was particularly important. (See Chapter 5 of this volume.)

28. This action has been characterized in scathing terms by the former White House Chief of Staff Donald Regan. He describes "amateurism . . . astounding gullibility," and "virtually foreordained failure." Quoted, *International Herald Tribune,* 10 May 1988.

5

U.S.-Soviet Relations

CONDOLEEZZA RICE

No legacy would make me more proud than leaving in place a bipartisan consensus for the cause of world freedom, a consensus that prevents a paralysis of American power from ever occurring again.—Ronald Reagan

For Ronald Reagan, no area of foreign policy has been more fundamentally linked to his goal of securing a bipartisan consensus for the cause of world freedom than relations with the Soviet Union. On the campaign trail, candidate Reagan made it clear that he blamed most of the world's ills on the combination of the decline in America's military might and will and Soviet exploitation of those circumstances. President Reagan wasted no time in assuring the world that he intended to take up the global challenge presented by the Soviet Union and that he would pursue a new relationship on his terms.

What, then, have the eight years of the Reagan approach to U.S.-Soviet relations wrought? If we are asking whether Ronald Reagan's imprimatur on U.S.-Soviet relations will outlast his administration, the answer, even on the surface, appears to be yes. In many ways he redefined the terms of the debate and set new points of departure for negotiation in the four agenda areas that he defined: human rights; regional conflict; arms control; and cultural and scientific exchange.

Ronald Reagan had the luxury of an uninterrupted eight years in which to pursue his goals for U.S.-Soviet relations. Richard Nixon was the last president to enjoy such stability, and his administration was truncated and then cut short by Vietnam and Watergate. Yet, when reviewing the Reagan record, it is not consistency but an about-face in policy after his 1984 reelection which is often noted. Undeniably, speeches about the "evil empire" were few and far between in Reagan's second term. The President attended four summits, a record for an American president and one that is particularly startling since there had been no summits until June 1985.

However, if Ronald Reagan became statesman-like in his rhetoric and took on the instruments of his predecessors—arms control and summitry—we ought not lose sight of one essential fact: the goals that he set more than eight years ago are remarkably close to today's agenda in U.S.-Soviet relations. The new equilibrium, if one is emerging, looks more like the one that Reagan defined than the one that was bequeathed to him.

From that point, it would be easy to move to a picture of cause and effect; but assessing the relationship of the Reagan strategy to the state of U.S.-Soviet relations is more complicated. First, there are still many unresolved issues, and there have been some outright defeats for the administration's policy. The problem is especially difficult because the eight years of stability in the White House were concurrent with extraordinary flux in the Kremlin. In marked contrast to a period in which Leonid Brezhnev outlasted three American presidents, Ronald Reagan held the White House during the last two years of Brezhnev's rule, the brief interludes of Yuri Andropov and Konstantin Chernenko, and the first three years of Mikhail Sergeich Gorbachev's tenure. Can it really be accidental that the Reagan approach began to succeed only after Gorbachev took the reigns of power in the Kremlin?

The problem is an epistemological one with which those who study power and influence are familiar. It is difficult to show that A has been influenced by B because the possibility always exists that A would have followed the course in question anyway. Yet the question, as difficult as it is, is critical because the Reagan legacy is not just a set of agreements. It is above all an approach to dealing with the Soviet Union. The approach is one of challenging the Soviets with what, at times, seem outrageous demands and holding to positions that would seem to have but a faint possibility of negotiability. In reviewing the Reagan years, it is far less surprising that Reagan proposed the things that he did than that the Soviets accepted some of them. The problem for future administrations is to know why the approach worked and whether it will continue to do so.

The Lessons of Détente

For Reagan and his core advisors, the lesson of détente was that the Soviet Union had taken advantage of America's desperation for cooperation and given nothing in return. They painted a picture of a relentless Soviet military buildup, unconstrained either by Soviet economic failings or the arms control process, the goal of which was to give the Soviet Union unquestioned military superiority over the United States. A central feature of this argument was that the Soviet Union did not accept "mutually assured destruction" as a condition of the nuclear age. Rather, the Soviet Union believed that it could fight and win a nuclear war and was preparing to do so.[1] Undeterred by the threat of mutual suicide, the Soviet Union aggressively pursued every opportunity to undermine, and at times, directly confront Western power around the globe.

The proponents of this view found considerable Soviet behavior to support their argument: Cuban troops were fighting in Angola; Soviet and East German generals commanded Cuban and Ethiopian forces in Eritrea in 1978; and, of course, there was Afghanistan. All were taken as signs of Soviet adventurism unchecked by an indecisive and insecure America.

The new administration served notice that it intended to call the Soviets to account for this behavior and that even cultural and technological exchange lacked value in this context. Technological exchange, according to administration officials, had been legalized spying. Limitations were placed upon exchange, and the principle of reciprocity for Soviets traveling in the United States would be strictly enforced in accordance with the treatment of Americans abroad. This led, for example, to the establishment of a twenty-five-mile circumference around sensitive areas (including Stanford University and the Silicon Valley), tight restrictions on consular personnel, and even charges against employees of the Soviet mission to the United Nations. There was even an ill-fated and highly controversial attempt to limit publication of basic scientific articles that had national security ramifications. Whatever the merits of the idea that Soviet scientists were benefiting from open exchange among the international community of scholars, any attempt to enforce screening of papers by the government was denounced by a wide spectrum of scientists, and the policy eventually unraveled.

At times, Reagan seemed to call into question the wisdom of any contact with the Soviet Union. The essential premise of détente had been that the Soviet Union was, for the most part, a state like any other with legitimate interests in the international system. The goal of détente, in its broadest sense, was to increase the stake of the Soviet Union in international stability. However, for Ronald Reagan, any effort to improve relations on the basis of mutual benefit was fraught with danger because the Soviet Union was a state that "openly and publicly declared that the only morality they recognize is what will further their cause—meaning they reserve unto themselves the right to commit any crime, to lie, to cheat, in order to attain that. . . . I think, when you do business with them . . . you keep that in mind."[2]

The image of the Soviet Union as immoral in its international behavior was married to a view of the Soviet system as internally weak and fundamentally unsound.[3] The prescription was clear: the Soviet Union was succeeding in the world because the United States refused to challenge it; but the Soviet Union was ultimately too weak to withstand a challenge from the morally and technologically superior West.

In this regard, Reagan reserved his most scathing criticism for arms control and what he viewed as the associated "decade of neglect" of American military strength. The critique had three parts. First, arms control had been at best a fraud and at worst an unmitigated set of defeats for the United States. The Interim Offensive Agreement of 1972 rather than constraining forces had permitted the two sides to increase their weapons inventories almost three times. More importantly, the Soviet Union had, under the guise of arms control, continued to build its forces, attained a position of military superiority, and was politically exploiting that advantage around the world.

Second, as noted above, while the United States had been paralyzed by the belief in the cataclysmic impact of nuclear war, the Soviet Union was busily preparing to fight and win a nuclear war. Thus, America's policy that was tied to a belief in mutual vulnerability might not deter at all because the perception of vulnerability was not shared by the U.S.S.R. Although operational American military strategy had long since abandoned mutual assured destruction (MAD), Reagan's advisors castigated past administrations for adherence to this "bankrupt strategy."[4]

Finally, the challenge was not to conclude arms control agreements but to reestablish a "margin of safety" in American military forces by rebuilding American military strength. American military spending had declined in the decade of the 1970s. The administration brought renewed commitment to military modernization even though sentiment for increases in the defense budget was already growing. The Carter administration's final projected defense buildup would also have increased resources significantly. Arguably, though, the initial infusion of resources (in fiscal year 1982 Congress approved a defense budget almost 12 percent larger than that of the previous year) and the sustained character of the buildup were undeniably Reagan. The program, a five-year plan costing 180 billion dollars, included restoration of the B-1 bomber that Carter had canceled and plans for accelerating the Trident II program. Improvements were also made in American force readiness and in pay for military personnel. The defense buildup was intended to be a strong signal to the Kremlin that "the decade of neglect" had come to an end.

In addition to new policies on cultural and technological exchanges, time and again the administration raised the abominable Soviet human rights record. Plans were laid to increase broadcasts that exposed these abuses to countries behind the Iron Curtain and to Soviet client states like Cuba. At the time of near civil war in Poland, the administration sponsored a program called "Let Poland be Poland" which featured prominent Polish Americans and American entertainment figures supporting the cause of the Polish workers.

Reagan denied that this was a policy of confrontation. Rather, he said he was trying to change the terms of cooperation to those that more closely matched the security interests of the United States and her allies. In the two most central areas—arms control and regional security—this translated into a policy that intentionally raised the ante and served notice on Moscow that cooperation would require a complete change in Soviet behavior. In retrospect, this was a very high-risk strategy indeed.

In the Third World, the policy was dubbed the "Reagan Doctrine." Essentially, the policy raised the stakes for the Soviet Union in a number of regional conflicts. It supported "freedom fighters" in Angola, Nicaragua, and Afghanistan. Although the fit was not very exact, the fates of Jonas Savimbi, the contras, and the Mujahadeen were linked in a policy that armed and aided rebels on one criterion alone: opposition to Soviet-backed governments in the Third World.

The most visible, and to date most effective, direct challenge to the Kremlin was in Afghanistan. As a candidate, Reagan had condemned Carter's grain embargo as an ineffective and weak response to Soviet aggression in Afghanistan. Appealing to the farm vote, Reagan promised to lift the embargo that he claimed penalized American farmers more than the Soviet Union. He carried through on that policy. Yet for the first two years of his administration, Reagan himself was without an effective response to Soviet policy in Afghanistan. What could the United States do after the Soviet Union decided to commit combat forces to conflict in a country with which it shared a border? At the time, the Mujahadeen looked like no match for the Soviet Union. Pictures and documentaries that began to leak out of Afghanistan showed a valiant effort by rebels using World War II vintage weapons.

Gradually, the administration increased aid to the rebels but did so covertly. A strategy began to emerge with the cooperation of Pakistan. Pakistan was encouraged to give safe haven to the rebels and to keep the supply lines open. The price was apparently an increase in military aid to Pakistan and, ultimately, a blind spot concerning Pakistan's nuclear weapons development capability. The turning point was the decision in 1985 to give antiaircraft Stinger missiles to the Afghan rebels. This undermined what had been the Soviet's most effective strategy: aircraft and helicopter fire against unarmed and completely exposed rebel installations. With diminished air superiority, Soviet ground forces and logistics columns were increasingly exposed. The degree to which this single technology turned the tide of the war will undoubtedly be debated for years to come. It can certainly be said that it made the battleground a more level one for the Afghan rebels.

Within months, the Soviet Union and the Afghan armies began to suffer reverses more consistently. We will never know when the Soviet leadership decided that the war was now a quagmire with no apparent solution. Not long after Gorbachev's rise to power, the first pictures of what was really happening to Soviet soldiers in Afghanistan—there on "training missions and patrols"—began to appear in the Soviet press. In 1986, Gorbachev referred to Afghanistan as a "bleeding wound." All that was left to the Soviets was to find a graceful exit.[5]

Initially, the Soviet position was that any coalition government that ruled after their departure had to be "acceptable" to the reigning Afghan government. A "timetable" for the removal of Soviet troops was tied directly to an acceptable government for Afghanistan. When Pakistan and the United States held firm on this issue, the Soviets eventually caved in. There is no other way to describe the change in Soviet policy. By January 1988, it was clear in the negotiations at Geneva that Gorbachev was ready to leave Afghanistan virtually without conditions. In spite of a last-minute effort by Pakistan, with American acquiescence, to tie an agreement to an acceptable government for the rebels, the final accord did not lay out a course for Afghanistan's political development after the war. The language used was that it would be "left to the Afghan people to decide." The United States and the Soviet Union jointly offered international guarantees against outside interference in the affairs of Afghanistan. Soviet troops completed their withdrawal in February 1989.

It is, of course, a defensible argument that the Soviet Union would have left Afghanistan with or without the Reagan Doctrine's commitment to the Afghan rebels. Cause and effect cannot be definitively established; but one thing is certain: the rebels, after the steadier and more directed infusion of arms, fared much better in this war. The Soviet Union faced the prospect of continued reverses or of increasing its commitment of forces to try to change the tide of the battle. The leadership decided to get out of Afghanistan while an international agreement was still possible; but that agreement leaves the fate of the government that the Soviet Union supported for almost ten years uncertain at best.

The Reagan Doctrine has not had such dramatic impact in other areas of the world. Although Jonas Savimbi and the contras may have had some effect on the Angolan government and the Sandinistas, these rebels are far less sympathetic characters than the Afghan rebels. It has been more difficult to defend the image of Jonas Savimbi who is so closely tied to the regime of apartheid in South Africa as having the interests of his people at heart. If anything, the contras have been the administration's thorniest foreign policy problem because they have engendered so much domestic opposition. The commitment to the contras which produced the administration's most embarrassing scandal, Irangate, cannot and need not be explored here.

This points out a problem with the Reagan Doctrine. Since it is not differentiated in response to regional and indigenous circumstances, it is bound to have less impact and, some might argue, negative impact in some regions of the world. The Reagan Doctrine's biggest flaw, even though it has had dramatic impact in Afghanistan, is that it globalizes and bilateralizes conflicts whose dynamics are complicated by regional and indigenous politics. Perhaps the reason that the policy worked so well in Afghanistan is quite simple: Soviet forces were the problem, and their presence was appropriately the target of American pressure.

Setting the Course for Arms Control

The problem of what to do in arms control was, in many ways, more difficult and more fundamental. It was not long before the Reagan administration's categorical rejection of arms control as strategy produced a backlash in Europe and in the United States. Reagan had made clear that he had no tolerance for the "fatally flawed" Strategic Arms Limitation Talks (SALT) approach. Moreover, the administration's first impulse was to rebuild American strength.

One year into Reagan's administration, it was clear that arms control enjoyed a broad public basis of support. Nervous allies, Congress, and an increasingly strong public movement were troubled by the President's "loose rhetoric" on nuclear weapons. Alexander Haig's reference to U.S. plans to fire a nuclear "warning shot" in response to Soviet aggression and Reagan's unrestrained cold war rhetoric only added fuel. Almost in self-defense, therefore, the administration countered with an arms control plan of its own.

Reagan laid out an agenda that was significantly different from the SALT approach. What is interesting for our purposes is that the agenda is remarkably close to the baseline in arms control today.[6] In November 1981, Reagan wrote a letter to Leonid Brezhnev, then general secretary of the Soviet Communist party, establishing the following goals for arms control:

> 1. The first and most important point concerns the Geneva negotiations [on intermediate-range nuclear forces]. The United States is prepared to cancel its deployment of Pershing II and ground-launched cruise missiles if the Soviets will dismantle their SS-20, SS-4, and SS-5 missiles. . . . Soviet spokesmen have suggested that moving their SS-20s beyond the Ural Mountains will remove the threat. That assertion is wrong.

This became the basis for the zero option and eventually the global zero option (including Asian and European forces).

> 2. The United States proposes to open negotiations on strategic arms. We will make proposals for genuinely serious reductions and will seek to negotiate substantial reductions in nuclear arms which would result in levels that are equal and verifiable. Our approach to verification will be to emphasize openness and creativity—rather than the secrecy and suspicion which have undermined confidence in arms control in the past.
> 3. The third proposal I have made to the Soviet Union is that we act to achieve equality at lower levels of conventional forces in Europe.
> 4. I have pointed out that we must reduce the risks of surprise attack and the chance of war arising out of uncertainty or miscalculation. At the current Madrid meeting of the Conference on Security and Cooperation in Europe, we are laying the foundation for a Western-proposed conference on disarmament in Europe. This conference would discuss new measures to enhance stability and security in Europe.

The United States and the Soviet Union agreed to begin negotiations in the fall of 1981, but little progress was made. Many proponents of arms control believed that the Reagan proposals were too ambitious and one-sided. This was particularly true of the global zero option for intermediate-range nuclear forces. There were time pressures operating because under the NATO "dual-track" decision, failure to reach agreement by December 1983 meant that NATO would proceed with the deployment of 464 ground-launched cruise missiles and 108 Pershing IIs. The deployments were extremely unpopular among the vocal left in Europe, and those governments were anxious to achieve agreement. As the time ticked away, the pressures for Reagan to meet the Soviet Union halfway mounted, including an attempt by Paul Nitze, special advisor to the secretary of state for arms control, and the Soviet negotiator V. Kvitzinsky to strike a deal in the "walk in the Vienna Woods." In the final analysis, the administration would not budge. Relations between the superpowers reached their nadir in December 1983 when the Soviets, as they had promised, walked out of the Intermediate Nuclear Forces (INF) talks.

Strategic arms control was not off to an auspicious start either. The first Reagan proposal for deep reductions in the arsenals of the two sides actually increased the ratio of Soviet weapons to American targets. Moreover, the proposals were, on the surface, patently one-sided. The original proposal did not include bomber forces (a preponderance of them belonging to the United States) and would have exacted a greater price from the Soviet Union than from the United States through penalties for throw-weight and severe restrictions on heavy missiles.

Then, in March 1983, Ronald Reagan delivered the speech outlining his vision for a defensive shield for the United States. In rereading the speech, it is circumspect and relatively modest. "Wouldn't it be better to save lives than to avenge them?" the President asked.[7] The call to American scientists to accept the challenge of creating a defensive shield to replace offensive-based deterrence cast a long shadow over strategic arms control. The prospect of strategic defense threatened the Anti-Ballistic Missile (ABM) Treaty of 1972, long considered the crowning achievement of arms control and the basis for offensive force limitations. The Soviets expressed extreme alarm. The reaction is perhaps best summed up by the statement of Yuri Andropov who claimed that the Strategic Defense Initiative (SDI) was designed to "disarm the Soviet Union in the face of the American nuclear threat."[8]

Arms control was in very deep trouble. Shortly after walking out of the INF talks, the Soviet Union suspended the START (Strategic Arms Reduction) talks as well. Against the backdrop of recrimination and countercharges, the superpower relationship was at low ebb. The Reagan strategy had apparently backfired.

Or had it? There have always been arguments that some in the administration intended to set such stringent terms for arms control that the Soviet Union would be forced to refuse them. The onus for the breakdown of arms control would then be on their shoulders, and the

United States could continue with its military buildup without fear of public ridicule, at least from the broad center in American and Western opinion. The Soviets, for their part, might have expected sympathy from world public opinion, but instead, the Reagan gamble—if it was one—did work. The broad range of public opinion, focusing less on the negotiability of the proposals than on the dramatic Soviet walkout, did not support the Soviet Union. In spite of demonstrations in Europe and the United States, the deployments of INF forces did begin. Conservative governments that feared that the missiles might bring defeat in general elections survived in the Netherlands and Germany.

By September 1984, the Soviets apparently came to the conclusion that their absence from the arms control table was having the opposite effect that they had intended. Perhaps they also saw clearly that Ronald Reagan was about to win a second term. Andrei Gromyko, then foreign minister, was dispatched to Washington to try and repair relations. Ronald Reagan, reelected in a landslide, agreed to resume arms control talks after the first of the year.

The first round of the talks recessed without success. Shortly after the new talks, now divided into three baskets (INF, strategic offensive forces, and talks on weapons in space), the administration launched another set of salvos at the Soviet Union. This time the issue was compliance, or rather noncompliance, with arms control treaties. Citing a "pattern" of cheating on arms control agreements, the administration began issuing reports to Congress on Soviet noncompliance with arms control. The charges ranged from trivial to the very serious and well supported charge that the Soviets had violated the ABM treaty through the construction of a phased-array radar at Krasnoyarsk. Although many noted arms controllers dismissed the violation as militarily insignificant, few argued that the charge was without merit.[9]

That particular charge coincided nicely with the President's contention, after the speech establishing SDI, that it was the Soviets, not the administration, who had put the ABM Treaty in danger.

The second round of the new and already stalled arms control talks was scheduled to begin in March 1985. It is most certainly coincidental that Konstantin Chernenko died on the morning of the first session, but it turned out to be an important symbol for the birth of a new phase in U.S.-Soviet relations and particularly in arms control.

Gorbachev, Reagan, and Arms Control

The mood and scenes from the Washington summit of December 1987 seem, in retrospect, very far removed from the confrontational days in U.S.-Soviet relations four years before. Earlier, in Reykjavik, U.S.-Soviet relations narrowly escaped another crash; but in the twists and turns that brought the relationship to where it was in 1987, that meeting was probably the turning point. It was, after all, at Reykjavik that the broad outlines for acceptance of the zero option and the 50 percent reduction formula for strategic offensive forces were developed. That both Reagan and Gorbachev left Reykjavik frustrated was easily detectable in their expressions as they left and in their first statements. The talks broke down because Ronald Reagan refused to accept constraints on SDI.

However, this time, instead of stormily denouncing the talks, the Soviets, like the administration, sought to put a positive "spin" on the Reykjavik talks. What could have been viewed as disastrous suddenly became the point of departure for the next round of talks at Geneva. From that point on, it was very clear that Gorbachev wanted arms control agreements, and little by little the Soviets made their peace with Reagan's arms control agenda.

So, did the Reagan strategy simply succeed, or did the same ideas emerge independently in the Soviet Union? Two points are fact: (1) the current arms control agenda at all levels resembles the one that Ronald Reagan laid out in 1981; (2) the INF Treaty is the zero option on a global scale with stringent on-site verification measures. The START talks proceeded on the basis of agreement to cut warheads, not launchers, and to reduce the arsenals by 50 percent. There is a penalty for heavy missiles and a sublimit on ballistic missiles (which Reagan always said are particularly destabilizing). It appears that there will not be a further penalty for land-based systems, but counting rules for bombers are extraordinarily liberal. Penetrating bombers carrying all of their weapons are counted as only one weapon. There is further discussion of a "discount" for bombers that are able to fire cruise missiles from outside of air defense range. It now appears that exploitation of these rules could take both sides well over the 6,000-warhead limit. Since it is the United States that has a preponderance of bombers and significantly more experience in operating them, the rules are undeniably favorable to the United States. Finally, talks will apparently begin soon on conventional force reductions though they will probably be protracted and difficult. It is now Gorbachev who has taken up the Reagan formula that the goal is to reduce the possibility for "surprise attack." In the meantime, the Conference on Security and Confidence Building in Europe produced a treaty with stringent notification and inspection measures, including one that allows inspection of Soviet forces deployed in the European Soviet Union. Ronald Reagan did not move very far from his November 1981 agenda.

The other point, though, is that the Reagan strategy was getting nowhere until Gorbachev came to power. Clearly, there was some interaction between the stubbornness with which Ronald Reagan held to his positions and the emergence of Gorbachev. In trying to untangle this relationship, it would be useful to be inside the black box that is Soviet decision making. Absent that possibility, we can frame the question in terms of the decisions that Gorbachev faced when he came to power and as he has pursued his goals of economic and social restructuring in the Soviet Union. In this regard, the Reagan challenge arguably played heavily as a constraint on options that were available to Gorbachev.

Gorbachev did not come to power primed to accept the terms of the Reagan arms control agenda. In fact, his first attempt to lay out an agenda of his own was a curious combination of old Soviet arms control proposals (like a nuclear-testing moratorium and the creation of nuclear-free zones) and wildly unrealistic proposals like the elimination of all nuclear weapons by the year 2000.[10] His first attempt to upstage Ronald Reagan was a unilateral moratorium on nuclear testing in 1986. The President said that a comprehensive test ban was unacceptable, and he held fast to that position. In spite of Soviet efforts, no ground swell of public opinion rushed to the defense of the Soviet proposal, and it was unceremoniously dumped eighteen months later.

Gorbachev came to power with an overwhelming economic and social agenda. The Soviet economy had experienced ten to fifteen years of stagnation and was, in Gorbachev's own words, in "a precrisis" stage. The prescription was initially acceleration of growth; but over time, the Soviets became more and more radical in their views of the task at hand. Acceleration was replaced with concerns for modernizing the base of the economy and ultimately by *perestroika,* a term that does not mean reform but rather transformation and restructuring.

The key problem was to break up the Stalinist system of heavily centralized labor- and resource-intensive development and to replace it with a system that can meet the rapidly expanding challenges of the postindustrial technological revolution.

It is that technological challenge that probably represented the link between Soviet willingness to adapt in arms control and Gorbachev's domestic goals. In the best of all worlds, Gorbachev would have been able to put military modernization issues on hold. The Soviet Union had engaged in a massive military buildup over the ten years between 1965 and 1975. Although there is a great deal of disagreement about the level of the Soviet defense budget, there is little evidence that they spent a great deal. Estimates range from 12 to 18 percent. Under *glasnost'*, the Soviets are now admitting that the size of their national income may have been overestimated and that owing to heavy subsidies to the defense sector, they do not know how much they have been spending on defense. In any case, this was an extraordinary peacetime military buildup.[11] The buildup brought significant benefits. The Soviet Union could certainly boast, as Leonid Brezhnev did, "we will be so strong that no one would dare disturb our peaceful way of life." They were in a position to dominate their allies militarily and thus politically as well as to present a formidable threat to NATO. Finally, the Soviet Union was undeniably a superpower with military forces in far corners of the globe and the Soviet flag displayed far from Soviet shores.

What must have been distressing for Gorbachev was that since the early 1980s his marshals and generals had been proclaiming loudly that this was not enough. Yes, parity had been reached; but parity was a dynamic concept, and the United States was engaged in another round of military modernization that challenged the very gains the Soviet Union had made.

The argument was two-fold. The Reagan buildup and plans to deploy D-5, MX, and the B-1 represented a new round of the arms race. This argument was not so troubling and might have been put to rest by a political leadership that simply said no. However, the military, represented most loudly by Nikolai Ogarkov, then chief of the general staff, focused on the Soviet Union's technological inferiority, warning that there was a "revolution in military affairs" taking place. This meant that old strategies like incremental improvement in Soviet weapons systems and compensation for quality through numerical superiority were inadequate. As the Soviets are prone to do, they reached back for historical analogies as articles appeared on the transformation that had taken place when tanks replaced horses on the battlefield.[12] The message was very clear. The information-processing revolution, the possibilities opened up by weapons based on "new physical principles" (lasers), and progress in miniaturization of guidance so that conventional "smart weapons" now achieved yields approximating those of small nuclear weapons threatened to make Soviet defense forces obsolete.

It is difficult to overstate how alarmist the rhetoric from the Soviet marshals had become. Even before SDI was announced, Ogarkov published a pamphlet that seemed to liken the situation to the late 1930s and warned that a failure to take up the challenge would produce similar results.

The evidence suggests that even before Gorbachev came to power, the Soviet leadership was in no mood to accept this challenge. It is widely accepted that his alarmist rhetoric and aggressive pursuit of resources probably cost Ogarkov his job in 1984. Even though his replacement, Marshal Sergei Akhromeyev, was less forceful and alarmist, his message was similar. The United States was challenging the Soviet Union to a duel at ever higher levels of technological sophistication.

In this atmosphere, SDI took on a different meaning. The Soviet Union had been involved in research into defensive technologies and possessed the world's only deployed ABM system. However, early concepts for SDI focused on the use of space, new sensor technologies, and supercomputing to handle the millions of calculations needed to direct ballistic missile defenses. There were also possibilities for exploiting these technologies on the conventional battlefield, adding fuel to the contention that that arena, traditionally an area of Soviet strength, was also under challenge.

Perhaps the military would have preferred a strategy of the old type: intensive devotion of resources to the defense sector to meet the threat. However, there is some evidence that the generals understood that this challenge was different because technological breakthroughs were being achieved on parallel fronts. The problem was not to meet the challenge of the atomic bomb, forcing all resources into that project, but to meet the challenge of a large and rapidly expanding American (and Western) technological base.

The shocking news for Gorbachev must have been that this economy that had served nothing well if not defense was now incapable of supporting even those demands. In these circumstances, Gorbachev's options were severely constrained. He could take on the challenge in a way that might not be effective and that would continue to distort the economy toward intensive development of defense industries at the expense of the base of the economy. Another approach might have been to wait and see if Reagan could sustain the buildup and the SDI challenge. Interestingly, that strategy might have worked, since by 1987 Reagan had lost control of the Senate, lost control of SDI and generally lost the consensus behind expansion of the defense budget. However, Gorbachev took another road. Rather than meeting the threat head on, he decided to redefine the threat and make a virtue of temporary Soviet weakness.

Step by step this led to the development of the "new thinking in foreign and defense policy." It is a loose collection of ideas that attempt to give the Soviet Union the high ground of being the power that "understands the demands of the nuclear age."[13] The policy has too many aspects to detail it here.[14] In short, it is critical both of continued American "militarism" and the policies of Gorbachev's predecessors who reacted without flexibility and attention to the objective conditions of nuclear weapons. If the United States is attempting to gain nuclear superiority, this policy would argue, it is a futile attempt. Squarely in the center of the policy is apparent acceptance of a view that marginal numerical or qualitative advantages do not add up to military advantage in the area of nuclear weapons. This made acceptance of the zero option for INF forces possible, although it required the Soviet Union to dismantle four times as many warheads as the United States.

There are other reasons that the Soviets might have adopted this policy. The Soviet Union's foreign policy, particularly *vis-à-vis* Europe, was in something of a box. The SS-20 decision and the heavy armored forces pointed at the heart of Europe had become an irritant in an important set of political relationships. The policy of threatening the Europeans over the issue of the INF deployments had been such a complete failure that a new course might have been chosen for that reason.

The point is, though, that as Gorbachev moved to a strategy that saw a broader political-military strategy in which the military balance was just one element, the Soviet Union was able to accept constraints on its military power which might have been unthinkable without that shift.

From the point of view of the Reagan legacy, the important point is that the constraints and the terms of agreement were overwhelmingly those that Ronald Reagan had set out. Had the baseline of acceptable proposals been different, the constraints on Soviet military power would have been less severe. For instance, if in 1983 the United States had accepted a limited deployment of SS-20s in exchange for a limited deployment of NATO INF forces, a treaty eliminating that class of missiles would probably never have come into being.

Reagan delivered on his promise to change the terms of cooperation. The United States and the Soviet Union now negotiate reductions in the strategic forces, not limitations. On-site inspection and stringent terms of verification are in place in one treaty and being negotiated in several others. The Soviet Union has left Afghanistan, and the Soviets appear to be anxious to settle conflicts in a number of other areas.

Reagan could probably not take credit for the liberalization that is producing a more tolerant policy of human rights in the Soviet Union. That has an internal dynamic having to do with the need to revitalize

Soviet society and to create a constituency for change in the intelligentsia. Similarly, the opening up of Soviet society which makes cultural exchange somewhat easier is more an instrument of their internal politics. This does not mean that the Soviets are unaware of the international recognition of these changes and of its impact on the Soviet Union's image and ability to form beneficial economic and technological relations with the rest of the world. Gorbachev was clearly stung by the Reagan speech of April 1988 in which he condemned the Soviet Union as unchanged. He must have been heartened by Reagan's admission a few weeks later that the Soviet Union was to be congratulated for some of the changes taking place and the "parallelism" in which he engaged in admitting that not all in the United States is perfect.

In sum, it took Reagan's commitment to a given agenda and Soviet recognition that adaptation to it could serve Soviet goals to bring U.S.-Soviet relations to where they are today. In retrospect, it is easy to forget that whatever the President's commitment to a set of goals, the administration often stumbled badly in trying to achieve them. The road was not smooth, and administration management of U.S.-Soviet relations had some woeful moments as well as some splendid successes.

By most accounts, Reykjavik should rank as the high-water mark for lack of preparation. Reports of American proposals being drawn up in the small hours of the night on a makeshift table in the bathroom do not inspire confidence. The post-Reykjavik assessment coming out of the hearings held by the House Armed Services Committee supported those claims.

More seriously, there is increasing evidence that American proposals were often tendered before they were worked out properly, leaving the United States in the embarrassing position of having to back away from its own proposals. The most egregious example was in the matter of on-site verification for the INF Treaty in which the United States proposed a regime of challenge inspections so stringent that American industry and the Pentagon balked. After years of assuming that on-site verification was nonnegotiable, it was suddenly negotiated, and the drawbacks and management problems that it entails are now becoming clear. It may be that stringent verification regimes introduce new contradictions and are open to more misinterpretation.

There are other cases too. Could the President really have intended to dismantle all ballistic missiles in the American arsenal when he proposed zero ballistic missiles at Reykjavik? If so, were the terms under which we could do so clear before the proposal was made just in case the Soviets said yes? Proposal making for public effect rather than military substance has been a consistent problem in recent years. The Soviets engage in it too, and it only serves to make the arms control process more difficult.

Finally, questions must be raised about the management of the SDI program under Reagan, whatever its effect on the Soviet Union. The failure to define a technologically and economically defensible program left SDI in deep trouble and the consensus for exploring reasonable uses for defense split. The most counterproductive policy by far in this regard was the flap over the "reinterpretation" of the ABM Treaty. There may have been strategies available, some bilateral or even unilateral ones, to allow testing of SDI technologies; but by forcing a constitutional argument on the grounds that a President can "reinterpret" a treaty without regard for the meaning at the time of ratification, the administration made certain that there would be a battle with Congress. It came back to haunt the President. Ratification of the INF Treaty was held up, in part, over this constitutional issue.

Nevertheless, issues of management aside, that there is a positive impact of the Reagan years on U.S.-Soviet relations seems clear. Future arms control agreements with the Soviet Union will be expected to reduce military forces, not simply limit them. Verification will be stringent and will include measures for on-site inspection. The Soviet Union will always face the Afghanistan reality in situations of regional conflict: the United States might choose to arm and equip forces fighting Soviet clients, even if the stakes are very high and Soviet forces are, themselves, involved. It will be difficult for future presidents to require less.

What of the part of the Reagan policies which sought not a set of agreements but a new approach for America in dealing with the Soviet Union? Can future American presidents embark upon high-risk strategies of confrontation and have the Soviet Union respond as it has? In part, the answer lies in how wedded Gorbachev is to the "new foreign policy" that reacts to threat in a different manner. It must be noted, though, that the Soviet Union has given no signs of being so desperate that its security interests, broadly defined, are sacrificed in return for agreements. This is not 1918; and even though the Soviet Union is surely a society in trouble, it remains a tough adversary with interests that it will defend.

In closing the book on the Reagan years, one philosophical question comes to mind: has Ronald Reagan, the great cold warrior, brought the cold war to its conclusion? Would we have dared to ask that question in 1980? Reagan could claim, with considerable justification, that he challenged the Soviet Union and established new terms of cooperation. In doing so, he broadened the bipartisan consensus for arms control as a strategy in meeting some of the security requirements of the United States. There are still those on the far right and the far left who disagree; but arms control and military modernization are linked in a way that they have never been before. It is incumbent on future presidents to maintain that linkage.

In a broader sense, the United States can claim, with some justification, that containment has worked long enough to force fundamental change in the Soviet Union and in its foreign policies as well. What remains is to manage the victory of containment and find the next steps in dealing with the Soviet Union.

The Reagan legacy is one that includes some achievements, matters that are still unresolved, and its share of mistakes. Moreover, it is surely a legacy shared with Gorbachev. There is a sense that both as a symbol of a new and broader domestic consensus on U.S.-Soviet relations and as one who offered the Soviets a set of severely constrained options, Ronald Reagan has been a truly historic figure. It is up to future presidents to show that they can do better.

NOTES

The epigraph is taken from "State of the Union Address, 25 January 1988," reprinted in *Department of State Bulletin* 88, no. 2132 (March 1988).

1. Perhaps the most influential article in support of this thesis was written by Richard Pipes in *Commentary* 65 (July 1977), "Why the Soviet Union Thinks It Can Fight and Win a Nuclear War." This theme was central to the arguments of the Committee on the Present Danger to which most presidential advisors-to-be belonged. For a compilation, see W. Scott Thompson, ed., *National Security in the 1980s: From Weakness to Strength* (New Brunswick, N.J.: Institute for Contemporary Studies, 1980).

2. "News Conference of January 29" (Excerpts), *Department of State Bulletin* 81 no. 2048 (March 1981):12.

3. A view much like that of those who saw extreme internal weakness of totalitarian systems as the source for their aggressive external behavior. Zbigniew Brzezinski and Carl Friedrich wrote the definitive study in *Totalitarian Dictatorship and Autocracy* (Cambridge, Mass.: Harvard University Press, 1956).

4. American operational strategy had long recognized the value of "militarily significant" targets. The definition of what was significant has shifted over time, but the idea that the United States was engaged in "city busting" in the late 1970s was indefensible. See Scott Sagan, *Moving Targets* (New York: Council on Foreign Relations, 1989).

5. The reports of Artem Borowvik in the journal *Ogonyok* were particularly telling. Eventually, more candid accounts of the problems of soldiers in Afghanistan and of returning veterans began to appear in the central press although there was never criticism of the Soviet decision to invade or to remain.

6. For an excellent discussion of the early Reagan approach to arms control, see Coit D. Blacker, *Reluctant Warriors* (New York: W. H. Freeman, 1987), 131–60.

7. Ronald Reagan, "Peace and National Security," televised address to the nation, Washington, D.C., 23 March 1983, Department of State, *Realism, Strength, Negotiation: Key Foreign Policy Statements of the Reagan Administration* (Washington, D.C.: U.S. Government Printing Office, 1984).

8. "Yu. V. Andropov Answers Questions from a Pravda Correspondent," *Pravda,* 27 March 1983.

9. See, for example, a report by Sidney Drell, David Holloway, and Phillip Farley, *The Reagan Strategic Defense Initiative: A Technological, Political, and Arms Control Assessment* (Stanford, Calif.: Center for International Security and Arms Control, 1984).

10. See Gorbachev's speech to the party Congress in January 1986 reported in *Pravda,* 19 January 1986.

11. There is an excellent report on the Soviet economic reform problem from the Joint Economic Committee of the Congress entitled *Gorbachev's Economic Plans* (Washington, D.C.: U.S. Government Printing Office, 1987) in two volumes.

12. Condoleezza Rice, "The Soviet Military under Gorbachev," *Current History* (October, 1986).

13. For Gorbachev's view of this, see Mikhail Gorbachev, *Perestroika.*

14. Steven Meyer has done so in a forthcoming paper for *International Security.*

PART THREE

Economic and Fiscal Policy

6

Constitutional Principles and Economic Policy

STEVEN M. SHEFFRIN

Prior to the beginning of the Reagan administration, a common theme began to emerge among some conservative economists and policymakers. The poor economic performance of the last part of the Carter administration was not viewed simply as a consequence of badly chosen priorities or poor implementation of economic strategies but as endemic to the normal operation of economic policy in the United States. The fundamental problem concerned the incentives that the institutional framework provided policymakers. Under the system that prevailed, these conservative thinkers argued that the system inevitably produced too high an inflation rate and a tendency toward permanent fiscal deficits. These problems could not be solved simply by changing the personnel inhabiting the offices of the government. Fundamental institutional change was required to alter the incentives that faced policymakers. These institutional changes essentially involved reducing the scope of discretionary policy by placing constitutional or similar restraints on policymakers.

Brennan and Buchanan (1981), in *Monopoly in Money and Inflation: The Case for a Constitution to Discipline Government,* outlined the case for constitutional rules governing monetary policy. Their argument began with a parable of an alchemist who devised a procedure to create gold while living in a country with a gold standard. The alchemist noticed that when he took his newly created gold to buy goods, he was able to acquire goods for the gold, but the prices of all other goods rose, and the other citizens in the country were made worse off by the alchemist's discovery. In Version *A* of the story, the alchemist exploited the profits from his discovery and lived a life of luxury in his castle. In Version *B*, the alchemist decided not to use his gold-creation process because it reduced the welfare of the other citizens of the land.

Brennan and Buchanan asked which version of the parable a ten-year-old girl would find most plausible. Through introspection, they argued that their ten-year-old girl would find Version *B* to be implausible. Assuming this is indeed the case, why should a government in a position of creating money through open market purchases be expected to refrain from the inflation tax? Brennan and Buchanan argued that governments will not be able to refrain from using the inflation tax with the result that excess inflation will result from an unconstrained government with the ability to create money. The remedy for this problem is some type of constitutional restraint on the government's money-creation ability. In their words, "Only by restraining the discretionary powers of the monetary authorities through enforceable constitutional rules will the inflation be controlled. It is the *monetary regime,* not *monetary policy,* that must be modified" (p. 65).

The argument for the emergence of persistent deficits in a democracy rests on the power of special interests, especially coalitions of special interests, to use the legislative process to provide benefits to themselves at the expense of general taxpayers. The benefits of special-interest legislation are highly valued to the recipients whereas the costs of any one of these benefits to the general populace appears small. The result is a proliferation of spending. Coupled with the electorate's aversion to tax increases, the result is persistent deficits.

Stubblebine (1980, 51) provided a succinct account of this process.

> For each of us, government spending on a program offers the least-cost-way of providing that service. Classic examples, of course, are programs whose benefits accrue to a narrow group of people, but which are funded by general taxation. The tax price of the marginal costs to the individual beneficiaries appears to be zero. That they should demand unlimited numbers of those programs, each of unlimited size, should come as no surprise. And this is true of all of us. We are all beneficiaries of some program, and so increased spending has its proponents. At the same time, taxes are painful and we prefer total lower taxes. . . . The conjunction of these two factors—opportunity to intervene and support for this or that intervention—leads to budget deficits.

The only way to prevent this phenomenon is some type of constitutional restraint on either spending or the budget.

In an essay about principles of monetary and fiscal policy, Robert E. Lucas Jr. (1986, 133), writing several years later, echoes the same themes. "The tendencies towards permanent deficit finance and inflation that have emerged in our economy in the last fifteen years have much deeper roots that [sic] a transition of transient external shocks and internal mistakes. They arose, I believe, because the implicit rules under which monetary and fiscal policy is conducted have undergone a gradual but fundamental change. If this diagnosis is accurate, then the situation will improve only if new rules can be found that bind policy decisions without committing them to permanent inefficiencies."

The last phrase in the Lucas quote is important. Rules that bind economic policy decisions can prevent policymakers from taking necessary actions in the face of unexpected circumstances and events. Situations will naturally arise in which all parties recognize that a discretionary response that violates the rule will improve welfare. How can binding rules be designed so as to allow policymakers the opportunity to take decisive steps in the face of undesirable economic circumstances?

Much of the literature on constitutional restraints on economic policy fails to address this point. This literature often presumes that the advent of rules will put an end to "politics as usual." As Allen Schick (1982, 96) expressed this point, "Recourse to the constitution is an attempt to negate or limit political action." Political pressures for desirable outcomes do not simply disappear. Faced with "permanent inefficiencies" or even obvious temporary inefficiencies, the political process will generate pressure to sidestep or avoid rules. Any constitutional or statutory scheme to limit policy choices must confront this problem.

During the Reagan administration, both monetary and fiscal policy were subject to controls that, in principle, were designed to limit discretionary policy choices. Monetary policy was subject to a monetary targeting regime from the beginning of the Reagan administration. Fiscal policy choices were restrained through the Gramm-Rudman process during Reagan's second term. This chapter examines the economics and politics of monetary targeting and the Gramm-Rudman process from the perspective of living experiments in rule-constrained economic policy. It examines both the particular circumstances in which the rules developed as well as the influence of the rules on the actual policy choices that were made during the period. By considering two diverse experiments in rule-constrained policy-making, we can look at the common features and difficulties that necessarily emerge in any rule-constrained political environment.

Some supporters of constitutional restraints on economic policy would want to ignore evidence from these two episodes because Gramm-Rudman was a statutory restraint, and monetary targeting was partly statutory and partly administrative restraint. However, the difference between these types of restraints can be easily exaggerated. As Allen Schick (1982) noted, New York City plunged into bankruptcy under a constitution that explicitly prohibited deficit financing for operating expenses and pulled itself out of financial disaster through statutory controls on its budget. More generally, to the extent that the same types of problems emerge from all rule-governed policy experiments, the lessons from monetary targeting and Gramm-Rudman should inform the larger debate on rule-constrained political systems.

To preview the conclusions, the actual operation of monetary targeting and Gramm-Rudman provided surprises to both supporters and critics of rule-governed macropolicies. Both experiments were successful in influencing the course of policy; but they operated within the normal political channels and did not put an end to "politics as usual." Monetary targeting and Gramm-Rudman also came to have important symbolic value in political debate which appeared to exert an independent force on political outcomes. The policies, however, were not fully binding; when a consensus appeared to change the policies, political actors were able to work around the limits imposed by the rules and laws. Finally, technical flaws in the design of both monetary targeting and Gramm-Rudman became evident rather quickly and limited their effectiveness. The two experiments suggest that "intermediate policies" that fall between constitutional amendments and normal laws may play an important and beneficial role in formulating macropolicy.

Monetary Targeting

HISTORY PRIOR TO THE REAGAN ADMINISTRATION

Monetary targeting officially began in the United States in 1975 with the passage of House Concurrent Resolution 133. Although some economists hailed the bill as a triumph of monetarism, the legislative history, as Woolley (1984) recounts, suggests less than a resounding victory. The bill began in the House as a move to lower interest rates during the 1975 recession and then was changed in the Senate to call for increased money growth in the first half of 1975 as well as to have the Federal Reserve report to Congress every six months on its plans for the economy. As the final resolution was debated in the House, sponsors of the resolution indicated that concerns about interest rates, not just the money supply, were expressed in the resolution.

Until 1978, the Federal Open Market Committee (FOMC) responded to the resolution by announcing target growth ranges for several monetary aggregates every quarter. Each quarter, the target growth ranges would begin from the current level of the money supply. This policy led to what has been termed "base drift": if the money supply exceeded its target in any quarter and the growth targets were not changed, the deviation of the money supply from its target would be permanent.

With the passage of the Humphrey-Hawkins Act of 1978, the FOMC was required to target growth ranges every February for the remainder of the calendar year. Instead of quarterly base drift, the system was subject to possible annual base drift. It is a fair assessment that at least until 1979, meeting the targets was not the Fed's top priority. Targets for M1 (currency plus demand deposits) were exceeded in both 1977 and 1978.

The situation changed dramatically in 1979. In the midst of deteriorating economic conditions and increased political vulnerability, President Carter made numerous cabinet changes and placed G. William Miller, who was then federal reserve chairman, into the position of secretary of the treasury. The search for a new Fed chairman eventually resulted in the appointment of Paul Volcker. Volcker was faced with surging inflation, due to both increasing nominal wage demands and the effects of the second major Organization of Petroleum Exporting Countries (OPEC) price, a falling dollar, and growing perceptions of a financial crisis.

In October 1979, Volcker announced a major shift in policy. Prior to this time, the Fed had been using the federal funds rate (the interest rate on short-term interbank loans) as the vehicle to meet its money supply targets. Essentially, the Fed estimated what interest rate in the federal funds market would be consistent with their money targets and then used open market operations to hit this interest rate. Under this operating procedure, the funds rate could, in principle, have to move quite substantially as conditions in the money market changed. As a practical matter, however, the Fed was not willing to let the funds rate move that dramatically, and the result was that the money supply would be allowed to deviate from its targets.

The new policy that the Fed announced involved using bank reserves (technically, reserves not borrowed from the Fed) as the intermediate targets. In practice, the Fed now set a wide range for the federal funds rate in order to generate a target level of bank reserves which would be consistent with the monetary targets. Although the Fed was criticized in some quarters for not moving fully toward reserve targeting, it is clear that the Fed was now willing to tolerate sharp gyrations in the federal funds market and in short-term interest rates to try to meet its monetary targets.

In switching to a new operating procedure in 1979, the Fed was, in effect, announcing that it now would take the monetary targets seriously and was willing to change its procedures in order to meet these goals. This was, in part, the price the Fed had to pay to restore credibility and try to limit fears of continuing increases in inflation. Another, perhaps inadvertent, effect of the change in the operating system was to limit some of the blame for high interest rates and thus to allow the Fed to raise interest rates substantially. As long as the Fed said it was just controlling reserves, it could argue that the "market" was effectively setting interest rates. Of course, the level of interest rates was inversely related to the level of reserves the Fed supplied to the system, and thus it could be held responsible for the level of interest rates. Nonetheless, at least some of the governors felt that the new system had provided "political cover" for raising interest rates.[1]

With the Fed's switch to the new operating strategy, short-term interest rates were allowed to rise through February and March 1980. In March 1980, President Carter promulgated credit controls. These controls had immediate effects in the financial markets and the economy. The economy soon plunged into an extremely sharp but very short recession. As loan demand fell both because of dampening economic activity and the effects of the credit controls, and as depositors moved some assets from deposits to interest-bearing assets, M1 fell dramatically in April. The new operating system dictated that the Fed should allow the federal funds rate to fall in order to stimulate the growth of bank reserves in order to meet the monetary targets. The Fed did indeed allow interest rates to fall, and the Funds rate plunged from a high of seventeen percent in April to nearly nine percent by midsummer.[2]

By midsummer, however, a recovery from the recession had begun (perhaps due to the elimination of controls and easier monetary policy), and the money supply began to soar again. Now the Fed was faced with the less pleasant consequence of its operating procedure: interest rates had to rise to limit money growth. The Fed pushed the federal funds rate upward through the election until it reached over eighteen percent by year's end.

The last year of the Carter administration had not been a good year for the Fed. The economy had entered a recession but was still plagued by high inflation and fears of increasing inflation. Interest rates had fallen from very high levels only to rise again; and the Fed still had not achieved credibility in its fight against inflation.

TARGETING IN THE REAGAN ADMINISTRATION

The first full statement of economic policy from the Reagan administration came in the bold White House publication *America's New Beginning: A Program for Economic Recovery*. This document outlined in considerable detail the economic strategy of the administration and discussed specific budget and tax changes. There was also some discussion of monetary policy which emphasized two key points. First, there was to be a gradual reduction in the inflation rate engineered by a gradual reduction in the growth of the money supply. Second, it was important for the Fed to hit its monetary targets in order to restore credibility to monetary policy and alleviate fears in the financial markets.

Although the Reagan program has been often criticized for embodying inconsistent goals, the stated inflation and money growth goals taken by themselves were not that radical. The inflation goals for the five years following 1981 were:

Year	1981	1982	1983	1984	1985	1986
Inflation	9.9	8.3	7.0	6.0	5.4	4.9

These goals were to be accomplished by gradual reduction in the growth of money and credit to half the levels that prevailed in 1981.

The statements about monetary targeting were also quite reasonable. "In that connection, success in meeting the targets the Federal Reserve has set will itself increase confidence in the results of policy. Otherwise, observers are likely to pay excessive attention to short-run changes in money growth and revise anticipations upwards or downwards unnecessarily" (p. 22). At the same time, there was a clear recognition of the inherent difficulties of monetary targeting. "A number of factors—such as the introduction of credit controls and their subsequent removal and frequent shifts in announced fiscal policies—have contributed to pronounced fluctuations in interest rates and monetary growth over the past year. At the same time, we need to learn from the experience with the new techniques and seek further improvement" (p. 22).

The sharp divisions among economic advisors in the early days of the Reagan administration, documented in David Stockman's book *The Triumph of Politics* carried over to monetary policy. Although the language about the Fed in *America's New Beginning* may have been rather mild, harsher language echoed in the halls of the Treasury and the Old Executive Office Building. The Reagan administration economic team included two strong advocates of monetarism: Beryl Sprinkel, undersecretary of Treasury for Monetary Affairs; and Jerry Jordan of the Council of Economic Advisors, who believed that the Fed had not gone far enough in October 1979 and was still failing to take all the measures necessary to control the money supply.

The full monetarist agenda included a number of institutional reforms and changes. Instead of controlling unborrowed reserves, the monetarists urged the Fed to control total reserves. The discount rate (the rate at which banks can borrow from the Fed) should be pegged slightly higher than market rates, and a penalty rate should accompany excessive borrowing. The monetarists also advocated that reserve requirements should be changed so that required reserves would depend on contemporaneous deposits, not deposits that the bank held two weeks prior. Although the Fed later adopted some of this program, they resisted changes early in the Reagan administration which provided opportunities for attacks by monetarists.

Monetary targeting moved to central focus in the early period of the Reagan administration. The central economic challenge for the administration was to reduce inflation without suffering through a recession. If the Fed could consistently meet its targets, administration theorists reasoned, the private sector would then believe that the Fed was indeed embarking on a gradual deceleration of money growth which would imply lower inflation. Inflationary expectations would then gradually be reduced, and the economy could manage the transition to lower inflation rates without suffering through a recession; instead, it would be possible to grow rapidly through supply-side stimulus. If the Fed erred on either side—either too rapid or too slow money growth—this delicate expectational game with the public would be upset and with it the prospects for painless disinflation. This partly explained the preoccupation with monetary targeting.

At the same time, the financial markets were also preoccupied with monetary targeting. Economists studied in detail the effects on financial markets when the Fed announced on Friday the weekly money supply numbers. When the money supply exceeded what the market anticipated (and these anticipations were actually circulated in the financial community), interest rates rose. The most plausible explanation for this increase in interest rates following the announcement was that under monetary targeting, higher money growth now meant lower growth later, and thus the market was anticipating future Fed tightening (see, e.g., Roley and Walsh 1985). The only problem with this argument was that interest rates on long-term bonds as well as implicit five-year and beyond forward rates rose on the basis of one week's money supply announcement. Is it plausible that noisy data about one week's money supply can cause a revision about the level of interest rates five years in the future? Psychological factors clearly played a role. Clearly, the financial markets were also preoccupied with monetary targeting which in turn reinforced the administration's concerns about the Fed's performance.

Perhaps the key issue with monetary targeting is whether its presence forced the Fed to take actions that it would not have taken without the existence of the targets. Carl Walsh (1987) examined this issue using econometric methods over the entire targeting period from 1975 to 1985 for M1 and found little effect from the targets. However, as Walsh recognized, the Fed's own allegiance to targeting and its own operating procedures changed several times over the sample period thereby reducing the scope for econometric analysis. The approach taken in this chapter is to look carefully at four key episodes in money management during the Reagan administration. In the first two episodes, April 1981 and February 1982, it appears that monetary targeting contributed directly to the Fed's decisions. In the latter two episodes, July 1982 and May 1984, the Fed proceeded in its own direction.[3]

Episode One

During the first few months of 1981, the Fed kept the money supply at moderate levels and reduced the federal funds rate gradually. In April, the Fed was faced with very rapid money growth rates. At a May 18 meeting, the Fed decided in favor of tighter policy. The federal funds rate rose sharply from 15.7 percent in April to 18.5 percent in May and remained above 19 percent through July. The money supply responded promptly, and money growth was negative through May and June and grew at extremely low rates through November. The National Bureau of Economic Research (NBER) dated July as the start of the severe recession that eventually led to unemployment rates exceeding ten percent.

A strong case can be made that the Fed would not have been inclined to raise interest rates so dramatically in the absence of monetary targeting. The rise in the money supply occurred in April when income tax transactions can cause distortions in the money figures. Perhaps more important was the introduction of NOW accounts. The Fed had to create a new monetary measure, "shift-adjusted M1B," which attempted to purify the M1 measure by removing the estimated savings components from the NOW accounts from M1. The FOMC directive to the New York Bank even went so far as to note that "shifts into NOW accounts will continue to distort measured growth in M1B to an unpredictable extent, and operational reserve paths will be developed in the light of evaluation of these distortions" (Greider 1987, 732). Faced with these uncertainties, why did the Fed respond to the April increase in the money supply even though money growth earlier in the year had been modest?

White House pressure for meeting the targets, the preoccupations of the financial markets with M1 and M1 targeting, and a desire to build credibility all combined to lead the Fed toward tightening in May 1981. At this point, there was a consensus among the Reagan economic team that Fed credibility was essential to their program and that credibility could only be established by meeting the targets. The same philosophy emanated from Wall Street. The Fed had been accused of tolerating too much volatility in M1 growth in the prior recession (which some blamed for the short recession) and had an interest in trying to prevent a surge in money growth even when the causes were extremely unclear. For the year, the target for M1 growth was in the 3.5 to 6 percent range; the actual growth for the year was 2.3 percent.

Episode Two

The second major decision point came for the Fed in early 1982. At this point, the economy had already entered into a recession, and the consumer price index (CPI) in late 1981 had already begun to increase at a slightly lower rate. By the end of the year, interest rates had begun to fall with the federal funds rate down to near 12 percent from a summer high near 19 percent and short-term Treasury securities falling from 15 percent to near 11 percent. Beginning in November, the money supply began to increase at a rapid rate and continued to increase through January and February. Despite the fact that the economy had now entered a recession and money growth in the previous year had been below target, the Fed was now faced in February with the prospect of increasing interest rates to stem the increase in the money supply.

Pressure from the White House this time was quite direct: in a January 19 press conference, President Reagan expressed dissatisfaction with the recent increase in the money supply which he feared would send the wrong signals to the market. With the Fed subscribing to monetary targeting, President Reagan was not viewed as abusing the independence of the Fed but specifically asking the Fed to adhere to its own targets. This gave additional legitimacy and concreteness to this event.

According to William Greider (1987, 443), some Republicans on Capitol Hill, including Senator Howard Baker, had been urging Volcker to lower interest rates, but the call from the White House was for control of the money supply.

In reaching a decision about monetary policy in February 1982, the FOMC had to weigh the risks of deepening the recession against those of losing its credibility and abruptly ending the recession as in 1980 with no lasting effect on inflationary expectations. Based partly on their belief, reported in the FOMC minutes, that a recovery would begin in the second quarter, the Fed chose to limit money growth sharply, and its directive called for no further M1 growth in the first quarter of 1982 and even indicated that declines in M1 would be tolerated.

Episode Three

In June 1982, it appeared that the February episode was about to be replayed. Since April of that year, money growth had exceeded the Fed's growth ranges, and growth in early June appeared to be very rapid. However, several factors made the situation quite different from the previous February. First, the recession had been under way for ten months, and the spring recovery had failed to materialize. The Congress was quite vocal about the effects of the Fed's tight money policies and grew concerned about the upcoming elections. Two other factors were perhaps more important: sharp policy divisions among the Reagan economic advisors, and the emergence of debt problems and financial fragility.

The divisions among the administration advisors can be seen through the pages of the *Wall Street Journal* during June. On June 11, a story on the credit pages (p. 39) expressed Beryl Sprinkel's concerns. "[He] renewed his criticism of the Federal Reserve, charging that money supply growth has been much too erratic. He added he is 'concerned' about the rapid increase in the money supply and the monetary base in recent months." He was also quoted as saying that the administration was against both raising the targets for money growth or the base for the targets.

On Friday, June 21, a page-three story appeared in the *Journal* entitled "Treasury Studies Curbs on Power of FRB; Worry Recovery is Being Undermined." This was a clear attempt to place additional pressure on the Fed. The article quoted Sprinkel as saying that "various options" were being considered about legislation to change the Fed's role. "The major issue is what we mean by independence." Sprinkel went on to complain about the money supply being on a roller coaster. Although the Fed was reducing the money supply on average, which was what the administration desired, there had been too much instability. The Reagan administration "has asked for stable money growth since arriving in office, and we don't think we are getting it." According to Sprinkel, this instability had made the recession deeper. In the context of April through June increases in the money supply and Sprinkel's previous statements, the cry for stability implied that the Fed should raise interest rates to prevent any further increases in the money supply.

These positions, however, were not shared by the rest of the administration. On Monday, Murray Weidenbaum and David Stockman downplayed the implied threats to the Fed and also disavowed a policy of immediate tightening. A story on Tuesday, June 25, in the *Journal* (p. 3) minimized the significance of the Treasury study on the Fed and stressed that it dealt solely with highly technical issues. More important, however, was the different slant on the desired course of monetary policy. Weidenbaum, Chairman of the Council of Economic Advisors, stated that the administration wants a "gradual pace" for monetary growth because it worries that above-average growth generates fears of inflation. "At the same time, however, the White House wants the Fed to avoid a sharp tightening of monetary policy, designed to bring the growth rate quickly down to the target range. . . . An abrupt contraction could create a 'liquidity crunch' Mr. Stockman said." In other words, they wanted precisely the opposite outcome that resulted from the similar situation in February. In addition to Weidenbaum and Stockman publicly disowning a strict monetarist line, Greider reports that James Baker also lost faith in monetarist prescriptions and did not want the Fed to tighten any further (Greider 1987, 490).

With the obvious divisions among the White House economic advisors, Volcker and the FOMC were under less pressure to take actions to bring money growth in line with the target ranges. The Fed now was witnessing visible strains in the financial system. Mexico was experiencing the first of several financial crises in the 1980s, and Volcker was involved in the first of many rescue attempts. The failure of Penn Square exposed the fragility of other major money center banks and raised the prospects of failures for major banking enterprises which were later realized in the failures of Seattle First and Continental Illinois.

In early July, the Fed raised its target range and began liberally supplying reserves to the system by lowering the Federal Funds rate (Greider 1987, 506–14). Short-term interest rates started falling in July, and by October, rates had fallen to 7.7 percent from 12.5 percent in June. The stock market began to rise in the summer as it began to understand that the Fed had eased. The bond market rallied as long-term rates fell

nearly three hundred basis points from June to October. A strict application of monetary targeting, such as in February, would not have allowed
these dramatic decreases in interest rates and the double-digit money
growth rates beginning in August.

Episode Four

The last episode under review indicates that strong White House
pressure on the Fed without the support of the monetary targeting framework was not sufficient to change Fed policies. In early 1984, the economy was now in the recovery phase and growing at a rapid rate. The Fed
was clearly worried that the expansion was proceeding too rapidly and
tightened slightly in late March allowing the Funds rate to rise above 10
percent for the first time since 1982.

The White House was dismayed by this action as it wanted no
potential interference with the President's reelection bid in the fall. In
May, an increase in the prime rate by large banks was taken as an
opportunity to criticize the Fed for not allowing the money supply to
grow sufficiently to accommodate the expansion. This effort was orchestrated by James Baker who was aided by Richard Darman, Larry
Speaks, and Donald Regan (Greider 1987, 621–23). However, without
any justification from a common shared framework such as was provided by monetary targeting, the pressure from the White House was
perceived as simply an election-year attempt to influence the Fed, and the
White House efforts were denounced on Wall Street and in the press.
Reagan was forced to hold a brief press conference to pledge support for
the Fed's efforts in difficult times. The federal funds rate remained high,
and there is no indication that the Fed's policy was changed by the White
House efforts.

The Fed continued to target M1 until 1987 when it totally abandoned
M1 as a target and only announced targets for broader aggregates. However, M1 targets did not appear to constrain the Fed's behavior after July
1982 in the sense of forcing policy shifts that the Fed would not have
been inclined to make. Most observers argue that the Fed essentially
based policy, certainly after October 1982, on its general readings of the
financial markets and the economy. When monetary targets became inconvenient, some device was found to eliminate their effects on fundamental policy choices. In July 1983 and 1985, for example, faced with
too rapid growth in M1, the Fed simply set a new base for its target range
without trying to counteract the prior growth.

Financial deregulation had so fundamentally changed the monetary
landscape that M1 targeting was no longer feasible. In 1986, the target

growth ranges for M1 were 3 to 8 percent. Actual money growth for that year was 15.2 percent! The Fed still announced targets for broader aggregates, but by 1985 even monetarists were doubting the wisdom of continued monetary targeting in any form (see, for example McCallum 1985).

Although generalizations from one extended period are inherently dangerous, there appear to be four lessons that emerge from the experience with monetary targeting:

1. Although monetary targets were "on the books" since 1975, it took a serious financial crisis and loss of confidence to force the Fed to take actions that treated the targets seriously. Adherence to the targets was the price that was paid for loss of confidence in the Fed.
2. The explicit guidelines and commonly accepted framework provided by monetary targeting became useful vehicles through which the White House could exert pressure on the Fed. Without reliance on the device of monetary targeting, White House efforts to pressure the Fed could more easily be perceived as attempts to limit the Fed's independence.
3. Rather than eliminating political influence on the Fed, the effectiveness of monetary targeting as a vehicle to influence the Fed depended dramatically on the ongoing political battles within the administration. When profound and transparent divisions appeared among White House advisors, the effectiveness of monetary targeting disappeared.
4. Institutional changes caused by a sustained period of high interest rates and rapid financial deregulation eventually led to the end of targeting for narrow aggregates. Although at the end of the period, this deficiency in monetary targeting was obvious to all parties, similar difficulties, although on a smaller scale, plagued monetary targeting from the beginning.

The Gramm-Rudman Experience

BACKGROUND

Monetary targeting was adopted in a time of economic crisis with growing panic in the financial markets over inflation. Gramm-Rudman was adopted more in the midst of a political crisis than an economic crisis. Economists had been warning for some time about the pernicious effects of persistent deficits, and these warnings had become a veritable litany in

Congress, especially in the Senate. Martin Feldstein, successor to Murray Weidenbaum as chairman of the Council of Economic Advisors, had articulated the case against deficits from within the administration. Deficits first raise short- and long-term interest rates as the additional government bonds compete with private financing. The higher domestic interest rates lead to both "crowding-out" of domestic investment and an appreciated dollar as foreign investors attempt to purchase domestic securities. An appreciated dollar leads to trade deficits as the relative price of U.S. goods increases in world markets.

Although the litany was well understood in Congress, there was considerable debate in the academic community about its accuracy. Perhaps the weakest link in the chain of reasoning was the very first: the connection between deficits and interest rates. This issue had been analyzed by economists in some detail. A Congressional Budget Office (CBO) review of the literature revealed that the evidence connecting budget deficits and interest rates was weak with as many studies failing to find links as those finding connections (Congressional Budget Office 1984, 99–102). The actual pattern of long-term nominal interest rates exhibited declines as deficits rose, and it is notoriously difficult to estimate long-term inflationary expectations to determine the behavior of long-term real rates. Perhaps most disconcerting for the theory was the behavior of the stock market. If government deficits were raising real interest rates in the bond market, then prices in equity markets should have been falling in the face of higher required yields. Yet, the U.S. stock market was booming.[4] Indeed, the rising stock market and the trade deficit could be jointly explained by theories that stressed the attractiveness of investment in the United States relative to abroad, assuming no effects from government deficits at all.

The boom in the stock market was indicative of a phenomenon that was more important than mere academic discontent with the traditional deficit story. It did not appear to the general public that the deficits were actually hurting the economy. To be sure, workers in firms in the tradeable goods sector were suffering from the higher dollar (just as they would be benefiting from the falling dollar several years later—with only a mild reduction in the deficit). However, total employment continued to grow, unemployment fell, trips to Europe and foreign goods in general were cheap, and the stock market continued to increase. Some economists warned that the effects of deficits would only be felt in future years in terms of either a diminished capital stock or a transfer of the ownership of domestic capital to foreign residents. However, these dangers were abstract; in 1985, the U.S. economy looked quite strong.

The strains on the political system in Washington from the deficits, however, were growing severe. There was a general feeling that the deficits had to be brought under control. This feeling was embraced by traditional conservatives, such as the Senate Republicans who were now in control, and the majority of the Reagan economic team. Democrats also favored deficit reduction. They had seen, over the past few years, how persistent deficits led inevitably to pressures to reduce spending, particularly on nonentitlement, nondefense programs. Reduced deficits, particularly through higher taxes, would alleviate pressure on these programs.

The first half of 1985 witnessed a complex three-ringed battle over deficit reduction with the key participants being the Senate Republicans, led by Senator Domenici, head of the Senate Budget Committee; the White House; and the Democrats from the House of Representatives.[5] These battles, however, produced little deficit reduction and led to the resignation of David Stockman in July. The Senate Republicans felt betrayed in the process because they had voted for cuts in cost of living for Social Security recipients, but President Reagan did not support these cuts.

It was in this atmosphere of political deadlock and frustration that Gramm-Rudman originated. The key precipitating event was a required vote on a new debt ceiling limit for the federal government, one that would allow the debt to exceed $2 trillion. The House had adopted procedures that obviated the requirement for a separate debt ceiling vote (it was part of their final budget resolution); but in the Senate, a separate vote was required (Ellwood 1987, 14).

Senator Phil Gramm, who had offered budget limitations proposals before, took this opportunity to place binding controls on Congress. He brought on as cosponsors a Republican moderate, Warren Rudman, and Senator Hollings from the Democratic party. To gain passage of the bill, Social Security was eliminated from any budget-cutting procedures. Although in principle, defense could be cut severely in the final outcome of the process, the President supported the bill perhaps largely to take symbolic action against the deficit and avoid partisan attacks associated with raising the debt limit.

The bill passed the Senate easily and also gained considerable support in the House. Although the House Democratic leadership did not like the bill, they hoped to change it substantially in conference. Indeed, the bill was effectively written in conference and, as we will see below, the House did exert important influence over its final structure.

THE LOGIC AND STRUCTURE OF GRAMM-RUDMAN

Is it ever rational for a person or group to decrease deliberately the options they have available? If an individual or group knows in advance that it is likely they will make incorrect or unadvised decisions under duress, then it may be valuable to limit the scope for decision making. Gramm-Rudman was a grand experiment in this tradition. Congress essentially imposed a series of rules that would automatically take over if certain deficit targets were violated. Like Ulysses, Congress tied itself to the mast.

How did Gramm-Rudman work? Table 6.1 contains deficit targets that Congress set for itself under both the initial Gramm-Rudman law and the second Gramm-Rudman law. Unless the Congress adopted binding budget resolutions to meet these targets (or, in some cases, come within $10 billion of the target), an automatic budget-cutting procedure known as sequestration would automatically go into effect. Borrowing the terminology from Dr. Strangelove, this was essentially a doomsday machine.

The heart of the Gramm-Rudman law was the automatic sequestration procedure, and there were many subtleties involved in its design from both political and budgeting perspectives. The first step in implementing the first law was to determine the target deficit reduction required under the law. This deficit reduction included any surpluses or deficits for Social Security and other off-budget activities. Then the budget was divided into two parts: defense and nondefense. Exempt activities including interest on the debt, Social Security payments, and a group of low-income programs were then excluded.

The next step was to reduce equally the defense and nondefense

TABLE 6.1 Deficit Targets for Gramm-Rudman

Fiscal Year	Gramm-Rudman I	Gramm-Rudman II
1986	171.9	
1987	144	
1988	108	144
1989	72	136
1990	36	100
1991	0	64
1992		28
1993		0

parts of the budget through reductions from eliminating the automatic cost of living adjustments to retirement and disability programs. In addition, a series of adjustments for special programs was made for the nondefense part of the budget. There were also special rules for health programs which limited their reductions and also required the reductions to be made in payments to health providers. Also exempt from both defense and nondefense were prior legal obligations incurred by the government. All these adjustments determined the necessary reduction in *outlays* to meet the targets.

The next step was to determine the uniform percentage reductions to apply to the spending resources in defense and nondefense programs. Spending resources included previously unobligated *budget authority* and any new budget authority. Congress actually determines budget authority—the right to spend money—not outlays. Since the actual sequestrations applied to budget authority and not outlays, the CBO and the Office of Management and Budget (OMB) were required to estimate the link between reductions in budget authority and outlays necessary to meet the deficit targets. For fiscal year 1986, the sequestration percentages were 4.9 for defense and 4.3 for nondefense.

Although there was a general intention to have an "across-the-board" philosophy and have most programs subject to the sequestration procedures, it is evident from this description that Congress modified this procedure to meet certain congressional priorities. In addition, the rules for 1986 were also modified. As an example, the President was given authority to remove military personnel accounts from the sequestration base. Congress also put in language protecting "congressional interest items" ensuring that no military bases were closed. We can, in part, explain some of the structural features of Gramm-Rudman by considering the problem of designing an ideal doomsday machine.

The designers of Gramm-Rudman did not wish to put the government totally on automatic pilot but designed their mechanism to force the Congress and the administration to make choices between tax increases and various forms of spending cuts. Designing a mechanism that would actually work, however, is not an easy task. An ideal mechanism would have to meet two essential tests in order to force a compromise agreement:

1. The outcome if an agreement is not reached must be well defined so that its consequences can be readily foreseen and distasteful enough to most parties so that an agreement is desirable. In other words, it must be *unpalatable*.

2. The default provisions must be *credible*. They cannot be so draconian that no one believes they would be allowed to remain in force if the deficit targets were not reached.

These two considerations strongly influenced the actual structure of the first Gramm-Rudman law. The across-the-board thrust of the law was essential so that proponents of both military and domestic programs would fear implementation of the sequestration provisions. The detailed sequestration procedures allowed interested parties to calculate the precise impacts if the automatic provisions actually went into effect. No major players looked forward to a major sequestration for fiscal year 1987.

At the same time, many features of the law could best be explained by the need to make the automatic features of the law credible. First, fiscal year 1986 had already begun by the time the law went into effect, which left very little time for any negotiations that first year. Thus, a limit was placed on the total funds to be sequestered. Second, there were special provisions in place just for fiscal year 1986 including, for example, additional flexibility within Defense Department accounts. Third, Social Security and interest on the national debt were exempt from all cuts. Fourth, there were safety valve features for both recessions and wars. One can plausibly argue that all these features were necessary in order to prevent Congress from simply passing a new law if the automatic cuts went into effect. If, for example, Social Security were not exempt, many members of Congress would not feel the automatic cuts would be credible because they would anticipate overwhelming pressures for them to adopt a new law, and if they believed that, there would be no real incentives to reach an agreement.

As we will discuss below, the first Gramm-Rudman law was ruled unconstitutional by the Supreme Court. A second Gramm-Rudman bill was passed in 1987. This second bill also had features ensuring credibility. The maximum amount cut or sequestered was severely limited for the first two years. This meant that the bulk of the deficit-cutting effort was postponed until after the 1988 presidential election. Although this could be viewed as mere political escapism, one could argue that foreknowledge of election-year pressures led all parties to soften deficit-cutting demands to reflect the maximum cuts that were feasible.

Not all of the important features of the law could be explained with reference to our two basic principles that are to make the automatic features unpalatable but credible. Many low-income programs were exempt, and there were special rules for health and retirement programs.

Many of these features—for example, the additions to the list of exempt programs—were added by House Democrats in the bargaining process in conference. To explain these features of the law, it is useful to borrow a concept from game theory: the notion of a "threat point."

In cooperative bargaining models, the threat point is the outcome if the parties fail to agree. In general, the nature of the threat point or fallback provisions will be an important determinant of the final outcome. The intense bargaining that occurred in conference between Democrats and Republicans reflected an awareness of the importance of the threat point. Even if everyone anticipated that a bargain would be struck, the threat point would still partially determine the outcome. The fifty percent defense and fifty percent nondefense cuts in Gramm-Rudman were reflected in the budget negotiations for fiscal year 1987, indicating the importance of the threat point.

This brief description of the Gramm-Rudman law gives some feel for its extraordinary complexity. Two areas (in addition to the intricate design of the actual sequestration mechanism) posed special problems for the designers of the legislation: the provisions for adjustments in the face of economic downturns, and the baseline definitions for determining the actual size of the projected deficits.

Critics of balanced budget proposals have always raised the Keynesian stabilization argument that in the event of a downturn, balancing the budget would just exacerbate the deteriorating economic conditions. This argument played an important role in the debate prior to final passage. In one of the earliest versions of the bill, the recession provisions were virtually nonexistent. In the event that the CBO and the OMB forecast a recession at the beginning of a fiscal year, Congress would be given several extra weeks to formulate a response, but the deficit targets would still be in force. These recession provisions were perceived to be much too weak.

In the conference committee, the House Democrats proposed that the targets be adjusted depending on economic conditions. If economic growth exceeded three percent, the target would be twenty percent per year below the actual fiscal 1985 deficit. However, for every 0.1 percentage point the growth rate fell below three percent, the required reductions would be reduced by one percentage point. For example, real economic growth of two percent would require a deficit target of only ten percent below the prior deficit.

The version that came from the Senate side and was finally adopted had fixed deficit targets but two safety valve features. First, if the CBO and OMB predicted negative real growth for two consecutive quarters, then an automatic vote would be taken in both houses on a joint resolution as to whether the deficit targets must be met. Second, the automatic vote would also be triggered if real economic growth were to fall below one percent for two consecutive quarters.

Both the House plan and the final law provided some protection from the Keynesian stabilization dilemma. The final law had the danger that economic growth could be sluggish but not quite fall to only one percent for two quarters. In this case, the actual deficit would increase, and to meet the targets would require larger cuts during weak economic conditions. The House plan would have avoided this problem but would have created considerable ambiguity as to the precise targets that would be required thereby making it difficult for all parties to focus on concrete alternative plans.

Charles Schultze (1987) argued that there were serious flaws in the recession escape clauses in Gramm-Rudman. The central problem he identified, which also applied to the House alternative, was that the escape mechanisms were geared to the *rate of change* of gross national product (GNP) rather than the deviation of GNP from some fixed target or forecast. Essentially, slow or erratic growth could lead to cumulative shortfalls of GNP and large budget deficits without triggering the escape clauses.

Schultze performed two interesting experiments to "test" the recession clauses in Gramm-Rudman. He first looked at the last eight recessions in the United States to determine if the escape clauses would have been triggered by two consecutive quarters of negative economic growth. He found that in seven of the eight cases, the law would not have been suspended in the first year of those recessions and would have been suspended in only half of the first years of the recovery periods.

Schultze also examined whether conventional forecasters would have predicted two quarters of negative economic growth in time to trigger the escape mechanisms. Looking at forecasting data for the last three recessions, he found that only in one episode were two quarters of negative growth predicted for the first year of the recession. Schultze concluded that the escape clauses were too weak to be effective. Either Congress would adhere to the targets and inflict substantial harm upon the economy, particularly in protracted recessions, or else would simply abandon the Gramm-Rudman process entirely by passing another law or resorting to budgetary tricks.

Projections of future deficits require an estimate of what the deficit would be in the absence of any further action. These projections are necessary in order to determine if the automatic sequestration provisions in the law are to be triggered. Both the CBO and the OMB use *baseline concepts* to project what the budget would be in the absence of changes in policy; but, of course, the term "changes in policy" is somewhat ambiguous. For example, the CBO assumes that no change in policy means that discretionary programs are kept constant in real terms. Baselines are a statement of the status quo but also involve predictions of what Congress will do within the current policy framework.

The first Gramm-Rudman law developed its own baseline concept. On the revenue side, the current tax law was assumed to remain in force, and provisions scheduled to expire were assumed to expire except for excise taxes dedicated to trust funds which were assumed to remain unchanged. On the spending side, the enacted levels for annual discretionary appropriations were to be used. If appropriation bills had not been enacted within five days of the reporting deadlines, last year's appropriations were to be assumed to continue but without any adjustment for inflation.

The zero inflation adjustment assumption did not, of course, preclude Congress from developing budgets that preserve programs in real terms. However, it implicitly set as the norm a situation in which program reductions were required if appropriation bills were not enacted. Compared with using the CBO baseline, it made sequestration less likely; but in the event that sequestration occurred, programs were reduced from a lower level. The zero inflation assumption was an attempt to set a tone for budget reduction.

The second Gramm-Rudman law changed the baseline to include inflation adjustments; that is, existing programs were projected to continue in real terms. The reason for the change was to minimize cuts in the event of any sequestration. Although the deficit targets for the first two years were modest and involved limited deficit reduction efforts, in the event a sequestration did occur, there was a common interest among all elected officials to minimize disruptions prior to the forthcoming 1988 elections.

During the debate of the Gramm-Rudman law, many members of Congress expressed reservations about the constitutionality of the process. Immediately after its passage, several suits were brought challenging its constitutionality. The law actually contained contingencies (described below) in case the sequestration feature of the law was found to be unconstitutional as the Supreme Court in fact ruled. The second Gramm-Rudman law was written to preserve the automatic sequestration procedures yet avoid constitutional difficulties.

Shortly after its passage, the District Court of Washington, D.C. ruled that the law was unconstitutional in *Synar v. the United States*. The sequestration for 1986, however, was allowed to go into effect, and the case went to the Supreme Court. The Supreme Court's decision followed the logic of the district court and it is therefore worthwhile to begin with an analysis of the ruling of the district court.

There were two principal arguments brought before the district court. First, the plaintiffs argued that the law delegated too much legislative power to the executive branch in the sequestration process in that legislative decisions and priorities were forfeited to the executive branch. Second, they also argued very nearly the opposite position. The law gave the comptroller general, the head of the Government Accounting Office, special duties including reconciling any differences between the reports of the CBO and OMB and preparing a final sequestration order for the president. The plaintiffs argued that this delegates executive functions to a legislative officer and again violates the separation of powers doctrine. The administration filed a brief in support of the latter argument.

The district court rejected the first argument that the law delegated too much power to the executive branch. The opinion noted that Congress had carefully spelled out the entire sequestration process including special rules and exemptions and that the executive branch was simply placed in the role of executing the law.

The district court did rule, however, that the comptroller general's role did render the law unconstitutional. The court ruled that the comptroller general performed executive functions under the Gramm-Rudman law which were not constitutional because the comptroller general is removable not only by impeachment but also by a joint resolution of Congress. According to the court's interpretation of prior Supreme Court cases, no other branch of government can have removal powers over officers who perform executive functions.

As the court itself recognized, their arguments on this point were quite scholastic: "It may seem odd that this curtailment of such an important and hard-fought legislative program should hinge upon the relative technicality of the authority over the Comptroller General's removal" (*Synar v. United States*, X-22). It appears that the court took a very narrow reading on this issue in contrast to its rejection of the first argument.

In fact, one can argue that the executive functions given to the comptroller general were very minor and carefully circumscribed by the law. The comptroller general was designated to resolve differences between the CBO and OMB, but the law indicated that these differences are to be resolved by averaging. The court noted that the president must issue the sequestration order precisely as presented by the comptroller general. However, almost all the work was to be done by the CBO and OMB, and careful directions were given for the comptroller general in this process.

The Supreme Court concurred fully with the district court ruling regarding the role of the comptroller general. The majority opinion stressed the continuity between their ruling in this case and the earlier Chadha case also involving separation of power issues. In a footnote, the opinion went out of its way to indicate that this ruling was not to be construed as an attack on independent agencies as some observers feared.

The Gramm-Rudman law contained within it provisions in case the Supreme Court found the sequestration procedure unconstitutional. CBO and OMB would now prepare their reports as before, but Congress must then vote in order to require sequestration. Sequestration would no longer automatically begin if Congress failed to act in accordance with the deficit targets. This dismantled the doomsday machine.

The second Gramm-Rudman law reinstated the automatic sequestration feature of the initial law and removed the comptroller general from the entire process. Under the terms of this law, the president would automatically issue a sequestration order based on a report by the OMB director. The OMB director's report would take into account a report from the CBO, but final authority would rest with OMB.

THE OPERATION OF GRAMM-RUDMAN

As the Gramm-Rudman law was passed initially, there was much speculation about the incentives created by its features. Some argued that since deficit targets in the early years only had to be met with a $10 billion leeway, this created incentives for compromise. Others pointed to incentives that could lead to delay or sequestration. If an appropriation bill was passed which implemented budget cuts yet sequestration still occurred, the sequestration would start from the new lower figure. Thus, no party would want to have its appropriation cut before everyone else went through the process. This potential problem was addressed in the second version of the law. A more basic problem is that some parties would prefer sequestration if the alternative were more drastic cuts in their favorite programs.

Rather than speculate about the possible incentive effects, it is more instructive to examine how Gramm-Rudman operated in practice. Since the budget process in four fiscal years (1986–89) was affected by Gramm-Rudman, there is at least a modest history that can be analyzed.

When the first Gramm-Rudman law was passed, fiscal year 1986 was already under way. Sequestration occurred on March 1, 1986 and was limited to $11.7 billion by the special rules that were constructed. In that year, sequestration was simply a useful device to obtain some deficit reduction, and these reductions were handled with surprisingly little outcry. Some agencies had more administrative difficulties than others: the Department of Agriculture had to make cuts in 13,000 separate field offices. Yet, the 4.3 percent sequestration in nondefense and 4.9 percent sequestration in defense accounts was not difficult for the system to handle.

At the time of this sequestration, Congress was in the midst of budget planning for fiscal year 1987 and faced the prospect of a larger and much more difficult sequestration in the fall if a budget compromise was not reached. However, the initial district court and then Supreme Court's ruling on the unconstitutionality of the automatic provisions clouded the picture. Congress would now have to vote affirmatively for sequestration. Moreover, economic performance deteriorated slightly over the summer which raised the deficit savings that were required.

Despite the lack of an automatic enforcement mechanism, Congress did adopt a budget plan that fell within $10 billion of the deficit target of $144 billion and thus avoided a vote on sequestration. The public spotlight on Congress from the entire Gramm-Rudman episode coupled with congressional elections in the fall led Congress to this course. However, in order to avoid a vote, budgetary loopholes in the law were heavily exploited. First, there were asset sales totaling $8.7 billion which did little to improve the overall fiscal picture yet lowered the deficit by that amount because the government is on a cash accounting system. Eliminating prepayment penalties on rural electrification loans led to a cash inflow of $1.1 billion. The most outrageous trick of all was to pay $680 million in revenue-sharing obligations for fiscal year 1987 on September 30, 1986, in order that these payments would fall into the previous fiscal year.

As fiscal year 1988 approached, Congress had passed the second Gramm-Rudman law, which eliminated many of these budgetary gimmicks and restored an automatic sequestration mechanism. As the fiscal year began, it appeared that substantial sequestration would possibly be required. On October 2, 1987, for example, the Senate Budget Committee (1987) prepared a report outlining the consequences of a $23 billion sequester. However, the budgetary picture was changed in the face of the dramatic stock market crash of October 19, 1987. Although public pressure forced an agreement, the amount that would have been sequestered set a floor for the first year of the budget plan.

Planning for fiscal year 1989 began with the idea that with presidential and congressional elections looming in the fall, no one wanted budget difficulties interfering with election campaigns. The budget committees initially adopted a plan that supposedly met the Gramm-Rudman targets, but these plans rested on economic assumptions of OMB which were extremely optimistic. At the time, the CBO forecast a deficit roughly $35 billion higher and which would not have met the Gramm-Rudman target. We thus had the ironic spectacle of the House Budget Committee accepting administration economic estimates over those of the CBO, whereas attempts to establish an equal role for the Congress in the Gramm-Rudman process was fundamental to the legislative history of the law.

During 1988, the economy grew more rapidly than most forecasters anticipated, and OMB's initial forecast no longer appeared as extreme. Sequestration was avoided for fiscal year 1989 as the target (with the $10 billion leeway) was met by less than $1 billion. Under CBO's estimates, Congress would have exceeded the Gramm-Rudman targets, but Gramm-Rudman II only required that the target established by OMB be met. The Bush administration faces a Gramm-Rudman target of $100 billion for fiscal year 1990.

Final Parallels

Monetary targeting and Gramm-Rudman are impure experiments in constitutional or quasi-constitutional rules; but some evidence, cautiously interpreted, is better than none. Three broad conclusions appear to emerge from our review of these experiences during the Reagan administration.

First, monetary targeting and Gramm-Rudman emerged in times of crisis. In the case of monetary targeting, a financial and credibility crisis led the Federal Reserve to adopt procedures signaling that they were serious about meeting the targeting procedures already on the books. Gramm-Rudman was born in the midst of a political crisis with all parties denouncing deficits but no concrete action appearing to be possible. Using the leverage provided by a required and potentially embarrassing vote on extending the federal debt limitation, the sponsors of Gramm-Rudman forced a dramatic restructuring of the budget procedures.

Second, both monetary targeting and Gramm-Rudman suggest that constitutional or quasi-constitutional rules are a continuation of politics, not its denial. These rules and laws were used as potent political symbols and means of exerting political influence. Gramm-Rudman targets influenced budget outcomes both in fiscal year 1987, when the automatic mechanism was not binding, and in fiscal year 1988, when the stock market crash forced an agreement in any case. Monetary targeting proved an effective weapon at times for the Reagan administration in its attempts to influence the Fed.

At the same time, these rules and laws had limited influence when some parties were in politically weak positions or when there was a general consensus to evade the rule or law. The Fed was able to abandon targeting, despite some criticism, in the face of a divided White House. Congress and the President initially chose unrealistic economic assumptions to avoid a budget fight in 1988.

Finally, technical flaws in designing monetary targeting and budgetary control measures became dominant considerations. Although there was heated academic debate about the desirability of monetary targeting of M1 in the early 1980s, financial deregulation eventually forced the total abandonment of targeting narrow aggregates. The government's cash flow accounting system could not have been better designed to provide escape from deficit control measures. Although many of the loopholes from the first Gramm-Rudman law were eliminated in the second law, there is a general understanding that Congress could, through mandated programs, regulations, credit guarantees or new off-budget gimmicks, find ways to evade the intent of budget control laws.

These are sobering lessons for advocates of constitutional mechanisms to control economic policy. There is perhaps one final paradox: despite the government's continued ability to create money (recall the alchemist parable), inflation was brought under control and appears to be stable; and despite the general belief of the power of special interest over the general welfare, Congress adopted two major initiatives—Gramm-Rudman and tax reform—which placed general interest over specific interests. Perhaps the original diagnosis that led to the constitutional prescriptions was too simplistic.

These experiments in rule-governed macropolicy can be viewed from another more optimistic perspective. It is clear that monetary targeting did help the fight against inflation in the early 1980s. It is also true that the Gramm-Rudman legislation did aid the Congress and the President in achieving some progress in deficit reduction. These experiments can be viewed as "intermediate strategies" for macropolicy operating between the realms of constitutional amendments and normal laws. The lessons from the Reagan administration suggest that strategic innovations in this middle ground can help the conduct of policy by coordinating action and focusing attention on key problems facing the country. They do not put an end to politics but channel political forces in productive ways. Viewed in this light, the Reagan legacy contains two impressive experiments in intermediate political strategies which may guide future administrations.

NOTES

This chapter was written while the author was a visiting professor at the Department of Economics, Princeton University. Tom Hazlett provided valuable comments.

1. This aspect of monetary targeting was recognized, at least after the fact, by several governors of the Federal Reserve. See the quotes from Henry Wallich in Greider (1987), 105–6 and from Nancy Teeters in Kettl (1986), 177.

2. Interest rate and money supply data are taken from the Appendix B in Greider (1987).

3. The narrative descriptions of the four episodes are based on Greider's (1987) detailed treatment as well as reports and stories in the *Wall Street Journal* and summaries of FOMC meetings in the *Federal Reserve Bulletin*. I have also relied on Kettl (1986) for background material.

4. Blanchard and Summers (1984, 273–334) discuss this point in detail.

5. Ellwood (1987) provides an interesting account of the politics leading to Gramm-Rudman from which part of this account is based.

REFERENCES

America's New Beginning: A Program for Economic Recovery. February 18, 1981. Washington, D.C.: White House.

Blanchard, Olivier, and Lawrence Summers. 1984. "Perspectives on High World Real Interest Rates," *Brookings Papers on Economic Activity* 84(2): 273–334.

Brennan, Geoffrey H., and James M. Buchanan. 1981. *Monopoly in Money and Inflation: The Case for a Constitution to Discipline Government.* Sussex: Institute of Economic Affairs.

Congressional Budget Office. 1984. *The Economic Outlook* (February): Appendix A.

Ellwood, John W. 1987. "The Politics of Gramm-Rudman." Mimeograph.

Greider, William. 1987. *Secrets of the Temple: How the Federal Reserve Runs the Country.* New York: Simon and Schuster.

Kettl, Donald F. 1986. *Leadership at the Fed.* New Haven, Conn.: Yale University Press.

Lucas, Robert E., Jr. 1986. "Principles of Fiscal and Monetary Policy." *Journal of Monetary Economics* 17:117–34.

McCallum, Bennett T. 1985. "On Consequences and Criticisms of Monetary Targeting." *Journal of Money, Credit and Banking* 27; no. 4, part 2:570–97.

Roley, V. Vance, and Carl E. Walsh. 1985. "Monetary Policy Regimes, Expected Inflation, and the Response of Interest Rates to Money Announcements." *Quarterly Journal of Economics* 100:1011–39.

Schick, Allen. 1982. "Controlling the Budget by Statute: An Imperfect but Workable Process." In *Reconciliation: The New Budget Process*. Princeton: Woodrow Wilson School of Public Affairs.

Schultze, Charles L. 1987. "The Economics of Gramm-Rudman." Mimeograph.

Senate Budget Committee. 1987. "The Estimated Effect of a 1987 Sequester under the Amended Gramm-Rudman-Hollings Law." October 2, 1987.

Stockman, David. 1986. *The Triumph of Politics*. New York: Harper & Row.

Stubblebine, William Craig. 1980. "Balancing the Budget versus Limiting Spending." In *The Constitution and the Budget,* edited by W. S. Moore and Rudolph G. Penner, 50–56. Washington, D.C.: The American Enterprise Institute.

Synar v. United States of America. 1986. Decision printed in *Daily Tax Reporter* (February 10): X1–X23.

Walsh, Carl E. 1987. "The Impact of Monetary Targeting in the United States: 1976–1984." Mimeograph.

Woolley, John T. 1984. *Monetary Politics*. New York: Cambridge University Press.

7

Ideology and Economic Policy

M. STEPHEN WEATHERFORD and
LORRAINE M. McDONNELL

Did the Reagan presidency produce an economic revolution, or did his eight years result in more of the same? This is the central issue in assessing the impact of the Reagan years. The President focused on economic policy and promised and claimed major changes. Early assessments generally supported these claims, emphasizing the comprehensive nature of Reagan's economic ambitions (Heclo and Penner 1983) or the unusual policy mix with which the administration attacked the American economy's stagflationary problems (Blinder 1987). Sympathizers and opponents alike appeared eager, although for different reasons, to show that the policies were both radical and efficacious. However, later assessment undermined that verdict. How radical could these policies have been, given that the primary initiatives—easing taxes on business, curbing federal budget growth, diminishing and stabilizing the growth of the money supply, deregulation—had precursors in the Carter years? Moreover, inflation and unemployment did not appear to respond any differently through recession and recovery from what conventional, even Keynesian, models would have predicted. Perhaps most surprising of all, as the historical record accumulated, it became clear that even the critical medium-term predictions have not been borne out: personal savings rates are lower and consumption higher, and neither business investment nor productivity growth has risen.

In the end, many commentators concluded that the emperor's new clothes turned out to be second-hand and slightly refurbished: "the Reagan administration's macroeconomic objectives have not differed sharply from those that had evolved under its predecessors, although under President Reagan some reweighting of these objectives has been accomplished and a clearer sense of priorities developed" (Sawhill 1986, 104). Others claim that Reagan's conservatism was indistinguishable from that of Nixon and Ford (Reichley 1982). Particularly given the supply-siders' early exaggerated assertions, the temptation has been to conclude that claims of a revolution or radical restructuring amounted to little more than campaign rhetoric carried into office by a president who was, in the final analysis, more actor than politician.

We argue that this assessment underestimates Reagan's impact on the economy by failing to take seriously the role political ideology plays in the administration's economic policy-making. The error is a difficult one to resist: underestimating Ronald Reagan has more than two decades of tradition behind it (cf. Wilson 1967); and although ideology is scarce enough in American electoral campaigns, the ideologue in power is an unprecedented occurrence. It is no wonder, for our pragmatic political culture, as much as institutional arrangements of shared power, make compromises and trade-offs the central facts of life in American politics.

Establishing the case for inferring an ideological presidency is not easy. Evidence must, for instance, go beyond the assertion of new ideas—the tradition of American incrementalism has assimilated generations of new ideas, but ideology connotes comprehensiveness in diagnosis and solution. Nor can the evidence be confined only to ideas—if a necessary condition of enactment is compromise, then pragmatism, not ideology, seems the proper description. Nor can the evidence be confined to conventional indicators of aggregate economic activity—for ideologies are not about inflation and unemployment, but about who does what, and who gets what. In our view, assessing Reagan's economic legacy entails evaluating his impact on these three dimensions of the American political economy: *ideas, implementation,* and *effects.*

The first part of this chapter outlines the President's economic ideology. The second describes the process of translating ideology into practice, focusing on the way the President used his advisory resources in economic policy-making. The final section reflects on this history to assess the legacy of the Reagan years as a source of guiding ideas; as an exemplar of effective leadership in economic policy-making; and as a cause of fundamental change in the American economy.

Economic Ideology and Policy

THE IDEOLOGY

Although operative ideologies are not expected to be tightly reasoned philosophical constructs, a pattern of family resemblances links the scholar's notion of ideology with the politician's. An economic ideology is a cluster of ideas about the relationship between government and the economy from which policy preferences can be readily drawn. These ideas are linked, largely by virtue of their common source in a smaller number of fundamental beliefs. These beliefs—for instance, a particular image of human nature or of the interplay between markets and politics—provide the lodestone against which options can be compared in particular situations.

Two central beliefs—individualism and populism—formed the core around which Reagan's economic ideology was organized; and two personality traits—self-confidence and optimism—shaped its application to particular political choices and his expectations about the efficacy of his decisions.[1] Cannon (1982) and others (Greenstein 1983; Gelb 1985) described the roots of these orientations in Reagan's boyhood and youth, but three aspects are worth underlining: (1) the sense of assurance, relentless cheerfulness, small town optimism which Reagan took from his boyhood experiences; (2) a style of interpersonal relations which combined affability with distance and emerged during his high school and college years; and (3) the impression Roosevelt's leadership made on Reagan during his politically formative years. The impression was not that of a formulator of policies but of a communicator whose sense of rhetoric (cadences, metaphor, dramatic quality, flair for the grand gesture) transmitted "a message in the darkest days of the Depression [which] was less an economic one than a call for renewed self-confidence and courage" (Cannon 1982, 32).

The family's experience in the Depression made it natural for Reagan to express his populism through Democratic partisanship, but the decade of the 1950s marked a transition—from well-paid actor, property rich but cash poor, in 1952 to prosperous, even wealthy, ten years later; the marriage to Nancy Davis, whose family ties brought Reagan into personal contact with businessmen as friends; and especially his experience as spokesman for General Electric and his adoption of increasingly pro-business, anti-New Deal stands—signaling both the beginning of his political career and the formation of his adult ideology. His support for big business capitalism was consistent with his populist beliefs; he con cluded that "if the reins of government were removed, business would boom, spreading prosperity to all the people" (Gelb 1985, 28; Cannon 1982, 88–97).

The conception of values that underlies this ideology is notable for its complete absence of any transcendent element. The motives for action, as the rewards for accomplishment, refer to interests rather than to passions or moral sentiments.[2] This is especially clear when Reagan is most idealistic and eloquent.

> We are not talking here about some static, lifeless econometric model— we are talking about the greatest productive economy in human history, an economy that is historically revitalized not by government but by people free of government interference, needless regulations, crippling inflation, high taxes and unemployment. (Reagan 1980)

> The production of America is the possession of those who build, serve, create, and produce. For too long now, we've removed from our people the decisions on how to dispose of what they've created. We have strayed from first principles. We must alter our course. (Reagan 1981)

It has become commonplace to note that Reagan is not a religious person and to draw the contrast with Carter's spirituality. Both the elevation of property and the appeal to the Protestant conception of salvation tapped deeply rooted branches of American populism. Yet it is remarkable that the leader ushering in the greater change envisioned its rewards as narrowly individual and superficially materialistic.

By the early 1960s, Ronald Reagan had become a prominent conservative spokesman, and by 1966, when he ran for governor of California, his ideas on major economic policy issues were fully formed and remained essentially constant thereafter (Deaver, quoted in Gelb 1985; Cannon 1982). James Baker noted that the President's great strength was "his inner compass. . . . He not only believes certain things strongly but has believed them for a long time" (quoted in Gelb 1985, 25). Tobin's (1988, 84) description of Reagan's economic ideology as "celebrating the miracle of Adam Smith's Invisible Hand—free markets . . . laissez faire . . . an extravagant version of the central paradigm of economic theory" is a fair summary, but it misses the nuances that distinguish different elements of the creed by their closeness to Reagan's core beliefs.

His subscription to monetarism and his aversion to fine-tuning the economy, for instance, were tenets adopted as part of a package of conservative Republican economic policy beliefs developed in opposition during the Kennedy and Johnson years; his antipathy to business regulation can be traced in a similar way to his experience as a spokesman for General Electric, the National Association of Manufacturers (NAM), and other big business organizations during the 1950s and early 1960s. High taxes and high spending are two sides of the "government as leviathan" against which Reagan took his stand, but his opposition to each had distinctive roots. His commitment to cutting tax rates sprang from personal experience: high marginal taxes in the 1940s had actually discouraged him from making movies; and by the 1960s, as a property-owning suburbanite trying to better his family's status, Reagan had felt the sort of diffuse personal anger against high taxes which allowed him to appeal so successfully a decade later to the sentiment of tax revolt (Cannon 1982, 96ff; Heclo and Penner 1983; Sears and Citrin 1985). Reagan's opposition to social spending was not the mirror image of his advocacy of tax cuts—its rationale owed much more to outrage at "welfare cheats" and waste than to direct experience with incentive effects and self-reliance. Reagan's mother's participation in church and other voluntary social welfare activities and his father's work for the Depression era welfare office in Dixon affirmed the importance of programs for the deserving poor, but the development of his political persona through the campaigns in California proved the effectiveness of attacking big government by denouncing welfare (Cannon 1982, 98–118).

Finally, it is worth noting how little personal meaning balanced government budgets and deficit spending held for Reagan. It is true that he spoke out against deficits for years, but there is little evidence in his background or in his core beliefs to support the inference that budget balancing was a primary priority that would constrain programmatic choices or that the public obeisance went much beyond ritualistic support for a traditional party demand. This aspect of Reagan's ideology combined with changing public and elite attitudes toward the economic effect of deficits (Peterson 1985–86) to foster a set of tax cuts and defense-spending increases which promoted the goals to which Reagan attributed higher priority. Other conservative presidents (although probably not many) subscribed to budget balancing much more firmly. Eisenhower, for instance, saw it as a close analogue to the family's monthly budget and as the burden of debt left to later generations.

Arraying major topics of American economic policy debates from those closest to those further from the center of the political ideology Reagan had formed by the mid-1960s would rank taxation as primary, welfare and social spending as second, followed by a nexus of typical conservative positions on such issues as stable monetary growth, business regulation, and deficit spending. The strength of this ideology is shown by the fact that "The president is easy to predict. . . . He's extraordinarily analytical to test options against his philosophy" (Howard Baker, quoted in Gelb 1985, 32).

THE POLICY CONNECTION

The central place of economic beliefs in Reagan's political persona and the role of economic ambitions in defining the administration's goals make this a historically unique economic presidency. Unlike Carter, and indeed most other presidents, Reagan did not undermine his plans by attempting to respond to each transient shift of major economic indicators; the clarity and salience of his economic ideology channeled his policy activities and gave them a unique degree of consistency and direction.

The Primacy of Ideology over Economic Theory

Because Reagan's positions were shaped to an unusual degree by the process of mobilizing popular support, their critical feature was their ability "not to convince intellectuals and experts, but to resonate with the deepest yearnings and dissatisfactions of ordinary people" (Heclo and Penner 1983, 25; Heclo 1986). That resonance depended on holding the focus on goals rather than means and on synthesizing ideas and blurring potential conflicts. With Reagan, the president in power was much closer to the candidate as campaigner than was the case for any chief executive in modern memory.

Thus, what economists denounced as theoretical promiscuity in Reagan's linking macroeconomic monetarism with microeconomic deregulation with supply-side's exaggerated version of rational expectations (Brooks 1982), defenders could see as an ideological eclecticism that raised no serious doubts about consistency—especially since his melding of different conservative theoretical streams was informed both by his core beliefs and his goals for the American economy. In this context, it should occasion little surprise that Reagan irreverently refused to defer to professional economists when their advice conflicted with that of his political aides. Peterson (1985–86) notes, moreover, that professional economists and political elites were coming to doubt that budget deficits should so severely constrain current policy goals, and this argument further softens the contrast between theoretically consistent and ideologically consistent. In the end, the allegation that Reagan was preaching voodoo economics revealed an important (but perhaps not fatal) fact about his economic theory and an interesting but much less important fact about his economic ideology.

The complex process of selection and testing which leads some politicians toward the executive and some toward the legislature incrementally matches experiences and skills to personal styles and belief systems; it seldom did so better than in Reagan's case. Reagan's political experience was not that of bargainer or negotiator, but as propagandist mobilizing popular support and shaping the issue from above the conflict rather than participating in the horse trading of policy formulation and passage. Reagan's combination of closeness to the public with distance from the policy-making process limned the persona of a movement politician (Wilson 1980).

Much of Reagan's success sprang from his intuition that effective economic policy-making combines economics with politics. The intention of economic policy, after all, is to change behavior; of a broad economic ideology, to reshape patterns of behavior. Typical government policies seek to alter economic behavior by changing the material incentives market participants face—for instance, to channel production, investment, or demand by altering subsidies, interest rates, or taxes. Yet economic behavior is also intimately affected by confidence—the balance of optimistic or pessimistic intuitions about future contingencies— and there are no policy levers or material incentives capable of altering expectations directly. The wedge this indeterminacy drives between instruments and targets is nowhere wider than in the puzzle of how to slow inflation. What the political campaigner understands but the economist underestimates is the role of expectations, confidence, faith in the government, and credibility—in short, the role of successful persuasion.

Consider the counterfactual: by 1980, Carter's top economic priority was clearly to lower the rate of inflation. Yet it is difficult to believe that inflation would have fallen as fast or as far under a second Carter administration as it did in Reagan's first term. Most of Reagan's inflation-fighting accomplishment can be attributed to a policy mix that no Democrat could have implemented; but some portion, it seems fair to say, is accounted for by credibility effects (cf. Blinder 1984; 1987; Cagan and Fellner 1984).

The Primacy of Allocative and Distributive Goals

Economic problems of stabilization and growth played a primary role in the electorate's retrospective rejection of Jimmy Carter in 1980 (cf. Kiewiet and Rivers 1985). The incoming administration diagnosed the inflation as a monetary problem attributable to excessive money supply growth, and although the Federal Reserve under Paul Volcker had already begun to lower the rate of monetary growth, it seems likely that monetary policy was tighter longer under Reagan than it would have been under a second Carter administration.[3] Bringing down the inflation rate was undoubtedly the administration's major economic victory. The slow rate of economic growth was attributed by the new administration to excessive government spending and taxing, which were viewed as disincentives to work effort and entrepreneurial initiative. Given this broad-gauge diagnosis, virtually all of Reagan's economic policy proposals could claim the intention of stimulating productivity growth.[4]

Nordhaus (1984) summarizes a number of separate studies of the Reagan program's probable effects on the growth rate over the period 1981–90. Taking into account the effect of policy changes on (1) private investment (net of crowding out due to the deficit), (2) public capital formation, (3) federal support for research and development, and (4) regulatory changes reveals that the net effect was a significantly diminished growth rate rather than an acceleration. The Reagan administration record on stabilization and growth can be described quite precisely by quantitative economic criteria: its successes and failures summed to a mixed report (cf. Summers 1984).

Yet surely this is not what is meant by the "Reagan Revolution," a notion that implies the accomplishment of fundamental political economic change, whereas stabilization and growth are technically complex but not revolutionary challenges. Moreover, Reagan's economic policy solutions proposed much more far-reaching changes than would have followed from any established economic model of stabilization or growth. The fit between problem and solution seems paradoxical if considered solely from the perspective of economic theory. Yet an economic ideology carries its own solution, and the state of the economy is less the cause for newly fitted policy to be formulated than the occasion for implementing policy already favored on political grounds. The key to understanding the impact of Reagan's economic policies lies less in econometric evaluations of the administration's stabilization and growth programs than in judgments of their allocative and distributive policies against political as well as economic criteria.

Unlike stabilization and growth, the government's role in allocating economic functions between the public and private sectors and in distributing income and wealth is shaped less by economic theories than by political economic ideology. Allocation raises powerfully politicized questions. Despite the fact, for instance, that the public finance literature is replete with theories about the optimal alignment of jurisdictional boundaries and public goods provision, issues of who does what are primarily settled by partisan or ideological beliefs about the desirable balance between public and private or between central power and states' rights.

Republican presidents typically come into office committed to the allocative goal of decentralizing the functions of government. For example, revenue sharing and the introduction of block grants to the states were motivated by the Nixon administration's theory of federalism—one that largely accepted the public sector's role as service provider but rejected both the Great Society's centralizing thrust and the resulting close nexus of federal-city relations. Reagan's allocative policies were also decentralizing, but they were animated by a political economic ideology quite different from the Republican conception of federalism which ran from Eisenhower through Ford.

Reagan's ideology posited two primary sets of actors: government and individuals. There was no variegated notion of intermediate levels of government varying systematically in their political complexion or administrative efficiency. Thus, most of the budgetary savings in the 1982 budget were in grants to state and local governments (Nathan et al. 1983). Far from pursuing decentralization of given public sector responsibilities to lower governmental levels, however, Reagan sought to reduce the role of government altogether. He consistently opposed revenue sharing, and block grants were intended as a step toward ending all federal aid (cf. Beer 1983).

Distributional policies translate beliefs about who should get what into laws that influence economic choices. Both in theory and practice they are more highly politicized and deeply embedded in long-standing ideological cleavages than any of the government's other economic interventions. Redistributing market-generated income and wealth influences incentives, and economic theory and analysis can parse many of the relevant economic effects (Bosworth 1984). Predicting the effects of future policy changes would be imprecise even if it only involved certain extrapolations from current data and models; but evaluating distributive initiatives is intrinsically political for it involves weighing the interests of payers against those of recipients, and economists have little to say about interpersonal comparisons (Cooter and Rappaport 1984). Resolving distributional questions inevitably implicates ethical beliefs about justice and the appropriate relation between market earnings and individual equality as distributive principles. These are matters at the core of an economic ideology but largely omitted from economic theories.

On distributional questions, even more than on allocative ones, Reagan's economic ideology differed radically from his predecessors'. The federal tax system that Reagan inherited had been modified by successive administrations; but on the whole, Democratic presidents have not been consistently progressive nor Republicans solely regressive. Indeed, Pechman (1985) and Page (1983) conclude that the tax system was essentially neutral with respect to market-generated inequalities. On the spending side, Republican candidates typically are staunch defenders of the market and profess opposition to government transfers that distort market incentives. However, in practice, Nixon and Ford accepted (and extended) the Great Society's redistributive spending programs, just as Eisenhower earlier had accepted those of the New Deal. The net effect of incremental changes in tax and transfer programs has been roughly to keep pace with the economy's generation of income inequality: from World War II to about 1960, income distribution in the United States was essentially stable; some slight movement toward greater equality occurred over the two decades before Reagan came to power (Thurow 1973).

No president since Hoover had called for substantially diminishing the government's role in redistributive social programs; Reagan accomplished it. Tax reductions were unabashedly regressive, and their cumulative value from fiscal year (FY) 1982 to FY 1985 was about $360 billion. Budgetary reductions in human services programs over the same period amounted to about $112 billion (Haveman 1984, Table 2). These reductions impacted especially hard on the working poor for whom more stringent needs tests and steeper implicit tax rates (benefit losses tied to increases in earnings) deprived low-earning families of cash and in-kind support (Meyer 1986). Poverty increased: in 1978, 11.4 percent of American families were living below the official poverty line; in 1985, the proportion was 14 percent. Inequality increased; Table 7.1 shows the average income for the 20 percent of Americans at the bottom of the income distribution, then for the next 20 percent, and so on, in 1980 and 1984.

The distinction between narrowly economic and intrinsically politicized economic policies helps to clarify the evaluative task by illuminating the line between rhetoric and intentions. Several policies proposed as solutions to the economic problems appeared, from an economic perspective, to be perverse or mistaken, but they often fit neatly as part of a political strategy. The most prominent of these was the deficit, whose dramatic growth should have worked as a circuit breaker to stop tax cuts and defense-spending increases or to switch the administration's position on tax increases. Most economists agree that the budget deficit

TABLE 7.1   Mean Income by Quintile (1984 Dollars)

Quintile	1980	1984	Change (%)
First	$ 5,026	$ 5,067	+0.8
Second	11,897	11,859	−0.3
Third	18,359	18,543	+1.0
Fourth	25,743	26,736	+3.9
Fifth	41,640	45,602	+9.5
Top 5%	57,808	65,546	+13.4

Source: Clark and Corrigan 1986, 2987; cf. Tobin 1988.

will hamper stabilization efforts in the future since it drastically restricts fiscal policy flexibility, and that it will slow productivity growth as its repayment (and especially to overseas holders of American debt) takes a large share of national savings. However, the deficit is understandable as the unavoidable residual of higher priority decisions.

Another example was the pattern of regulatory changes sponsored by the administration. The Carter administration had made considerable progress in deregulation, lowering entry barriers to new firms eager to compete with established companies, and strengthening the operation of market mechanisms in a number of ways. The Reagan administration was much less forceful in pressing its expressed deregulatory intentions, particularly in trucking; and although the administration eased government rules, the abandoned regulations were mainly environmental and safety restrictions rather than those that directly affect competition. It is difficult to see how this pattern of policy decisions could have been consistent with maximizing economic efficiency. A political explanation might locate the rationale in long-run ideological beliefs about the appropriateness of government regulation of health and safety or perhaps in short-run constituency politics.

SUMMARY

Two sets of inferences summarize this section on Reagan's economic ideology: one looking backward toward its correlates in personality attributes and family experiences, the other forward toward its influence on policy selection. The fit is strikingly logical—*ex post*—between Reagan's personal self-confidence and optimism and the elevation of individualism and self-reliance in his economic ideology. We have no special insight into the personality sources of political beliefs, and we are mindful of the methodological pitfalls to causal inferences in this area, but the atypicality of this combination should not go unremarked. Ideologues and holders of extreme political views tend to be inflexible, and that inflexibility can be traced to personal traits such as low self-esteem, insecurity, and suspiciousness which stifle healthy interpersonal relations and impede social learning. Reagan manifested none of those traits. In fact, given his "intellectual passivity" (a senior White House aide quoted in Gelb 1985, 112) when it came to tasks like reading and studying reports, Reagan's ability to flourish, even with the mistakes, in the hyper-informed environment of Washington politics was a tribute to his sensitivity to interpersonal cues. This quite singular fit between personality and ideological core beliefs grounded Reagan's policy preferences in a strong, stable base of maxims to which he could return when temporarily defeated, and it provided the personality resources to compromise at the margin without the perfectionist's chagrin at sullying principle.

The other inference tracks the President's ideology from abstract issue preferences to decisions about setting priorities and advocating policies. We argue that the criticism commonly made of Reagan for his economically unsophisticated concatenation of policy rationales taken from theoretically inconsistent models misses the distinction between economic and political idea systems. Intended to explain or predict and tested through scientific debate and verification, an economic theory must measure up to logical consistency. Intended to mobilize in a context of loosely examined competing claims, an economic ideology is tested against criteria that show less deference to professional authority and logical canons and more to the leader's ability to understand and address popular concerns in terms the public understands as harmonious with its own values. Reagan's political education as the spokesman for the emerging conservative movement of the 1960s and 1970s shaped his economic ideology as the servant of his political goals. So long as policy proposals were consistent with his own core beliefs and manifestly advanced the goals of Republican conservatism, their eccentric intellectual parentage did not prevent their being integrated into the belief system. The strongly politicized nature of this economic ideology also underlay Reagan's ordering of initiatives in economic policy. Although Reagan came to power largely as a result of the public's rejection of Carter's economic stabilization program, the emphasis in his administration was not on the more economic of the government's interventions— stabilization and growth—but on the more political—allocation and distribution.

In the next section, we turn to an examination of the way these beliefs and policy goals shaped the legislative strategies of the President and his advisors.

Operationalizing Reagan's Economic Ideology: The Role of His Advisory Network

A president's ability to pursue effectively his economic ideology requires careful policy selection and coordination: his economic advisory network shapes the translation of ideological goals into concrete policy proposals and the promotion of those initiatives through the policy-making process. The president typically draws the members of this network from senior White House staff, the Council of Economic Advisors (CEA), the Office of Management and Budget (OMB), and the Department of the Treasury. In doing so, he confronts the tension between maintaining openness to maximize information and to aid in building support for subsequent proposals, and advancing tightly focused policies that reflect a consistent set of priorities. The pursuit of policy coherence presses an administration toward centralization and hierarchy.

In the case of Ronald Reagan, the tension was largely resolved in favor of an economic advisory network that stressed control of agenda and strategy through a two-tiered system. The first tier consisted of senior White House staff and Cabinet officers who functioned as pragmatic political managers, mediating the views of a second tier of advisors who represented several diverse schools of economic thought. The emergence of a centralized hierarchical structure dominated by political rather than economic advisors allowed Reagan to advance his economic ideology in a focused and consistent manner. In this section, we analyze the composition of Reagan's economic advisory network and its strategies for furthering his ideology, focusing particularly on the 1981 tax and budget cuts, the 1986 tax reform, and the deficit reduction efforts of the past few years.

THE ECONOMIC ADVISORS

Reagan's ideology was such that no one economic theory could be used to operationalize all of his major goals. Consequently, the administration included in its initial group of advisors advocates of three conservative theories: neoclassical, monetarist, and supply-side. Monetarists were represented in the early years of the administration by Beryl Sprinkel, the treasury undersecretary for monetary affairs (and later CEA chair), and on the CEA by Jerry Jordan. Those espousing supply-side approaches included Norman Ture, treasury undersecretary for tax policy; and Paul Craig Roberts, treasury assistant secretary for economic policy. Those who could be categorized as neoclassicalists included Murray Weidenbaum, the first CEA chair; and his successor, Martin Feldstein.

Although espousing different theories about the most effective way to stimulate economic growth, they all shared a belief that government's role in the economy should be limited. Some, like Feldstein, were respected academic economists before joining the administration; others such as Roberts (a former associate editor of the *Wall Street Journal's* editorial page) were less economic experts than popularizers and disseminators of a theory. However, most shared two traits: they were more concerned with economic than political issues; and each tended to espouse policies and concentrate on indicators that represented only one part of Reagan's economic ideology (e.g. the supply-siders focused on tax rates; the neoclassicalists, on inflation and the budget deficit; and the monetarists, on the money supply).

The narrow focus of each school and the inherent contradictions among them are somewhat comically illustrated in David Stockman's description of how economic forecasts were prepared in 1981. Stockman described it as getting out "our economic shoehorn and try[ing] to jimmy the forecast numbers until all the doctrines fit" (1986, 102). Supply-siders such as Ture and Roberts wanted to show real gross national product (GNP) growth around 5 to 6 percent (as compared with historical rates of 3 percent) to demonstrate the effect of the proposed tax cut. On the other hand, monetarists such as Sprinkel wanted to show the lowest possible numbers for money GNP because that was the litmus test of sound anti-inflationary monetary policy. To accommodate movement on these two indicators consistent with each theory, the forecast would have had to show inflation of only 2 percent by the third or fourth year. However, Weidenbaum, a more eclectic, conservative economist, was concerned about the professional credibility of such low inflation figures. Stockman described the result of combining all these economic theories into a single forecast:

> The inflation-saturated and -battered U.S. economy we inherited in 1981 was going to do what? Why, just leap up on its hind legs and start growing at a 5 percent annual rate. And it would do so at the same time it was going through the shakes and shivers of taking the monetary restraint cure and experiencing the tremors of disinflation.

> The whole proposition eventually shattered within twenty-four months. The 1982 numbers made it clear as a bell. When you added the supply-siders' assumptions of 5.2 percent real growth for that year to Weidenbaum's 7.7 percent inflation, you got a mountain of money GNP—and phantom tax revenues [of nearly $200 billion]. The gold standard, hard money crowd ended up forecasting 13.3 percent money GNP growth for 1982; they would have had to put three shifts on the Fed's printing presses to achieve it. (1986, 106–7)

Examples of advisors' attention to economic indicators at the expense of political ones include Feldstein's public advocacy of swift action to curb the budget deficit in the face of criticism from both senior White House staff and the then-Secretary of the Treasury Donald Regan, who were opposed to any tax increases (Jaroslovsky and Blustein 1983; Blustein 1984), and Sprinkel's vocal opposition in 1982 to U.S. intervention in currency markets which subsequently led Regan to amend his aide's statement in order to placate European allies (Pine 1982).

Although the administration successfully pursued policies reflecting the preferences of these advisors, most had only marginal influence, and many left the administration early. During Reagan's first term, the CEA had very limited influence and focused its day-to-day work on micro-economic issues such as trade and agricultural policies. In the one instance in which it prevailed in the debate on economic forecasts, Feldstein convinced the administration to scale back its public optimism and use an economic growth rate of 3 percent for 1983. As it turned out, the actual growth rate for that year was twice Feldstein's prediction. After Feldstein returned to Harvard, Reagan even considered trying to abolish the CEA and waited some six months before appointing a successor. Economic theorists within the Treasury encountered similar fates. Ture's aggressive pursuit of supply-side economics to the exclusion of other concerns resulted in his being excluded from top-level meetings within the agency (Campbell 1986). He left government in 1982, and his position and that of Sprinkel were abolished after their departures.[5]

THE POLITICAL ADVISORS

The explanation for this seeming disjuncture between policy and advice lies in the predominant influence of another group of advisors. Their effectiveness stemmed not from their economic expertise but from strong allegiance to Reagan's ideology coupled with the political skills to choose selectively from policy initiatives premised on different economic theories. Their loyalty was to a successful Reagan presidency, not to any particular economic theory, and their task was to integrate day-to-day tactics with the administration's longer term policy goals (Heclo and Penner 1983). This group included the trio who headed Reagan's White House staff during his first term: Edwin Meese, counselor to the President and later attorney general; James Baker, the chief of staff and later secretary of the Treasury; and Michael Deaver, the deputy chief of staff. Also included were David Stockman, the director of OMB; and Donald Regan. Further down in the formal hierarchy but still key to furthering the administration's policy goals were men such as Max Friedersdorf, the assistant to the President for legislative affairs; and Staff Secretary Richard Darman (later deputy Treasury secretary).

Charles Schultze, CEA chair during the Carter administration, argues the limits on purely economic advice for any president: "The economist turned policy advisor will quickly discover that in the councils where economic advice for the policymaker is formulated, one-half to two-thirds of the discussion has little to do with economics, at least in the conventionally defined sense. A large part of the discussion centers around political feasibility, legislative strategy, optimum timing, effects on public opinion" (as quoted in Bonafede 1982, 248). This preeminence of the political over the economic was particularly true for the Reagan administration because Reagan's economic strategy was founded on a political, not an economic, theory (cf. Heclo and Penner 1983). Furthermore, "the array of offsetting advice from the economics profession created a kind of vacuum providing an opportunity for the political ideology of the Reagan administration to predominate" (Heclo and Penner 1983, 28). Reagan himself indicated the preeminent role that these political experts would play in mediating the advice and interests of the various agencies concerned with economic policy in his September 9, 1980 speech: "Crucial to my strategy of spending control will be the appointment to top government positions of men and women who share my economic philosophy. We will have an administration in which the word from the top isn't lost or hidden in the bureaucracy" (Reagan 1980).

Not only did Reagan enter office with a limited number of well-defined priorities that all focused on changing the relationship between government and the economy, but his aides understood that the opportunity for accomplishing fundamental change was a very brief one (Smith 1981). Consequently, by the time the administration entered office, it not only had a set of policy proposals but also the mechanisms in place to further that agenda. The operations of several groups were critical to that strategy. One was the trio of Meese, Baker, and Deaver. Together they regulated the flow of information into the Oval Office and orchestrated all staff activities. A second group was the Economic Affairs Council that was chaired by Donald Regan and met 271 times during Reagan's first term—more than the other six Cabinet councils combined (Kirschten 1985a). At the beginning of Reagan's second term, the number of Cabinet councils was reduced from seven to three, but the reorganized Economic Policy Council continued as a forum for administration policy development.

A third group was the Legislative Strategy Group (LSG) headed by Baker. This group consisted of eight to ten aides who met daily (sometimes two to three times a day) to plan the administration's congressional tactics. By keeping the group small and meeting frequently, the administration was able to keep pace and react quickly to legislative developments on Capitol Hill. Cabinet officers were brought into the group's meetings on an as-needed basis; and in keeping with its top-level status, the LSG avoided dealing with stand-ins for Cabinet secretaries (Kirschten 1982).

This group's activities were key to Reagan's major legislative victories in economic policy. For example, the LSG spearheaded the 1981 tax cut negotiations with Congress, and key members of the group played a similar function during the shaping of the tax reform bill. Some first-term administration officials have even argued that the LSG, together with David Stockman, set virtually all significant domestic policy in the first term, often ignoring or overturning Cabinet council decisions (Brownstein and Kirschten 1986). According to one former White House official: "There were many instances where the Cabinet councils were sitting around discussing things and Stockman couldn't make the meeting because he was on the Hill negotiating a settlement of the exact same issue they were discussing" (as quoted in Brownstein and Kirschten 1986, 1583). This vehicle for promoting the President's legislative program was continued in his second term by his new chief of staff, Donald Regan.

TRANSLATING IDEOLOGY INTO POLICY

Two tenets guided the work of Reagan's political advisors. The first is what Heclo and Penner (1983) have called the strategic management of Reagan economic policy. Although the basic ideology behind Reagan policy was never open to question or debate, his aides had considerable latitude within which "to thrust and parry depending on circumstances"—bargaining and accommodating within the broad parameters established by Reagan's ideology. This approach, dating back to Reagan's tenure as governor of California, was described by his long-time aide

Edwin Meese in this way: "to stand firm on principle but be flexible enough to negotiate within the framework of principle" (as quoted in Smith 1981, 48).

A second tenet was a corollary of the first. During the period in which the inevitable political bargaining occurred, Reagan was distanced from the process. At the same time, he was positioned to intervene actively as soon as a workable compromise was close at hand. As alternative proposals were presented and considered, Reagan would either be portrayed as "resisting counterpressure" (Heclo and Penner 1983), desiring "to hear a frank and unimpeded debate" (Kirschten 1985b, 384), or challenging Congress to meet its responsibilities by offering constructive alternatives to the administration's original proposals or budgets (Kirschten 1982). Only after a compromise likely to ensure passage of essential elements of the President's proposal had been reached would Reagan attach his personal judgment or approval to it. The objective was to keep him above the debate, thus husbanding his personal political resources until they were most needed. At that point, Reagan would become an active participant in the process, to the point of negotiating with congressional leaders directly (Smith 1981) or even lobbying some members before a key budget vote by telephone while on a foreign trip (Kirschten 1982). Although they were implemented by different actors and with varying degrees of success, these strategic principles were applied quite consistently in the pursuit of Reagan's major economic policy initiatives.

The 1981 Tax and Budget Cuts

Central to Ronald Reagan's ideology was a desire to decrease the growth of nondefense expenditures and to reduce taxes in order to create greater incentives for private producers. In moving toward these goals, the administration assumed office with a two-pronged program that ultimately (1) reduced $35.1 billion from the FY 1982 budget and significantly altered the scope of many federal programs; and (2) reduced individual tax rates by 25 percent over a 33-month period and provided business with a variety of tax breaks including accelerated write-offs for capital investment. These dramatic economic policy successes resulted largely from the skilled application of the two strategic principles described above. The effectiveness of these strategies was further magnified by the administration's decision to concentrate on basically just two legislative initiatives during Reagan's first year. As Friedersdorf, the head of the White House's congressional liaison office, noted: "the President was determined not to clutter up the landscape with extraneous legislation" (as quoted in Wayne 1982, 56). The intensity of this focus was reflected in the fact that Reagan delivered more public remarks about his economic process than about any other topic, and two-thirds of the 1981 recorded votes in the Senate involved budget-related matters (Schick 1982).

The centralizing features of Reagan's advisory network and its pragmatism were illustrated in the negotiations that surrounded passage of the tax cut legislation and the budget resolutions. To deal with budgetary reductions inside the executive branch, a budget working group evolved which included Baker, Meese, Stockman, and Regan who together negotiated directly with relevant Cabinet secretaries and their immediate ideas. Stockman described the group as "strong keepers of the central agenda" (as quoted in Greider 1981, 33). The process was quick and relatively decisive because Cabinet secretaries had little time to marshal opposition, and they knew that the group essentially spoke for the President.

Similarly, when negotiations began with members of Congress, any deals could only be authorized by Baker, Meese, Stockman, or in some cases, Friedersdorf (Wayne 1982). Deals were indeed made: the tax bill contained the proverbial ornaments (Wehr 1981; Cohen 1981; Stockman 1986), and the pet projects of key congressmen were spared in the budget resolutions (Sinclair and Behr 1981; Stockman 1986). When faced with the realization that it could not build a coalition in favor of its proposals without such trades, the White House acted pragmatically within clear limits. Stockman describes the President's reaction to advice that the tax cut could not pass without compromises:

> As Regan and the others talked, I studied the President's face. He looked pained. Obviously, he hadn't anticipated that his own advisors would be counseling him on the need to compromise on his most cherished reform. But Ronald Reagan was a politician. He was willing, up to a point.
>
> "Going with some of their ornaments," he pondered. "Well, yes. . . . But on the rate cut, we have to draw the line. Twenty-five percent is as low as we can go. I don't want you fellas asking me to go under that figure. We'll take it to the people if we have to." (1986, 259)

The costs of compromise were a myriad of tax expenditures including peanut price supports, reduced estate and gift taxes, and tax breaks for oil and gas producers; but Reagan got his 25 percent reduction in individual rates and a liberalized depreciation schedule for business.

The administration's second strategic principle of distancing Reagan from specific negotiations combined with his intervention at critical points was well implemented during the 1981 legislative battles. In contrast to Jimmy Carter's frequent involvement in shaping the specific details of legislation, Reagan never allowed himself to be pulled into negotiating particulars or ratifying administration deals struck with Congress. Yet he spent considerable time lobbying key members of Congress at White House meetings and Camp David barbecues. Equally important was his televised address prior to the House vote on the Gramm-Latta budget resolution and another two days before the House voted on the tax cut legislation. The well-orchestrated outpouring of public support which resulted from each provided the Republican gypsy moths and the Democratic boll weevils who constituted the swing votes in Reagan's legislative coalition with a grass roots rationale for voting with him.

Tax Reform

Reducing marginal tax rates was the cornerstone of Reagan's economic ideology. However, the strategy for achieving that goal, although ultimately successful, was less straightforward than when used in 1981. Still, the themes of advice centralized through a political network, pragmatism in pursuit of ideological goals, and the strategic use of presidential influence persisted. In January 1984, Reagan asked the secretary of the treasury "to develop a plan of action with specific recommendations to make our tax system fairer, simpler, and less of a burden on our Nation's economy" (Council of Economic Advisors 1984, 7). The plan was not to be presented until after the 1984 election; and according to Reagan aides, the timing was politically motivated: the White House wanted to deflect attention from the deficit during the campaign and to have a major policy offensive ready for 1985 (Blustein 1985).

The development of what came to be called Treasury I and its subsequent transformation into Treasury II—the proposal Reagan ultimately supported and presented to Congress—are prime examples of expert technical advice mediated through the political advisory network. By the time the department began its work, the supply-siders primarily concerned with capital formation (e.g. Ture) had left the Treasury. Consequently, much of the development work on Treasury I was done by senior career staff in the office of tax policy, whose organizational norms stressed an efficient tax system that maximized the base, minimized tax expenditures, and emphasized a fair distribution of the tax burden (Clark 1985a). A working group of top treasury officials (including Regan) began with the individual tax code and then moved on to business taxation. It was only after all provisions had been considered on simplification grounds that the group asked for an economic analysis of the effects of the proposed changes. Both the Wharton and the Data Resources, Inc. econometric models predicted that Treasury I would not help economic growth and would encourage consumption at the expense of investment. However, Regan, after briefing Reagan, decided to make the study public, saying that he would be the lightning rod for ensuing protest (Clark 1985a). He was careful, however, to make clear that the plan was only a starting point that would need to be modified: it "was written on a word processor [and] can be changed" (as quoted in Cohen 1985, 953).

Treasury I reduced individual marginal tax rates to 15, 25, and 35 percent from a top rate of 70 percent and the maximum corporate tax rate from 46 to 33 percent. To offset these reductions, Treasury I eliminated individual tax preferences such as the deduction for state and local taxes and various tax shelters; and on the corporate side, it repealed the investment tax credit and replaced the accelerated cost recovery system (ACRS)—a major feature of the 1981 tax cut—with a less generous depreciation schedule.

Once Treasury I was announced, the process changed from one focused on applying uniform technical criteria to one of political bargaining and compromise. The administration avoided the comprehensive approach to tax overhaul outlined in Treasury I and responded to traditional Republican business and investor interests. The administration's goal was to make the plan economically sound yet politically salable (Blustein and Birnbaum 1985). This latter condition meant that for the plan to succeed, it needed to respond to powerful political interests while still retaining an aura of fairness. Furthermore, the plan had to acknowledge the particular concerns of a few key congressional leaders—for instance, Robert Packwood, chair of the Senate Finance Committee, who did not want employer-paid health insurance premiums to be taxed.

These political choices were reflected in the plan that the administration sent to Congress. Over a five-year period, it would reduce individual taxes by $131.8 billion and raise corporate taxes by $118.4 billion as compared with Treasury I which would have reduced individual taxes by $148 billion and raised corporate taxes by $165 billion. The largest benefits of the individual rate reductions were to go to those at either end of the income distribution—those earning under $10,000 a year would have their taxes reduced by 35.5 percent, and those earning over $200,000 a year would receive a 10.7 percent reduction as compared with those earning $20,000 to $30,000, who would only receive an 8.7 percent reduction (Clark 1985c). The plan relaxed the depreciation rules proposed in Treasury I and compensated for some of the revenue loss with a corporate minimum tax.

As with the 1981 tax and budget cuts, the process by which this final plan was shaped was a highly centralized one. Although the trio of Baker, Meese, and Deaver had been replaced by Regan, and the formal White House advisory structure had been simplified somewhat, major decisions were made in essentially the same way. As Kirschten describes the process: "big decisions still get made by small ad hoc groups of heavyweight advisors who get things resolved by narrowing the debate—in effect, shutting other interested parties out of the process" (1985d, 1418). In the case of tax reform, the changes in Treasury I were made not by the Economic Policy Council, but by Regan, Baker, Darman, and Assistant Treasury Secretary for tax policy Ronald Pearlman, with Vice President Bush and several other White House aides including Patrick Buchanan participating less actively. Excluded from the discussions were CEA Chair Beryl Sprinkel; OMB Director Stockman; and Commerce Secretary Malcolm Baldridge (Kirschten 1985d).

Despite the centralization of the advisory process, consensus among Reagan's key advisors was more difficult to reach than it had been in 1981, and their disagreements were sometimes aired in public. For example, once the House Ways and Means Committee began to consider the President's proposal, Baker and Darman made it clear that they were willing to negotiate a bill acceptable to the Democratic majority on almost all features except the 35 percent top rate proposed by the President. Other advisors regarded Baker and Darman's approach as appeasement. Some, like Buchanan, stressed the profamily aspects of the tax proposal which they believed would be in jeopardy if the personal exemption were reduced (Mayer and Murray 1985); others such as Sprinkel focused on the economic growth implications of the tax bill and argued that Ways and Means counterproposals would increase the cost of raising capital (Blustein and Mayer 1985). However, Baker, Darman, and Regan continued to argue to Reagan that compromises were necessary if he were not to be blamed for killing the bill.

In the six months between the announcement of Treasury I in November 1984 and May 1985 when the administration sent its tax reform plan to Congress, Reagan was careful once again to distance himself from the negotiations. In his state of the union speech on February 6, he outlined some general principles that were to guide his advisors during their negotiations: the top personal tax rate should be reduced from 50 to 35 percent; the home mortgage deduction should be retained;

individuals near the poverty line should be exempt from income taxes; incentives for capital formation should be retained; and the plan should be revenue neutral. Beyond that, however, Reagan remained aloof from the process and was not briefed on the specifics of the plan devised by Baker and Darman until April 30. At that point, Reagan chose a top rate of 35 percent and a $2000 personal exemption over a 34 percent rate and a $1900 exemption. He also vetoed Baker's proposal to allow charitable deductions only above 1 percent of income, arguing that the private sector should be encouraged "to do things so that government won't have to" (as quoted in Blustein and Birnbaum 1985). Before that time, however, Reagan professed to know nothing about the details of the developing Treasury plan and cited only general principles, as he did in a February *Wall Street Journal* interview, when he was asked about the proposed increase in overall corporate taxes:

> I haven't even made an attempt to study that bill in detail that much to know that. I assume that that would mean things that would be taken away from them that are present deductions. No, I would have to be convinced of the need to do that because I'm a believer that one day we must recognize that only people pay taxes. And someday I would hope that we could arrive at a tax structure that would recognize that you can't tax things, you only tax people.

Just as Reagan's distancing himself from negotiations was typical of the administration's approach to economic policy-making, so was his strategic intervention to remedy the miscalculations of his advisors and to save the tax reform bill in the House. In their efforts to seek accommodation with House Ways and Means Committee Chair Rostenkowski, Baker, Darman, and Regan failed to anticipate the anger and frustration that Republican members would feel when the President lukewarmly supported Rostenkowski's version—one they viewed as antifamily and harmful to business investment (Merry 1985; Fessler 1985a). Although Reagan had made clear that overhaul of the tax system was the major domestic priority for his second term, only 14 of 182 House Republicans voted for a rule that would allow debate on the tax bill. At this point, Reagan stepped in, making an unusual trip to Capitol Hill to plead for their help and promising in a letter to each that he would veto the final legislation if it did not contain specific changes consistent with their preferences (Fessler 1985b). The bill was passed on a voice vote; Reagan's personal intervention and assurances had saved the administration from what could have been its major domestic policy setback (Weinraub 1986).

Deficit Reduction

The interplay between ideology and advice in attempts to reduce the federal budget deficit looks quite different than it did for tax policy, largely because this area was not central to Reagan's economic ideology. For Ronald Reagan, reducing the budget deficit provided yet another rationale for shrinking the size of the federal government, but he never regarded it as an economic policy goal in and of itself. For most of his administration, Reagan viewed deficit reduction as a lever he could use to further his goal of decreasing domestic expenditures. Again and again he made clear that deficit reduction could only be thought of in terms of spending reductions, not tax increases. His response to the recommendation of Stockman and Feldstein that a contingency tax be included as part of the FY 1985 budget submission is typical:

> There has not been one tax *increase* in history that actually raised revenue. . . . And every tax *cut,* from the 1920s to Kennedy's to ours, has produced more.
>
> We have always warned that the problem is *deficit spending.* . . . But "they" had this theory that it didn't matter because we just owed it to ourselves. So this deficit isn't our fault. It was here before we got here. Now they're all just waiting for us to admit we were wrong so they can go back to tax and spend. . . .
>
> There was a time when government took less than ten percent from the people. But that has gone up and up and up. And that's where all the trouble started. I remember some economists warned about it at the time. . . .
>
> So that never has worked. Carter tried it, He came up with the largest tax increase in history for Social Security and it was already bankrupt when we got here.
>
> No, we have to keep faith with the people. Everywhere I go they say, Keep it up! Stick to your guns! Well, isn't that what we came here to do? (as quoted in Stockman 1986, 406)

This quote also embodies two other basic themes that Reagan used continuously in talking about the deficit: his administration had inherited a problem that was not of their making; and the fault rested with Congress because it refused to make the spending cuts Reagan had requested (Kirschten 1985c). As Stockman (1986) indicated, no amount of information or arguments to the contrary were going to convince Reagan to change his basic interpretation of either the causes of or solutions to budget deficits.

Given the secondary importance of deficit reduction in his ideological framework, it is not surprising that Reagan's advisory network was considerably less effective in this policy area. First, not only did its low presidential priority provide little incentive to pursue a viable solution, but unlike either the 1981 initiatives or the 1986 tax reform, meaningful deficit reduction required sustained action: quick victories with a large political payoff were unlikely. Second, deficit reduction more than any other economic policy concern generated major splits among members of Reagan's advisory network. As early as fall 1982, Stockman began to argue that some type of tax increase was necessary to offset the effects of the 1981 tax cut and increased defense spending. Baker was also willing to support such a policy, but Regan argued strenuously that the deficit numbers were exaggerated and would go away without raising taxes (Frontline 1986). Feldstein's concern about the long-term effects of the deficit caused him to weigh in on the side of increased taxes and to incur the ire of Regan. Early in Reagan's second term, U.S. Trade Representative William Brock argued that budget deficits were leading to an overvalued dollar, which in turn was increasing trade deficits to record levels. On the other hand, CEA member William Niskanen argued that deficits have little discernible effect on interest rates, and reducing the budget deficit would have only a marginal effect on the trade balance (Clark 1985b).

The low priority given deficit reduction and the splits within the administration were particularly evident when it was forced to deal with the impending passage of the Gramm-Rudman-Hollings deficit reduction plan (which became the 1985 Balanced Budget and Emergency Deficit Control Act). Regan and the reconstituted LSG convinced the President to give the measure an early and enthusiastic endorsement. This action was taken at a time when James Miller, Stockman's successor at OMB, had not yet been confirmed by the Senate. Consequently, the administration lacked an active negotiator who was sensitive to the plan's implications and risks for the President's priorities and who could play a key role in the measure's development. Furthermore, Baker and Defense Secretary Weinberger opposed the plan. At the same time, careful consideration of the deficit problem was crowded off the presidential agenda by issues of greater importance to the administration such as passage of the tax reform bill and the upcoming Geneva summit with Soviet leader Gorbachev. As a result, the White House was unable to exert much influence on the final form of Gramm-Rudman-Hollings. Particularly troublesome was Weinberger's decision to absent himself from negotiations with Congress, which meant that the administration lost flexibility in coping with mandatory defense cuts (Kirschten and Rauch 1985).

With Gramm-Rudman-Hollings, the administration was in a reactive mode. After blaming Congress for not taking decisive action to reduce federal spending in the past, it could not now oppose such action. Its strategy was to try and minimize damage to the defense budget—a clear presidential priority—and to portray the measure as an alternative to the inevitable call of a growing number of congressmen for increased taxes. This posture contrasted sharply with the one taken for the 1981 tax and budget cuts and for the tax reform bill. In both those cases, the administration seized the initiative and maintained it throughout the legislative process. Publicly voiced opposition from within the administration was minimized, and the President used his political resources strategically for the two initiatives central to his ideology. The lesser importance of deficit reduction, however, meant that key advisors were freer to express divergent positions publicly and that Reagan was not actively involved in effecting the final shape of the legislation.

SUMMARY

It is a truism to argue that a president needs both economic and political advice in shaping his economic policy initiatives. Expert advice on the degree to which a particular policy option will produce economic effects consonant with a president's ideological goals is only useful to the extent that it also includes an assessment of the initiative's political and administrative feasibility including potential sources of support and opposition, its distributional effects on constituencies of importance to the President and Congress, and the likelihood that the initiative can be implemented consistent with its intent. The need for such advice presses for an integration of the economic and the political.

However, presidents may choose to organize their advisory networks to meet that requirement in a variety of ways and to strike a balance between economic and political concerns at different points. John Kennedy and Dwight Eisenhower were presidents with clear economic goals and for whom the economy was an important policy focus but who chose to organize their advisory networks very differently from Reagan's. The members of Kennedy's CEA and his key advisors within the Treasury acted as sources of both economic and political advice. They were sensitive to political constraints in formulating their advice to Kennedy; viewed themselves as a political interest group (Stein 1969); often were the ones to float trial balloons to obtain congressional and public reaction (Flash 1965); and above all, were considered part of Kennedy's inner circle with direct access to him. Unlike Reagan, Eisenhower chose to place greater weight on purely economic advice by the status he accorded the CEA and its chair, Arthur Burns. This was the case, even when Burns's empirical, although still conservative, approach to economics caused him to disagree with the ritualistic big business conservatism of Treasury Secretary George Humphrey and most Republican party leaders (Weatherford 1987).

The preeminence of political over economic advice and the two-tier structure that separated economic experts from decision making in the Reagan administration are quite understandable in light of the President's ideology. No one economic theory could operationalize all of his major goals without identifying the trade-offs inherent in reducing taxes and simultaneously increasing defense spending. Such an organizational structure is also understandable if we think of Reagan's economic ideology not as guidelines for managing the economic but as a blueprint for advancing a set of deeply held political principles. Thus, the artfulness of Reagan's advisory network lay in its ability to be guided strongly by a political ideology yet act pragmatically in pursuing its agenda using the President's own political resources strategically. This critical difference between leadership in pursuit of a political ideology and effective management of the national economy suggests that Reagan's economic policy legacy must be assessed on two very different dimensions.

The Triumph of Ideology

After a series of failed presidencies, Reagan's economic policy accomplishments proved that national government can work. Yet, the evidence of efficacious presidential leadership is more mixed in other policy areas. Indeed, the concentration of presidential attention and resources that promoted dramatic economic policy changes resulted in neglect of issues ranging from the environment to foreign affairs. Thus, the generalizations we draw from this chapter will not necessarily typify the administration's actions elsewhere. Nevertheless, Reagan's economic legacy is clear: the nation will inherit an economy changed not only in its operation but in its political significance. Much of the explanation for this stems from Reagan's ability to meld a simple but powerful economic ideology with a leadership style that coordinated ideas and personal strengths to unparalleled political advantage.

Presidents are not allowed the luxury of experimenting with different management styles, so if a predecessor's approach appears to produce results, later presidents may consider emulating it. How much difference did Reagan's ideology and style make? Can the ingredients of Reagan's success be copied? Reagan's leadership significantly contributed to his economic policy accomplishments, but it is important not to lose sight of the political and economic context of those successes. The credit that goes to the President must also be shared with a number of idiosyncratic events which made for unusually favorable political circumstances: Carter's unpopularity, resulting in an exaggerated impression of Reagan's electoral mandate; the intellectual disarray among Democratic party elites in the face of Reagan's initial onslaught; a series of favorable supply shocks; a strengthening dollar; an accommodative Federal Reserve to assist in reducing inflation; and foreigners eager to accumulate American debt to minimize the short-run constraint of a rising deficit. However fortunate the President, policy accomplishments of this magnitude cannot be attributed only to timing and luck. Reagan's economic ideology fostered these achievements by providing the strength of conviction and clear standard to evaluate virtually every economic policy initiative against larger political economic ambitions. The President's guiding ideas led him to concentrate his resources not only on the economy as opposed to other issue areas, but narrowly within economic policy—on reducing marginal tax rates and secondarily on directly diminishing the government's role in redressing market inequalities. Reagan may have owed his election to the stabilization challenges summarized in the "misery index," but his economic policy initiatives paid scant attention to short-run stabilization goals, focusing instead on a set of dramatic initiatives in the most political of economic policies: allocation and distribution.

The conventional wisdom about ideology in American politics asserts that the marriage of comprehensive plans to political institutions produces incrementalism. It certainly seemed reasonable to expect more of the same as Reagan entered office facing a recession, high popular cynicism about governmental effectiveness, and an ideologically divided Congress. His administration's ability to orchestrate the major changes in policy direction embodied in the 1981 tax and budget cuts and in the 1986 tax reform is thus equally a credit to policy management. Again, the lesson—in the eclectic mix of policy rationales, in the habitual refusal to defer to professional economic advice, in the strategy of cutting taxes first—lies in the politicization of economic policy-making.

The Reagan administration's economic policy success affords us a unique opportunity to observe a concerted attempt to govern by ideas in a political system where pragmatism has always been a way of life. We conclude by turning from close observation of politics and policy-making to reflect on the potential significance of Reagan's powerful advocacy of a distinct economic ideology.

The Reagan administration shaped the political economic dialogue both by posing the central questions and by circumscribing the range of possible answers. The result has been to curb and, we think, strictly limit future growth of the government's role in redistributing income and in equalizing individuals' competitive opportunities. The historical significance of this triumph of ideas should not be underestimated; Reagan's was not a regime of conservative consolidation but an innovative, even radical, attempt to define the public philosophy. Define rather than re-define seems the appropriate notion, for Reagan's economic ideology was more explicit and more alive to the political power of ideas than the congeries of policy nostrums it would replace.

Scholars and commentators speak of the clash of ideologies, and it is natural to imagine that the impact of ideas on politics works through the symmetrical opposition of synthesis and antithesis. Yet neither the New Deal nor the Great Society was an expression of a grand plan. Their policies were essentially limited attempts to ameliorate particular problems, expanded program by program over time as much by a sort of interest group liberalism of the social service professions as by a considered partisan rationale. The absence of any clearly articulated communitarian ethic to provide intellectual justification of this accumulation of programs meant that their maintenance depended on keeping the issue of willingness to pay at the periphery. Reagan's economic ideology placed the question of cost first, and it did so not through a negative wholesale attack on redistributive programs, but rather by bringing to the fore traditional American values of individualism and property. This rationale for shrinking the government's approach did not deny compassion but rather supplanted it by appealing to even more deeply engrained images.

It is too early to tell whether this altered frame of reference will take root as an enduring change in the American public philosophy. However, whether the ideological legacy persists or not, the significance of the attempt tells an important historical lesson for it is not only the consciously ideological style but the substance of the ideas themselves that mark a departure from past presidencies. The great presidents of American history have always taken advantage of the bully pulpit they occupied to speak for a larger conception of social purpose and individual responsibility, to take the side of the weak and the less privileged. The Franklin Roosevelt and Lyndon Johnson presidencies marked watersheds in American history because they conceived of government as the instrument, in an increasingly complex industrial economy, for carrying out the community's good intentions toward its disadvantaged members. Reagan's is not a purposely selfish public philosophy, but its twin pillars—suspiciousness of government and faith in individual acquisitiveness—define its significance. By failing to rise above the immediate values of individual material ambition, Reagan forfeited the opportunity, offered by his position and considerable skills, to advance a broader conception of the good society.

NOTES

Prepared for the conference on the Legacy of the Reagan Presidency, sponsored by the Institute of Governmental Affairs, University of California, Davis, 24–26 May 1988. We wish to acknowledge the valuable research assistance of Mary McKenzie.

1. Our thinking about ideology and policy preferences in their social, cultural, and personality context has been influenced by Wildavsky (1987a), Barber (1972), and Greenstein (1969).

2. The contrast is elegantly elaborated by Hirschman (1976).

3. In part, this is due to the administration's (and especially the President's) strong support for the Fed's tight policy; in part, monetary tightening by the Fed was the appropriate stabilizing response given the administration's loosening of fiscal policy in 1981. (The tax cut and defense-spending increases were predicted to amount to a net stimulative shift of 5 to 6 percent of GNP for the first three years.)

4. Several economists have analyzed the economics of the Reagan administration's policies, including Hulten and Sawhill (1984), Bosworth (1984), and Boskin (1987).

5. The current consensus is that the CEA under Sprinkel fared somewhat better. After ending administration censure for his initial outspokenness, Sprinkel became a low-profile team player while still adhering to his monetarist views. This role allowed him to position the CEA as a participant in the administration's economic decision-making process, although not necessarily to exert a major influence on it (Murray 1985; Kirschten 1986).

REFERENCES

Barber, J. D. 1972. *The Presidential Character: Predicting Performance in the White House.* Englewood Cliffs, N.J.: Prentice-Hall.

Beer, S. H. 1983. "Ronald Reagan: New Deal Conservative?" *Society* 20, no. 2: 40–44.

Blinder, A. S. 1984. "Reaganomics and Growth: The Message in the Models." In *The Legacy of Reaganomics: Prospects for Long-Term Growth,* edited by C. R. Hulten and I. V. Sawhill, 199–228. Washington, D.C.: Urban Institute Press.

———. 1987. "Tight Money and Loose Fiscal Policy." *Society* 24, no. 4: 80–83.

Blustein, P. 1984. "Feldstein's Call for a $50 Billion Tax Rise Will Be Opposed by Reagan's Top Aids." *Wall Street Journal,* 6 January.

———. 1985. "The Reagan Tax Plan: Economics or Ideology?" *Wall Street Journal,* 1 July, 1.

Blustein, P., and J. H. Birnbaum. 1985. "Give and Take: President's Tax Plan Took Shape in Months of Talks, Compromises." *Wall Street Journal,* 30 May, 1, 11.

Blustein, P., and J. Mayer. 1985. "Battle Lines Form within White House over Ways and Means Tax Revision Bill." *Wall Street Journal,* 26 November, 1.

Bonafede, D. 1982. "Reagan's Economic Advisors Share Task of Shaping and Explaining Reaganomics." *National Journal* 14, no. 6: 245–48.

Boskin, M. J. 1987. *Reagan and the Economy.* San Francisco: ICS Press.

Bosworth, B. P. 1984. *Tax Incentives and Economic Growth.* Washington, D.C.: Brookings Institution.

Brooks, J. 1982. "Annals of Finance." *New Yorker,* 19 April, 96–150.

Brownstein, R., and D. Kirschten. 1986. "Cabinet Power." *National Journal* 18, no. 26: 1582–89.

Cagan, P., and W. Fellner. 1984. "The Cost of Disinflation, Credibility, and the Deceleration of Wages 1982–1983." In *Essays in Contemporary Economic Problems: Disinflation 1983–1984,* edited by W. Fellner. Washington, D.C.: American Enterprise Institute.

Campbell, C. 1986. *Managing the Presidency!* Pittsburgh: University of Pittsburgh Press.

Canon, L. 1982. *Reagan.* New York: Putnam.

Clark, T. B. 1985a. "Strange Bedfellows." *National Journal* 17, no. 5: 251–56.

———. 1985b. "For Those Who Blanch at Sight of Red Ink." *National Journal* 17, no. 6: 298–99.

———. 1985c. "Retreating to Tax Reform." *National Journal* 17, no. 22: 1267, 1298–99, 1302–12.

Clark, T. B., and R. Corrigan. 1986. "Ronald Reagan's Economy." *National Journal* 18, no. 50: 2982–87, 2990–99.

Cohen, R. E. 1981. "A Reagan Victory on His Tax Package Could Be a Costly One Politically." *National Journal* 13, no. 24: 1058–62.

———. 1985. "Congress, Awaiting Reagan's Tax Reform Proposal, Is Bracing for a Battle Royal." *National Journal* 17, no. 18: 952–55.

Cooter, R., and P. Rappaport. 1984. "Were the Ordinalists Wrong about Welfare Economics?" *Journal of Economic Literature* 22: 507–30.

Council of Economic Advisors. 1984. *Economic Report of the President.* Washington, D.C.: U.S. Government Printing Office.

Excerpts from the "Interview with President Reagan." 1985. *Wall Street Journal,* 8 February, 6.

Fessler, P. 1985a. "GOP Defeats Attempt to Consider Tax Bill." *Congressional Quarterly,* 2613–16.

———. 1985b. "House Reverses Self, Passes Major Tax Overhaul." *Congressional Quarterly,* 2705–11.

Flash, E. S., Jr. 1965. *Economic Advice and Presidential Leadership.* New York: Columbia University Press.

Frontline transcript 412. 1986. *The Disillusionment of David Stockman.* Boston: WGBH Educational Foundation.

Gelb, L. H. 1985. "The Mind of the President." *New York Times Magazine,* 6 October, 20ff.

Greenstein, F. 1969. *Personality and Politics*. Chicago: Markam.

————. 1983. "Reagan and the Lore of the Modern Presidency: What Have We Learned?" In *The Reagan Presidency*, edited by F. I. Greenstein, 159–187. Baltimore: The Johns Hopkins University Press.

Greider, W. 1981. "The Education of David Stockman." *Atlantic Monthly* (December): 27–54.

Haveman, R. H. 1984. "How Much Have the Reagan Administration's Tax and Spending Policies Increased Work Effort?" In *The Legacy of Reaganomics: Prospects for Long-Term Growth*, edited by C. R. Hulten & I. V. Sawhill, 91–126. Washington, D.C.: Urban Institute Press.

Heclo, H. 1986. "Reaganism and the Search for a Public Philosophy." In *Perspectives on the Reagan Years*, edited by J. L. Palmer, 31–64. Washington, D.C.: Urban Institute Press.

Heclo, H., and R. G. Penner. 1983. "Fiscal and Political Strategy in the Reagan Administration." In *The Reagan Presidency: An Early Assessment*, edited by F. I. Greenstein, 21–47. Baltimore: The Johns Hopkins University Press.

Hirschman, A. 1976. *The Passions and the Interests*. Princeton: Princeton University Press.

Hulten, C. R., and I. V. Sawhill. 1984. *The Legacy of Reaganomics: Prospects for Long-term Growth*. Washington, D.C.: Urban Institute Press.

Jaroslovsky, R., and P. Blustein. 1983. "Feldstein is Put under Intense Pressure for Publicly Voicing Qualms on Economy." *Wall Street Journal*, 1 December, 3.

Kiewiet, D. R., and D. Rivers. 1985. "The Economic Basis of Reagan's Appeal." In *The New Direction in American Politics*, edited by J. E. Chubb and P. E. Peterson, 69–90. Washington, D.C.: Brookings Institution.

Kirschten, D. 1982. "Reagan's Legislative Strategy Team Keeps His Record of Victories Intact." *National Journal* 15, no. 26: 1127–30.

————. 1985a. "With Regan Coming in at Quarterback, White House Ready to Field New Team." *National Journal* 17, no. 3: 148–51.

————. 1985b. "As Contradictions Become More Heated." *National Journal* 17, no. 7: 384–85.

————. 1985c. "Reagan's Feisty New White House Crew." *National Journal* 17, no. 13: 704–5.

————. 1985d. "Once Again, Cabinet Government's Beauty." *National Journal* 17, no. 24: 1418–19.

————. 1986. "Sprinkel Finds a Better Market." *National Journal* 18, no. 22: 714–15.

Kirschten, D., and J. Rauch. 1985. "Political Poker Game over Deficit Bill Calls Bluff of Reagan and Congress." *National Journal* 17, no. 50: 2855–60.

Mayer, J., and A. Murray. 1985. "Substance, Tactics of Tax Revision Cause Conflict among Administration Hard-Liners, Pragmatists." *Wall Street Journal*, 8 October, 64.

Merry, R. W. 1985. "Reagan's Plight: Tax Overhaul Becomes Political Predicament for the White House." *Wall Street Journal*, 6 December, 1, 27.

Meyer, J. A. 1986. "Social Programs and Social Policy." In *Perspectives on the Reagan Years*, edited by J. L. Palmer, 69–90. Washington, D.C.: Urban Institute Press.

Murray, A. 1985. "Sprinkel, Trouper at Treasury, Earns Reward as Top Reagan Economic Aide." *Wall Street Journal,* 22 February, 14.

Nathan, R. P., F. L. Doolittle, and Associates. 1983. *The Consequences of Cuts: The Effects of the Reagan Domestic Program on State and Local Government.* Princeton: Princeton Urban and Regional Research Center.

Nordhaus, W. D. 1984. "Reaganomics and Economic Growth: A Summing Up." In *The Legacy of Reaganomics: Prospects for Long-Term Growth,* edited by C. R. Hulten and I. V. Sawhill, 253–62. Washington, D.C.: Urban Institute Press.

Page, B. 1983. *Who Gets What from Government?* Berkeley and Los Angeles: University of California Press.

Pechman, J. A. 1985. *Who Pays the Taxes: 1966–1985.* Washington, D.C.: Brookings Institution.

Peterson, P. E. 1985–86. "The New Politics of Deficits." *Political Science Quarterly* 100, no. 4: 475–601.

Pine, A. 1982. "Beryl Sprinkel Irritates Many Europeans but Stays Influential in His Treasury Post." *Wall Street Journal* 13 July, 54.

Reagan, R. 1980. Speech before the International Business Council, 9 September. Chicago.

———. 1981. *America's New Beginning: A Program for Economic Recovery.* Washington, D.C.: White House.

Reichley, A. J. 1981–82. "The Conservative Roots of the Nixon, Ford, and Reagan Administrations." *Political Science Quarterly* 96, no. 4: 537–51.

Rockman, B. A. 1988. "Conclusions: An Imprint but Not a Revolution." In *The Reagan Revolution?* edited by B. B. Kymlicka and J. V. Matthews. Chicago: Dorsey Press.

Sawhill, I. V. 1986. "Reaganomics in Retrospect." In *Perspectives on the Reagan Years,* edited by J. L. Palmer, 91–120. Washington, D.C.: Urban Institute Press.

Schick, A. 1982. "How the Budget Was Won and Lost." In *President and Congress: Assessing Reagan's First Year,* edited by N. J. Ornstein, 14–43. Washington, D.C.: American Enterprise Institute.

Sears, D. O., and J. Citrin. 1985. *Tax Revolt: Something for Nothing in California.* Cambridge, Mass.: Harvard University Press.

Sinclair, W., and P. Behr. 1981. "Horse Trading." *Washington Post,* 27 June, A1.

Smith, H. 1981. "Taking Charge of Congress." *New York Times Magazine,* 9 August, 12–17, 19–20, 47–50.

Stein, H. 1969. *The Fiscal Revolution in America.* Chicago: University of Chicago Press.

Stockman, D. 1986. *The Triumph of Politics.* New York: Avon Books.

Summers, L. H. 1984. "The Legacy of Current Macroeconomic Policies." In *The Legacy of Reaganomics: Prospects for Long-Term Growth,* edited by C. R. Hulten and I. V. Sawhill, 179–98. Washington, D.C.: Urban Institute Press.

Thurow, L. C. 1973. *Generating Inequality: Mechanisms of Distribution in the U.S. Economy.* New York: Basic Books.

Tobin, J. 1988. "Reaganomics in Retrospect." In *The Reagan Revolution?* edited by B. B. Kymlicka and J. V. Matthews, 85–103. Chicago: Dorsey Press.

Wayne, S. J. 1982. "Congressional Liaison in the Reagan White House: A Preliminary

Assessment of the First Year." In *President and Congress: Assessing Reagan's First Year,* edited by N. J. Ornstein, 44–65. Washington, D.C.: American Enterprise Institute.

Weatherford, M. S. 1987. "The Interplay of Ideology and Advice of Economic Policy-Making: The Case of Political Business Cycles." *Journal of Politics* 49: 925–52.

Wehr, E. 1981. "White House's Lobbying Apparatus." *Congressional Quarterly,* 1 August, 1372–76.

Weinraub, B. 1986. "How Donald Regan Runs the White House." *New York Times Magazine,* 5 January, 12–14, 27, 31–32, 36–37, 52, 54.

Wildavsky, A. 1987a. "Choosing Preferences by Constructing Institutions: A Cultural Theory of Preference Formulation." *American Political Science Review* 81, no. 1: 3–21.

———. 1987b. "President Reagan as Political Strategist." *Society* 24, no. 4: 56–62.

Wilson, J. Q. 1967. "A Guide to Reagan Country: The Political Culture of Southern California." *Commentary* 43, no. 5: 37–45.

———. 1980. "Reagan and the Republican Revival." *Commentary* 70, no. 4: 29–32.

8

Reagan's Tax Policy

CHARLES E. McLURE JR.

The most obvious feature of Ronald Reagan's tax policy can be summarized in three words: lower marginal rates. This is by far the most important and most symbolic tax change made during the Reagan years, the one that will have the most important impact around the world, and perhaps the one most likely to endure. Perhaps almost as important is the triumph of the philosophical viewpoint which rate reduction symbolizes: reducing the impact of tax policy on the working of the economic system.

Then there is the agenda of unfinished business Reagan leaves, dominated by the need to reduce the federal budget deficit. Almost as important is the pressing need to reduce the complexity of the tax system, another legacy of the Reagan years, perhaps by switching to a simpler alternative to the income tax. Finally, if we are to retain the income tax, I would add to the agenda of unfinished business the need to realize the promise of fundamental tax reform which was lost between the Treasury Department's 1984 tax reform proposals to Reagan and passage of the 1986 Act.

These five items—rate reduction, Reagan's philosophy and goals in the area of tax reform, deficit reduction, reducing complexity, and realizing the promise of tax reform—are discussed in this chapter. It will be convenient for expositional reasons, however, to present them in a somewhat different order. Following a brief statement of Reagan's philosophy and goals for tax policy in the remainder of this introduction, the next section provides a more detailed interpretation of the practical implications of that philosophical viewpoint. Then follows a discussion of rate reduction. The descriptions of the unfinished agenda of income tax reform and the complexity of the 1986 Act in the subsequent sections provide the background for the consideration of an alternative and simpler approach to direct taxation. Some of the techniques that might be used to accomplish deficit reduction and finally an examination of the place of tax reform in the Reagan legacy conclude this chapter.

Ronald Reagan's basic conservatism and dislike for government interference in the economy could be seen clearly in both the rhetoric with which he announced his 1981 tax program and his 1985 tax reform proposals to the Congress—although not in the interventionist tax policies he actually endorsed in 1981. On February 18, 1981, less than a month after taking office, Reagan said, "the taxing power of government must be used to provide revenues for legitimate government purposes. It must not be used to regulate the economy or bring about social change." Three years later, in his 1984 state of the union message, Reagan said, "Let us go forward with an historic reform for fairness, simplicity, and incentives for growth."

These two statements—although not totally consistent with each other—provide a useful bench mark for assessing the Reagan impact on structural tax policy. This is true not just because these are Ronald Reagan's words; I and many other scholars of tax policy would accept them as a shorthand description of generally appropriate tax policy. Taken together, these two statements suggest that to the extent consistent with the mutual achievement of other goals, the tax system should be fair, economically neutral, simple, and conducive to economic growth. (To these goals for tax structure I would add another dealing with the level of taxation: tax receipts should be adequate to pay the bills; this is the topic of the section on reducing the deficit.)

Implications for Tax Policy

Like any shorthand description, these brief statements of Ronald Reagan must be interpreted, extended, and qualified if they are to provide an adequate basis for deliberations on tax policy. My own interpretation of our bench mark statements is that *all real economic income should be taxed uniformly and consistently at low rates, under a system that is as simple as possible, given these other goals.* Although this statement is somewhat more precise, it too requires interpretation, elaboration, and justification. This clarification can perhaps best be provided by focusing on selected groups of words.[1]

All income must be taxed if the system is to be fair and economically neutral. If some income escapes tax or benefits from preferential taxation, those who receive it will be treated unfairly relative to those who pay tax on all their income; moreover, too many economic resources will be devoted to those activities that are undertaxed. Finally, economic decision making will be simpler if all sources and uses of income are taxed uniformly and consistently rather than differentially; if all income is taxed in the same way, economic decisions can be made without consulting one's tax advisor.

Taxing all real income has another important simplification benefit, especially given political realities in the United States. Congress appears to be schizophrenic in its attitude toward tax favoritism. It makes preferential treatment of various sources and uses of income generally available and yet is reluctant to allow unrestricted access to such treatment. The result is complexity that could be avoided through the adoption of a comprehensive definition of income. An example that creates complexity for many middle-income taxpayers is the phaseout of the deductions for contributions for Individual Retirement Accounts (IRAs) contained in the 1986 Act. Another is the limitation on the use of home equity loans to circumvent the intent of the elimination of the deduction for interest on consumer debt. For upper-income Americans, complexity of this type involves mostly income from capital, timing issues, and tax shelters. For example, accelerated depreciation, the expensing of intangible drilling costs in the oil and gas industry, and full deduction of nominal interest expense are generally allowed, but limits on investment interest, limits on the deductibility of so-called "passive losses," at-risk rules, and the alternative minimum tax (AMT) prevent excessive use of these provisions. These antishelter provisions contribute significantly to the complexity of the income tax but would be unnecessary under a comprehensive definition of income.

Reasoning such as this prompted the Treasury Department in its 1984 report to President Reagan entitled *Tax Reform for Fairness, Simplicity, and Economic Growth* (hereafter Treasury I) to propose the elimination of a long list of exclusions, exemptions, deductions, and credits. (Proposals involving timing issues are discussed below.) Among the most important and controversial of these were the exclusion of many employer-provided fringe benefits and the deductions for all state and local taxes.

Where labor income is concerned, it is relatively easy to understand the prescription to tax all income uniformly and consistently, although the inclusion of fringe benefits in the previous list may raise some eyebrows. By comparison, when capital income is considered, the implications of this same prescription are far less obvious, especially to a lay audience. The problem can be traced to two basic sources of difficulty: timing and inflation.

Economic income is the tax base only if timing issues are handled satisfactorily. Issues of timing arise because it can make a great deal of difference when income is recognized and when deductions are allowed for expenses. Consider for example the case of a defense contractor constructing a multimillion dollar warship over a period of years. In order to minimize the present value of tax liability, the taxpayer would generally want to claim deductions for expenses immediately while deferring recognition of income as long as possible. Similar issues arise in a surprising range of other areas including timber, orchards and vineyards, natural resource industries, and the accounting for inventories and installment sales. Thus the question of depreciation allowances, although perhaps the most familiar timing issue, is far from unique. If, because of timing issues, taxable income does not approximate economic income as closely as possible, given administrative realities, the very concept of taxing all income uniformly and consistently is meaningless.

Real income must be the base of a true income tax. The tax system of the United States, like many others, reflects an implicit assumption that prices are stable—that is, that there is no inflation. If this assumption is not valid, the interaction between an unindexed tax system and inflation creates economic distortions and inequities. For this reason, Treasury I proposed a comprehensive system of inflation adjustment for interest income and expense, depreciation (and similar allowances), capital gains, and cost of goods sold from inventory. The purpose was to assure that the measurement of real income would be independent of the rate of inflation.

Simplification involves at least three aspects. Most obvious is the elimination of onerous burdens of understanding complex tax laws, keeping records, and completing returns. This is probably what most people have in mind when they use the term. A second type of simplification is the removal of tax influences on economic decision making. This is likely to be especially important for high-income taxpayers and businesses. Finally, it appears that some Americans are not interested in simplification so much for themselves as for others because they are annoyed to see those whose income is as great as theirs paying less tax. Although this third form of "simplification" is important from a political point of view, it is merely tax reform by another name and need not be discussed further.

The questions then are: (1) how well did tax policy fare during the

Reagan years in achieving these announced goals of public policy? and (2) what are the likely implications for the future of tax policy? These two questions are addressed in the four sections that follow.

Rate Reduction

One of the outstanding accomplishments of the Reagan administration was the reduction of marginal tax rates. Whereas marginal rates paid by individuals reached as high as 70 percent (50 percent under the maximum tax on earned income) when Reagan assumed office in 1981, the highest marginal rate is now 33 percent (and only 28 percent at the top of the income scale). For most corporate income, the rate was reduced from 46 to 34 percent.

It is difficult to overstate the importance of this achievement. Not only are there substantially less disincentives—for work, for saving, for investment, and for innovation—but the distortions and inequities that remain are less important at these lower rates. Even if tax shelters might otherwise have survived tax reform, they simply have little attraction at rates this low.

It seems likely that this aspect of the Reagan Revolution will endure even if rates rise slightly from the low point reached in the 1986 Act. (It does not seem unlikely that the 28 percent rate levied on income above the range to which the 33 percent rate applies may be raised in order to eliminate this strange "humpbacked" rate schedule. However, as noted below, there is fear that such a change might cause tax reform to unravel.) There is growing realization among both politicians and tax experts that high marginal rates do a great deal of mischief and accomplish little. Even before the submission of the Treasury Department's tax reform proposals to the White House in late 1984, rate reduction was occurring elsewhere. For example, on January 1, 1984, Indonesia reduced the top individual rate from 50 to 35 percent and the corporate rate from 45 to 35 percent. In May 1984, the United Kingdom announced a reduction of its corporate rate from 52 to 35 percent.

While the U.K. example was important in helping sell rate reduction in the United States, there is little doubt that it will be the U.S. rate reductions that will have the most influence in the rest of the world. Whether because of the persuasiveness of the intellectual arguments for lower rates, because of mere emulation, because of the fear of brain drain, because of competitive pressures from U.S. firms subject to lower rates, or because of fear that U.S. firms would not be able to take full credit for taxes paid to high-tax countries, nations around the world have become subject to "rate reduction fever." This tendency is perhaps most visible in the nations of the Third World, where the harm caused by high tax rates may be every bit as great as that in more advanced countries. Colombia has reduced its corporate rate and its top individual rate to 30 percent (from 40 and 49 percent, respectively), and Jamaica has reduced its top individual rate from 57.5 to 33⅓ percent. The United Kingdom has recently announced that it will reduce its top individual rate from 60 to 40 percent, and other developed countries have adopted more modest rate reductions.

The Lost Promise of Tax Reform

Measured by the standards of what had been achieved in prior tax reform efforts and what could reasonably have been expected, the Reagan record in tax reform was spectacular. Yet on an absolute scale, the tax reform acts of the Reagan years have done poorly at achieving the basic objective of taxing all income uniformly, consistently, and simply. Some of the loopholes that were plugged in 1986 had been placed in the tax code only in 1981; the investment tax credit (ITC) and highly accelerated depreciation are among the most important examples. Many of the most important gaps and inconsistencies in the tax base which survived tax reform have existed since the income tax was first enacted 70 years ago. These include the exclusion of interest on general obligations of state and local governments, the exemption of most employer-provided fringe benefits, and the deductions for home mortgage interest and the income and property taxes levied by state and local governments. In addition, the United States remains one of the few advanced countries to provide no relief from the double taxation of corporate dividends.

On the other hand, progress has clearly been made in a few areas. All unemployment compensation is now subject to income tax. Consumer interest is no longer deductible. Many other previously available deductions have been eliminated or combined and made subject to floors. The elimination of the deduction for state and local sales taxes, although inappropriate when seen in isolation, at least establishes the principle that broad-based taxes levied by subnational governments are no longer off limits to federal tax reform. Perhaps more important, the 1986 and 1987 Acts established and then extended limits on the deductibility of home mortgage interest. Various antishelter provisions as well as low rates may make tax shelters a thing of the past.

Substantial progress has been made in the resolution of timing issues. Among the provisions added to the tax code or tightened significantly during the Reagan years are those dealing with installment sales, completed contracts, inventories, and other accounting changes. The AMT has also been tightened and extended to corporations. As a result of these changes, the definition of income for tax purposes approximates economic income more closely than at the beginning of the 1980s. The tax system is thus fairer than before, it distorts economic decisions less, and there are fewer opportunities for tax shelters. Yet the tax code is also much more complicated than before. Whether the system is perceived to have been improved is not clear. Certainly the increase in complexity has not enhanced that perception.

No direct progress was made during the Reagan years in removing the influence of inflation from the measurement of real income from business and capital. (Monetary values such as personal exemptions and the limits of rate brackets have been indexed, however.) As a result, the basic measurement of income remains as vulnerable to inflation as in 1980. A rise in the rate of inflation would cause the overstatement of real interest income and expense, the overstatement of real capital gains, and the understatement of depreciation and similar allowances.

Several of the antishelter provisions adopted in 1986 do, however, have the indirect effect of reducing the damage that would otherwise result from the overstatement of real interest deductions during an inflationary period. Because of the limitations on the deductions for investment interest and passive losses, excess interest deductions arising from investment activities and tax shelters generally cannot be used to offset other income. Although overall this should have a salutary effect on the equity and neutrality of the system, it is an extremely poorly targeted mechanism to use for this purpose. Moreover, it does nothing to remedy the misstatement of real capital gains and depreciation allowances which occurs during inflationary times. Finally, this approach is almost certainly more complicated than direct assault on the inflation problem along the lines described in Treasury I.[2]

Although the Treasury I proposals for inflation adjustment were given short shrift in the political and legislative process that began at the White House and continued on Capitol Hill, they may ultimately have an important impact both here and abroad. By highlighting the inequities and distortions that are caused by the interplay between inflation and a tax system that makes no allowance for inflation, they have caused greater awareness of the problem. If inflation is expected to be a problem, this awareness may contribute to the consideration of either an inflation-adjusted income tax or the Simplified Alternative Tax described in a later section.

The Complexity of the 1986 Act

Simplification was an early victim of the political process that produced the Tax Reform Act of 1986. As a result, the U.S. income tax is vastly more complicated now than in 1980, so much so that some practitioners as well as public policy experts have expressed fears about a "compliance meltdown."

Numerous reports in the press about increased complexity and increased error rates confirm personal experience that the new tax law is too complicated to be generally understood. Confronted with a system they can no longer understand and facing the prospect of having to pay someone else who (they hope) does understand the system to prepare their returns, average taxpayers may adopt an attitude of deliberate neglect of the more complicated provisions. That is, they may feel that they have no moral obligation to comply with a law as complicated as the 1986 Act. They are likely to realize that since many taxpayers are in the same boat, there is little chance that they will lose the audit lottery and be forced to pay increased taxes, penalties, and interest. Such an attitude is likely to be fostered by official IRS statements that penalties will not be assessed in cases in which underpayments can be traced to new complexities.

Some of the increased complexity is undoubtedly the result of the mere fact that the law was changed; after taxpayers have a few years to learn the new rules these problems should fade away. Moreover, some complexity occurs because new rules were implemented for income from prior investments. This complexity should also diminish over time as such investments are unwound and replaced by different investment vehicles with simpler tax consequences. However, some of the added complexity is likely to be permanent and to be diminished little by the passage of time.

Some complications result from efforts to prevent abuse of the system or to limit the benefits of generally available preferences. For example, new rules now prevent the shifting of nonlabor income to children in order to take advantage of the graduated rate structure and the use of home equity loans to circumvent the limitations on (and eventual elimination of) the deduction for consumer interest. The benefits of deductions for IRAs, the 15 percent rate, and personal exemptions are phased out for middle-income taxpayers.

To some extent, increased complexity is the result of efforts to measure economic income more accurately; the provisions intended to deal with timing issues discussed above fall in this category. As undesirable as such complications are, at least they can be rationalized as inevitable in a system that takes as its objective the taxation of economic income—an objective that is necessary if an income tax is to be fair and neutral. As has long been known, simplicity is not always compatible with fairness and neutrality.

Other complications result from efforts to eliminate opportunities for tax shelters; these include the rules for passive losses, limits on investment interest deductions, at-risk rules, and the AMT. It might be thought that these complications can be justified in the same way as those just discussed. In fact, they generally would not be necessary in a system based more nearly on real economic income—that is, a system in which timing issues and inflation were handled satisfactorily. In short, if taxable income closely tracks real economic income, there are few opportunities for shelters and therefore no need for complex antishelter legislation. In this sense, simplicity complements fairness and neutrality.

For high-income individuals with complicated financial dealings, the problems of complexity are especially great. The various provisions intended to produce a more accurate measure of economic income and to prevent opportunities for tax shelters complicate compliance tremendously. For someone in this position, tax reform has made full compliance expensive, if not impossible. Moreover, this increased complexity may very well deter some activities that would make economic sense in the absence of taxation; to the extent that this happens, tax reforms intended to foster economic neutrality do just the opposite.

Even worse, the new tax system is not even immune from the effects of inflation. A renewal of double-digit inflation would create inequities and distortions if nothing is done to reflect it in depreciation (and similar) allowances, in the calculation of capital gains, in interest income, and in deductions for interest expense. Acceleration of depreciation allowances, restoration of the investment tax credit, and the partial exclusion of long-term capital gains, the traditional ad hoc means of dealing with this problem, would not be an appropriate response. They do nothing to correct the mismeasurement of real interest income and expense. Besides providing the proper offsets for inflation only for (at most) one inflation rate, such techniques would have a quite uneven impact across sectors of the economy and across taxpayers. Moreover, they would place even more pressure on the antishelter devices in the 1986 Act and therefore add further to the complexity for many taxpayers. On the other hand, the conceptually correct approach—inflation adjustment for these items of income and expense—would also add to the complexity.

A Simplified Alternative

Faced with this "catch 22" situation in which the complexity of the income tax has become intolerable and is likely to grow worse, it is reasonable for the nation to examine alternatives to the traditional income tax.[3] One such alternative would abolish most of the problems of timing and the need for inflation adjustment by making the following fundamental changes: all business receipts (except interest and dividends, which would not be taxable) would enter the calculation of taxable income when received; all business expenditures (except for interest and dividends) would be deductible immediately, whether for raw materials, capital goods, inventories, or whatever; interest and dividends would be neither taxable nor deductible; and nonbusiness capital gains would not be taxed.

Under this system, which I have elsewhere called the "Simplified Alternative Tax," there would be separate taxes on individuals and businesses.[4] Individuals would pay tax under a graduated rate schedule but only on labor income; thus interest and dividends would be tax-exempt. All businesses would be subject to a flat-rate tax, presumably at a rate equal to the top individual rate, regardless of their organizational form (that is, regardless whether organized as corporations, partnerships, or proprietorships). Business losses could not be used to offset individual income. Integration of the business and individual taxes could be achieved at the discretion of the taxpayer in the case of closely held companies by the simple expedient of paying wages and salaries (taxable to the individual but deductible to the business) rather than paying dividends (exempt and nondeductible) or retaining income in the business (no tax consequences except payment of the higher business tax).

This alternative is vastly simpler than the existing income tax. Timing issues would virtually disappear under this regime since all receipts would be recognized immediately for tax purposes, and all expenditures would be deductible immediately. Inflation adjustment would not be necessary since inflation would have no chance to cause mismeasurement of the tax base under this system. There would be no need to allocate interest expense among various categories or to limit deductions for investment interest since none would be deductible. Because of the treatment of interest expense and business expenditures as well as the separation of the individual and business tax bases, there would be no tax shelters. The "kiddie tax," the provision of the 1986 Act under which the nonlabor income of minor children is taxed at the marginal rate of the parents, would be unnecessary, since nonlabor income would not be subject to the individual tax. (Opponents of this scheme will point out that there are no shelters and the kiddie tax is not needed because all income from business and capital is sheltered. I return to this contention immediately below. A more daunting problem is the possibility that interest deductions would continue to be allowed in some sectors.)

Although far from complete, this list of ways in which the Simplified Alternative is simpler than the income tax should cause taxpayers traumatized by the complexity of the 1986 Act to drool. Opponents of a consumption-based direct tax object to its distributional implications. The Simplified Alternative Tax would, in effect, be a tax on labor income plus economic rents since it effectively exempts income from investments that do not yield extraordinary returns.[5] The usual response is to note that almost any degree of progression desired can be achieved by altering the rate structure. More important, the distributional implications of any consumption-based direct tax depend crucially on how gifts and bequests are treated. If no deduction is allowed for such transfers, the tax base of the Simplified Alternative Tax is "lifetime endowment," arguably a better tax base than annual income. Moreover, progressivity would be substantially greater than if deductions were allowed for such transfers.

Whether the Simplified Alternative Tax will actually be adopted anytime soon cannot be predicted with certainty. However, it seems likely that it—or something like it—will be discussed much more widely than if there had been no Tax Reform Act of 1986. That Act has created so much complexity and discontent among taxpayers that a search for a simpler alternative is almost certain. This dialogue—and the adoption of a radically different system, if that should occur—may be among the most important bequests of the Reagan years in the tax area.

Unlike the reduction in rates, which was a conscious and much publicized policy objective of the Reagan administration, public debate of a simpler alternative to the post-1986 income tax almost certainly was not a conscious objective. Yet it can hardly be said that Reagan and his supporters would have not welcomed such a debate. There were probably many in and around the administration who would like to have seen something akin to the Simplified Alternative Tax proposed in Treasury I.[6]

This approach was not followed in Treasury I for a number of reasons. First, the leading proposal for such a tax contained only a single individual rate. Although a single rate would have important administrative advantages, it would reduce the progressivity of the tax system significantly—so much so that the alternative was deemed to be unacceptable on equity grounds as well as politically infeasible.[7] Even worse, there was uncertainty about how gifts and bequests would be treated. As noted above, a tax that applies to gifts and bequests of the decedent/donors as well as to consumption has the advantage of being levied on lifetime endowments. A tax levied on consumption alone rather than on lifetime endowments would reduce progressivity so much as to be unacceptable.

Second, relatively more attention was focused on a different consumption-based direct tax in the preparation of Treasury I, one that allowed a deduction for saving and included proceeds of borrowing in the tax base.[8] There was an additional concern that because of the inclusion of borrowing in taxable income this version would be unacceptable for both political and constitutional reasons. Whether constitutional arguments could be made successfully against a tax that allowed no deduction for interest was (and is) unclear. However, whichever approach to the direct taxation of consumption was chosen, it was felt that a Treasury Department proposal to shift the basis of taxation from income to consumption would be so radical as not to be taken seriously. Now that the 1986 Act has shown how difficult it is to tax income even if no effort is made to allow for inflation in the measurement of income, there may be less resistance to the idea of a consumption-based direct tax.

Reducing the Deficit

The second area in which the Reagan legacy is one of unfinished business is the need for deficit reduction. For most of the period that Reagan has been in office, responsible observers have recognized that the United States should not—and could not—continue indefinitely to run large federal budget deficits. My guess is that a concerted effort will be made during the next four years to find a way to reduce the deficit. Since it will be extremely difficult to cut spending, I believe attention will focus primarily on ways to increase revenues despite President Bush's election promise of "no new taxes."

It is possible that the income tax will be made to carry this increased burden, but I doubt it. There appears to be widespread fear in Washington that rate increases might cause tax reform to unravel. By this it is meant that if rates are raised significantly there will be irresistible political pressure to restore tax preferences eliminated or curtailed in 1986.

Base broadening appears to be a promising avenue for long-term increases in revenues. As noted above, many large gaps in the definition of income survived the 1986 Act. These include the exclusion for interest on general purpose obligation bonds of state and local governments and for employer-provided fringe benefits; deductions for state and local taxes on income and property and for home mortgage interest; and various tax preferences for particular industries such as oil and gas and timber. Yet I doubt that much will be done in this area quickly (except in the case of preferences for particular industries); nor should it, given the inequities that would result.

Another approach would be to adopt a variety of provisions, mostly outside the income tax area, which would make sense even if there were no great demand for higher revenues. For example, Professor Larry Summers (1987) has suggested that we should raise taxes on alcohol and tobacco products, tax the capital income of foreigners, tax what Summers calls "financial engineering" (actually the turnover of financial securities), limit income tax deductions for advertising, auction off import quotas, raise gasoline taxes, and improve tax compliance. According to Summers, this package would raise $70 billion. Space does not permit exhaustive treatment of these proposals. (I would, however, argue that taxing the advertising of alcohol and tobacco products, despite its administrative difficulties, appears preferable to merely increasing existing excises on these products.) One can imagine the Congress biting the bullet and adopting some of these proposals, especially once it considers the alternatives.

One of the alternatives that is most mentioned as a means of reducing the deficit is the adoption of a federal sales tax such as a value added tax (VAT) or a retail sales tax. Whether the United States is likely to adopt a national sales tax is hard to know. Both the pros and the cons of such a move are formidable.[9] The primary advantages of the VAT are its economic neutrality and its ability to raise large amounts of money relatively easily. A federal retail sales tax would do almost (but not quite) as well on both scores and have the added advantage of greater familiarity to American business.

Liberals might oppose a national sales tax as regressive. Excluding food and other "necessities" from the tax base is a crude and inappropriate way of dealing with this problem. Increasing transfer payments would be a more promising approach, but even it is not adequate because of the large number of poor who do not receive transfers. Burdens on low-income families could be essentially eliminated through extension of the earned income tax credit device to make it a de facto negative income tax; of course, such a step would have quite far-reaching implications.

Conservatives may also oppose introduction of a national sales tax in the absence of constitutional limits on the taxing and spending powers of the federal government. There is good reason to believe that federal spending will be greater if the United States adopts a national sales tax than if it does not.

Finally, officials of state and local governments can be expected to oppose introduction of either a federal VAT or a national sales tax. It appears that either would reduce the fiscal sovereignty of subnational governments (see McLure 1987b, 1988a).

In short, it is hard to know what to expect. A national sales tax seems to be the only way to raise the enormous amounts of revenue needed to close the budgetary gap. Yet, it is hard to see the United States actually adopting such a measure.

Suppose for the moment that a VAT is eventually adopted. Although a VAT has long been advocated by many conservatives in this country (usually as a replacement for the corporate income tax), one can only assume that adoption of a federal VAT as a deficit reduction technique is not something Ronald Reagan would be proud of; after all, he opposed tax increases consistently throughout his term in office. Yet it would not be unreasonable to consider that landmark fiscal measure part of the Reagan legacy, if it should occur.

Concluding Remarks

In many ways, the administration of Ronald Reagan is likely be seen as a watershed in the history of tax policy in the United States. Reagan enjoyed one spectacular success in tax policy—the reduction of marginal rates. This was perhaps his most important imprint in the area of structural tax policy. However, also important is the triumph of his philosophical view that tax policy should not be used for social engineering or industrial policy. One can only guess how long this part of the Reagan legacy will survive.

On the other hand, a spectacular failure—the increase in complexity of the U.S. income tax—also occurred "on his watch." It will be interesting to see whether we learn to live with the increased complexity or change the law again, perhaps by adopting the Simplified Alternative Tax described earlier.

Finally, Reagan left us with a deficit problem that by common consensus must be resolved in one way or another. Given Reagan's aversion to increased taxes, it would be ironic indeed if part of the Reagan legacy were the economic and political forces that would lead to introduction of a national sales tax—a measure that once introduced, would almost certainly be a permanent and growing part of the fiscal landscape.

NOTES

The author is a senior fellow at the Hoover Institution, Stanford University. From 1983 to 1985 he was deputy assistant secretary for tax analysis of the U.S. Treasury Department. In that capacity, he had primary responsibility for development of *Tax Reform for Fairness, Simplicity, and Economic Growth,* the tax reform proposals submitted to President Reagan by the Treasury Department in November 1984 which became the basis of the Tax Reform Act of 1986.

1. For a more detailed discussion of these objectives, see McLure (1986).

2. For further discussion along these lines, see McLure (1987a).

3. For a more detailed discussion of the need to consider an alternative to the traditional income tax, see McLure (1988b). For further discussion of the complexity created by attempting to deal with timing issues and the need for inflation adjustment in an income tax, see McLure (1989).

4. This alternative will be recognized as a variant of the plan proposed by Hall and Rabushka (1983) and (1985) and modified by Bradford (1986). For further discussion, see Zodrow and McLure (1988).

5. For a demonstration of this proposition and further discussion of distributional issues including alternative methods of treating gifts and bequests, see Zodrow and McLure (1988).

6. See, for example, the editorial by Hall, Hume, and Rabushka (1986) which proposed a tax modeled after that discussed above as an improved AMT.

7. See U.S. Department of the Treasury (1984, 1: 21–24).

8. See U.S. Department of the Treasury (1984, 1: 30–35). For further discussion of such a tax, which was modeled after that in U.S. Department of the Treasury (1977), see Aaron and Galper (1985).

9. For a complete discussion of these issues, see McLure (1987b). McLure (1988b) suggests that use of the Simplified Alternative Tax to replace the income tax would allow greater revenues to be raised without resorting to a VAT.

REFERENCES

Aaron, Henry J., and Harvey Galper. 1985. *Assessing Tax Reform.* Washington, D.C.: Brookings Institution.

Bradford, David F. 1986. *Untangling the Income Tax.* Cambridge: Harvard University Press.

Hall, Robert E., and Alvin Rabushka. 1983. *Low Tax, Simple Tax, Flat Tax.* New York: McGraw-Hill.

———. 1985. *The Flat Tax.* Stanford: Hoover Institution Press.

Hall, Robert E., Jaquelin H. Hume, and Alvin Rabushka. 1986. "End Deductions and Have Them, Too." *Wall Street Journal,* 4 March.

McLure, Charles E., Jr. 1986. "Where Tax Reform Went Astray." *Villanova Law Review* 31, no. 6 (November): 1619–63.

———. 1987a. "U.S. Tax Reform." *Australian Tax Forum* 4, no. 3: 293–312.

———. 1987b. *The Value Added Tax: Key to Deficit Reduction?* Washington, D.C.: American Enterprise Institute.

―――. 1988a. "State and Local Implications of a Federal Value Added Tax." *Tax Notes* 38, no. 13: 1517–35.

―――. 1988b. "The 1986 Act: Tax Reform's Finest Hour or Death Throes of the Income Tax?" *National Tax Journal* 41, no. 3 (September): 303–15.

―――. 1989. "Lessons for LDCs of U.S. Income Tax Reform." In *Tax Reform in Developing Countries*, edited by Malcolm Gillis, 347–90. Durham, N.C.: Duke University Press.

Summers, Lawrence. 1987. "A Few Good Taxes." *The New Republic*, 30 November: 14–15.

U.S. Department of the Treasury. 1977. *Blueprints for Basic Tax Reform*. Washington, D.C.: U.S. Government Printing Office. Also available as Bradford, David F., and the U.S. Treasury Department Staff. 1984. *Blueprints for Basic Tax Reform*. Arlington, VA: Tax Analysts.

Zodrow, George R., and Charles E. McLure, Jr. 1988. "Implementing Direct Consumption Taxes in Developing Countries." World Bank Working Paper WPS131, December 1988.

PART FOUR

Institutional Change

9

From Nixon's Problem
to Reagan's Achievement:
The Federal Executive Reexamined

JOEL D. ABERBACH and BERT A. ROCKMAN

with Robert M. Copeland

More than a decade ago we wrote an article entitled "Clashing Beliefs Within the Executive Branch" (Aberbach and Rockman 1976). The article was based on interviews done in 1970 with top-level appointed and career officials in the federal government. Our findings documented that during the Republican presidential administration of Richard Nixon, the senior American career civil service was little disposed toward Republican presidents and their policy initiatives. Moreover, the Republican appointees (noncareer executives) who were the superiors of these career officials—particularly those appointees who were in the departments with social service missions—also were inclined toward more liberal policy postures than those pursued by the Nixon administration, especially in the period after our study. In Nixon's view, in fact, much of the bureaucracy represented hostile territory for his administration's plans. Nixon sought very aggressively to gain control over the bureaucracy. In the fall of 1970, for example, he established a "White House counterbureaucracy for domestic affairs" headed by Frederick Malek (Nathan 1983, 39). This was only part, however, of a series of well-known actions designed to achieve greater political control of the bureaucracy by the White House.

Beginning in 1986 and continuing into 1987, we again interviewed samples of top-level appointed and career officials in the federal government. The interviews, as before, ranged broadly, but once again we had measures of party affiliation and views on the role that government should play in economic and social affairs. We again also had a Republican administration, although as we will outline below, its situation and approach differed in important respects from those of the Nixon administration.

Our objective here is to compare and contrast the federal executive in the Nixon and Reagan administrations, with emphasis on the changes that have taken place and what they suggest. We concentrate here on comparing over time federal executives' party affiliations and attitudes about the role of government in the nation's economy.

We begin with a brief description of our data followed by a discussion of the different settings of the Nixon and Reagan administrations in which we take note of those factors particularly relevant to each administration's relations with top federal executives. We then analyze the data on executives' party affiliations and their beliefs about the role government should play in the nation's economy. Finally, we discuss the implications of our findings for understanding bureaucratic responsiveness in the American political system.

The Data

Data for this chapter are drawn from two surveys of top-level executives (career and noncareer) conducted in 1970 and 1986–87.

In 1970, we interviewed 126 administrators from eighteen federal agencies within the Washington, D.C. metropolitan area. The administrators all came from agencies whose primary responsibilities are in the domestic policy areas; administrators in defense and foreign affairs were excluded from the sample frame. Officials were stratified by position. Samples were drawn from those formally designated as "political executives" and from career civil servants with supergrade status (GS 16–18).

Political executives were defined as persons holding "policy" positions at approximately the level of assistant secretary and who were formally appointed by the President and passed with the advice of the Senate (PAS) or persons who were officials on executive level schedule C or held NEA (noncareer executive assignment) job designations with GS rankings of 16 or higher. The career civil servants all held career executive assignment (CEA) status. In order to be considered in the sampling universe, each supergrade CEA had to be the *top* career official within a particular administrative subunit. Sixty-one political executives and sixty-five supergrade career civil servants were interviewed.

Our aim for the 1986–87 sample was to draw comparable respondents plus an additional subsample of officials with staff analytic responsibilities. Given changes in the universe of domestic agencies (additions and deletions) and changes in the personnel system brought about by the

Civil Service Reform Act of 1978 (PL95-454), we had to take into account the new designation of officials (the senior executive service) and new options available to political managers. We once again sampled personnel in domestic agencies, drawing a group of PAS appointees, a group of noncareer executives in the senior executive service (SES-NA) created by the 1978 Act, a group of SES career officials who were the top career officials within their particular administrative subunits (and, therefore, most comparable to the 1970 career officials sampled), and a sample of the rest of the SES. All SES officials held "general" as opposed to "reserved" positions.[1]

"By law, no more than 10 percent of total SES positions, governmentwide, may be filled by noncareer appointees. The proportion of noncareer appointees may, however, vary from agency to agency (up to a limit of 25 percent) within the overall total" (Senate Governmental Affairs Committee, 1984, 255). Under the new law, therefore, positions previously filled by career employees could in 1986–87 be filled by noncareer officials if the positions were on the general list and if certain other conditions were met. In the changing bureaucracy, the top civil servant in a particular unit may have been at a different level than in 1970; and because of the greater flexibility the new law allowed in moving SES executives around in a given agency, individuals who might have been found in what we classified as the top slot under the conditions holding in 1970 would not necessarily have been in that position in 1986. This makes it particularly interesting to compare top career SES executives with other SES career executives, and we designed our study to allow us to do so.

Interviews were completed in 1986–87 with 199 administrators from twenty-one federal agencies in the Washington, D.C. metropolitan area. As in 1970, administrators came from agencies whose primary responsibilities were in the domestic policy area. Of the administrators interviewed, sixty-five were classified as political executives (eighteen PAS and forty-seven SES-NA), sixty-six were in the top career group we call SES-CA-I for purposes of this chapter, and sixty-eight were others with career status, mainly in SES (eight were at GS 15 acting in SES positions), whom we designate SES-CA-II. Fifty-seven of the total (at all levels) were classified as staff analysts. However, we have consolidated the staff and line respondents in this chapter because there are no significant effects of staff as opposed to line status on the variables we examine here.

In both 1970 and 1986–87, most of the interviews were tape-recorded. This allowed us to use and code open-ended questions comfortably and to code for wide-ranging and complex answers to our probes (Aberbach, Chesney, and Rockman 1975, 1–27).[2] The data for 1986–87 used in this chapter came from an initial and cursory coding of a very limited number of variables from the 199 interviews completed. Among these are variables comparable to those used in the 1976 "clashing beliefs" article.[3]

Settings

We began the "clashing beliefs" article by pointing out that tensions always arise within the bureaucracy when presidential administrations change since the change brings new program priorities, new emphases, and new personnel. Tensions, we noted, "are exacerbated when a change in the White House is accompanied by a change in party control. This is especially true when the changeover is from Democratic to Republican control because of Republican suspicions that the career bureaucracy is heavily infiltrated by Democrats" (Aberbach and Rockman 1976, 456). We noted more specifically that

> The Nixon administration . . . came to power suspicious of the existing bureaucracy. The tone of the administration's rhetoric stressed the philosophy of decentralization and substantial curtailment of some of the directions undertaken in the previous eight years of Democratic rule. . . . Suspicious of the responsiveness and loyalty of the administrators, the Nixon administration's litmus test of loyalty often went beyond even the partisan affiliations of the administrators to rather exacting ideological standards of loyalty. (Aberbach and Rockman 1976, 457)

Although Nixon was clearly suspicious of the federal bureaucracy from the beginning, and he very often proposed domestic policies that, in Richard Nathan's words, would "weaken the federal bureaucracy . . . [by] taking power away from the specialized bureaucracies of the federal government" (Nathan 1983, 27), it is also fair to say, as Nathan does, how difficult it is to summarize the Nixon domestic program ideologically, especially in the early years. The Family Assistance Program (a guaranteed annual income), he notes for example, would most likely have weakened the federal bureaucracy, but it was an issue that was more on the agenda of liberals than conservatives, which may explain why Nixon did not back it with great passion.

Nixon's early behavior *vis-à-vis* the domestic bureaucracy and the Congress was not marked by unrelieved hostility. He tried the traditional practice at first of appointing cabinet members "to *represent* the major interests in the inner councils of government" (Nathan 1983, 30), and he allowed them to choose their own subcabinet subordinates. He worked to develop legislative proposals for presentation to the Congress which would put his own stamp on domestic policy but signed bills dear to the hearts of liberals on environmental and regulatory matters. Over time, however, beginning in earnest during the period of our 1970 interviews, he slowly developed the "administrative presidency" strategy so graphically described by Nathan. In this, he would aim to bypass the Congress, put "loyalists" into appropriate positions, and deal ruthlessly with the career bureaucracy. He fell from power before his strategy could be put to a full test—although his fall and the strategy were not unrelated.

By comparison, President Reagan had an easy time of it. Like Nixon, Reagan was hostile to the domestic bureaucracy and to the thrust of much prior domestic policy, but he had numerous advantages. First, his victory in the 1980 presidential election was much more definitive than Nixon's 1968 victory. Second, and perhaps more importantly, he carried a Republican Senate in with him, leading Washingtonians to view his victory as an indicator of deep-seated political change in the country. Third, his advisors had learned something from the Nixon experience, and they set out from the beginning to appoint Cabinet and especially subcabinet members "loyal" to the President and his program. (The Republican majority in the Senate was a help in this regard.) Fourth, his program was more coherent than Richard Nixon's and more conservative from the very beginning, and both were advantages in guiding his own appointees and the career civil service. Fifth, he came to office after the enactment of the Civil Service Reform Act, and the new rules supplemented his already considerable political leverage. Finally, he came to power in a changed political atmosphere. Whereas Nixon was in office at the end of the regulatory boom, deregulation was already in full swing when Reagan took office. Confidence in big government was low. This created an environment more favorable to an aggressive conservative agenda.

Reagan, in short, knew better what he wanted, had learned from Richard Nixon's experiences, and had several advantages in resources and political strength from the beginning.

Shifting, Yet Still Clashing, Beliefs of the Federal Executive

When Richard Nixon came to office, he did not find many Republicans in the top reaches of the career bureaucracy. As the data in Table 9.1, "1970," show, in fact, only 17 percent of the supergrade career civil servants whom we sampled in 1970 reported that they nor-

TABLE 9.1   Party Affiliation by Job Status

| Formal Job Designation[a] | Party Affiliation[b] | | | Totals | |
	Republican (%)	Independent (%)	Democrat (%)	(%)	N
1970 (Aberbach and Rockman)					
High political appointee (PAS designation)	81	6	13	100	16
	⟩ 66	⟩ 10	⟩ 24		
Middle-level appointee (NEA, schedule C designation)	59	12	29	100	41
Supergrade career	17	36	47	100	58
		$\gamma = .58$			115
1976 (Cole and Caputo)					
Political appointees	61	19	19	99[c]	57
Supergrade career	16	46	38	100	111
		$\gamma = .59$			168
1986–87 (Aberbach, Copeland, and Rockman)					
High political appointee (PAS designation)	89	6	6	101[c]	18
	⟩ 94	⟩ 3	⟩ 3		
Middle-level appointee (SES-NA)	96	2	2	100	47
Career I (SES-CA-I)	44	14	41	99[c]	63
Career II (SES-CA-II)	27	24	49	100	63
		$\gamma = .67$			191
	($\gamma = .82$ excluding CA-IIs; $N = 127$)				

[a] Because of the small number of PAS-designated appointees in our samples hereafter analyses involving the job status variable will collapse PAS and SES appointees into a general category.

[b] Party affiliation for 1970 and 1986–87 in our studies was measured by asking the administrators whether they normally voted for one party or the other. Those who said they did not normally vote for one party or the other were coded as Independents. Party affiliation for 1976 in the Cole and Caputo study was measured by party identification rather than voting behavior.

[c] Totals do not equal 100% because of rounding.

mally voted Republican. This contrasts with 47 percent who said that they normally voted Democratic, and 36 percent who characterized themselves as Independents. A study undertaken in 1976 by Cole and Caputo, published in 1979, used "party identification" rather than voting behavior to measure party affiliation. It indicated relatively modest change after six years of Republican control of the White House (Table 9.1, "1976"). The percent Republican remained about the same compared with 1970 (17 to 16 percent), although the percentage Democrat dropped about nine points (from 47 to 38 percent). Independents replaced Democrats as the modal group, and they apparently showed stronger pro-Republican policy leanings than had the Independents in our 1970 study, who were much closer to Democrats in their attitudes. Even among top career executives selected for their posts after the 1968 election, however, only 24 percent were clear Republican identifiers (Cole and Caputo 1979, 405). The sustained period of Republican rule evidently did not change the overall partisan makeup of the career bureaucracy that much, although Cole and Caputo certainly show that the relatively small number of top career executives in their sample appointed after 1968 were more likely to be Republicans or Independents than those who were already supergrades in 1968 (Cole and Caputo 1979, 404).

The 1986–87 data do show a much stronger Republican representation among career executives, especially among the top category of SES career executives (CA-I). Actual Republican affiliation was up to 44 percent for the CA-Is, more than two and one-half times the percentages in 1970 and 1976. Democrats showed a modest drop over 1970, and Independents faded to 14 percent (from 36 percent). This may not have been the top career bureaucracy of Reagan's dreams, but its Republican plurality is a sharp contrast to the strong Democratic plurality under Nixon in 1970 and even to the evident plurality of Independents in the 1976 Cole-Caputo sample.

The contrast between the career SES-CA-I and career SES-CA-II samples in 1986–87 is equally interesting. The SES-CA-II people had about the same percentage of Democrats as the 1970 supergrade sample and showed only a modest 10 percent Republican shift contrasted with a 27 percent gain (from 17 to 44 percent) for Republicans among SES-CA-I executives. The flexibility given to political appointees by the 1978 Civil Service Reform Act to shuffle career executives about may well be at least partially manifested in these data. In order to get a good picture of why CA-IIs were less Republican than CA-Is, we will need more information as to when and how the different types of career executives in our survey were selected for their current jobs, what their career patterns were, and also what were their reasons for retirement or separation after Reagan took office. The fact that SES-CA-Is were more likely to have worked for more than one agency (46 percent) compared with SES-CA-IIs (31 percent) leads one to think that a link between the civil service reform and Reagan administration personnel policies may be found.[4]

The possible import of the reform is further reinforced by some comparative data on the social service agencies. As Cole and Caputo show, by the end of the Nixon-Ford administrations, an extraordinary number of vacancies in the ranks of the social service agencies had occurred (perhaps brought on by political pressure) and been filled— enough to eliminate the relationship between partisanship and agency type found in our 1970 study. Indeed, according to the Cole and Caputo data, 46 percent of the top noncareer and career officials in the social service agencies were appointed in the post-1968 period (18 out of 39) as opposed to 23 percent (29 out of 127) of the comparable group in other agencies. They ascribe this success to Nixon's "administrative presidency" strategy; his administration may well have concentrated on the social service agencies and eventually forced out an extraordinary number of officials. We should note, however, that their data also show that turnover was proportionally heaviest among political appointees and not civil servants in the social service agencies, and they indicate that proportionately most of the change in political makeup in these agencies came from the percentage of Republicans among the post-1968 political appointees (Cole and Caputo 1979, 407).

As Table 9.2 shows, our data also indicate that the relationship between agency and partisanship in 1986–87 was very low by comparison with 1970.[5] We are not yet in a position to look at turnover among civil servants, but the utility of the Civil Service Reform Act to the Reagan administration in producing this result in the 1980s is suggested by the following figures from Table 9.3. Of the career officials classified in CA-I in 1986–87, two-thirds (67 percent) of those in the social service agencies were Republicans as opposed to 39 percent of CA-I officials in other agencies. Of the career officials classified in CA-II in 1986–87, only 11 percent in the social service agencies were Republicans compared with 33 percent in the other agencies. As a consequence, the direction of the γ coefficient between agency and party is reversed for the two groups of career officials, and the relationship is a significant one in each case. It is +.36 for CA-I officials (social services more Republican) and −.48 for CA-II officials (social services more Democratic). It appears that the Reagan administration was able to sort out SES career personnel in the social service agencies very well, putting Republicans at the very top and placing the SES Democrats in those agencies in slightly lower positions. More analysis of how this was done should prove valuable to understanding the impact of the civil service reform.

TABLE 9.2 Party Affiliation by Agency

	Party Affiliation			Totals	
	Republican	Independent	Democrat		
Agency[a]	(%)	(%)	(%)	(%)	(N)
1970 (Aberbach and Rockman)					
Social service agencies (HEW, HUD, OEO)	24	30	46	100	33
Other agencies	46	21	33	100	82
		$\gamma = -.32$			
1976 (Cole and Caputo)					
Social service agencies (HEW, HUD)	30	37	33	100	43
Other agencies	30	38	32	100	141
		$\gamma = -.002$			
1986–87 (Aberbach, Copeland, and Rockman)					
Social service agencies (ED, HHS, HUD)	54	9	37	100	46
Other agencies	56	15	29	100	145
		$\gamma = -.08$			

[a]Hereafter, the agency variable will be dichotomized as indicated in the table. HEW, Health Education and Welfare; HUD, Housing and Urban Development; OEO, Office of Economic Opportunity; ED, Education; HHS, Health and Human Services.

Turning back to Table 9.1, this time to examine political level officials in detail, a look at the high (PAS) and middle-level appointees (NEA in 1970 and SES-NA in 1986–87) reveals the impact of the Reagan appointment strategy. PAS level appointees were strongly Republican in the Reagan administration, but at the middle level there is a vast difference. Fifty-nine percent of the middle-level appointees in 1970 were Republicans as opposed to 96 percent in 1986–87. Some of this difference may be due to the fact that Nixon had some Johnson holdovers he had not yet replaced in 1970, but both the magnitude of the difference and a comparison with the Cole and Caputo data showing that only 61 percent of the political appointees were Republicans in 1976 lead one to the conclusion that the Reagan personnel system was particularly effective in reaching its goals. The Reagan administration was solidly Republican at the appointee level. Few Democrats or Independents were selected to satisfy program constituencies or even to provide specialized expertise.

Ironically, although there is evidence of a general Republican shift at all levels, there remained a marked clash in party affiliations between

TABLE 9.3 Party Affiliation by Agency (1986–87 Career Executives Only), Controlling for Job Status

| | | Party Affiliation | | | Totals | |
		Republican (%)	Independent (%)	Democrat (%)	(%)	N
Job Status	Agency					
SES-CA-I	Social service agencies (ED, HHS, HUD)	67		33	100	12
	Other agencies	39	18	43	100	51
	$\gamma = .36$					
SES-CA-II	Social service agencies (ED, HHS, HUD)	11	22	67	100	18
	Other agencies	33	24	42	99[a]	45
	$\gamma = -.48$					

[a]Total does not equal 100% because of rounding.

political appointees and career civil servants. This is reflected in the correlation coefficients between job designation and party affiliation in each of the years. The coefficient is actually highest in 1986–87 because the percentage Republican of political appointees was so high and the percentage Democratic so low in comparison with 1970 even though career officials at all levels were more Republican than in 1970. So, we may have a situation in which a great deal of "success" did not breed happiness because the solid Republican group of political appointees at the top looked down on a more marbled set of layers below them.

It may be, however, that for the Reagan administration, party affiliation represented only a necessary yet not a sufficient test of success. The real test of sufficiency would have rested with the political beliefs of the administration. The Reagan administration, after all, started with a set of conservative goals and wanted administrators in tune with its program.

To test its success in this regard, we looked at a measure of the role administrators thought the government should play in the nation's economy. The actual item is reproduced in note a to Table 9.4. Administrators who strongly supported an active role in the nation's economy are coded at one end of the scale (designated "left" for ease of discussion). Those who strongly opposed an active government role in the nation's economy, preferring instead that decisions in this area be left to the private sector, are coded at the other end of the scale (designated "right"). Other categories run from "supports with reservations," through a center "pro/con" view, to "opposes with reservations."[6]

A look at Table 9.4, "marginal distribution," indicates a startling change from 1970 to 1986–87 in the beliefs that top administrators held about the role government should play in the nation's economic affairs. Whereas 16 percent of all respondents were to the right of center on this measure in 1970, in 1986–87 over half were. This is more than a threefold increase.

And as Table 9.4, "party affiliation," indicates, the shift is still very strong even when we controlled the party affiliation variable. Almost 70 percent of Republican affiliators in 1986–87 were to the right of center compared with 25 percent in 1970 (a ratio of 2.71 : 1). The comparable figures for Independents and Democrats were 40 percent to 10 percent (4 : 1) and 24 percent to 10 percent (2.4 : 1), respectively. The correlation between party and beliefs about the role of government is even stronger in 1986–87 than in 1970. One graphic indication of the magnitude of the change in beliefs is the fact that Democrats in 1986–87 were as likely to be right of center on this measure (24 percent) as Republicans were in 1970 (25 percent).

TABLE 9.4 Role of Government in the Nation's Economy,[a] Overall, and by Party Affiliation, Agency, and Job Status

	Strongly Supports Active Government Role (Left)		Supports, with Reservations, Active Government Role (Left-Center)	Pro/Con Views, Balance Between Positive and Negative (Center)	Opposes, with Reservations, Active Government Role (Right-Center)		Strongly Opposes Active Government Role (Right)	Totals	
	(%)	(total %)	(%)	(%)	(%)	(total %)	(%)	(%)	(N)
Marginal Distribution for Role of Government in the Economy Measure									
1970	28	52	24	32	15	16	1	100	115
1986–87	4	22	18	28	39	51	12	101[b]	196
Party Affiliation									
1970									
Republican	7	32	25	43	25	25	0	100	44
Independent	36	50	14	41	5	10	5	101[b]	22
Democrat	46	77	31	13	10	10	0	100	39
				$\gamma = -.50$					
1986–87									
Republican	5	10	5	22	49	69	20	101[b]	105
Independent	0	24	24	36	40	40	0	100	25
Democrat	5	41	36	35	22	24	2	100	58
				$\gamma = -.58$					
Agency									
1970									
Social Service	39	60	21	30	9	9	0	99[b]	33
Other	23	49	26	33	17	18	1	100	82
				$\gamma = .27$					

								Total	N
1986–87									
Social service	4	24	20	26	41	50	9	100	46
Other	4	21	17	28	38	51	13	100	150
				$\gamma = .05$					
Job Status 1970									
Political appointees (pooled)	17	40	23	42	19	19	0	101[b]	53
Career super-grades	37	63	26	24	11	13	2	100	62
				$\gamma = -.35$					
1986–87									
Political appointees (pooled)	2	8	6	20	47	72	25	100	64
SES-CA-I	3	20	17	30	41	50	9	100	66
SES-CA-II	8	38	30	32	29	31	2	101[b]	66
				$\gamma = -.49$					

[a] The role of government in the nation's economy item is as follows: It is argued by some people that government must play a greater role in the nation's economic affairs, while others say that decisions in this area should be left to the private sector. On the whole, which of these positions comes closest to yours? (*Probe:* How strongly do you feel about this?)

[b] Totals do not equal 100% because of rounding.

Not surprisingly, given the results in Table 9.2 and the data on agency presented in the text, Table 9.4, "agency," shows that the agency link to beliefs about the role of government in the nation's economy, quite evident in 1970, had just about disappeared by 1986–87. The correlation (γ) between agency and the role of government indicator dropped from .27 to .05.

The last entry on Table 9.4, "job status," reinforces what we have seen so far. Given the relationship between party and role of government and the extraordinary proportion of Republicans among political appointees in 1986–87, it is not too surprising that job status continued to be a strong predictor of where an administrator stood on the role government should play in the nation's economy. This relationship, in fact, was even stronger in 1986–87 than in 1970, and leads us to paraphrase our conclusion about party and job status: although there is evidence of a general shift to the right at all levels (and political appointees and CA-I level career administrators both moved to the right by identical 3.8 : 1 ratios), there remained a marked clash in beliefs between political appointees and career civil servants.

Finally, Table 9.5 shows that both party and job status had independent effects on beliefs about the role of government in the nation's economy, although the very small numbers for some cells in the 1986–87 political appointee pool (due to the overwhelming number of Republican appointees) must caution us about the results. However, it is clear that for both career and noncareer executives, even including CA-II level civil servants, the relationship between party and beliefs about the role of government was robust in every instance and was actually stronger in 1986–87 than in 1970. Within each job status category in each year, Republicans were to the right of comparable Democrats, and, with one minor exception, Republicans, Independents, and Democrats in each job status category in 1986–87 were to the right of comparable party affiliators in each category in 1970.[7]

In addition, the differences between the CA-I and CA-II civil servants in the 1986–87 data discussed above are reinforced. CA-I people were consistently to the right of CA-II people, controlling for party affiliation.

Again, we should stress *both* the shift to the right at all levels *and* the clash in beliefs that continued to exist.

TABLE 9.5 Role of Government in the Nation's Economy by Party Affiliation, Controlling for Job Status

Party Affiliation	Political Appointees (Pooled)				
	Left and Left-Center (%)	Center (%)	Right-Center and Right (%)	Totals	
				(%)	(N)
1970					
Republican	30	47	24	101[a]	34
Independent	0	75	25	100	4
Democrat	83	8	8	99[a]	12
		$\gamma = -.57$			
1986–87					
Republican	5	20	75	100	60
Independent	50	0	50	100	2
Democrat	50	50	0	100	2
		$\gamma = -.79$			
Career Executives					
Supergrade Career					
1970					
Republican	40	30	30	100	10
Independent	61	33	6	100	18
Democrat	74	15	11	100	27
		$\gamma = -.29$			
Career I					
1986–87					
Republican	7	25	68	100	28
Independent	11	33	56	100	9
Democrat	31	38	31	100	26
		$\gamma = -.53$			
Career II					
Republican	29	24	47	100	17
Independent	29	43	29	101[a]	14
Democrat	50	30	20	100	30
		$\gamma = -.34$			

[a] Totals do not equal 100% due to rounding.

Conclusions

The data are remarkably clear. We had shifting yet still clashing beliefs within the executive branch. We will look first at the shift, then at the clash, and finally say a few words about the implications of our findings.

An interlocking set of factors probably accounts for the shift.

We mentioned earlier the systematic recruitment and selection efforts of the Reagan administration—the checking on the views of possible appointees and drawing on the burgeoning network of conservative think tanks. The fruits of these efforts were readily apparent in the proportion of Republican conservatives at the appointee level, and they were probably important in producing the differences we found in party and belief between the CA-I and CA-II levels in our career samples.

For the latter, especially, we believe that the law—the Civil Service Reform Act of 1978—was an important asset for the Reagan administration. The administration apparently took great advantage of the new flexibility the law provided. In addition, we should also note that the natural attrition of civil servants through retirement plus the ravages of program cuts and reorganizations probably also took their toll and gave the Reagan administration the opportunity to use the provisions of the Civil Service Reform Act effectively.

In addition, the Reagan administration had the advantage of six years of Republican control of the Senate. This provided it with a much better chance of pushing through appointees it wanted, no matter what agency clientele groups might think, and of shielding its appointees from the effects of congressional pressure.

However, for recruitment, selection, opportunities for manipulation, and even for control of the Senate to be effective, the Reagan administration had to know what it wanted; and, by the beliefs of its appointees, there is evidence that it did know what it wanted and knew more consistently and to a greater extent than did the more traditional and pragmatic Nixon administration. Those factors gave it clearer guidelines from the beginning and provided clearer signals for all concerned.[8]

It also had a legitimacy the Nixon administration never achieved—a legitimacy borne of its more complete electoral victories and the fact that it appeared to be more in tune with its time and through its electoral victories, better suited to write the tunes. The term *mandate* is sometimes used (often wishfully in the face of confounding data) to describe such a condition. Although Reagan barely won more than 50 percent of the vote in the 1980 election, the Republicans' takeover of the Senate and their gains in the House of Representatives plus their early legislative successes and Reagan's high popularity level, particularly among the young, gave the aura of a substantial shift in the tides of opinion. If we assume that bureaucrats read both the election returns and the political spin given to them by other members of the Washington cognoscenti, then we may have a better grasp of the reasons for the shift in bureaucrats' views.

We should add to that the idea of concordance (Aberbach and Rockman 1986), the notion that bureaucrats are part of an elite that is intimately involved with the world of ideas, especially ideas about public policy, and that changes in their ideas correspond to alterations in the intellectual climate of public policy. In this view, bureaucrats are idea retailers. They are often familiar with a few key ideas that are percolating through the social science and applied public policy literature. To an increasing extent, and quite expectedly, we are beginning to see the products of the schools and institutions of public policy which have spread throughout the country's universities in the last two decades now reaching high positions. Mirroring changes in social science itself, the play of ideas and their analytic logic seems to have shifted among bureaucrats from sociological to economic notions.

Next to the academic community itself, bureaucrats at this rarified level are the natural hosts for ideas floating around in the environment. They are attentive to ideas and interested in them, and not surprisingly, they articulate exceedingly well changes in the dominant set of ideas. If in the midst of the New Deal and the Fair Deal, the Democrats were perceived as the party of ideas and direction and the Republicans as mere defenders of a no longer legitimized status quo, those conceptions had nearly reversed themselves for many administrators at the time of our present interviews. In this regard, one of our respondents put the question of his political identity (Independent) nicely: "In the 1960s, the Democrats espoused ideas that moved and inspired the country. Now it's the Republicans who are doing that while the Democrats drift about."

If these factors help to explain the shifts at all levels, why the continued clash?

First, although career civil servants may reflect changes in the political climate—a fact that, if correct, should give comfort to those concerned about bureaucratic responsiveness in a democratic society—they are generally a more cautious and skeptical lot than the types a zealous administration is likely to appoint. This is evident in our data in the differences between the beliefs of Republican political appointees and Republican careerists in our CA-II sample. Second, and relatedly, an administration can, with a favorable political climate, work its will at the political appointee level much more rapidly than at the career level. It can force the rate of turnover in personnel up at the career level, but it still must allow time to work; and the necessary time is likely to be greater than a presidential administration's life. Third, administrators live in a world that extends beyond the president. They have congressional committees and program constituencies with which to contend; and in the case of career civil servants, they must look to the future as well as to the present.

An implication of all this is that an activist administration, whether Democratic or Republican, with strong views that represent a break with the past is likely always to have beliefs that clash with those of its civil servants. One solution to this, if a solution is needed, would be a political/ideological spoils system that allows each administration to select whomever it pleases for any position it wishes to fill. The SES system pushes somewhat in this direction but clearly not enough to satisfy those who want near total control by the president. A second possibility would be a civil service of neutrals in the most basic sense, neutral tools who would salute any order. Twentieth-century history suggests that we probably do not want that. We could also have a law mandating a civil service of Independents or a bipartisan civil service split 50-50 between the parties or one-third Democratic, one-third Independent, and one-third Republican, or some such arrangement, but enforcing it would create immense problems, and the clash of beliefs problem would not be solved except where balance was an administration's goal.

The question of what kind of political profile, if any, the civil service should have in the United States is not an issue on which we can reach closure here. However, our data suggest a rather adaptable civil service and civil service system. When the rare situation in the American political system occurs in which an administration has a substantial degree of coherence in its overall program goals and its personnel system and appears for the moment to have strong political momentum (quasi-party government), the career bureaucracy seems moved by the same forces. It does not move all the way, of course, so that the views of the career service exactly mirror those of the presidential administration. Although that may present a problem for the administration in power, it should not otherwise be a matter of concern. Far from it. Indeed, the career bureaucracy is probably able to do its job best when it provides some equilibrium to the system and when it cautions political officials by drawing on reserves of experience, conviction, and dedication to following the law. When it behaves in this way, the top civil service is well positioned for a return to the normal conditions of American politics—a state characterized by its legal division of authority, its lack of a clearly defined decisional apparatus, its consequent confusing directional signals, and its strong incentives to the bureaucracy to seek political support outside the executive in behalf of its programs and clienteles.

NOTES

The authors wish to thank the National Science Foundation (Grant SES 85-17167) for research support and The Brookings Institution for its generosity in housing this project. We also thank Joseph Seman, Kerry Manning, and Julio Carrion of the University of Pittsburgh and David D'Lugo and Peggy Dembicer of UCLA for their able assistance.

Joel D. Aberbach thanks the Academic Senate and the Institute of Social Science Research at UCLA for support.

Bert A. Rockman is grateful for support from the Center for International Studies at the University of Pittsburgh.

Robert M. Copeland is completing his doctoral work at the University of Michigan.

1. General positions may be filled by career or noncareer people, whereas career reserved positions, as the designation indicates, may be filled only by career people. Career reserved positions are positions in which impartiality or the public perception of impartiality is considered essential (such as audit or certain law enforcement positions).

2. In 1986–87 we used close-ended questions more extensively than in 1970 in order to expand our earlier work and to gain new information in as efficient a manner as possible.

3. Some of the items had to be coded directly from the tapes since not all of the interviews had been transcribed. The data presented here are basically very accurate but minor adjustments in the data are still possible.

4. Twenty-two percent of the career supergrades in the 1970 sample had served in more than one agency. See Aberbach, Putnam, and Rockman (1981, 71).

5. $\gamma = -.08$ in 1986–87 versus $\gamma = -.32$ in 1970. A negative coefficient indicates more Democrats in social services agencies. See Aberbach and Rockman (1976); Cole and Caputo (1979).

6. We chose this scale rather than the left-right social services continuum used in our "clashing beliefs" article mainly for practical reasons. The left-right social services continuum is coded from an examination of the answers to many questions on our interview transcript. We coded a quick version of this item for the 1986–87 interviews, often based on listening to the tape only, but we are not yet confident enough of the variable for 1986–87 to allow a category-by-category comparison of the distributions to the responses. However, we should note that the "role of government and social services" continuum measures were strongly related in 1970 ($\gamma = .62$) and were even more strongly related for our rough coding of the left-right social services con-

tinuum in 1986–87 ($\gamma = .86$). Therefore, most of what we say about analysis of one measure is likely to be valid for the other.

7. The exception is for Democratic political appointees. However, reflecting the Reagan appointment practices, there were only two Democratic political appointees in the 1986–87 sample.

8. The clearer signals also may have sped up "voluntary" departures of senior career officials in certain agencies in which the Reagan administration radically reversed prevailing directions. If so, that also would help account for a more compatible set of career officials. Such an interpretation was suggested to us by two career officials, one in the Energy Department and one in the Justice Department.

REFERENCES

Aberbach, Joel D., James D. Chesney, and Bert A. Rockman. 1975. "Exploring Elite Political Attitudes: Some Methodological Lessons." *Political Methodology* 2: 1–28.

Aberbach, Joel D., and Bert A. Rockman. 1976. "Clashing Beliefs Within the Executive Branch: The Nixon Administration Bureaucracy." *The American Political Science Review* 70: 456–68.

Aberbach, Joel D., Robert D. Putnam, and Bert A. Rockman. 1981. *Bureaucrats and Politicians in the Western Democracies*. Cambridge: Harvard University Press.

Aberbach, Joel D., and Bert A. Rockman. 1986. "A Changing Federal Executive? Early Surmises With Some Surprises." Paper for the IPSA conference on the structure and organization of government. Pittsburgh, PA, December 11–13.

Cole, Richard L., and David A. Caputo. 1979. "Presidential Control of the Senior Civil Service: Assessing the Strategies of the Nixon Years." *The American Political Science Review* 73: 399–413.

Nathan, Richard P. 1983. *The Administrative Presidency.* New York: John Wiley and Sons.

Senate Governmental Affairs Committee. 1984. *United States Government Policy and Supporting Positions*. 98th Cong., 2d sess.

10

The Presidency after Reagan:
Don't Change It—Make It Work

RICHARD P. NATHAN

Ronald Wilson Reagan was not a great president, but perhaps greatness may not be possible without a major national crisis. He was, however, a very successful president, serving out two full terms and leaving office as a respected national leader with a great reservoir of good will among the people, much as was the case with Dwight David Eisenhower. The purpose of this chapter is to examine both the Reagan presidency as an institution and the case for making fundamental changes in the office.

The presidency is much more than one person; "it is," said Albert De Grazia, "a Congress covered with skin."[1] We need to assess presidents in these terms as the leaders of a large system. Actually, there were two Reagan presidencies: a first term, during which the Reagan system worked relatively smoothly, considering the immensity of the challenge; and a second term, in which the presidency as an institution fell short of this earlier standard. I derive lessons from both of them to argue in favor of keeping the presidency as an institution in its present form and against those who want basic constitutional changes in the office.

This is not to say that we should take a head-in-the-sand attitude toward all modifications in the role of the president and the office of the presidency. I distinguish two types of changes: (1) constitutional—in the role, term, and duties of the president and the principle of the separation of power; and (2) procedural—in the organization and staffing of the office of the president and in the selection process for the presidency. Changes of the latter type may indeed be desirable. In fact, they are happening all the time.

I take specific issue with the scholarly opinion among some contemporary presidency watchers, much of which opinion dates from the Carter years, that we should make fundamental alterations in the American presidency. These opinions can be identified easily by associating them with Lloyd N. Cutler, a distinguished Washington attorney and counsel to President Carter; and government expert James L. Sundquist. My position is that we should not adopt their proposals for constitutional changes that vary the basic character of the American presidency.

The Basic Character of the Presidency

The presidency is a quintessentially American institution. Its operation reflects the competitive, often confrontational, style and spirit of American government. It can and often does work well as the focus for policy-making and in its execution of the American governmental system despite the inevitable criticisms leveled at presidents and the rocky moments that are bound to occur. For much of the first term of Ronald Reagan's presidency (to the surprise of many president watchers) Reagan operated successfully to get his way in this intense political milieu. I can best convey the spirit of my assessment with an anecdote.

A newspaper reporter interviewing people about a primary election asked a man on the street how he would vote. "Oh, I never vote," the man replied, "it just encourages them."

The reason many people think this story is funny is that it has a familiar ring to it, reflecting the idea that in the United States politics is not the most venerated of professions. We love to make fun of, and trouble for, our politicians, perhaps out of envy for the excitement of their work and the attention they receive when they are riding high.

Personally, my bias is that I think we are too hard on our politicians. The fear that voting "just encourages them" reflects the tendency that bad press for politicians is good press for the media; many citizens know more about the foibles than the fineness of our political leaders. We do not give enough credit to the thousands of men and women who dedicate their lives to the profession of politics in this country.

The pluralistic American political system and culture have much to do with this love-hate relationship with our politicians. The character of U.S. politics makes every citizen a potential political player and critic. In De Tocqueville's terms, our political system is "full of striving and animation," but at the same time it is responsive and vibrant in a way De Tocqueville clearly admired.

The framers of the Constitution may have had a little secret among themselves—which James Madison never recorded—to the effect that they should make the presidency a beguiling office. They surely did so. The dominant view in the literature is that the framers resisted assigning a clear strong role to the presidency because of their fear of England's last powerful king, George III, against whom the colonists saw themselves fighting the Revolutionary War. Tom Paine called George III "the Royal Brute of Britain." The king stood in the minds of the framers as a symbol of the dangers of lodging executive power in a single person. As a result, some of the framers did not want to have an executive; and Forrest McDonald says that one fourth of the delegates at the constitutional convention advocated a plural executive.[2] McDonald added that the lack of a knowledge base and different opinions among the delegates were the reasons for "the curious manner" in which executive powers are divided and distributed in the U.S. Constitution.[3]

The result is that Article II created a relatively weak executive branch in terms of the president's relationships with the Congress. In his brilliant study of the Jeffersonian presidencies, James Sterling Young said that when it came to presidential leadership of Congress, the president's cupboard was bare:

> It seems beyond argument that the Constitution provided a wholly inadequate vehicle for presidential leadership of Congress. That the framers made the Chief Executive independent of the representative body was no inconsiderable accomplishment in a nation whose colonial experience gave every reason for mistrusting executive power. Nothing would have been more out of character with the organizing principles of the Constitution than for the framers to have admitted into it the concept of presidential leadership of the legislative branch.[4]

The original conception of the American national government put the force of government in the legislature. Article I of the Constitution, dealing with the legislative branch, is the longest and most specific article. It contains the enumerated powers of the new national government, which are explicitly assigned to the Congress.

Now in the twentieth century, this earlier conception that regarded the presidential office as having a limited role in the political process has been supplanted by a greatly strengthened presidency that has acquired new and broad powers. The Rooseveltian communications power of the modern presidency, the executive budget, the creation of the executive office, and the expansion of its staff and duties have all contributed to the growth in the role of the modern president as a policy initiator and leader. Under and since the FDR presidency, the fear has often been expressed that now an "imperial presidency" threatens our liberties and our political system.

There is also another contemporary view that rises to the surface in periods of stress. It was evident with Lyndon Johnson during the Vietnam War; with Jimmy Carter on his retreat to Camp David to ponder the national malaise; with Richard Nixon in the Watergate affair; and with Ronald Reagan for much of his second term. At the height of the Iran-contra affair, Larry Speakes, serving as the chief White House spokesman for President Reagan, said, referring to the presidency, "when you stumble, you're immobilized."[5] His comment reflects this second view of the presidency as a vulnerable and isolated office, beset by pressures and inflated expectations; this is a view that coexists, often in the same formulation, with the idea of an imperial presidency.

Elements of the opinion of an isolated and vulnerable presidency can be seen in some of the proposals for changes in the office. Lloyd Cutler, in a now famous 1980 article in *Foreign Affairs,* emphasized what he saw as the perennial problem of stalemate in the American policy process. The focus of his analysis was Jimmy Carter's failure to win ratification of the SALT II treaty—not necessarily a good example since, historically, the Senate has ratified about 1,000 treaties and has turned down twenty, only five in this century.[6] Unfortunately for Jimmy Carter, the Soviets invaded Afghanistan just before the SALT II treaty came up for a vote.

Lloyd Cutler's essential complaint is that the existing system prevents the government from "making those decisions *we* all know must be made."[7] The problem with this analysis is the assumption that there is a group of people that knows what is best and that the political process, in synthesizing the values and views of the citizenry, is unable to do what that omniscient "we" know should be done.

Another reason, according to Cutler, for reform of the presidency is the related tendency for the American political system to reflect "a sort of permanent centrism."[8] I do not so much quarrel with this part of Cutler's analysis as I would raise a question about whether this tendency is a weakness at all. One can argue quite to the contrary that it is the very key to the stability and longevity of the American constitutional system.

On the basis of his analysis, Lloyd Cutler calls for changes that would convert the presidency into an office resembling that of the prime minister in a parliamentary form. Among his chief recommendations are permitting as many as half of the members of the Cabinet to be chosen from among sitting members of the Congress; allowing for a vote of confidence during each presidential term; and changing the duration of presidential and congressional terms so that they are coterminous.

In much the same way as Lloyd Cutler, James L. Sundquist, in a Brookings Institution book on constitutional reform published in 1986, takes aim at the condition of divided government in which one party controls the Congress and the other the executive branch. Under these conditions, he says, "the normal difficulties of attaining harmonious and effective working relationships between the branches are multiplied manifold."[9] Sundquist urges reforms similar to those advocated by Cutler.

I base my case against these and similar non-quick constitutional fixes on two arguments:

1. The Edmund Burkean argument: be very careful about changing institutions.
2. The experience of the Reagan presidency offers guidance for the future which supports the conclusion that the presidency can and does work. This is, I believe, the major thrust of this chapter.

An important idea associated with the Burkean argument fits the subject at hand: Burke's respect for institutions. Referring to the dangers of institutional change, Burke said, "By this unprincipled facility of changing the state as often and as much, and in as many ways, as there are floating fancies or fashions, the whole chain of continuity of the commonwealth would be broken. No one generation could link with another. Men would become little better than flies of summer."[10]

I believe it is just as well that no important political leaders are currently pressing for constitutional changes of the type advocated by Cutler and Sundquist. Many politicians would like to amend the Constitution to require a balanced budget (a dubious constitutional tenet), to permit prayer in the schools, or to ban abortions, but as far as I know, no important active politician supports opening the Pandora's box of constitutional change to permit congressmen to serve in the Cabinet, to provide for votes of confidence, or to have combined executive-congressional tickets.

In dealing with the second argument, I wish to draw on Ronald Reagan's experience to support the position on the presidency taken here and as stated in the chapter title. The modern president is the nation's most powerful leader, a teacher, and a human being all wrapped up in one. He must be skillful in structuring and managing the office if the institution is to succeed and stay on an even keel amid the great pressures that swirl around it. The president cannot let the machinery take on a life of its own. He must be in control, but he cannot control everything. The fact that there is constant political bargaining in our governmental system does not mean that we cannot make important decisions; however, decisions take skill and time and they often require a triggering event or issue to produce broad agreement on a new or significantly changed course of action.

The first term of the Reagan administration was a good period for the American presidency in which the office and the officeholder stood in high regard and in which Reagan's policies had a profound effect on many areas of our national life.

More than anything else, Ronald Reagan was viewed at the outset of his presidency as a great communicator—although in point of fact, I do not believe this was or is his strongest suit. Reagan's greatest strengths, as demonstrated by the experience of his first term, are three-fold: (1) his excellent sense of timing; (2) his ability to select and deploy effectively his chief subordinates; and (3) what Fred Greenstein calls "his propensity to act on principles" and to stick to them.[11]

Principles of Effective Presidential Leadership

There are three principles about the way the presidency works which I believe were the keys to the effectiveness of the presidency in Reagan's first term.

The first principle is that the president must be *selective* in choosing the issues on which his or her personal decisions and leadership are required. This, of course, is where Carter and Nixon were said to have had their greatest problems: they were not very selective; both were detail men. As presidents, they tended to take too many subjects and issues to themselves. In Carter's case, so the barbs went, he was said to view the role of the presidency as being similar to that of the captain of a nuclear submarine.

The second principle for organizing the presidency is that the president must *consider dissenting views* but not allow them to swamp the system and prevent action. The Bay of Pigs fiasco very early in Kennedy's presidency is a case in which dissent could not get through. Afterward, the President said, "How could I have been so off base?"[12]; but it was too late.

The third, and I believe most important, principle is that in dealing with the issues the president selects for his own attention and leadership, he must have a *balanced group of trusted advisors* who bring a range of experience and viewpoints to dealing with them. There are a number of dimensions to presidential issues which need to be represented in the advice of the president's associates. One is the capital "P"olitical dimension in the broad sense of what the times call for and what the public wants. A second dimension is that of intellectual or substantive input. A third is the political dimension with a small "p" in the sense of getting things done, working with friends, and watching out for opponents and detractors.

Reagan's first-term troika of Edwin Meese, James Baker, and Michael Deaver was a balanced and smooth-working system in these three-dimensional terms. Edwin Meese represented the "P"olitical dimension—what Reagan was about, and what he had stood for. He had been a close associate of the President's when he was governor of California and knew the agenda and the man in these terms. James Baker, although not an intellectual or scholarly person in his own right, brought to the group substantive ideas as well as a keen organizational sense in handling issues and executing decisions. Michael Deaver was the keeper of the political person—i.e. with a small "p." Although I was not privy to the inner workings of the Reagan White House, I understood Deaver's role to be that of the person who knew both of the Reagans (Mr. and Mrs.) in terms of their personal preferences; their work style; preferred schedule; whom they liked and whom they did not; with whom they wanted to share time, when, and on what basis.

It needs to be remembered that this threesome—despite the destructive problems Meese and Deaver later faced—brought the needed range of inputs to the President's decisions and winnowed out opinions that could disrupt or distort the presidential decision process. I credit Reagan himself for this system; the presidency cannot be delegated. This blend of people and process would not have worked had it not above all reflected the style and personality of the President.

To underline this theory of *how* the presidency works *when* it works, I submit that Nixon, with his very strong intellect and deep substantive knowledge, failed to have this kind of a balance of political, substantive, and personal inputs. When he was off base, his worst instincts tended to predominate because so many of the people around him shared his uneasy view of the world. I have always believed that if a balanced group of advisors had been involved in the planning of Nixon's reelection campaign, the Watergate break-in would not have occurred. If Melvin Laird or Elliott Richardson had been in the room when John Mitchell and others were discussing campaign shenanigans, the planning group very likely would not have considered the Watergate caper as a fit subject for discussion, much less approval.

The theory of how the presidency works when it works well, grounded in these three principles, is supported in Reagan's case by what happened in his second term. In order to keep James Baker on his team, Reagan made a decision that cost him dearly because it went against these principles. Reagan picked Secretary of the Treasury Donald Regan to be the White House chief of staff. In terms of the institution of the presidency, this was a serious error for which the President was clearly and personally responsible, and which now, in retrospect, he must regret mightily. Donald Regan was not suited to this position, much less capable of replacing a three-person system. He demonstrated in this office—as he had done beforehand—tendencies to mistrust independent-minded people and particularly politicians, which was a fatal flaw in a person in so central a political role.

Martin Anderson, in his book entitled *Revolution,* said of Donald Regan: "he did not have the political sensitivity and eye for political danger of any of the three men he replaced. His style was straightforward, abrupt, and somewhat impetuous. When in doubt, he charged. In many worlds, he was extraordinarily effective, but in his new job he was handicapped by a lack of political finesse that was compounded by his lack of expertise in foreign policy."[13]

Nothing demonstrates Donald Regan's political ineptitude and naiveté better than does his own book *For the Record.* The book, which destroyed what was left on the credit side of the ledger for Regan, revealed him as utterly lacking a concept of both the institution of the presidency and the role of the White House chief of staff. If we can believe his own account, he came to the conclusion that "the mystery" of the office made it necessary for him to "hold his tongue" rather than attempt to engage the President on critical issues such as tax policy, Central America, or our approach to trade negotiations.[14] This amazing confession of his own failure to set and manage a decision agenda for the President (and his apparent unwillingness to ask his predecessors how to do so) indict him more than anyone else could have, Nancy Reagan included.

The replacement of Donald Regan by former Senate Majority Leader Howard Baker brought a strong set of political skills to this key White House position. Howard Baker's performance and that of Frank Carlucci, who succeeded Vice Admiral John Poindexter as the director of the National Security Council, steadied the Reagan presidency and contributed to what in his final year in office was a better situation.

I hope and believe that in retrospect we will be more willing to look at the whole of the Reagan record and to credit him for the way his principles and aims made their mark on national policy at home and abroad. There is already a tendency to resuscitate Reagan's modern predecessors—Eisenhower, Nixon, Carter, and Ford—in this longer perspective.

There are other important ways to view the institutional functioning of a given presidency. In what follows, I consider the successful (though unheralded) personnel policies of the Reagan presidency, Reagan's approach to major areas of public policy, and his relations with the Congress and the judiciary.

Personnel Policies

In an area in which I have a special interest—the selection and deployment of Cabinet and subcabinet level officials—Reagan's presidency was much more effective from the vantage point of Reagan's main principles and objectives than most people realize. From the very start, Reagan (principally through Edwin Meese) selected people whose views were in accord with his own and who were made to understand that they were expected to hew the line for the administration's objectives. This administrative presidency strategy involved penetrating the bureaucracy in order to push Reagan's policies into administrative processes.[15] The Aberbach and Rockman chapter in this book is an important corroboration of this position. Martin Anderson's book on the Reagan presidency takes a similar stance. I believe that such a strategy is both wise and appropriate as a way to exercise political influence in the American governmental system, and I credit Reagan for his achievement in this area. I would add that this is not only a good strategy for conservatives, but makes just as much sense for a more liberal Democratic administration.

Major Policy Areas

In economic affairs, the operation of the Economic Policy Council chaired by the Secretary of the Treasury worked well, especially with James Baker in this lead role. By contrast, in the national security arena, the bad experience of allowing the National Security Council (NSC) to be operational rather than relying on Secretary of State George P. Shultz to play the lead operating role in foreign policy wreaked its special brand of havoc in the Iran-contra affair. This last point bears elaboration. Many president watchers, observing that in the presidency one cannot avoid having something go wrong, cite this need to prevent mistakes as an argument for changes in the system. In my opinion, however, this opinion does not give enough weight to the competitive character of American government. It reflects too high a standard for any human-run activity, even one restructured by Lloyd Cutler and James Sundquist.

In domestic affairs, Ronald Reagan put his mark on the nation for reasons having to do with his approach to the office itself. Reagan maintained his principles of favoring limited government and greater reliance on the states, and he pushed these ideas into the bureaucracy in a way that had a much more pervasive impact than is commonly realized. In particular, Reagan achieved success in shifting budget priorities, increasing spending, and shifting the dialogue on domestic programs so that it focused on warding off cuts rather than devising new programs. This last accomplishment was seen in a plateauing of domestic spending in the aggregate, encompassing some increases (as for Medicare and Medicaid) which mask cuts in other domestic areas such as revenue sharing (eliminated under Reagan), employment, education, and training, and welfare.[16]

Relations with Other Branches

Reagan, especially in his first term, had an exemplary staff and system for congressional relations. House Speaker Tip O'Neill seemed not to know whether to laugh or cry about Reagan's early successes on Capitol Hill. The administration also was aggressive in pushing its ideas in the judicial process. One way this was done was through the positions the administration took on issues that were before the courts. William Bradford Reynolds is not a household word, but he did make a mark. Reagan also put his stamp on the courts through his appointments, especially his younger appointees to the federal district courts. He should also be given credit for trying in the conservative jurist Robert Bork's appointment to the U.S. Supreme Court, although the controversy over this appointment came at what was surely the low point in the Reagan presidency—the period beginning with the Iran-contra affair.

A closer look at the way these bad moments were presented in the media gives substance to the points already made—that earlier in Reagan's tenure, the office worked well. Referring to the problems associated with the nomination of Judge Douglas H. Ginsburg to succeed Bork, an article in the *New York Times* said they "added to the case of those who argue that the President has lost his once flawless touch."[17] The story continued, "They used to say that it never rained on Ronald Reagan, but in recent months he has been drenched by an unremitting monsoon."[18] In this period, Reagan was caricatured as out of touch, aging, and uninformed. Sometimes he appeared to be all of these things.

My thesis, to reiterate, is that despite this rocky period and the reversals it involved, Ronald Reagan had more than his share of successes and good moments in office. No president can fail to be controversial. Success in the presidency is appreciated more in hindsight than in the present tense. That Reagan has weaknesses is undeniable. My argument is that for much of his tenure and in a number of areas, Ronald Wilson Reagan demonstrated qualities that made the office, especially in the first term, work well. Many president watchers were chagrined, some embarrassed, and others surprised by Reagan's record up until the Iran-contra affair. His presidency, as I see it, reflected the strengths of America's political system. It was a yeasty exciting period with ideas clashing and clanging in our polity.

Conclusion

I am not arguing that any alterations in the way the presidency operates are ill advised—only that our standards and aspirations should be human-scaled and that in this spirit, fundamental constitutional changes in the office should not be adopted at this time. I said earlier, and I repeat, that procedural changes in the operation of the presidency and changes in the presidential selection process are being made all the time, and in many cases they are needed. As an example, I believe we have overstaffed both the executive office of the president and the Congress and that this top-heaviness makes it harder for the two branches to work together. The two branches often appear, as British political expert James Douglas has suggested, like two huge armies that are extremely hard to maneuver on the field. However, changes in the procedures and staffing of the Congress or the presidency are a far cry from constitutional changes that alter the separation of powers and the role and structure of either.

In sum, my balance sheet for the Reagan presidency shows many pluses; and to me, they support my thesis: we should not fundamentally change the presidency as an institution of the American governmental system. It can be made to work, not perfectly; but, as Edmund Burke surely would have asked, what does work perfectly?

NOTES

Appreciation is expressed to James Ceasar, John J. DiIulio, James Douglas, Fred I. Greenstein, and John Lago for assistance in the preparation of this paper.

1. Alfred de Grazia, "The Myth of the President," in *The Presidency*, ed. Aaron Wildavsky (Boston: Little, Brown, 1969).

2. Forrest McDonald, *Novus Ordo Seclorum: The Intellectual Origins of the Constitution* (Lawrence: University Press of Kansas, 1985), 240.

3. Ibid., 249.

4. James Sterling Young, *The Washington Community, 1800–1828* (New York: Harcourt, Brace and World, 1966), 157.

5. Bernard Weintraub, "Speakes: So Near But So Far Away," *New York Times*, 18 March 1987, 10.

6. I am indebted to my Princeton colleague John D. DiIulio for assistance here and to the work of James Q. Wilson, "Does the Separation of Powers Still Work?" *The Public Interest*, no. 86 (Winter 1987): 36–52.

7. Lloyd N. Cutler, "To Form a Government," *Foreign Affairs* 59 (1980): 127.

8. Ibid., 131.

9. James L. Sundquist, *Constitutional Reform and Effective Government* (Washington, D.C.: Brookings Institution, 1986): 75. See also Donald L. Robinson, *"To the Best of My Ability," The Presidency and the Constitution* (New York: W. W. Norton, 1987). This book arrives at conclusions similar to those of Cutler and Sundquist.

10. As quoted in Russell Kirk, *The Conservative Mind* (Chicago: Henry Regnery Co., 1953), 39.

11. Fred I. Greenstein, "The Need for an Early Appraisal of the Reagan Presidency," in *The Reagan Presidency, An Early Assessment*, ed. Fred I. Greenstein (Baltimore: The Johns Hopkins University Press, 1983), 4.

12. Theodore Sorenson, *Kennedy* (New York: Harper and Row, 1965), 294.

13. Martin Anderson, *Revolution* (New York: Harcourt Brace Jovanovich, 1988), 318.

14. Donald T. Regan, *For the Record: From Wall Street to Washington* (New York: Harcourt Brace Jovanovich, 1988), 267.

15. See Richard P. Nathan, *The Administrative Presidency* (New York: John Wiley and Sons, 1983); and idem, "Institutional Change under Reagan," in *Perspectives on the Reagan Years*, ed. John L. Palmer (Washington, D.C.: Urban Institute Press, 1986), 128ff.

16. Richard P. Nathan, Fred C. Doolittle, et al., *Reagan and the States* (Princeton: Princeton University Press, 1987); and Richard P. Nathan and John R. Lago, "Intergovernmental Relations," *Public Budgeting and Finance*, 31 May 1988.

17. *New York Times*, 7 November 1987, 33.

18. Ibid.

11

Reagan's Judicial Strategy

WALTER F. MURPHY

A person who specialized in cost-benefit analysis and knew little of the details of the American political system would predict that when a President had a free hand in selecting judges, he would consider not only candidates' intellectual power, integrity, and experience, but also the degree to which they agreed with his constitutional philosophy as well as with his specific policies. Looking at appointments positively, a dispassionate analyst would predict that by choosing officials to serve for "good behavior," a president could continue to shape the country's political future long after his administration was history. A cost-benefit analyst would also be impressed with the potential price of choosing unsympathetic judges,[1] for the American constitutional structure appears to give them what is in effect an item veto on much domestic and some foreign policy.

Detailed investigation would show that such costs and benefits are indeed present in the way the system operates. One need look no further than the New Deal to see what havoc hostile judges can wreak on a president's policies or the Warren Court on the loyalty-security programs of Truman and Eisenhower.[2]

As for benefits, John Marshall, John Adams's choice for chief justice, presided over the Supreme Court, doing his best to preserve the Federalist view of the Constitution, until the final year of Andrew Jackson's second term. Stephen Field, the last of Lincoln's nominees for the Court, did not resign until 1895. William O. Douglas, whom Franklin Roosevelt chose in 1939, retired in 1976, thirty-one years after FDR's death. And William J. Brennan, Jr., whom Eisenhower appointed in 1956, was still a force on the Court thirty-three years later. The selection of judges as young as Sandra Day O'Connor (fifty-one), Antonin Scalia (fifty), and Anthony Kennedy (fifty-two) were when they were nominated pretty much ensures that Ronald Reagan's mark will be on the Supreme Court until well into the twenty-first century.

Most presidents seem to have been acutely aware of what was at stake in such a situation.[3] Richard Nixon summed it up neatly when he said about his judicial nominees: "First and foremost, they had to be men who shared my legal philosophy." George Washington set the pattern by staffing the first Supreme Court[4] with six Federalists; he apparently felt no need to assuage anti-Federalists by choosing any of their number. John Adams continued to choose Federalists and even practiced nepotism at one remove by nominating his predecessor's nephew, Bushrod Washington, for the Supreme Court.

After watching the lame-duck sixth Congress create new judgeships and Adams use the closing hours of his lame-duck administration to put party men on the bench, Jefferson complained[5] that the Federalists "have retired into the judiciary as a stronghold. . . . [A]nd from that battery all the works of republicanism are to be beaten down and erased. By fraudulent use of the Constitution, which has made judges irremovable, they have multiplied useless judges to strengthen their phalanx." There was, of course, much to this accusation. The Judiciary Act of 1801, Adams's "midnight judges," and his talking Oliver Ellsworth into resigning the chief justiceship so a younger, healthier Federalist might serve—one who could outlast Republican regimes—did smack of court packing. Moreover, the convoluted constitutional construction Marshall used in *Marbury v. Madison* (1803)[6] to justify judicial review forged a weapon that judges have ever since wielded to beat down and erase the works of *any* administration that has incurred their displeasure.

Once in office, Jefferson showed that the Federalists had taught him well. He behaved as a model partisan: refusing to deliver the signed commissions of Federalist judges; signing into law the Judiciary Act of 1802, which, contrary to Article III of the Constitution, deprived newly appointed (and thus Federalist) circuit judges of their offices and salaries; pushing the House to impeach other Federalist judges; and choosing his own judicial nominees from the ranks of deserving and committed Republicans, whose party loyalty he vetted.[7] Many years later, disappointed that one of his nominees had shown insufficient Republican zeal, the former president felt free to write that their mutual devotion to the Constitution would allow his "unbosoming" himself of criticism.[8]

Even less subtly, Lincoln is reported to have said when considering a replacement for Chief Justice Roger Brooke Taney: "We cannot ask a man what he will do, and if we should, and he should answer us, we should despise him for it. Therefore we must take a man whose opinions are known."[9] The records of other presidents read much like those of Washington, Adams, Jefferson, and Lincoln. Indeed, in the nineteenth century, Andrew Jackson, Martin Van Buren, James Polk, Millard Fillmore, Franklin Pierce, and James Buchanan selected federal judges exclusively from the ranks of their own parties.[10] Among the ten most recent chief executives, only Herbert Hoover chose less than 90 percent of judges from his own party, and he still culled the GOP's membership for more than 80 percent of judicial nominees.

William Howard Taft seems to stand out as one of the exceptions to this general pattern, rising above partisan lines, at least with respect to selections for the Supreme Court. He chose three Democrats: Edward Douglass White of Louisiana as chief justice, and Horace Lurton of Tennessee and Joseph R. Lamar of Georgia as associate justices. Those nominations prompted one Washington wag to comment that had Taft been pope he would have appointed a Protestant to the College of Cardinals.

Taft, however, was less ecumenical than shrewd. First, by honoring southern Democrats he probably hoped to loosen their party's grip on the South, and by selecting a Catholic, to woo Romans from their Democratic allegiance.[11] Second, and more fundamentally, he deemed political philosophy more important than party label and strongly preferred Democrats who were rock-ribbed conservatives to wishy-washy Republicans. It was a policy he had begun when, as governor general of the Philippines, he had appointed Filipinos wherever possible. "We can," he had explained to a friend, "select the men who will be as orthodox in matters of importance as we are. . . ."[12] And, when Taft became chief justice, he continued to influence judicial selection by pushing the candidacies of honest, intelligent men, even Democrats like Pierce Butler,[13] with whom he politically agreed, and doing his utmost to sabotage the chances of honest, intelligent men, even Republicans like Learned Hand, with whom he politically disagreed.[14]

Of all presidents, James Earl Carter gave the strongest appearance of depoliticizing judicial selection, carrying out a campaign promise by establishing judicial nominating commissions to propose, on grounds of merit alone, candidates for the courts of appeals. He also pressured senators, who often control appointments to district courts, to follow his lead, although his success there was spotty. But whatever Carter's criteria for "merit" were, they indicated that Democrats were far more deserving than Republicans, for slightly more than 90 percent of his nominees were from his own party.[15] As Jon Gottschall puts it, "Carter's initial pledge of non-partisan judicial selection was reduced in practice to merit selection among Democrats."[16]

Reagan's[17] Policy of Judicial Selection

Ronald Wilson Reagan came into office with unusual opportunities. First, in January 1981, there were more than ninety vacancies on the federal bench; second, the Republicans had just won a majority of seats in the Senate, something they had not been able to do since 1952;[18] third, both Reagan's enormous majority in the electoral college and his party's winning control of the Senate seemed to many journalists and professional politicians to constitute a mandate for significant, perhaps even radical, change in the direction of public policy.[19] Reelection in 1984 by an even larger popular majority meant that Reagan, unless death or accident intervened, would be the first President since Eisenhower to finish eight years in office; and length in office is a great asset if one wishes to change the collective jurisprudence of the federal bench, for, as the old saw has it, judges seldom die and never retire. In fact, by the end of his first seven and a quarter years in the White House, Reagan's nominees held 338 judgeships on district courts and courts of appeals—almost half the total number of judges on those tribunals. In addition, he selected three of the nine members of the Supreme Court (four of the nine if one counts William H. Rehnquist's promotion as a new appointment).

Just after coming into office, Reagan's administration had taken steps to exploit its advantages by centralizing the process of selecting judges. At least since Harding, presidents had largely delegated responsibility in this area to the attorney general, who in turn had delegated it to the deputy attorney general and his staff. Reagan's people, however, created the Committee on Federal Judicial Selection to control nominations. That group included the White House chief of staff, one or more presidential counselors, and the presidential assistant for legislative affairs, as well as the attorney general, deputy attorney general, associate attorney general, and the assistant attorney general for legal policy.[20] Demoted was the American Bar Association's (ABA) Committee on the Federal Judiciary, who no longer received a short list of candidates to evaluate—only the final choice.[21]

By involving the White House directly in recruitment and placing the President's chief of staff in command, this institutional arrangement allowed a high degree of coordination. According to Sheldon Goldman, the leading expert on judicial selection, never before had an administration so systematically taken into account questions of patronage, legislative relations, and public policy.[22] Although occasionally, as in the case of Judge Douglas H. Ginsburg, something went to pot, scrutiny of candidates was usually thorough. Stories persisted that members of the committee or its staff closely interrogated candidates about their views on specific public policies and constitutional issues[23] as well as their general jurisprudence. Indeed, some sitting judges being considered for "promotion" reported having been asked to defend some of their decisions.

In addition, Reagan's centralization of command enabled his administration to bargain more effectively than most presidents with Republican senators and occasionally representatives[24] over judicial appointments. Nevertheless, Reagan was unable to persuade these people to surrender their ancient prerogatives, and many of his nominations for the district bench were the result of compromises with Republican legislators. Therefore, this chapter will focus on Reagan's choices for the various courts of appeals and the Supreme Court, where the bargaining power of senators is much reduced.

REAGAN'S NOMINEES FOR COURTS OF APPEALS

Although Carter usually had chosen as judges people who had been committed to partisan political goals, he did broaden the base of recruitment. Historically, federal judgeships had been the almost exclusive domain of WASP males who had typically been prosecutors or corporate counsel and, in this century at least,[25] attorneys for the wealthy, not for the poor or defendants in criminal prosecutions. Yet one of every five of Carter's nominees for the courts of appeals was female and one out of six was black. Furthermore, he chose two Hispanics and one person of Asian ancestry. More than 20 percent of his nominees had been members of firms of moderate size (more than five but less than twenty-five partners), small firms (less than five partners), or in solo practice. About a third had been prosecutors, a reduction from the approximately 50 percent of Johnson's and Nixon's nominees.

The professional backgrounds of Reagan's nominees did not significantly differ from Carter's, as Table 11.1 demonstrates. The average ages of the two sets of judges were almost identical: Carter's fifty-two, Reagan's fifty. Moreover, both sets of judges had been well-educated professionals, upper- or middle-class in socioeconomic status. Patterns of party affiliations were also similar, though, of course, the signs were reversed: A bit more than 90 percent of Carter's choices were Democrats, while just under 95 percent of Reagan's were Republicans. This difference looks

TABLE 11.1 Professional Backgrounds of Appointees to Courts of Appeals

	Nominated by	
Major Occupation	Carter N = 56 (%)	Reagan[a] N = 74 (%)
Politics	5.4	6.8
Judiciary	46.4	54.0
Large law firm (>25)	10.8	12.2
Moderate law firm (5–24)	16.1	10.8
Solo or small firm (<5)	5.4	1.4
Professor	14.3	13.5[b]
Other	1.8	1.4

Source: Sheldon Goldman and Austin Sarat, *American Court Systems,* 2d ed. (New York: Longman, 1989).
[a] Confirmed as of March 30, 1988.
[b] Fifteen percent if one includes Robert H. Bork.

smaller when one keeps in mind that almost three-quarters of Carter's choices had been politically active while only two-thirds of Reagan's had been much engaged in partisan politics.

On some dimensions, however, the two groups display quite different characteristics, as Table 11.2 indicates. Although the numbers are smaller than one would like as a basis for generalization, it is clear that Reagan was more likely than Carter to choose from among the very rich, slightly more likely to nominate Catholics, and slightly less to nominate Jews. These data may reflect differences in the pools from which the two parties draw their support. Wealth has always been closely correlated with Republicanism; and a majority of Catholics left the Democratic ranks in 1980 and 1984 to support Reagan, as they had Eisenhower in 1956. On the other hand, Jews remained overwhelmingly Democratic; but, even under Reagan, they got about twice as many judgeships as their fraction of the nation's total population.

The most striking differences pertain to race, ethnicity, and sex. Reagan chose only one black, one Hispanic, and no Asians[26] for the courts of appeals. Again, these figures may partly reflect ethnic distributions of party loyalty. Very few blacks were able to find it in their hearts to support a man who was routinely indifferent and sometimes opposed to continued federal protection of their civil rights.

More difficult to explain via party affiliation is the fact that Carter picked proportionately almost four times as many women as Reagan,

TABLE 11.2   Demographic Characteristics of Appointees to Courts of Appeals

	Nominated by	
Characteristic	Carter N = 56 (%)	Reagan[a] N = 74 (%)
Ethnicity or race		
White	78.6	97.3
Black	16.1	1.4
Hispanic	3.6	1.4
Asian	1.8	0.0
Sex		
Male	80.4	94.6
Female	19.6	5.4
Religion		
Protestant	60.7	55.4
Catholic	23.2	31.1
Jewish	16.1	13.5
Proportion millionaires	10.3	17.6

Source: Sheldon Goldman and Austin Sarat, *American Court Systems,* 2d ed. (New York; Longman, 1989).
[a] Confirmed as of March 30, 1988.

although in the latter's defense it should be said that he nominated more women than any president except Carter. Moreover, Reagan selected the first woman to sit on the U.S. Supreme Court. Still, it is plain that he cast aside Carter's policy of trying to break the monopoly of non-Hispanic white males on federal judgeships.

It is not clear, incidentally, how much effect judges' ethnicity or gender has on their decision making. It is difficult to get the right kinds and amount of data, but the most systematic study found that

> black and white judges displayed remarkably similar decision-making records. In none of the areas probed did significant differences associated with race emerge. Gender comparisons yielded no male/female differences of significance in areas of criminal policy and women's rights. However, females were less apt to support personal liberty and minority policy claims and more prone to uphold the economic regulatory role of the federal government than were male judges. Overall, the women displayed a pronounced tendency to rule in favor of government entities.

> No differences were found on any of our measures of judicial acceptance. Female and black judges had similar appeal and reversal rates and were

about as likely to have their opinions cited favorably as were their male and white counterparts. . . .[27]

Yet, even if the gender or ethnic backgrounds of judges do not greatly affect the substance of their decisions, judges' gender and ethnic backgrounds may significantly affect the way in which some groups perceive and evaluate not only those particular decisions but also the larger political system as well. The phenomenon of political representation and any consequent feeling of having participated in government can include the fact of officials' being "chosen from" a given group as well as being "chosen by."[28]

REAGAN'S NOMINEES TO THE SUPREME COURT

There were no retirements or deaths among the justices during Carter's four years in the White House, but three retired during Reagan's two terms. To fill these vacancies, he nominated five different people. His initial selection in 1981 was Sandra Day O'Connor, a fifty-one-year-old judge of Arizona's intermediate appellate court, who, although a former Republican state legislator, had been appointed by a Democratic governor. (Her name had been bruited about the White House[29] while she was still a trial judge when Ford was considering a replacement for William O. Douglas.) Like many of Reagan's nominees, she was a millionaire.

When, in the summer of 1985, Warren Earl Burger retired as chief justice, Reagan "promoted" William H. Rehnquist, whom Nixon had put on the Supreme Court in 1971, to the center chair. A former "Goldwater Republican" from Arizona whom the NAACP had accused of antiblack activity and whom other civil-liberties groups had opposed because of his narrow views of rights to privacy and freedom of speech and association, the new chief had served in Nixon's administration as assistant attorney general in charge of the office of legal counsel, among the most technically demanding posts in the Department of Justice. He had gone to the Court at the age of forty-seven, and the chief justiceship came when he was sixty-two.

To replace Rehnquist as an associate justice, Reagan chose Antonin Scalia, whom he had earlier nominated for the Court of Appeals for the District of Columbia. Son of an Italian immigrant and former professor at the University of Chicago Law School,[30] Scalia had served as an assistant attorney general under Gerald Ford and had also practiced in a large firm in Cleveland.

When Lewis F. Powell announced his retirement in 1987, Reagan's first choice was Scalia's colleague on the Court of Appeals for the District of Columbia, Robert H. Bork, former professor of law at Yale and solicitor general who had, with deep personal misgivings, presided over Nixon's "Saturday Night Massacre" in October 1973. After what were probably the most acrimonious confirmation proceedings ever for a judicial nominee, the Senate finally rejected Bork, 58–42. The administration then turned to Douglas H. Ginsburg, another judge on what seemed to have become the Supreme Court's farm team. Although only forty-one, he had served on the faculty at the Harvard Law School, as an assistant attorney general, and as a senior official in the Office of Management and Budget. When questions arose about his use of marijuana years earlier and about conflicts of interest (later resolved in his favor), the judge bowed to pressure from within the Cabinet and asked the President to withdraw his name.

The administration's third choice was Anthony M. Kennedy, a judge whom Gerald Ford had selected for the Court of Appeals for the Ninth Circuit in 1975. He and Scalia were both born in 1936; and both are Catholics. A graduate of Stanford and Harvard Law School, he had spent most of his professional life in private practice, although he had also worked extensively as a lobbyist and had had close ties with Reagan and Edwin Meese III during their days in California's politics.

THE QUALITY OF REAGAN'S APPELLATE JUDGES

It is far easier to tabulate judges' net worth or ethnic backgrounds than it is to evaluate their intellectual, professional, or moral fitness for their work. Indeed, it is not likely we shall ever have enough data—even assuming agreement on standards—to make judgments on the collective moral fitness of a group of human beings engaged in such complex and controversial work as judges. The individual judges we are apt to know most about are the pathological cases such as Martin Manton in the 1920s and Harry E. Claiborne in the 1980s. Moreover, with the cumbersome process of impeachment as its cornerstone, the federal government's system of supervising judicial conduct is not likely to produce fine evaluations.

To assess intellectual and professional fitness, we do have some data, even though they are only partial and impressionistic. On the positive side, it would be difficult to find judges more intellectually able and professionally skilled than Robert Bork, Frank Easterbrook, John Noonan, Richard Posner, Kenneth Ripple, Antonin Scalia, or Ralph Winter, all of whom had been highly respected professors at nationally ranked law schools. On the other hand, few judges in recent decades have gone to the bench with less impressive credentials than Daniel Manion, whom Reagan nominated for the Court of Appeals for the Seventh Circuit.[31]

One might look on the evaluations of the ABA's Committee on the Federal Judiciary as providing a more objective standard, although in fact, those assessments reflect the subjective views of members of the legal profession whom the committee contacts. The distribution of these ratings, at least for the appellate judges whom Reagan selected during his first term, is quite similar to those for nominees of other recent presidents, as Table 11.3 shows. Reagan's choices received a larger share of ratings as "exceptionally well qualified" than any judicial cohort had since Lyndon Johnson was in the White House; on the other hand, Reagan's nominees had proportionately more judges who received ratings of merely "qualified." If one lumps the top two categories together. Reagan's nominees, as a group, scored somewhat lower than those of Carter, Nixon, and Johnson but somewhat higher than Ford's.[32]

TABLE 11.3   ABA Rankings of Nominees for Courts of Appeals

	Nominated by				
Ratings	Reagan[a] N = 31 (%)	Carter N = 56 (%)	Ford N = 12 (%)	Nixon N = 45 (%)	Johnson N = 40 (%)
Exceptionally well qualified	22.6	16.1	16.7	15.6	27.5
Well qualified	41.9	58.9	41.7	57.8	47.5
Qualified	35.5	25.0	33.3	26.7	20.0
Not qualified	0.0	0.0	8.3	0.0	2.5
No report sought	0.0	0.0	0.0	0.0	0.0

Source: Sheldon Goldman, *Reaganizing the Judiciary*, 68 *Judicature* 313:325 (1985).
[a]Only through end of first term.

One might use other criteria to evaluate professional ability—and all are similarly problematic. During his first term, Reagan's thirty-one selections for the courts of appeals included nineteen judges, sixteen of whom were sitting on federal district courts—a far higher proportion of "promotions" than Carter, Nixon, or Johnson had made but somewhat lower than that of Ford. If one assumes that most federal district judges are initially appointed principally because of merit, "promotion" is a sign of a well-qualified appellate nominee. Alas, what evidence we have does not support that assumption. Furthermore, there are problems with "promotion," the chief one being the temptation it dangles before district judges to make themselves attractive through their decisions and opinions to present or future administrations.

One might look on a professorship as an indication of competence. And, if one counts Robert Bork as an academic—shortly before his nomination he had left Yale for private practice—during Reagan's first term, about one of six of his selections for the courts of appeals had been a professor of law. Teaching at a leading law school would certainly evidence professional knowledge; but, as anyone who has ever attended a faculty meeting knows, that datum tells nothing whatsoever about judgment, temperament, or basic values.

Among the most controversial criteria of excellence would be a degree in law from an Ivy League school. Reagan's nominees contained by far the smallest proportion of such graduates among recent cohorts of judges. Whatever the worth of that sort of training (or selection for it) as an indicium of ability, it is interesting that populists like Johnson and Carter would have chosen so many judges (28 and 41 percent) from the alumni of the most prestigious schools and a supposed conservative like Reagan so few (16 percent).

THE QUALITY OF REAGAN'S NOMINEES FOR THE SUPREME COURT

It was the political and legal philosophies of Reagan's justices that critics challenged, not their professional competence. By standards of educational pedigree, his nominees to the Supreme Court would certainly rank as high as any cohort with the possible exception of Franklin D. Roosevelt's. All had impeccable academic credentials: Rehnquist and O'Connor stood at the top of their class at Stanford Law School; Bork received his training at the University of Chicago's law school; Scalia, Ginsburg, and Kennedy were products of the Harvard Law School. Bork had been a professor at Yale, Ginsburg at Harvard, Scalia at Chicago, and Kennedy had been an adjunct professor at the McGeorge Law School in Sacramento. Moreover, all had had considerable experience in public affairs.

The ABA's committee gave O'Connor, Rehnquist, Scalia, Bork, and Kennedy its highest ranking. Bork, however, caused a division that became public. Ten of the fifteen members had voted for "well qualified," four for "not qualified," and one simply said "not opposed." (Ginsburg withdrew before the committee could complete its work.)

What Difference Does It Make?

To analyze considerations presidents weigh in selecting judges responds in only a small part to the broader—and more important—question of what difference those selections make. To gauge a president's success, we have to know his goals as well as how his nominees have reacted to the various problems they have faced. It is obviously far too early to make definitive judgments, but there is enough evidence to allow some tentative assessments.

JUDGESHIPS AS PATRONAGE

One may, of course, look on judgeships as patronage. They are truly, as the Wizard of Ooze, Everett Dirksen, once called them, "grand political plums." And one can see from the discussion above—if one needed a reminder—that most presidents have so looked on judgeships.

It is also apparent, however, that presidents have viewed judgeships as more than patronage. "We feel that we owe certain people jobs," one of the men who handled judicial nominations during the Kennedy administration remarked, "but we do not feel we owe them *specific* jobs."[33] Not only does fear of or hope in judges' power constrain presidents to try to choose people of intelligence, integrity, and competence, but so does judicial prestige. To stack the bench with incompetent sycophants would make a president and his party very vulnerable at the polls—at least, so might he reasonably believe—and bring down a wrathful judgment from historians.[34]

In using judgeships as patronage, Reagan had a mixed but largely successful record. On the one hand, the active role that the White House's Committee on Federal Judicial Selection played in choosing district judges irritated some Republican senators; and the choice of Daniel Manion was an embarrassment to the party. Reagan's nomination of Robert H. Bork, failure to mount a grass roots campaign for the nominee, and refusal to take the opposition seriously until the attack was in full swing split the GOP. Although only six of the forty-six Republican senators voted against confirmation, the most effective of Bork's senatorial inquisitors had been Arlen Spector, Republican from Pennsylvania; and few of the forty Republicans who voted for the President's man tried hard to recruit additional supporters.

On the other hand, embarrassment over Manion was short-lived; and after the administration's mishandling of Bork's confirmation and its stumbling and fumbling immediately following that defeat, it soon produced a candidate in Anthony Kennedy behind whom the party could unite. Moreover, most of Reagan's nominees did not divide or even greatly displease Republican senators or, as far as one can divine such, the GOP generally. Installing more than three hundred deserving Republicans—almost all of whom seemed professionally competent and honest—provided strong nourishment for a political party, the loaves and fishes that keep such organizations healthy.

REAGAN'S POLICY GOALS

It was always difficult to divine what Ronald Reagan or his advisors had in mind; and, although judicial appointments were no exception to that rule, here he was probably little different from most presidents in that he wanted judges to play several not easily reconciled roles. In general terms, his administration favored a judicial philosophy that came close to being a parody on legal positivism,[35] that is, where individual rights were concerned,[36] judges should follow the narrowest possible interpretation of the constitutional document's plain words as modified—usually restricted—by what judges imagined to be "original intent." More specifically, his White House adamantly opposed earlier decisions of the Supreme Court that: recognized constitutional rights to privacy and abortion; broadly construed rights of the criminally accused; read the Constitution and federal statutes as mandating and/or permitting affirmative action; interpreted the First Amendment to protect much material that had historically been considered obscene or pornographic; construed the antiestablishment clause to forbid prayers in public schools; and allowed the federal structure of Congress to serve as the principal bulwark against national encroachment on state authority.[37]

In sum, Reagan wanted judges to defer: to Congress on questions of civil rights or social policy; to the states on such issues when they disagreed with Congress as well as on most matters of federal-state relations;[38] to the President when he and Congress differed on their respective authority;[39] to previous courts by following precedents, except when those precedents stood in the way of the administration's goals; and to what Attorney General Meese imagined was the "original intent"[40] of the framers of the document of 1787 or its amendments, again except where, as with affirmative action, that supposed "intent" might trump policies the administration favored. In effect, Reagan's regime wanted judges to undo much of the constitutional jurisprudence of the last half-century affecting civil rights, tip the balance of the constitutional power toward the presidency rather than Congress, construct a new national history, and creatively interpret—or flatly ignore—the plain words of certain inconvenient constitutional clauses such as the Preamble and the Ninth Amendment.

But playing verbal games with the constitutional text, deferring but only eclectically to other agencies of government, rewriting history, and selectively overruling precedents all smack of "judicial activism,"[41] supposedly a naughty word in Reagan's political vocabulary. What he seemed to want was "judicial restraint" when he agreed with a governmental policy and "judicial activism" when he disagreed—a very human set of desires.

Plainly, the unifying feature of this conglomeration of conflicting items for a judicial agenda was support for the bundle of public policies associated with Ronald Reagan. Such an agenda might be called conservative, but only if one's definition of that term is esoteric. Insofar as one wishes judges to respect the past, be suspicious of centralizing political power, foster religious sentiment, oppose pornography, show concern for society's interests in preventing crime as well as punishing criminals, one can legitimately claim to be following a traditional conservative path. Insofar as one opposes a constitutional right to abortion on demand, one also professes a conservative faith, although by no means do conservatives have a monopoly on such opposition.

Nevertheless, however far European conservatives have leaned toward monarchy, preference for the relatively efficient authority of the president over that of a more cumbersome, slow-moving, typically compromising legislature has not been a hallmark of American conservatism. Indeed, since Lincoln, Republicans have tended to nominate presidential candidates whose concepts of executive power have been more passive than those of their opponents.

Moreover, insofar as one is not suspicious of all governmental power, whether state or federal, insofar as one wants to vest in the popular will, expressed through elected officials, plenary authority to define, limit, or even erase almost all civil rights, and, most significant of all, insofar as one proclaims a positivistic separation of morality from law and politics, one contradicts tenets fundamental, from Edmund Burke and Alexander Hamilton to Russell Kirk and George Will, to the dominant American version of conservatism.

Obviously, not all of Reagan's nominees to the appellate bench agreed with the administration on each of these points. Some of his judges—Bork, Posner, and Rehnquist, for instance[42]—espoused, at least *for judges*, a separation of law and morals; but others—Noonan and Ripple, for example—thought such a cleavage unacceptable. In addition,

Reagan's nominees have often publicly disagreed with each other. As Bork's chances for confirmation were fading, Posner launched a thinly veiled attack on his colleague's view of judicial decision making.[43] In 1984, Scalia bitterly attacked as too capacious Bork's interpretation of the First Amendment's protection of freedom of the press,[44] a specific illustration of what, as we shall presently see, is the fact that, although Reagan's nominees typically vote together, they do not always do so.

THE VOTING STUDIES

We have several close examinations of the voting records of Reagan's nominees to the courts of appeals comparing them with nominees of other presidents. These studies differ in some important aspects, but they tell much the same story.

Rowland et al.

Using a sample of 1,500 criminal cases decided between 1981 and 1984, Rowland, Songer, and Carp[45] found that Reagan's nominees were almost twice as likely as Carter's to vote against defendant's claims. In decisions that divided a court, Carter's judges were apt to support defendant's claims almost five times as often as were Reagan's. The conclusion of Rowland et al., however, is not merely that Reagan had chosen efficiently. To them, the data "also suggest that implicit ideological criteria affected the allocation of values by Carter appointees more strongly than would be predicted by most descriptions of the Carter appointment process."[46]

Gottschall

Jon Gottschall[47] came up with somewhat similar findings after analyzing a sample of 3,752 decisions of the courts of appeals from July 1, 1983 through December 31, 1984. In 1,037 of those cases, nominees of both Carter and Reagan sat together, and they agreed 74 percent of the time.

If, however, one extracts from the sample the cases that divided a particular court—whether or not nominees of both presidents were sitting—differences between the two cohorts appear huge. Carter's nominees were almost twice as likely as Reagan's to vote for a liberal result—with "liberal" defined as being pro (1) defendants' claims in criminal cases or the media's where the First Amendment was involved; (2) women or racial or ethnic minorities where they alleged discrimination; (3) the poor when they asserted a right to welfare benefits; (4) labor unions against management; and (5) plaintiffs in personal injury suits.

Among the more fascinating of Gottschall's findings is that Reagan's nominees agreed with each other 91 percent of the time as compared with Carter's nominees' voting together in 82 percent of the cases, figures that hardly indicate a high rate of disagreement within either cohort and reinforce the conclusions of Rowland et al. about policy considerations[48] also being reflected in Carter's selections. Curiously, however, it was judges chosen by Nixon and Ford who displayed the highest rate of cohesion, although by only a trivial amount more than Reagan's nominees (92 percent to 91).

Recognizing that findings based on such a small slice of time must be tentative, Gottschall concluded:[49]

> Reagan's appointees are not clearly or dramatically more conservative than Nixon's or Ford's appointees, although they *are* clearly more conservative than appointees of the Carter, Kennedy and Johnson administrations.

> Moreover, despite the dramatic influx of supposedly more politicized appointees of the Carter and Reagan administrations and an apparent increase in the frequency of dissent, consensus still prevails for the most part in voting on the courts of appeals.

Tomasi and Velona

In yet another study,[50] two students at Columbia Law School analyzed all 1,347 cases that divided the courts of appeals during the two-year period from January 1, 1985 through December 31, 1986. The results largely support but partially contradict Gottschall's. First, this sample of Reagan's judges disagreed with judges nominated by Democratic presidents in almost three-quarters of nonunanimous cases decided by panels but only in a little more than half the cases disposed of en banc—a ratio of disagreement quite similar to those registered by judges nominated by Nixon and Ford.

Second, as did Gottschall, Tomasi and Velona found that, in all the nonunanimous cases, Reagan's people supported liberal results—with liberal defined pretty much as by Gottschall—about half as often as did Carter's cohort. On a third point, however, Tomasi and Velona disagreed with Gottschall. He had found that, when judges nominated by Reagan sat in the same case with judges nominated by Carter and the decision was not unanimous, Reagan's nominees supported liberal results only 5 percent of the time. Tomasi and Velona's figure was 22 percent, hardly a large score but one vastly higher than Gottschall's. The different ways in which the two studies classified judges can account for part, but only part, of this variance. The basic explanation probably lies in judges' responding differently to different cases at different times.

Table 11.4 compares some of the findings of these voting studies on one issue, criminal justice, an issue whose importance Reagan had stressed time and again as a central factor in his choice of judges. "I'll tell you what I believe," he said on the campaign trail in 1984, "and that is we ought to appoint judges who restore respect for the laws and make criminals think twice before they commit a crime";[51] and, after each of his many nominations of a justice for the Supreme Court, the President had emphasized that his candidate would be tough on accused criminals.

The numbers in Table 11.4 indicate that Reagan succeeded rather well in his attempts to put on the bench judges who would be more concerned than were nominees of Carter and Johnson with punishing the criminally accused—which is not to say that he succeeded in having the law radically changed, only that he got judges who were less sympathetic to putative rights of the criminally accused.

Wilson

James G. Wilson has published a finely detailed two-part analysis[52] of the scholarly writings and judicial opinions of five of Reagan's more notable nominees for U.S. courts of appeals: Bork, Easterbrook, Posner, Scalia, and Winter. Wilson concluded that these judges' academic writings—like the administration's own goals described above—do not in some very significant respects fit the traditional American model of conservatism. In particular, Bork's peculiar brand of positivism, Easter-

TABLE 11.4 Support for Claims of Defendants in Nonunanimous Criminal Cases (by President)

	Judges Nominated by		
Study	Nixon/Ford (%)	Reagan (%)	Carter (%)
Rowland et al.[a]	35	35	67
Gottschall	23	31	61
Tomasi and Velona[b]	21	25	(62)+

[a] Rowland et al. report data only for Nixon's nominees.

[b] Tomasi and Velona lump together as "Democrats" judges nominated by Kennedy, Johnson, and Carter. Fifty-eight of the seventy-five Democratic judges were Carter's nominees.

brook's refusal to temper legal rules with considerations of justice, Posner's fascination with maximizing wealth, Winter's opposition on abstract theoretical grounds to plans to reallocate resources, and Scalia's ignoring history and context in attacking affirmative action all violate precepts central to a Burkean approach to politics.

Moreover, their writings and judicial work do not reflect a uniform ideology or even the same approach to political-legal problems. These judges, Wilson argued, "are torn between moralism, free marketeering, statism, positivism, libertarianism, and historicism."[53] Thus, some of their opinions "are acceptable by most contemporary 'liberal' standards. A few are even generous interpretations of constitutional rights."[54] Furthermore, the extent to which these jurists had engaged in constitutional theorizing about a limited judicial role was not a reliable indicator of their relative hostility to claims of individual rights. It was Scalia, in academia the least theoretical of the five, who was the most inhospitable to such claims.

On the whole, the five jurists followed relevant rulings of the Supreme Court defining constitutional rights. Although in doing so they "occasionally expressed regrets" at the law's liberal values, they sometimes "creatively expanded or redefined rights."[55] Nevertheless, Wilson found that the "overall direction of these opinions . . . is clear: individual constitutional rights are the exception, grudgingly given. After all, these men believe that judicial review is presumptively illegitimate."[56]

IDEOLOGY AND POLICY PREFERENCES

The data summarized here demonstrate that, when a federal appellate panel has been divided, Reagan's nominees have tended to vote together and to disagree with judges chosen by Democratic presidents, although at about the same rate as judges nominated by Nixon and Ford. To say, however, that party background accounts for a significant share of the variance in the decision making of federal judges on lower courts is to carry stale news.

More important, these studies indicate that Reagan's judicial cohort has acted in a relatively antiliberal ("conservative" seems the wrong word) fashion. Nevertheless, the evidence now available does not suggest that these people are, as a group, ideologues. Insofar as the term "ideology" refers to a coherent view of the world, it is probably not logically possible for those who fully support Reagan's peculiar mix of public policies to be ideologues in any strict sense of that term,[57] even though they may be fervent advocates of his policies.

One must say much the same thing about Reagan's nominees for the Supreme Court. A single term does not provide enough data to judge Kennedy, but O'Connor, Scalia, and Rehnquist represent prudent efforts to implement the White House's judicial objectives. Reagan's advisors followed Lincoln's prescription: They recommended people whose views were known. Furthermore, although the three justices have not yet encountered the full range of problems on the GOP's agenda, each deserves high, but not perfect, marks for handling the issues they have confronted. They have demonstrated that they share many of the administration's judicial goals, although none seems quite as devoted as Bork to democratic theory or deference to legislatures.[58]

On several occasions after her confirmation, Reagan said, "I'd be pleased to stand on the record of Sandra Day O'Connor on the Supreme Court";[59] and well he should have been. She has frequently displayed skepticism toward claims of liberty against government, a quality Reagan seemed to admire in judges. Moreover, she has raised a powerful critique of *Roe v. Wade*,[60] arguing that technological developments have left that ruling's framework "clearly on a collision course with itself."[61]

Rehnquist comes closest to having publicly formulated a coherent judicial philosophy. His special brand of legal positivism, narrow interpretation of individual rights, hostility to claims to a right to abortion, and customary although not unswerving deference to Congress when its authority does not clash with that of a state[62] were crystal clear and directly in line with much of Reagan's avowed objectives.

It is, however, always risky to read the future through the past, and sitting in the center chair may have unsettled some of the chief's views.[63] He had given fair warning of such a possible shift in a speech delivered in 1984, when he spoke of the way the Court could change a justice's thinking:

> The Supreme Court is to be independent of the legislative and executive branches of the government; yet . . . it is to be subjected to indirect infusions of the popular will in terms of the President's use of his appointment power. But the institution is so structured that a brand-new presidential appointee, perhaps feeling himself strongly loyal to the President who appointed him . . . is immediately beset with the institutional pressures which I have described. He identifies more and more strongly with the new institution of which he has become a member.[64]

There is some evidence that Rehnquist has experienced a perceptible change. For instance, in the 1987 term, he wrote the opinion for a unanimous Court in *Hustler Magazine v. Falwell,* holding that the First Amendment protected publication of obviously false information that was designed to ridicule a public figure. In almost every previous case involving libel, Rehnquist had taken a very narrow view of the reach of the First Amendment.[65] During the same term, he wrote the opinion for a divided Court, ruling that federal courts had jurisdiction to review the CIA's dismissal of a homosexual employee as a security risk.[66] Never before had he been noted for sensitivity to the claims of homosexuals,[67] but he had been noted for deference to the federal government's powers to carry on diplomatic relations and wage war. Rehnquist was also the author of the Court's opinion in the most far-reaching decision of 1988, *Morrison v. Olson,*[68] upholding the constitutionality of the provision in the Ethics in Government Act allowing federal judges, in certain instances in which federal officials were suspected of criminal activity, to appoint special prosecutors. Reagan's administration had waged a long and bitter campaign to have this part of the law invalidated as an invasion of executive power and had won in the court of appeals.[69] Defeat with the concurrence of two of the three sitting justices whom the White House had chosen was a hard blow to the President's effort to reshape constitutional doctrine.

Both in academia and on the court of appeals, Scalia had avoided grand theorizing, a course he has continued on the Supreme Court. As Wilson reported, however, Scalia's record on the court of appeals was unclouded; and one must suppose that it was precisely that record that endeared him to the administration. His first two terms on the Court show that the President's advisors had more accurately read this particular collection of judicial tea leaves than they had Rehnquist's, for Scalia produced no major surprises. Most important, he was the sole dissenter in *Morrison,* arguing that prosecutors, special or otherwise, fell outside the category of "inferior Officers," for if a president could not control them, he could not "take care that the laws be faithfully executed."[70]

Adherence, to a given set of objectives for public policy is, however, not the same as an ideology. O'Connor was by no means a constant pillar of support for the administration's positions, as her joining the chief justice in *Morrison v. Olson* dramatically demonstrated. Moreover, her votes, as partially summarized in Table 11.5, show that although she usually joins her Stanford classmate, she had also been very likely to agree with Lewis F. Powell, supposedly a centrist when he was on the Court, and agrees more than half the time with William J. Brennan, Jr., who, along with Thurgood Marshall, speaks for (and sometimes beyond) the jurisprudence of the old Warren Court. Furthermore, her differences

TABLE 11.5 Frequency of Justice O'Connor's Agreement with Other Justices[a]

Term	Rehnquist N = 1,080 (%)	Powell N = 888 (%)	Brennan N = 1,079 (%)
1981	82	72	49
1982	86	80	55
1983	92	85	57
1984	91	86	61
1985	85	87	57
1986	86	83	45
1987	83	—	60

Source: Annual article on the Court's previous term in HARV. L. REV. 96–101 (1982–87) for the 1981–86 terms; I am responsible for the data on the 1987 term.
[a] All cases decided by full opinion or per curiam with lengthy explanations of reasoning. N = number of cases.

with the chief justice have included significant issues of individual rights such as equal protection and freedom of speech and assembly.[71]

Nor does Scalia, despite his overall voting record, respond in a programmed fashion. For instance, he joined the majority in: *Griffith v. Kentucky* (1987), making retroactive the rule that a prosecutor's peremptory challenges of black jurors may deny equal protection;[72] *Cruz v. New York* (1987), tightening the rules on admissibility of one defendant's confession against another;[73] and *Lakewood v. Plain Dealer* (1988), striking down a local ordinance allowing the mayor to determine which newspapers could be displayed in coin-operated racks.[74] (O'Connor dissented and Rehnquist did not participate in *Lakewood*.) In addition, Scalia wrote the opinion of the Court in *Arizona v. Hicks* (1987),[75] limiting the scope of warrantless searches.

Not only do these three sometimes disagree among themselves on important issues, but they also frequently find themselves—individually and as a group—in the company of the Court's liberals. The justices were unanimous, for instance, in sustaining both New York's and California's laws against sexual bias in "private" social clubs.[76] (Although O'Connor did not participate in the case from California, she had written a strong concurring opinion in an earlier case from Minnesota involving a similar statute.[77])

During the 1986 term, the first term during which three of Reagan's nominees were on the Court, they voted together in 105 of the 145 cases (72 percent) decided by full opinion on which all three sat. But, in 50 of those 105 instances (48 percent), all three joined—or were joined by—

Brennan. During the 1987 term, the three voted together in 106 of 138 cases decided by full opinion (77 percent) and agreed with Brennan in 71 of those (67 percent). Of the 63 cases in which Kennedy participated during the 1987 term, he linked with the three in 48 (76 percent). Brennan voted with this four-judge group in 32 of those decisions (67 percent). If these be ideologues, they be a strange collection.

Appointments and the Changing Face of Constitutional Interpretation

The appointing process is an integral part of the constitutional system. Presidents have regularly used it for one or more of four purposes:[78] (1) as a source of patronage; (2) as an opportunity to increase or decrease the symbolic representation of certain groups in government; (3) as a means to maintain or improve the professional quality of the bench; and (4) as a chance to shape or reshape the long-term course of law and public policy. One can see Reagan's selections as efforts to serve all four purposes, although not necessarily with each carrying equal weight.

The fact that almost nineteen of every twenty vacancies went to Republicans is rather strong evidence that something was at work beyond random chance or a nonpartisan search for merit. Yet patronage can account for only part of the pattern of nominations. Certainly the resentment of some Republican senators indicates that the White House was not merely oiling its legislative wheels. Nor do the names of O'Connor, Scalia, Winter, Noonan, Posner, Kennedy, Ginsburg, or Easterbrook read like a Who's Who of party workhorses who deserved rewards. Furthermore, no astute strategist would have believed that any of them, or most of Reagan's other judicial nominees, were known by enough voters to affect Republican chances at the polls.

There is also evidence of the second purpose. The reversal of Carter's policy of selecting some judges from among women and previously ignored racial and ethnic minorities indicates an effort to restore the bench to its status as the preserve of white males—though, as indicated above, some of this pattern may be the creature of ethnic political allegiances, importing again an element of patronage.

The third purpose, to maintain or even improve the professional quality of judicial personnel, may be motivated by the public good—the importance of having truly qualified people on the bench—or narrow, partisan, self-interest—selecting able judges makes the president and his party look good and so might attract voters or at least historians. I have already said enough about the quality of Reagan's nominees for it to be evident that, on the whole, he chose people who were, according to the more obvious though problematic criteria, professionally very well equipped.

The fourth purpose, to influence the course of judicial decision making, increases in importance as one moves up the judicial hierarchy. Every president has had such concerns, but Reagan's people were more determined in their efforts to influence public policy, more thorough in their searches, and usually more careful in vetting candidates. His advisors worked from a script two centuries old, but they played their roles more skillfully—or ruthlessly, if one does not like the results—than had any of their predecessors.

Speaking of judicial selection, James McClelland said that "this is the most lasting and significant achievement of the Reagan administration."[79] He may well be correct. Barring nuclear holocaust or rampant plague, a large share of Reagan's nominees will still be on the bench well into the twenty-first century; and, as a disgruntled Anti-Federalist complained, the constitutional document gives federal judges a "stupendous magnitude of power."[80] Who is on the bench can make an immense difference.[81] Had Adams, for instance, not persuaded Oliver Ellsworth to resign the chief justiceship, Jefferson would probably have given the post to Spencer Roane, the ardent states-righter from Virginia; and the course of American history might have been very different.

Nevertheless, as we have seen with Rehnquist, it is difficult to predict judicial behavior from pre-judicial careers and also difficult to predict the performance of a justice from service as a judge on a lower court. Even though Reagan's advisors did their work assiduously, almost by definition no one can do it perfectly. Moreover, as Rehnquist pointed out,[82] one of the critical variables is the changing nature of the problems judges must face. After 1937, Franklin Roosevelt chose his nominees for their views on federal regulation of the economy, not for their thinking about racial discrimination or the Bill of Rights; and it was those latter issues that formed the battleground of constitutional interpretation for the next generation.

To forecast at any given moment that the Supreme Court will change some ruling doctrines is almost as safe as forecasting that the weather will change. Constitutional law has never been static, nor is it ever likely to be. It is always, snakelike, in the presence of shedding or growing new skin. These developments usually come slowly, often imperceptibly until the adjustment is an accomplished fact. Judges, Jefferson complained, move "on noiseless foot." The central—and difficult—questions pertain to the direction in which and extent to which the Court will change its collective mind; and the nation's shifting problems, chance events, and other institutions' reactions to those happenings help shape that change.

In the short run, Reagan's presidency did not effect a judicial revolution, but we shall not know for decades what the longer range impact will be. Still, one can confidently assert that his choices of O'Connor and Scalia and promotion of Rehnquist increased the odds of decisions that are more generous toward governmental—especially state—authority and less protective of the constitutional claims of those litigants who are accused of crime, are invoking a general right to privacy, or, more specifically, are asserting a right to abortion.

If Reagan's advisors chose Kennedy with the astuteness they demonstrated in most other selections, the odds for such decisions escalated.[83] Indeed, Justice Harry Blackmun, author of the Court's opinion in *Roe v. Wade* (1973),[84] publicly said in September 1988: "The next question is, 'Will *Roe v. Wade* go down the drain?' I think there's a very distinct possibility that it will, this term. You can count the votes."[85] The records of Reagan's nominees to the courts of appeals indicate that they would respond with enthusiasm to this sort of reshaping; and there is no reason to believe that the district judges Reagan nominated would react differently.

In one important sense, Reagan's not choosing ideologues obsessed with democratic theory may have increased his long-run influence on constitutional development. It is shrewd for a president who brings about an electoral realignment to select judges who will defer to his new majority. If, however, a president fails to carry out such a realignment— and in this respect, Reagan failed badly—then his substantive policy goals might well be better served by judges who share those goals but are less than pure in their commitment to judicial deference to legislative decisions.

NOTES

I am indebted to Bernard Roberts, Jr., of the Princeton class of 1988; Mark Brandon, Esq., of Princeton; and Suzette Marie Hemberger of the American Bar Foundation for research assistance and to Mark Brandon and Robert George of Princeton, Sheldon Goldman of the University of Massachusetts, and Gary L. McDowell of the Center for Judicial Studies for critical readings of earlier drafts. The Center of International Studies, Princeton University, supported my research.

1. It might well be rational for a president to assent to the selection of a doctrinally unsympathetic judge providing the benefits gained would outweigh the costs, although the president would have to discount any short-run gains by the judge's probable length of service and the relative importance of the judgeship.

2. See C. Herman Pritchett, *Congress versus the Supreme Court, 1957–1961* (Minneapolis: University of Minnesota Press, 1961); and Walter F. Murphy, *Congress and the Court* (Chicago: University of Chicago Press, 1962).

3. For general studies of the appointing process and its products, see Henry J. Abraham, *Justices and Presidents*, 2d ed. (New York: Oxford University Press, 1985); Harold W. Chase, *Federal Judges: The Appointing Process* (Minneapolis: University of Minnesota Press, 1972); Elliot E. Slotnick, "Federal Judicial Recruitment and Selection Research: A Review Essay," *Judicature* 71 (1988): 317; W. F. Murphy and C. Herman Pritchett, eds., *Courts, Judges, and Politics*, 4th ed. (New York: Random House, 1986), chap. 4 and bibliography cited.

4. At that time, justices of the Supreme Court were also the principal trial judges and spent more of their time riding circuit than hearing appeals in the capital. In 1796, George Washington nominated Samuel Chase for the Supreme Court. He had opposed ratification of the Constitution, but, in addition to having apparently repented that sin, during the Revolution he had been a strong supporter of Washington in the Continental Congress, defending him against efforts to remove him as commanding general.

5. To John Dickinson, 19 December 1801, *The Writings of Thomas Jefferson*, ed. Andrew A. Lipscomb (Washington, D.C.: The Thomas Jefferson Memorial Association, 1903), 10: 301f.

6. 1 Cr. 37.

7. See Donald G. Morgan, *Justice William Johnson: The First Dissenter* (Columbia: University of South Carolina Press, 1954), chap. 3.

8. Jefferson to William Johnson, 27 October 1822, *The Works of Thomas Jefferson*, ed. Paul L. Ford (New York: Putnam's, 1905), 12: 247.

9. George S. Boutwell, *Reminiscences of Sixty Years in Public Affairs* (New York: McClure, Phillips, 1902), 2: 29; I read, perhaps wrongly, David M. Silver, *Lincoln's Supreme Court* (Urbana: University of Illinois Press, 1956), 207–8, as being a tad skeptical of Congressman Boutwell's perfect recall.

10. Kermit L. Hall, "Social Backgrounds and Judicial Recruitment: A Nineteenth-Century Perspective on the Lower Federal Judiciary," *Western Political Quarterly* (1976): 243, 254; see also his "240 Men: The Antebellum Lower Federal Judiciary, 1829–1861," *Vanderbilt Law Review* 29 (1976): 1089.

11. See Daniel S. McHargue, "President Taft's Appointments to the Supreme Court," *Journal of Politics* 12 (1950): 478. Both before and after coming to the Court, Taft, an Ohio man who always kept his plate up, was keenly conscious of the leverage patronage gave the executive. See Henry F. Pringle, *The Life and Times of William Howard Taft* (New York: Farrar and Rinehart, 1939), esp. 1: 424. It was hardly sheer coincidence that, in 1956 during the middle of a heated campaign for reelection in which it appeared that Catholics might play a decisive part by abandoning their traditional Democratic loyalty, Eisenhower gave a recess appointment to an Irish Catholic—and moderate Democrat—William J. Brennan, Jr. Whether or not this choice was the product of a deliberate piece of campaign strategy, it is worth noting that 1956 was the first time, for which we have reliable data, that a Republican presidential candidate won a majority of Catholic votes.

12. Quoted in Pringle, *Life and Times*, 1: 205.

13. Again, it was not mere happenstance that, in an election year, Taft had urged Coolidge to name a Catholic conservative Democrat.

14. See generally, Walter F. Murphy, "In His Own Image: Mr. Chief Justice Taft and Supreme Court Appointments," *Supreme Court Review* (1961): 159; and "Chief Justice Taft and the Lower Court Bureaucracy," *Journal of Politics* 24 (1962): 453. For an exhaustive study of the appointment of a single justice, see David J. Danelski, *A Supreme Court Justice Is Appointed* (New York: Random House, 1964).

15. Here, as often where I offer no other citation, my source for the backgrounds of judges has been Sheldon Goldman's writings. See esp. Goldman and Austin Sarat, *American Court Systems*, 2d ed. (New York: Longman, 1989).

16. "Carter's Judicial Appointments: The Influence of Affirmative Action and Merit Selection on Voting on the U.S. Court of Appeals," *Judicature* 67 (1983): 164, 173.

17. For lack of a better term, in this essay I shall say "Reagan" or "Reagan's administration" fully realizing that there is no reason to suspect that he paid any more attention to or had more knowledge of judicial selection than any of his other duties. But, whether academics like it or not, Ronald W. Reagan was president of the United States from January 1981 until January 1989 and officially responsible for the government's actions and inactions. For accounts of what in the armed services is called "attention to duty," see generally, David A. Stockman, *The Triumph of Politics* (New York: Harper and Row, 1986); Donald T. Regan, *For the Record* (New York: Harcourt Brace Jovanovich, 1988); Larry Speakes, *Speaking Out* (New York: Scribner's, 1988); and Doyle McManus and Jane Mayer, *Landslide: The Unmaking of the President, 1984–1988* (Boston: Houghton Mifflin, 1988).

18. Senatorial courtesy exacts a price from the president for his party's controlling the upper house. On the whole, however, an astute president can ensure that the benefits far exceed the costs; and, as noted below, Reagan's administration created more freedom for itself in dealing with senators than had recent governments.

19. Stanley Kelley, Jr., *Interpreting Elections* (Princeton: Princeton University Press, 1983), has closely examined responses to surveys of voters' attitudes and concluded that people tended to vote *against* Carter rather than *for* Reagan. In politics, however, truth is often far less important than perceptions of truth; and journalists as well as professional politicians widely interpreted the election as a mandate *for* Reagan. This (mis)perception added to the new President's political clout, making many Republican legislators think they were beholden to him for election and would be for reelection and many Democratic legislators view him as nearly invincible.

20. See Sheldon Goldman, "Reaganizing the Judiciary," *Judicature* 68 (1985): 313, 315–16.

21. After the ABA's committee had leaked its poor evaluation of Judge G. Harrold Carswell when Nixon was about to nominate him for the Supreme Court, the White House for a time snubbed the committee; but, under Ford and Carter, relations again became close.

22. Goldman, "Reaganizing the Judiciary," 315. See also his "Judicial Appointments and the Presidential Agenda," in *The Presidency in American Politics*, ed. Paul Brace, Christine Harrington, and Gary King (New York: New York University Press, 1989).

23. For a general and very critical account, see Herman Schwartz, *Packing the Courts: The Conservative Campaign to Rewrite the Constitution* (New York: Scribner's, 1988). For a particular instance, see the *New York Times*, 8 July 1981, asserting that an "Administration official" said that when considering Judge Sandra Day O'Connor, White House aides had questioned her about such matters as the exclusionary rule and to whom on the Court she felt closest. As a state legislator, she had taken a stand on abortion which caused the National Right to Life Committee and the National Pro-Life PAC to oppose her confirmation and Rev. Jerry Falwell to call it "a disaster." In response to a reporter's direct question, however, the President claimed that after interviewing her, he was "completely satisfied" with her views of that issue. Transcript of Presidential Press Conference announcing the nomination, 7 July 1981; *New York Times*, 8 July 1981. As it turned out, he had good reason to be satisfied.

24. Reagan's administration continued the policy of consulting about judicial vacancies with Republican representatives from states for which there was no Republican senator.

25. For an argument with heavy supporting data that federal judicial appointments from 1829 to 1861 took in a somewhat broader segment of the white male social spectrum, see Hall, "Social Backgrounds."

26. Carter's choosing a single Asian makes him look far more catholic on this count than perhaps he deserves.

27. Thomas G. Walker and Deborah J. Barrow, "The Diversification of the Federal Bench: Policy and Process Ramifications," *Journal of Politics* 47 (1985): 596, 614. For a study producing evidence that white and black judges at the state level follow different patterns in sentencing, see Susan Welch, Michael Combs, and John Gruhl, "Do Black Judges Make a Difference?" *American Journal of Political Science* 32 (1988): 126.

28. See W. F. Murphy and Joseph Tanenhaus, *The Study of Public Law* (New York: Random House, 1972), 37–38.

29. See Pat Lindh to Doug Bennett, memorandum, 14 November 1975, the Ford Library. (I am indebted to Fred I. Greenstein for a copy of this memorandum.) Douglas, of course, did not retire until 1976, but his precarious health had given the White House a long time to search for a successor.

30. Scalia had also taught at the law schools of Georgetown, Stanford, and Virginia.

31. Manion's record as a judge may turn out to be better than anyone had any reason to expect. See Stephen J. Adler, "Not That Dumb," *The American Lawyer* (January/February 1988): 32ff.

32. Ford and Johnson each nominated one judge whom the ABA rated as "unqualified." The small number—twelve—of appellate judges Ford chose makes this one selection a large portion of the whole. Moreover, because Ford nominated some judges actually selected when Nixon was in the White House, one should hesitate to make much of the differences between the two presidents' nominees.

33. Quoted in Harold W. Chase, "Federal Judges: The Appointing Process," *Minnesota Law Review* 51 (1966): 204.

34. To be sure, presidents have, on occasion, put on the bench people whose

greatest claim to merit was being a friend or a friend of a friend. One need look no further back than Lyndon Johnson's nomination of Homer Thornberry for the Supreme Court or Truman's choice of Fred Vinson, Sherman Minton, Harold Burton, and Tom Clark.

35. My positivist (and even some natural-law) colleagues are quick to deny that the version of positivism espoused by Reagan's nominees is closely akin to the versions of H. L. A. Hart or Joseph Raz. Some even deny that what Rehnquist, Bork, et al. advocate is positivism at all.

36. For a critique of the conception of individual rights employed here, see Robert P. George, "Natural Law, the Common Good, and American Politics," *Proceedings of the Fellowship of Catholic Scholars* 10 (1988): 9.

37. The Republican platform of 1980 spelled out some of these goals, the most notable exception being opposition to affirmative action. See *Congressional Quarterly Almanac 1980,* esp. 62b, 74b.

38. See esp. the Republican party's platforms of 1980 and 1984. *Congressional Quarterly Almanac 1980,* 62b, 74b; ibid. *1984,* 55b. Reagan's campaign speeches and occasional remarks on judicial appointments echoed and went beyond these planks.

39. For example, the administration's opposition to the War Powers Act, its arguments against: the legislative veto in *INS v. Chadha,* 462 U.S. 919 (1983); Congress's delegating in the Gramm-Rudman Act authority to the comptroller general to cut budgets, *Bowsher v. Synar,* 478 U.S. 714 (1986); and congressional authority under Article II, section 2, to vest appointments in the courts of law, *Morrison v. Olson,* 101 L.Ed.2d 569 (1988). My point is not that any of these positions is prima facie wrong, only that: As far as the War Powers Resolution was concerned, the President claimed interpretive authority superior to that of Congress; and, in each of the other instances, the administration asked judges not to defer to Congress's interpretation of the Constitution.

40. See, for instance, Edwin Meese III, "The Attorney General's View of the Supreme Court: Toward a Jurisprudence of Original Intent," *Public Administration Review* 45 (1985): 701.

41. I do not think that this term or its putative antonym, "judicial self-restraint," is particularly meaningful or even useful, but judges, elected officials, journalists, and legal scholars continue to make these fuzzy distinctions. For my critique, see Walter F. Murphy, James E. Fleming, and William F. Harris, II, *American Constitutional Interpretation* (Mineola, N.Y.: Foundation Press, 1986), chap. 8, esp. 314–15.

42. Rehnquist has been the most direct on this point—see his article "The Notion of a Living Constitution," *Texas Law Review* 54 (1976): 693—although Posner's celebration of economic efficiency as the driving force of law is hardly subtle. Bork has taken a rather complex view—not that Posner's and Rehnquist's are simple—favoring society's authority to determine its values and impose them on dissenters. See his "Tradition and Morality in Constitutional Law" (Washington, D.C.: The American Enterprise Institute, 1986), partly reprinted in Murphy and Pritchett, *Courts, Judges, and Politics,* 635–40. As Bork put it: "In a constitutional democracy the moral content of law must be given by the morality of the framer or the legislator, never by the morality of the judge. The sole task of the latter—and it is a task quite large enough for anyone's wisdom, skill, and virtue—is to translate the framer's or the legislator's

morality into a rule to govern unforeseen circumstances. That abstinence from giving his own desires free play, that continuing and self-conscious renunciation of power, that is the morality of the jurist" (ibid., 640).

Elsewhere in this lecture, Bork attacked the notion of judges' importing philosophical notions into constitutional or statutory interpretation without (apparently) realizing that he himself was importing his own—and controversial—notions about moral philosophy.

The issues here are extremely complex. Even Justice William J. Brennan, Jr., who is surely no positivist, made some comments during the hearings on his confirmation which strongly implied his belief in a separation of law and morality. U.S. Senate, Committee on the Judiciary, *Hearings on the Nomination of William J. Brennan, Jr., To Be an Associate Justice of the U.S. Supreme Court*, 85th Cong., 1st sess., 1957. In their first edition (1961), Murphy and Pritchett, 96–101, excerpted some of the relevant colloquy.

43. "What Am I? A Potted Plant?" *The New Republic*, 28 September 1987, 23–25.

44. See Bork's concurrence and Scalia's dissent in *Ollman v. Evans*, 750 F.2d 970 (1984).

45. C. K. Rowland, Donald Songer, and Robert A. Carp, "Presidential Effects on Criminal Justice Policy in the Lower Federal Courts: The Reagan Record," *Law and Society Review* 22 (1988): 191. The authors stratified their sample to overrepresent 1983 and 1984. This study also reports a similar investigation of district judges with similar results.

46. Ibid., 198.

47. "Reagan's Appointments to the U.S. Courts of Appeals: The Continuation of a Judicial Revolution," *Judicature* 70 (1986): 48.

48. For reasons discussed below, I do not think the term "ideology" is appropriate.

49. Ibid., 54. The italics are in the original.

50. Timothy B. Tomasi and Jess A. Velona, "All the President's Men? A Study of Ronald Reagan's Appointments to the U.S. Courts of Appeals," *Columbia Law Review* 87 (1987): 766.

51. "Remarks at a Reagan-Bush '84 Rally, November 2, 1984," *Weekly Compilation of Presidential Documents* 20 (1984): 1738, 1741.

52. James G. Wilson, "Justice Diffused: A Comparison of Edmund Burke's Conservatism with the Views of Five Conservative, Academic Judges," *University of Miami Law Review* 40 (1986): 913; and idem, "Constraints of Power: The Constitutional Opinions of Judges Scalia, Bork, Posner, Easterbrook and Winter," ibid. 40 (1986): 1171. Wilson included all opinions published until May 28, 1986, and a few others announced later that year.

53. Wilson, "Constraints of Power," 1265.

54. Ibid., 1174.

55. Ibid., 1266.

56. Ibid.

57. Thus, I think that Rowland et al., as quoted in n. 46, are correct only insofar as they use the term "ideology" in the very loose sense of general political orientation.

58. All three, of course, are charter members of this sect. See, for example, Antonin Scalia's exchange with Richard Epstein: "Scalia v. Epstein: Two Views on Judicial Activism," reprinted from *Cato Journal* 4 (1985) as a pamphlet by the Cato Institute, Washington, D.C., 1985; and Sandra Day O'Connor's "Trends in the Relationship between the Federal and State Courts from the Perspective of a State Court Judge," *William and Mary Law Review* 22 (1981): 801; and Rehnquist's "The Notion of a Living Constitution."

59. "Remarks at a Reagan-Bush '84 Rally," *Weekly Compilation*, 1741. See also "Question and Answer Session with Reporters, October 11, 1984," ibid., 1496.

60. 410 U.S. 113 (1973).

61. *Akron v. Akron Center for Reproductive Health*, 462 U.S. 416, dis. op., 458 (1983).

62. For Rehnquist's approach to constitutional interpretation, see his "Notion." For examples of his deferring to the states instead of Congress on issues of federalism, see his opinion for the Court in National League of Cities v. Usery, 426 U.S. 833 (1976), and his dissent in *Garcia v. SAMTA*, 469 U.S. 528 (1985); for his deferring to the states instead of Congress on an issue of civil rights, see his dissent in *Rome v. United States*, 446 U.S. 156 (1980). In the last case, he, the usual prophet of judicial deference to the legislature, complained that the Court's decision "requires the judiciary to cede far more of its power to interpret and enforce the Constitution than ever envisioned." See, generally, Sue Davis, *Justice William H. Rehnquist and the Constitution: The Quest for a "New" Federalism* (Princeton: Princeton University Press, 1989).

63. For interesting speculation, see Stuart Taylor, Jr., "Rehnquist's Court: Tuning Out the White House," *New York Times Magazine*, 11 September 1988, 38ff.

64. Speech delivered at the College of Law, University of Minnesota, 1984; reprinted in part in Murphy and Pritchett, *Courts, Judges, and Politics*, 173–76; the quotation appears at 176.

65. See, for example, *Time v. Firestone*, 414 U.S. 448 (1976). On the other hand, Rehnquist had held that, when *the police* libeled an innocent man with a public claim that he was a "known criminal," they had not violated the victim's constitutional rights. *Paul v. Davis*, 424 U.S. 693 (1976).

66. *Webster v. Doe*, 100 L.Ed.2d 632 (1988).

67. Rehnquist had joined the majority in two previous decisions upholding state authority to punish consenting adult homosexuals for engaging in sexual relations in the privacy of their own homes—Doe v. Commonwealth's Attorney, 425 U.S. 901 (1976), and *Bowers v. Hardwick*, 478 U.S. 186 (1986)—a different but related issue.

68. Meese, "The Attorney General's View."

69. *In re Sealed Case*, 838 F.2d 476 (D.C. Cir. 1988).

70. When on the court of appeals, Scalia had wanted to undercut much of the limitations on presidential power *vis-à-vis* that of Congress, which the Steel Seizure Case, 343 U.S. 579 (1952), had found in the Constitution. See his separate opinion in *Rainbow Navigation, Inc. v. Department of the Navy*, 783 F.2d 1072 (D.C. Cir. 1986).

71. See, for instance: Equal protection—O'Connor delivered the opinion of the Court in *Mississippi University for Women v. Hogan*, 458 U.S. 718 (1982) relying on a "three-tiered" test to invalidate a state regulation based on sex; Rehnquist continued

his long rejection of anything but reasonableness as a test and dissented. In *Roberts v. Jaycees,* 468 U.S. 609 (1984), pitting freedom of association against a state statute against discrimination, O'Connor produced a concurring opinion that in some ways offered stronger protection for both rights than did the majority's opinion. Rehnquist noted only that he concurred in the result. In *Rogers v. Lodge,* 458 U.S. 613 (1982), O'Connor joined the majority to invalidate the electoral system of a county in Georgia for violating the rights of black voters; Rehnquist dissented.

Freedom of speech and assembly—in *Boos v. Barry,* 99 L.Ed.2d 333 (1988), O'Connor and Scalia were part of a 5-3 holding invalidating a federal statute making it a crime to display within 500 feet of a foreign embassy a sign that would bring the foreign government into "public odium" or "disrepute." Rehnquist dissented.

72. 479 U.S. 314. Although O'Connor dissented against retroactive application of the new rule, she had joined the majority in the basic case, *Batson v. Kentucky,* 476 U.S. 79 (1986). Rehnquist dissented in both *Batson* and *Griffith.*

73. 481 U.S. 186.

74. 100 L.Ed.2d 771.

75. 480 U.S. 321. Rehnquist and O'Connor dissented.

76. *New York State Club Ass'n v. New York City,* 101 L.Ed.2d 1 (1988); and *Rotary International v. Rotary Club,* 481 U.S. 537 (1987).

77. *Roberts v. Jaycees.*

78. For an examination of presidential motivations, see William E. Hulbary and Thomas G. Walker, "The Supreme Court Selection Process: Presidential Motivations and Judicial Performance," *Western Political Quarterly* 33 (1980): 185; and Rayman L. Solomon, "The Politics of Appointments and the Federal Courts' Role in Regulating America: U.S. Courts of Appeals Judgeships from T. R. to F. D. R.," *American Bar Foundation Research Journal* (1984): 285.

79. Quoted in the *Wall Street Journal,* 1 February 1988.

80. William Grayson in Virginia's ratifying convention; quoted in Alpheus Thomas Mason, *The Supreme Court: Palladium of Freedom* (Ann Arbor: University of Michigan Press, 1962), 72.

81. See, generally, Laurence H. Tribe, *God Save This Honorable Court: How the Choice of Supreme Court Justices Shapes Our History* (New York: Random House, 1985).

82. "Presidential Appointments to the Supreme Court," in Murphy and Pritchett, *Courts, Judges, and Politics.*

83. If four judges vote together and the other five vote randomly, the four will win thirty-one out of thirty-two times. Judges, of course, do not vote randomly; but, as the Court is constituted at the beginning of its 1988 term, the odds are high of picking up a fifth vote for the specific legal policies Reagan endorsed.

84. 410 U.S. 113.

85. Quoted in the *New York Times,* 14 September 1988, from a speech given at the law school of the University of Arkansas.

PART FIVE

Electoral and Congressional Relations

12

After the Reagan Revolution:
A Postelectoral Politics?

BENJAMIN GINSBERG and MARTIN SHEFTER

Ronald Reagan won landslide Electoral College victories in the presidential contests of 1980 and 1984. Republicans, nevertheless, failed to win control of the House of Representatives, and though they captured the Senate in 1980 they lost their majority in the middle of Reagan's second term. Republican control of the presidency and Democratic control of Congress were confirmed in the elections of 1988.

This pattern of divided outcomes is generally seen as the chief electoral legacy of Reaganism. What is even more noteworthy, however, is that the Reagan era confirmed a major change that has been taking place over the past two decades in the very role and significance of elections in American politics. Rather than continuing to rely primarily upon voter mobilization, contending forces have come increasingly to use such mechanisms as congressional investigations, alliances with foreign governments, and judicial proceedings to gain political power.

The growing use of one nonelectoral weapon of political combat—the criminal sanction—is suggested by the tenfold increase between the early 1970s and the mid-1980s in the number of indictments brought by federal prosecutors against national, state, and local officials (see Figure 12.1). Although many of those indicted were lower level civil servants, large numbers were prominent figures—among them more than a dozen members of Congress, several federal judges, and a substantial number of high-ranking executive officials including Michael Deaver and Lyn Nofziger, and Labor Secretary Raymond Donovan. These data, of course, do not even take into account the many other top-ranking officials such as Attorney General Edward Meese and House Speaker Jim Wright who

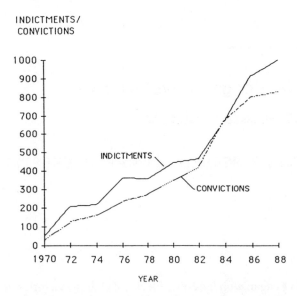

FIGURE 12.1. Federal indictments and convictions of public officials, 1970–86. Reporting procedures were modified in 1983 so that pre- and post-1983 data are not strictly comparable. *Indictments* are of federal, state, and local officials by U.S. prosecutors; *convictions* are of federal, state, and local officials in the U.S. courts. (*Source:* Reports of the U.S. Department of Justice Public Integrity Section, 1971–88.)

were the targets of investigations that did not result in indictments.

There is no reason to believe that the level of political corruption in the United States has actually increased tenfold over the past decade and a half, but it could be said that this sharp rise in the number of criminal indictments of government officials reflects a heightened level of public concern with governmental misconduct. However, both the issue of government ethics and the growing use of criminal sanctions against public officials have been closely linked to struggles for political power in the United States. In the aftermath of Watergate, institutions were established and processes created to investigate allegations of unethical conduct on the part of public figures. Increasingly, political forces have sought to make use of these mechanisms to discredit their opponents. When scores of investigators, accountants, and lawyers are deployed to scrutinize the conduct of an Ed Meese or a Jim Wright, it is all but certain that something questionable will be found. It is the creation of these processes more than changes in the public's moral standards which explains why public officials increasingly are being charged with ethical and criminal violations.

Three arenas of nonelectoral conflict have become especially important in the United States over the past two decades. First, contending political forces have sought to make use of the powers of Congress and the presidency as political weapons and to that end have attempted to strengthen the branch of government to which they have access while weakening the branch controlled by the opposition. Second, competing groups have undertaken to gain control over other institutions such as the judiciary and the national security apparatus and to use these as instruments of governance and political combat. Third, competing groups have used techniques including exposés, lawsuits, covert operations, and the imposition of regulatory controls to disrupt and undermine organizations and social forces upon which their opponents depend for support while strengthening the organizations and forces with which they are allied.

Institutional Combat: Congress and the Presidency

Institutional conflict is built into the American governmental structure by the separation of powers. This form of political struggle has intensified over the past two decades, however, as the Republicans have gained a solid hold on the White House, and the Democrats have strengthened their grip on Congress. The GOP has reacted to its inability to win control of Congress by seeking to enhance the powers of the executive branch and to circumvent legislative restrictions on presidential conduct. The Democrats, in turn, have responded to the Republican presidential advantage by seeking to strengthen the Congress while reducing the powers and prerogatives of the presidency through legislative investigations, media exposés, and judicial proceedings as well as through the imposition of statutory limits on executive power. Ironically, the very techniques that allowed the Republicans to dominate presidential elections left them vulnerable to these tactics. The GOP depended for its electoral success on money and the new capital-intensive techniques of polling, television, advertising, and direct mail fund-raising, which enabled them to win elections without engaging in the long and arduous task of constructing grass roots electoral organizations. Had they possessed strong organizational ties to their supporters, the Republicans would not have been as vulnerable to investigations and allegations aired through the media. At any rate, the two parties now have become locked in a struggle whose outcome will be decided more by the institutional weapons and power at their disposal than by their capacity to mobilize additional voters.

INSTITUTIONAL POWER AND POLITICS

The power of any governmental institution is a function of both the strength of its alliances with social forces or with other institutions that can support its assertions of authority, and its internal capacities for coercion, extraction, distribution, and administration. These two sources of institutional power may be mutually reinforcing because an institution can use the support of its constituency to increase its coercive or extractive authority and then employ this enhanced authority to add new groups to its constituency.

For example, the presidency gained power in the 1930s and 1940s through both of these processes. The first has been emphasized by Samuel P. Huntington (1973). As he notes, presidents during the New Deal and postwar eras pursued domestic and foreign policies that won the support of a nexus of powerful national political forces: national labor unions, corporations, banks, law firms, news media, foundations, and universities. These political forces were thus prepared to support presidential policy initiatives—initiatives that characteristically added to the power of the executive branch—and to back the president in his conflicts with Congress and other governmental institutions. The votes, campaign assistance, money, publicity, and expertise they brought to bear on behalf of the president and his initiatives often enabled him to prevail over (or reach acceptable accommodations with) his opponents in other governmental institutions.

Equally important to the building of presidential power, however, was the second of the mechanisms mentioned above: the enormous growth of federal revenues, expenditures, and employment during the Depression and World War II gave the president access to resources he could use to induce members of Congress, state and local officials, party politicians, and private interests to follow his lead. At the same time, the growth of the federal government's coercive capacity—a capacity recorded in the Code of Federal Regulations and the corpus of federal statutory, administrative, and case law and enforced by an army of administrators, investigators, attorneys, special agents, and military personnel—enabled presidents to compel would-be resistors to come to terms. To enhance their control over this new federal leviathan and limit the ability of their opponents to draw resources and political advantages from it, Franklin Roosevelt and his successors created the "institutionalized presidency" and undertook to reorganize the executive establishment (Milkis 1985). Precisely because they recognized that questions of institutional and political power were at stake, forces that enjoyed better access to the Congress, administrative agencies, or courts than to the White House often resisted these efforts at executive reorganization. This conflict over the expansion of presidential power during the 1930s and 1940s is a useful backdrop for examining the institutional struggles of the past twenty years.

FROM WATERGATE TO CONTRAGATE

As just indicated, during the New Deal and postwar periods efforts to strengthen the presidency had received the support of a broad coalition of national political forces. In the late 1960s, however, this constituency split over the issue of Vietnam. The Nixon administration retained the backing of those elements that believed the United States should use its military resources to fight communism in Southeast Asia. At the same time, President Nixon attacked what he regarded as costly and socially disruptive excesses in federal domestic programs. Opponents of the Vietnam War and defenders of domestic social programs looked to Congress to support their point of view.

Many congressional Democrats, and some Republicans as well, allied with these dissident forces and sought to prevail over the White House on issues of both foreign and domestic policy. A combination of developments in the 1960s and 1970s enabled these members of Congress to fight, and ultimately defeat, the president. In the first place, during this period, Congress essentially acquired a distributive capacity of its own. As Morris Fiorina (1977) has noted, Congress enacted an enormous number of new domestic programs in these years; its members regularly intervened in the bureaucracy to channel the benefits generated by these programs to their constituents and then claimed credit for this largess. Fiorina attributed to this process the increased electoral advantage that incumbents came to enjoy at this time—an advantage that largely insulated congressional from presidential elections. This made it politically possible for congressmen to take on the president.

In addition, by establishing close linkages with other institutions, Congress effectively acquired administrative, mobilizing, and coercive capacities during the 1960s and 1970s. In a return to nineteenth-century practice, Congress enacted very detailed regulatory statutes and authorized private citizens to sue in the federal courts to secure their implementation (Rabkin 1988); that is, by allying with the judiciary, Congress was able to assure the interests enjoying access to it that the policies they favored would be implemented regardless of the political sympathies of the administration in power.

In a similar fashion, by establishing linkages with the national news media—especially through nationally televised hearings—members of Congress were able to mobilize nationwide constituencies in support of various policy initiatives and to stampede Congress into enacting and the president into signing legislation designed to remedy the evils the hearings in question publicized (Wilson 1984). The 1962 thalidomide hearings, chaired by Senator Estes Kefauver, was a pattern-setting example of this technique. Televised hearings could also be used to mobilize national constituencies against the White House. The 1967 Senate Foreign Relations Committee hearings on Vietnam, chaired by William Fulbright, for example, played a crucial role in legitimizing opposition to presidential policies in Southeast Asia.

Finally, alliances with the media and the judiciary provided Congress with a coercive capacity. In the 1950s, Senators Kefauver, McCarthy, and McClellan had demonstrated how televised hearings could be used to harass—and, in conjunction with perjury trials, imprison—gangsters, left-wingers, and union leaders. In the 1960s and early 1970s, other senators used these precedents to pillory and politically weaken employers of migrant labor, corporate polluters, and Nixon administration officials. After the Watergate episode entered its final stages and a special prosecutor was appointed, the congressional-media-judicial nexus achieved its full coercive capacity and was able to imprison errant administration officials.

These developments enabled Congress to strengthen its base of political support by increasing the range of governmental services it was in a position to provide to members of its constituency. Liberal political forces benefited especially from this and, in a reversal of their prior stance, became quite vocal in defending the prerogatives of Congress and attacking the "imperial presidency" (Schlesinger 1973). Thus, they were prepared to rally in support of Congress as tensions between the legislative and executive branches increased during the Nixon years.

President Nixon, especially after his reelection in 1972, responded to these developments by attempting to undermine the new capacities of Congress and the institutions with which it was allied. The President impounded billions of dollars appropriated by Congress and sought to sever its ties with the bureaucracy by reorganizing executive agencies without seeking legislative approval. The White House established the plumbers squad to plug leaks of information to Congress and the press, and, its opponents claimed, it sought to undermine the legitimacy of the Supreme Court by appointing justices who were completely unqualified. The administration's opponents also claimed that it sought to limit Congress's influence over foreign policy by keeping vital information from it, most notably in the so-called "secret bombing" of Cambodia.

The President's opponents declared these actions to be abuses of power, and this animated their attack upon Richard Nixon in the Watergate controversy. Congress scored a total victory in that institutional conflict. It won because the bulk of the constituency that had supported assertions of presidential power during the New Deal and postwar period ultimately abandoned Richard Nixon and because the combination of media exposure, congressional investigation, and judicial process enabled the President's opponents to divide, delegitimate, and disrupt his administration. During the course of this constitutional conflict and in its immediate aftermath, Congress undertook to institutionalize its victory by imposing statutory limits on executive power in the War Powers Act, the Budget and Impoundment Act, the Freedom of Information Act, the Arms Export Control Act, and the Ethics in Government Act and by subjecting domestic and foreign intelligence agencies to much stricter congressional scrutiny. These restraints were quite effective and contributed to the difficulties that Gerald Ford and Jimmy Carter faced in asserting their leadership in the mid- and late-1970s.

After his election in 1980, Ronald Reagan undertook to strengthen the presidency by putting together a new constituency for presidential power and rebuilding the capacity of the executive to act independently of Congress. This endeavor enjoyed reasonable success during his first half-dozen years in office until Congress and the institutions with which it is allied counterattacked in the Iran-contra affair.

The budget and tax cuts enacted at the President's behest were at the heart of the Reaganite effort to solidify Republican control of the White House (Shefter and Ginsberg 1986). The Reagan spending cuts diminished the flow of resources to—and promised to weaken politically—groups and organizations that had a stake in federal domestic expenditures and were closely tied to the Democrats. Chief among these were the poor and near-poor, public employees and their unions, blacks (who disproportionately are poor or employed in the public sector), and those members of the middle class who were working for universities and other institutions in the nonprofit sector of the economy (institutions that depend upon federal grants and tax subsidies). At the same time, the Reagan tax cuts generated enormous budget and trade deficits. The economic dislocations caused by these deficits weakened two other institutions linked to the Democrats: labor unions in import-sensitive industries, and municipal governments in the nation's industrial belt.

On the other hand, those members of the middle class who were working in the private sector—and even more clearly, upper-income individuals—benefited from the Reagan tax cuts. The President's tax and budget policies thus divided the middle class and joined the largest segment of it with the upper class. In addition, the administration's assault on unions broke the entente between labor and management which had emerged in many sectors of the economy during the late 1930s and 1940s and, as much as anything, explains the overwhelming support the Republicans now receive among businessmen. As a result, the GOP not only won two-thirds of the votes of the middle and upper classes in the 1984 presidential election, but also through Political Action Committees (PACs) and direct contributions, it solidified its enormous advantage in campaign finance (Edsall 1984; Jacobson 1985). By weakening established centers of power and reorganizing interests in these (among other) ways, the Reaganites sought to solidify Republican control of the White House and create a new constituency for presidential power.

In addition, the Reaganites sought to restrict the distributive and extractive capacities of Congress. The tax cuts enacted in 1981 were designed to serve the first of these purposes (Stockman 1986). The enormous budget deficits created by those tax cuts limited Congress's ability to enact new spending programs by subjecting such proposals to the charge of exacerbating the deficit problem, and the 1986 tax reform reduced the extractive capacities of Congress by eliminating many of the exemptions, deductions, and preferences that in prior decades had made it politically possible to increase tax rates. Just as Lyndon Johnson discovered after eliminating selective service student exemptions that when you must draft everybody you can draft nobody, so too Congress may discover if it attempts to raise tax rates that when you must tax everybody you can tax nobody.

At the same time, the Reaganites undertook to increase the coercive and administrative capacities of the executive branch, especially in the realm of national security policy. Reagan sought to reassert the prerogative of the president unilaterally to deploy military force abroad by invading Grenada and bombing Libya. In both of these episodes, the duration of American involvement was brief, casualties were minimal, victory was assured, and hence public support for the President was extremely high. Senators and representatives who disapproved of the President's conduct thus found it politically impossible to criticize him, and he was able to act without securing the prior approval of Congress. In addition, the administration undertook to rebuild the CIA's capacity to engage in covert operations by greatly increasing its budget and personnel and by attempting to circumvent congressional scrutiny of intelligence operations.

During Ronald Reagan's first six years in office, these efforts enjoyed considerable success. Congress did not enact a single major new social program; the administration oversaw the largest peacetime military buildup in the nation's history; and the President demonstrated that it was possible, despite the trauma of Vietnam, for a politician to increase his popularity at home by using American forces abroad. Observers generally agreed that Reagan had gone a long way toward restoring the prestige and power of the presidency (Chubb and Peterson 1985).

Nonetheless, the President did suffer a number of reversals. After 1982, the Congress refused to cut domestic spending any further and required the administration to slow the pace of its rearmament program. In addition, Congress restricted the President's efforts to aid the contras in Nicaragua by enacting a series of amendments—the Boland amendments—to foreign military assistance bills. Congressional Democrats further limited that effort by compelling the CIA to stop mining Nicaragua's harbors, insisting that the agency withdraw a training manual that advocated the assassination of Sandinista cadres, and publicizing charges that the contras violated human rights.

THE IRAN-CONTRA AFFAIR

It was in this context that the Reagan administration undertook to build an alternative intelligence apparatus, attached to the National Security Council. This apparatus enabled the White House to conduct covert operations (such as aid to the contras) which the Congress had refused to approve and activities (such as the Iranian weapons sales) which Congress almost certainly would not countenance.

Critics in Congress called the network put together by Oliver North and others a "state within the state." This characterization is not inappropriate because that apparatus had some of the administrative, extractive, and coercive capacities of a governmental intelligence agency. North's network was able to conduct covert operations because it was staffed by retired military officers and CIA operatives with experience in this realm and had ties to foreign intelligence officials and arms merchants. Lacking access to tax revenues, it was financed by gifts from foreign governments, contributions from wealthy American conservatives, and the profits from weapons sales to Iran. Furthermore, depending upon how one chooses to characterize its relationship with the anti-Sandinista forces to which it provided political and military guidance as well as financial and logistical support, it might be said to have had coercive capacities as well.

The eruption of the Iran-contra scandal did more than destroy this intelligence network. It disrupted the entire Reagan administration and to a significant degree shifted the balance of the national political power toward institutions that compete with the presidency. The President's difficulties cannot, however, simply be attributed to the fact that his administration committed a major blunder in selling arms to Iran in exchange for the release of American hostages and in diverting some of the proceeds from those sales to the contras. Scandals such as the Iran-contra affair must be understood as political events. Politically damaging revelations are a consequence of efforts by investigators to uncover facts that will embarrass an administration politically as much as they are a source of that administration's difficulties. After all, prior to November 1986, there were reports in the press that Israel was shipping arms to Iran and that Oliver North was helping the contras secure weapons, but neither the media nor Congress undertook to discover the source of these arms. As with Watergate, one must look to changes within political constituencies and to institutional factors to account for the emergence and success of challenges to the Reagan presidency.

As for changes within political constituencies, two developments weakened the coalition Ronald Reagan had constructed and served to energize the institutions through which his opponents operated. The first of these was the Democratic recapture of the U.S. Senate in the midterm elections of 1986. (The great benefits of incumbency in House elections had enabled the Democrats to retain control of that chamber, of course, despite the GOP landslides in the 1980 and 1984 presidential elections.) The Democrats' success in 1986 emboldened the President's opponents in Congress. In addition, it emboldened the press, which up to that point had treated the Reagan administration quite gingerly for fear of alienating its middle-class audience.

The second development weakening the President was the emergence of a cleavage between the White House and the nation's foreign policy establishment. The institutions comprising that establishment—the State Department, Council on Foreign Relations, organs of elite opinion—had been upset by the White House's actions during and after the Reykjavik summit, which had caused strains in the Atlantic alliance, and they were appalled by revelations of the extent to which the White House had made policy and conducted sensitive operations in the Mideast and Central America through Oliver North's alternative foreign policy network. The communications media most closely associated with the foreign policy establishment denounced the "cowboys" in the White House for constructing this alternative network, supported the State Department's virtual declaration of independence after the Iran scandal erupted, and joined in the attack on the Reagan administration.

As for institutional factors, the President was weakened by the very way in which the Iranian weapons deal was conducted. The White House made use of a network of retired military officers and arms merchants to deal with Iran because its policy was opposed by the State and Defense Departments and would certainly have evoked the same hostile reaction in Congress. This expedient was self-defeating, however, because after the weapons deal was revealed and the President came under attack, that network was not powerful enough to sustain him. Reagan could neither rely upon it to maintain his Iranian initiative (which he continued to insist was a good idea), nor was that network linked to powerful social forces to which he could turn for political support.

The administration's opponents, by contrast, were able to make use of the formidable iron triangle of institutions—Congress, the national news media, and the federal judiciary—which had triumphed over the White House in the Watergate affair. The extent to which this nexus has become institutionalized is indicated by the fact that after the diversion of funds to the contras was revealed, it was almost universally assumed that Congress should conduct televised hearings and the judiciary should appoint an independent counsel to investigate the officials involved in the episode. Yet this procedure is really quite remarkable: officials who in other democracies would merely be compelled to resign from office are in the United States threatened with imprisonment. The threat of imprisonment plays a crucial role in legislative-executive conflicts because it leads administration officials to testify against one another, that is, it gives Congress the coercive capacity to do battle with the imperial presidency.

By making use of these weapons of institutional combat—coercion, investigation, and publicity—in the Iran-contra affair, congressional Democrats were able to weaken the Reagan administration during its final two years. For example, the President was compelled to appoint a national security advisor, director of central intelligence, White House chief of staff, and ultimately to select a nominee for the Supreme Court acceptable to the opposition in Congress. In the realm of policy, the President was unable to advance his conservative agenda any further. Indeed, he only found it possible to take major initiatives—most notably arms control—when these coincided with the agenda of his liberal opponents. Thus, through institutional combat, the Democrats were able to contain the effects of Reagan's 1984 landslide electoral victory. By the same token, of course, the effects of the Democrats' success in the arena of congressional elections have been limited by the deficits that Reaganite fiscal policies produced. In these ways the consequences of each party's electoral victories have been contained by the weapons of institutional combat its opponents have developed and deployed.

Institutional Combat: Courts and the National Security Apparatus

In addition to exploiting the powers of the presidency and Congress, competing forces in recent years have sought to develop other weapons of institutional combat. In particular, liberal political forces have undertaken to gain control over or ally themselves with the courts and conservatives with the national security apparatus—institutions whose personnel and decisions are not directly subject to electoral review or challenge.

Of course, the use of such institutions as instruments of governance and political struggle is not without precedent in the United States. During the decades prior to the 1930s, for example, business interests relied upon the federal courts to check the hostile forces that controlled state legislatures, particularly in the Midwest and West. It was precisely to circumvent the influence that business exercised through the courts that Progressive reformers sponsored the creation of what then was a novel institution—the independent regulatory commission. Despite these precedents, what is distinctive about the present period is the extent to which competing forces have come to rely upon nonelective institutions and the scope of the powers that these institutions have come to exercise.

The alliance between liberal political forces and the federal judiciary dates back to the late 1930s and 1940s (Shapiro 1986). Faced with the threat of Franklin Roosevelt's court-packing plan, the Supreme Court found it prudent to abandon its ties to the conservative camp and align itself with liberals on issues of economic policy, civil rights, and freedom of speech. During the 1950s, 1960s, and 1970s, the federal judiciary took a leading role on behalf of school desegregation, reform of the criminal justice system, women's rights, affirmative action, and environmental and consumer regulation. The courts have been a valuable ally for liberal forces because they provide a channel for exerting influence that is not (at least in the short run) contingent upon victories in the electoral arena.

From the perspective of the judiciary, this alliance has been valuable because liberals—including important members of Congress—have been willing to defend the courts in struggles with opponents who seek to limit their jurisdiction or enforcement powers. In recent years, efforts to limit the power of the federal judiciary have been resisted by coalitions of civil rights organizations, women's groups, educators, liberal Jewish and Protestant organizations, bar associations, law professors, and congressional liberals.

The support that the federal judiciary has received from these quarters enabled it to expand its powers greatly over the past twenty-five years (Silverstein and Ginsberg 1987). Beginning in the 1960s, the Supreme Court substantially changed the rules governing justiciability— the conditions under which courts will hear a case—to permit the federal judiciary to play a larger and more active role in the governmental and political processes. For example, the Court liberalized the doctrine of "standing" to permit taxpayers' suits where First Amendment issues were involved. Similarly, the Supreme Court effectively rescinded the "abstention" doctrine which had called for federal judges to decline to hear cases that rested on questions of state law not yet resolved by the state courts. Moreover, the Supreme Court relaxed the rules governing determinations of "mootness" and, for all intents and purposes did away with the "political question" doctrine that for many years had functioned as limits on judicial activism. This liberalization of the rules governing justiciability gave a wider range of litigants access to the courts, rendered a wider range of issues subject to judicial settlement, and made the courts more valuable as an institutional ally.

Equally important in expanding access to the judiciary was the Supreme Court amending the federal rules of civil procedure to facilitate class-action suits. Claims that might have been rejected as *de minimis* if asserted individually could now be aggregated against a common defendant. Class-action suits became critical weapons in the arsenals of the civil rights consumer and of the environmental, feminist, and antinuclear movements.

Accompanying this increased use of class actions was an expansion of judicial remedies including injunctions and the broad use of equitable powers for innovative forms of relief. Class actions challenging conditions in mental institutions, prisons, and other public facilities, for example, produced a host of detailed judicial decrees setting forth the minimum standards of care required of public agencies. Increasingly, judges made use of special masters under the control of the court to take charge of the day-to-day operations of institutional defendants such as the Boston school system and Alabama state prison system. Thus, by the 1970s, the federal judiciary provided litigants with remedies of the sort that were previously only available from either the executive or legislative branches. The chief beneficiaries of these new judicial powers were liberal political forces that, in turn, could be counted upon to rally to the support of the federal judiciary when it came under fire.

The support of the federal judiciary became critically important to liberal forces during their struggles with the Nixon and Reagan administrations. During the Nixon presidency, the Supreme Court refused to halt the desegregation of southern school districts. Most important, of course, was the Court's decision in the Watergate tapes case which compelled Nixon to resign from office or face certain impeachment. During the Reagan era, the Supreme Court opposed the administration on abortion rights, church-state relations, voting rights, and affirmative action, thus helping to block the implementation of important segments of the conservative agenda. The Supreme Court also served the interests of liberal forces by offering the media substantial protection from the laws of libel and increasing the liability of officials of the executive branch to civil suits.

Both the Nixon and Reagan administrations sought to disrupt this alliance between the federal judiciary and liberal political forces. During his six years in office, President Nixon appointed a number of conservatives to the district and circuit courts as well as four justices including Chief Justice Warren Burger to the Supreme Court. Because of the importance liberals attached to the federal judiciary, especially to the Supreme Court, they resisted these efforts to create a more conservative bench. Liberal forces scored their most significant victories when Democrats in Congress blocked Nixon's efforts to appoint Clement Haynsworth and G. Harrold Carswell, both of whom were likely to oppose liberal interests, to the Supreme Court. The judges Nixon was able to appoint were, for the most part, moderate Republicans whose views on key issues were not sufficiently intense to impel them to seek to move the federal judiciary from its alliance with the liberal camp.

President Reagan, for his part, attempted to curb the ability of liberal forces to exercise influence through the federal judiciary by appointing notable conservative legal scholars such as Ralph K. Winter of Yale and Richard Posner of the University of Chicago to federal appeals courts. Through such appointments, Reagan sought not simply to ensure that conservative judges would replace liberals on the federal bench, but sought also to stage an intellectual revolution by enhancing the impact of conservative ideas on American jurisprudence. In the case of the Supreme Court, Reagan was able to appoint Sandra Day O'Connor, a Republican moderate; Antonin Scalia, a conservative appeals court judge and former University of Chicago law professor; and to elevate Nixon appointee William Rehnquist to the position of chief justice. However, after a bitter campaign, Senate Democrats defeated Reagan's next nominee, arch-conservative Judge Robert Bork; and conservative Judge Douglas Ginsburg, whom Reagan nominated in Bork's place, was compelled to withdraw his name from consideration. Reagan was forced to name a moderate, Judge Anthony Kennedy, to fill the Court's vacant position. As a result of this victory and some successful efforts to block conservative appointments to the lower federal courts, liberal forces were able to limit the success of the Reagan administration's efforts to disrupt their alliance with the federal judiciary.

Just as liberal forces have been able to exercise influence through the federal courts, conservatives have sought to use the military and national security apparatus as political weapons. From the 1940s into the 1960s, America's "military-industrial complex"—the national security apparatus and the economic sectors associated with it—had ties to both the Democratic and Republican parties. At the end of World War II, the dominant forces within the two major parties were able to achieve an accord on questions of foreign and military policy. This bipartisan consensus included the need to contain the Soviet Union and to maintain a powerful military establishment for this purpose. Presidents and members of Congress, Democrats and Republicans alike, supported high levels of military spending, the construction of new weapons systems, and the use of American military force abroad. Indeed, if there was any difference between the parties during this period it was the Democrats who were more consistent advocates of high levels of defense spending. Prior to the Vietnam War, the two largest military buildups of the postwar decades were sponsored by the Democratic administrations of Harry Truman and John F. Kennedy, whereas it was the Republican administration of Dwight Eisenhower which was most diligent in seeking to economize on defense.

Conflict over the Vietnam War shattered this bipartisan consensus. Factions that eventually came to play a dominant role in the Democratic party turned against the use of American military force abroad and sought to slash defense spending. Conservative Republicans saw the new Democratic stance on defense issues as a threat to America's security and at the same time as an opportunity to expand the GOP's social and political base.

By promoting an enormous military buildup, the Reagan administration moved to attach to the Republican party political institutions, social forces, and economic interests with a stake in defense programs. The goal of this endeavor was not simply to secure campaign contributions and votes; the administration's larger purpose was to create a governing apparatus that could supplant the institutions of the domestic state linked to the Democrats. During the New Deal and postwar periods, Democrats had constructed a number of domestic welfare, regulatory, and fiscal institutions through which they could manage the nation's economy, shape its social structure, and provide a steady flow of public services and benefits to their party's constituent groups. The institutions of the domestic state fashioned by the Democrats thus served both as mechanisms of governance and as the political institutions through which the party perpetuated its power.

Although the Reaganites might have wished to do so, the experience of the Nixon administration revealed that any effort to seize control of these institutions and use them for their own purposes would have encountered overwhelming resistance. The president, to be sure, can appoint top agency administrators, but the commitment of domestic agencies to liberal programs is fiercely defended by congressional committees and by the constituency groups the agencies serve. Thus, when the Nixon administration sought to reorganize and reorient a number of domestic bureaucracies, it generated a firestorm of opposition. Indeed, this effort was one of the major reasons that President Nixon's opponents undertook to drive him from office. Similarly, when President Reagan attempted to bring about major changes in the policies of the Environmental Protection Agency (EPA), the congressional and constituency forces that supported existing EPA programs launched a counterattack that not only blocked Reagan's efforts but also resulted in investigations of two of the President's top EPA appointees, Rita Lavelle and Ann Burford Gorsuch—investigations that in Lavelle's case led to criminal indictment, prosecution, and imprisonment.

Recognizing that at least in the short term, it would be unable to seize control of the agencies of the domestic state, the Reagan administration endeavored, instead, to weaken and supplant them. The first of these aims was served by the administration's budget and tax policies that reduced the revenues and resources available to domestic agencies and thereby limited their administrative and political capabilities.

In addition, however, the Reagan administration sought to enhance the size and power of America's military and national security apparatus and to use it as an instrument for governing and perpetuating the power of the GOP in a manner parallel to the Democratic use of the agencies of the domestic state. Democratic administrations used domestic spending programs to solidify the party's ties to its numerous constituency groups. At the same time, as specified by Keynesian theory, these federal spending programs stimulated economic growth and employment, thereby identifying the Democrats as the party of prosperity. Thus, even many interests that were not direct recipients of federal spending were given reason to support the Democrats. Although professing to reject the economic theory associated with Democratic spending programs, the Reagan administration adopted what might be described as "military Keynesianism." The administration's military programs directly benefited segments of the business community, regions of the country, and elements of the electorate whose fortunes were tied to the military sector. At the same time, the Republicans expected that the economic growth, high levels of employment, and healthy corporate profits promoted by these programs would provide Americans more generally with reasons to support the GOP.

In addition to this program of military Keynesianism, the Reagan administration sought to develop a military version of the "industrial policy" often espoused by the Democrats. The stated goal of such a policy was to enable American corporations to compete more effectively against their foreign rivals. Toward this end, the federal government would provide loans to industrial corporations for new plants and equipment. Moreover, under most variants of industrial policy, a board composed of labor, management, and "public" members would oversee efforts to alter work rules, investment decisions, and the organization of the workplace; that is, under the rubric of industrial policy, decisions regarding the allocation of capital and industrial production which had been the exclusive prerogative of businessmen would now involve union and public influence as well. In addition, most versions of industrial policy included plans for worker retraining, thus providing a windfall for both government and nonprofit social service agencies.

The Reagan administration sought to enhance competitiveness of American industry through means that reinforced rather than limited the prerogatives of corporate management. The administration's defense buildup was central to this endeavor. Reaganite military programs emphasized the production and procurement of new weapons systems rather than bolstering personnel or enhancing readiness and maintenance. The purchase of new weapons provided subsidies to business and promoted the development of new technologies that could increase the strength and competitiveness of American industry. The Reagan administration's Strategic Defense Initiative (SDI) or "Star Wars" was the most ambitious effort in this regard. As liberal economist Robert Reich noted, the SDI program, "could create whole new generations of tele-communications and computer-related products that could underpin information-processing systems in the next century" (Reich 1985). This enhancement of American industrial competitiveness, it should be noted, would be achieved without infringing upon the power of corporate executives.

The Reagan administration also undertook to use military programs as a form of social policy. While seeking to slash domestic social spending, the Reaganites largely maintained existing funding levels for the health care, educational, and income maintenance programs administered by the Veterans Administration (VA). These are identical to domestic welfare programs in all respects but one: historically, they have been linked to conservative veterans' organizations rather than to liberal political forces. Thus, under the rubric of putting an end to waste, fraud, and abuse, the Reaganites cut the welfare programs that were politically beneficial to their opponents. At the same time, however, they were happy to continue funding programs that served their political friends. Veterans' groups, for their part, were more than willing to endorse the administration's military ventures and lobby on behalf of its foreign policies.

In addition to these uses of military and national security policy, the Reagan administration made a novel effort to employ as political weapons nonelectoral institutions linked to the nation's foreign policy apparatus. In particular, the administration sought to develop alliances with foreign governments which could help it to achieve political goals it was unable to realize through America's own governmental institutions.

The most important of these alliances was with the government of Japan. Through the fiscal policies it pursued during the President's first four years in office (which sharply increased the value of the dollar) as well as its staunch support of policies of free trade, the Reagan administration opened America's borders to a flood of foreign—most notably, Japanese—goods. At the same time, by pursuing policies that contributed to the maintenance of high real interest rates, the administration encouraged foreign investors—most notably, Japanese financial institutions—to purchase U.S. Treasury securities with the profits their nation's manufacturers made by selling goods in the United States. The effect of these policies was that during the early 1980s what might be called "autodollars" were recycled by Japanese banks, much as "petrodollars" were recycled by American banks in the 1970s. Japanese industrialists and bankers served as the equivalent of tax collectors for the Reagan administration. Although Americans, in their capacity as voters, demonstrated in 1984 that they opposed increased taxation as a means of financing the federal government's expenditures, as consumers they willingly—indeed, enthusiastically—handed over billions of dollars that were used for this purpose when they purchased Japanese goods. These auto-dollars, invested by Japanese financial institutions in U.S. government securities, financed the Reagan deficits. In essence, the administration's alliance with the Japanese permitted it simultaneously to slash tax rates and carry out its enormous and costly military buildup.

A second set of foreign alliances used by the Reagan administration involved Israel and Saudi Arabia. In the first case, the White House used the Israelis to channel arms to Iran. In the latter case, the Reaganites strongly supported the sale of advanced weapons to Saudi Arabia while the Saudi royal family helped to finance the Nicaraguan contra forces. In both instances, an alliance with a foreign government allowed the White House to circumvent the opposition of its foes in Congress.

The Democrats, of course, sought to block each of these Reaganite efforts to use the national security apparatus as a political weapon. First, congressional Democrats resisted the president's military buildup and ultimately succeeded in reducing the growth rate of military spending to a level considerably below that desired by the President. Liberal Democrats argued that by provoking an arms race with the Soviets, Reaganite military policies diminished, more than they enhanced, American security. Democrats asserted that the nation's security would be better served by arms control agreements and demanded that the administration pursue serious negotiations with the Soviet Union to achieve reductions in both nuclear and conventional forces. To this end, they gave their support to what became the largest peace movement since the end of the Vietnam War and to its key proposal—the nuclear freeze. During the course of the Reagan administration, arms control became a central issue for the Democrats not only because of its implications for the prevention of war but also because it promised to reduce Reagan's ability to derive political benefits from the military and at the same time, to make more money available for domestic programs. Ultimately, these efforts were successful. After the Iran-contra debacle, the President found that the only policy initiative he could successfully pursue was negotiations with the Soviet Union to eliminate intermediate-range missiles in Europe.

Second, liberal forces sought to turn veterans' programs to their own political advantage. In particular, they created organizations of Vietnam veterans separate from the leading veterans' groups—the American

Legion and the Veterans of Foreign Wars. Whereas traditional veterans' groups serve the conservative cause by extolling the American military and supporting a strong defense, the new Vietnam veterans' groups portray soldiers who served in Southeast Asia as victims of American military policy. Rather than glorify the military establishment, they emphasize the suffering it imposed upon even its own soldiers, for example, by exposing them to the toxic herbicide, Agent Orange. At the same time, these liberal veterans' groups sought to gain access to the resources of the VA, for example, by demanding that the VA fund programs for the treatment of "post-traumatic stress disorder," a condition they asserted was common among Vietnam veterans.

Finally, congressional Democrats worked to undo the administration's foreign alliances. The Iran-contra investigation put an end to the ability of the White House to channel arms and funds through Israel and Saudi Arabia. The weapon chosen by the Democrats to attack the administration's alliance with Japan was protectionism: if they could block Japanese imports, Democrats would, of course, protect the jobs of workers in a number of major American industries. At the same time, however, a reduction in the flow of Japanese goods into the United States also promised to reduce the capacity of the Reagan administration to rely upon the Japanese as revenue agents. Thus, protectionist legislation represented a serious threat to the administration's fiscal programs and to its capacity to finance its military buildup.

In 1985–86, the Reaganites responded to the threat protectionism posed to their entire program by undertaking, in concert with America's major trading partners, to reduce American interest rates, drive down the value of the dollar, and thus to stimulate American exports. Over the next two years, the dollar fell by nearly half against both the Japanese yen and German mark. However, the United States continued to run an enormous trade deficit. Moreover, the declining dollar threatened to revive domestic inflation, while at the same time America's foreign creditors were appalled to see the value of their holdings in U.S. dollar-denominated securities shrink. As the value of the dollar continued to fall, foreign private investors became reluctant to purchase additional U.S. Treasury notes and bonds, threatening the administration's capacity to finance its budget deficit. Therefore, in the Louvre Accords of 1987, America and the other leading industrial nations agreed to stabilize the value of the dollar and to seek to reduce the U.S. trade deficit by having the Japanese and Germans stimulate their own economies. To this end, the United States promised to raise its interest rates and reduce its budget deficits, thus strengthening the dollar. In return, the Germans and Japanese would reduce their interest rates and pursue expansionary fiscal policies. This would improve the U.S. trade deficit by increasing the market for American goods in Germany and Japan while reducing German and Japanese exports to the United States.

Following the Louvre accords, the United States did increase its interest rates; however, disagreements emerged over the extent to which the major participants fulfilled their other commitments. The Germans and Japanese asserted that the Americans had failed to reduce the U.S. budget deficit, whereas the Americans claimed that the other two—in particular the Germans—had not sufficiently stimulated their domestic economies.

In the fall of 1987, rising interest rates together with the failure to improve the U.S. trade deficit weakened the American stock market. In addition, investor confidence was shaken by the continuing conflict between the United States and its trading partners over their respective obligations under the Louvre accords. This conflict came to a head in mid-October when Treasury Secretary James Baker threatened to allow the dollar to resume its fall unless Germany cut its interest rates. Investors feared that a further decline in the value of the dollar would lead foreigners to abandon the American stock and bond markets. This fear sparked the stock market collapse of October 19, 1987. In the wake of this crash, both the administration and Congress came under pressure to reduce the budget deficit; however, the White House remained adamantly opposed to significant tax increases or cuts in military spending while congressional Democrats opposed any substantial reductions in domestic spending. Consequently, negotiation between the White House and Congress following the crash failed to produce major deficit reductions.

This entire sequence of political and economic events grew out of conflicts between the administration and its opponents over the President's military buildup and fiscal policies. The administration's political standing was certainly not helped by the stock market crash and its aftermath. However, it is notable that despite all that transpired, the President's opponents were not able to destroy the administration's alliance with Japan. Japanese goods continued to flood American markets, and Japanese financial institutions (including Japan's Central Bank) continued to finance the American budget deficit. Thus, its alliance with the government of Japan—an institution most certainly not responsible to American voters—enabled the Reagan administration to maintain its key fiscal and military policies in the face of enormous political opposition.

Social Combat

In addition to institutional combat, political forces in recent years have engaged in another mode of struggle outside the electoral arena. They have used such weapons as criminal prosecutions, domestic intelligence operations, and media exposés to attack organizations and social forces linked to their opponents while employing subsidies, regulation, and deregulation to strengthen organizations and social groups with which they are allied.

After entering the White House, President Reagan and his supporters systematically began to attack the organizational bases of their opponents. Reagan appointees in executive agencies sought to "defund the left"—for example, halting the flow of federal funds to legal services agencies that file class-action suits on behalf of the poor. In addition, the Internal Revenue Service threatened to withdraw the tax exemptions of nonprofit organizations that engaged in political activism. These advocacy groups sought to defend themselves and their constituents by conducting a major voter registration drive among the poor in 1984, and President Reagan's appointees on the board of the Legal Services Corporation responded by initiating an investigation to determine whether this constituted a violation of the rights of poor people to make their own decisions concerning whether or not to register and vote.

In a similar vein, the Reagan administration launched a systematic campaign of criminal investigations and prosecutions of Democratic mayors, legislators, and judges. Thus, Republican United States attorneys initiated investigations of corruption and wrongdoing in such Democratically controlled cities as Chicago, New York, Washington, D.C., and Atlanta. Several of these probes were aimed at prominent black elected officials including Marion Barry, Julian Bond, Andrew Young, and Harold Ford. Investigations by the Justice Department's Public Integrity Section targeted federal judges such as Frank Battisti of Ohio and Alcee Hastings of Florida.

The Reagan administration also sought to weaken organized labor— probably the most important organizational mainstay of the Democratic party. It encouraged employers to resist union demands, itself setting an example by destroying the Professional Air Traffic Controllers Organization (PATCO). In addition, the President appointed individuals hostile to organized labor to the National Labor Relations Board (NLRB), an agency formerly dominated by union sympathizers. Moreover, the fiscal and monetary policies that Reagan pursued in his first term drove up real interest rates and the value of the dollar, eroding the international competitiveness of the most heavily unionized sectors of the American economy, increasing unemployment in these sectors, and reducing labor's bargaining power.

Finally, the administration supported policies of deregulation which provided business firms with a strong incentive to seek to rid themselves of their unions. During the New Deal period, the federal government had established a regime of regulation over numerous sectors of the American economy—airlines, telecommunications, petroleum, coal, banking, securities, railroads, and trucking. Characteristically, regulation was used to restrict price competition among firms within regulated industries and to create barriers to the entry of new firms. To the extent that firms within such industries could pass added costs on to their customers without having to worry about being undersold by competitors, they lost an incentive to control their labor costs. Consequently, union-management relations in most regulated industries were less adversarial than cooperative in character: rather than fight one another over wages and work rules, unions and employers entered the political arena as allies to defend and extend the regulatory regime and to secure direct or indirect public subsidies for their industry.

During the late 1970s, an unlikely coalition of conservatives and consumer advocates, asserting that these accommodations served special interests at the expense of the public interest, secured a substantial measure of deregulation in these industries. Through deregulation, conservatives sought to get business to break its accommodations with organized labor, and consumer advocates sought to weaken the labor unions and business interests that were among their chief rivals for influence within the Democratic party. Conservatives have had more reason to be satisfied with the consequences of deregulation. Especially in airlines, telecommunications, and trucking, deregulation led to the emergence of nonunion firms that sought to undersell the established giants in their industry, and this in turn compelled those giants to demand "give-backs" from their unions so as to lower their labor costs. It is little wonder then that the Reagan administration sought to maintain the momentum of deregulation and thereby to undermine the economic and political power of organized labor.

The national news media also became targets of conservative political forces during the Reagan era. Conservatives regarded the media as among the chief institutions through which their opponents exercised political influence. The key conservative weapons in this campaign were libel suits filed against the national news media, the best known example of which was the Westmoreland suit against CBS in the early

1980s. These suits were encouraged and often financed by conservative organizations such as the Capitol Legal Foundation, the American Legal Foundation, and Accuracy in Media Inc. When journalists and liberals charged that the threat of such suits could discourage attacks on public officials, these conservative organizations were quite forthright in saying that this was precisely their intention. For example, in a December 11, 1984 letter to the *New York Times* on the Westmoreland case, Reed Irvine, head of Accuracy in Media, asserted that Westmoreland's legal bills were "footed by contributions by individuals and foundations who believe that CBS deserves to be chilled for the way it treated the general. . . . What is wrong with chilling any propensity of journalists to defame with reckless disregard of the truth?"

Finally, through its domestic spending restrictions, the Reagan administration attacked urban service bureaucracies and municipal governments—agencies controlled overwhelmingly by the Democrats. The domestic programs whose budgets suffered the deepest cuts were those that had provided local governments with funds and the capacity to dispense a large number of jobs such as the Comprehensive Employment and Training program. In addition, the administration's 1986 tax reform package reduced the deductibility of local sales taxes and restricted the ability of local governments to issue tax-free bonds. These changes in the tax code further diminished the resources available to the administration's foes.

In recent years, liberals as well as conservatives have sought to strengthen organizations and groups with which they are allied while seeking to undermine those upon which their opponents depend. Liberals, of course, rely upon the support of labor unions and civil rights and women's groups. In addition, among the most important instruments of social combat they have fashioned in recent decades are public interest groups—organizations devoted to political reform such as Common Cause and Ralph Nader's Public Interest Research Groups, environmental groups such as the Sierra Club and Friends of the Earth, and consumer and health groups such as the Center for Auto Safety and Action for Smoking and Health. Public interest groups and other liberal organizations have sustained themselves not only through membership contributions and foundation grants but also through grants from the federal government. The recipients of federal funding have included such liberal groups as the Reverend Jesse Jackson's Operation PUSH, the Women's Equity Action League and the Conservation Foundation.

One weapon that these organizations have used very effectively has been the exposé alleging wrongdoing on the part of their foes. The best-known of these was Ralph Nader's book *Unsafe at Any Speed,* which asserted that the American auto industry was indifferent to the safety defects of its vehicles. The nuclear power industry has been another major target of such exposés. Indeed, this industry has been brought to its knees by highly publicized changes of safety hazards in nuclear plants.

Litigation is an equally important weapon in the arsenal of liberal organizations. Most obviously through federal court suits, civil rights groups launched a successful assault on southern school systems, state and local governments, and political arrangements that they could not possibly have altered in the electoral arena. In a similar vein, environmental groups have used the courts to block the construction of highways, dams, and other public projects that not only threatened to damage the environment but would also have provided money and other resources to their political rivals. Similarly through the courts, women's groups have succeeded in overturning state laws that restricted abortion as well as statutes discriminating against women in the labor market.

In a number of ways, Democrats in Congress helped liberal interest groups make use of the federal courts for these purposes. For example, regulatory statutes enacted during the 1970s gave public interest groups legal standing—the right to bring suits—challenging the decisions of executive agencies in environmental cases. Congress also authorized public interest groups to serve as "private attorneys general" and to finance their activities by collecting legal fees and expenses from their opponents—generally business firms or government agencies—in such suits.

Politics in the Post-Reagan Era

Political analysts both in the press and in academe devote an enormous amount of attention to analyzing America's national elections. America, however, has now entered an era in which institutional combat has increased in importance relative to electoral competition. This is not to say that electoral outcomes can make no difference. If the Republicans were able to break the Democratic stranglehold on Congress or the Democrats were able more than occasionally to overcome the GOP's advantage in the presidential arena, the stalemate that has characterized American electoral politics for the past quarter-century would be broken, and the patterns of institutional combat we describe would become less prominent.

Even under present conditions, elections can have an impact. In 1980, the Republican capture of the White House and Senate and the party's unusually strong gains in House races enabled Ronald Reagan to secure the enactment of major changes in tax and budget policy. President Reagan's dominance of American government lasted for little more than a year, however, before the momentum of the Reagan Revolution was broken by institutional struggles.

The one election in the past two decades which gave a single party control over the presidency and both houses of Congress—the election of 1976—had little effect on prevailing patterns of American government. Although a member of their party occupied the White House, congressional Democrats had acquired such a stake in legislative power and had so little confidence in their ability to maintain control of the presidency that they refused to follow Carter's leadership and continued their attack on presidential power. More than a short-term break in the electoral deadlock that has endured now for nearly a generation would be required to shift the focus of American politics from institutional combat back to the electoral arena.

REFERENCES

Burnham, Walter Dean. 1982. *The Current Crisis in American Politics.* New York: Oxford University Press.

Chubb, John, and Paul Peterson. 1985. *The New Direction in American Politics.* Washington, D.C.: Brookings Institution.

Edsall, Thomas. 1984. *The New Politics of Inequality.* New York: W. W. Norton.

Ferejohn, John, and Morris Fiorina. 1985. "Incumbency and Realignment in Congressional Elections." In *The New Direction in American Politics,* edited by John Chubb and Paul Peterson. Washington, D.C.: Brookings Institution.

Fiorina, Morris. 1977. *Congress: Keystone of the Washington Establishment.* New Haven, Conn.: Yale University Press.

Huntington, Samuel P. 1973. "Congressional Response to the Twentieth Century." In *Congress and America's Future,* edited by David Truman. Englewood Cliffs, N.J.: Prentice-Hall.

Jacobson, Gary. 1985. "The Republican Advantage in Campaign Finance." In *The New Direction in American Politics,* edited by John Chubb and Paul Peterson. Washington, D.C.: Brookings Institution.

Milkis, Sidney. 1987. "The New Deal, Administrative Reform, and the Transcendence of Partisan Politics." *Administration and Society* 18 (January, 1987): 433–72.

Rabkin, Jeremy. 1988. *Public Law, Constitutional Disorder.* New York: Basic Books.

Reich, Robert. 1985. "High Tech, a Subsidiary of Pentagon Inc." *New York Times,* 29 May:A23.

Schlesinger, Arthur. 1973. *The Imperial Presidency.* Boston: Houghton Mifflin.

Shapiro, Martin. 1986. "The Supreme Court's Return to Economic Regulation." *Studies in American Political Development* 1: 91–142.

Shefter, Martin, and Benjamin Ginsberg. 1986. "Institutionalizing the Reagan Regime." In *Do Elections Matter?* edited by Benjamin Ginsberg and Alan Stone. Armonk, N.Y.: M. E. Sharpe.

Silverstein, Mark, and Benjamin Ginsberg. 1987. "The Supreme Court and the New Politics of Judicial Power." *Political Science Quarterly* 102: 371–88.

Stockman, David. 1986. *The Triumph of Politics.* New York: Harper and Row.

Wilson, James Q. 1984. "The Politics of Regulation." In *The Political Economy,* edited by Thomas Ferguson and Joel Rogers. Armonk, N.Y.: M. E. Sharpe.

13

The Ruptured Legacy: Presidential-Congressional Relations in Historical Perspective

DAVID BRADY and MORRIS P. FIORINA

Think back half a century to the waning days of the second Roosevelt administration. If an early-day Larry Berman had organized a book on the Roosevelt legacy, would he have commissioned chapters with phrases in their titles like "The Ruptured Legacy," "Meager Patrimony," and "A Postelectoral Politics?" Probably not. Even granting that hindsight and the perceptions of contemporaries often differ, FDR's political legacy probably seemed more impressive in 1939 than Reagan's does today.

The contrast is all the more interesting because the Republicans had more reason for optimism in 1980 than the Democrats had in 1932. After all, Roosevelt was only the second Democrat to win the presidency in 40 years. Moreover, it was obvious to all that the Democrats owed their victory to Republican association with the Great Depression, not to popular enthusiasm for bold new Democratic programs (the platform did not mention any); and, lest we forget, the new administration faced an economic catastrophe. As FDR prepared to take office in 1932, an objective observer would have found little reason to believe that the Roosevelt legacy would last a generation or more.

Although the 1980 election, too, was largely a negative evaluation of the incumbent administration (Abramson, Aldrich, and Rohde 1982), it gave rise to much talk of a turn to the right or resurgence of conservatism. Moreover, the Republicans had controlled the presidency for 16 of the preceding 28 years, during which time scholars and pundits churned out books and articles on emerging Republican majorities, the end of the fifth-party system, and the breakup of the New Deal coalition (Phillips 1969;

Burnham 1970; Sundquist 1983). Finally, whatever the country's objective problems in 1980, they were not so pressing as in 1932. In 1980, the Republicans looked at least as well positioned to bequeath an impressive patrimony as were the Democrats in 1932. What happened?

A common answer is that Reagan failed to translate his personal popularity into support for the Republican party. During his first year, Reagan's dealings with Congress called forth comparisons with FDR's "hundred days." However, the 1982 elections eliminated the working conservative majority in the House, the 1984 House gains were disappointing, and the 1986 elections took away control of the Senate. The denouement of the Reagan era found a beleaguered president facing hostile majorities in both houses of Congress. In contrast, Roosevelt was able to translate his personal popularity into support for the Democratic party sufficient to ensure Democratic control of Congress through the life of his administration. By effective leadership he was able to induce these partisan majorities to adopt programs that met with popular approval, which in turn brought support for the Democratic party sufficient to make it the nation's majority party for a generation. So goes the conventional wisdom.

The trouble with such explanations is that they merely restate the question. To say that Reagan's patrimony is meager because he failed to translate his personal popularity into Republican support is akin to saying that Mondale lost in 1984 because he did not get as many votes as Reagan. It is true, but it does not give us much to work with. Why was the Republican party in the 1980s unable to capitalize on the personal success of its charismatic leader?

We argue that the answer to this question hinges on presidential success in dealing with Congress. Presidents who are fortunate enough to have partisan control of Congress, who can persuade their copartisans to adopt their programs, and whose programs successfully address national problems will translate their personal popularity into an enduring legacy. If any of the three conditions fails—if there is divided government, if fellow party members in Congress refuse to follow, or if programs are poorly conceived or the problems they address intractable, then historians will write of meager patrimonies and ruptured legacies.

We have stated the three conditions in this order: (1) electoral, (2) leadership, (3) effectiveness, because that is their logical sequence. One cannot see whether policies work unless Congress adopts them. Whether Congress adopts them depends on many factors, among them the president's leadership abilities. Jimmy Carter to the contrary notwithstanding, we believe that partisan majorities in Congress are a major factor in leadership. Other things being equal, it is easier to appear skilled if there are more of your party than the opposition in the House and Senate (Bond and Fleisher in press). Thus, for us, the electoral consideration has logical priority; and as an empirical matter, we believe that structural differences in electoral conditions are a principal element in the differential success of the Roosevelt and Reagan administrations. The remainder of this chapter develops that argument. We will begin with a brief review of presidential-congressional relations during the Reagan administration, then proceed to a discussion of the changes in electoral conditions which underlie the differences in the Roosevelt and Reagan legacies.

Reagan and the Congress: From Mastery to Impotence

By most measures, the first year of the Reagan presidency was extremely successful. After observing passage of the Gramm-Latta amendments that mandated reductions in federal expenditures and the tax cut that reduced both individual and corporate rates, pundits pronounced that the presidency was not an impossible job, that our institutions were "not broken," and that the problems of the 1970s were only transitory, not systemic. What developments produced such an outpouring of optimism?[1]

In February 1981, the President submitted to Congress a budget that called for a reduction of over $100 billion in spending over three years. Most of the proposed reductions required changes in existing law, and the conventional wisdom held that Congress, especially the House, would subvert the President's initiative. Instead, the Congress considered and passed the budget under special reconciliation procedures, giving the President most of what he wanted. The special procedures were critical in allowing myriad controversies to be submerged in a few specific votes, thus enabling the President to appeal to the nation with a "share the sacrifice" message. For our argument, the important aspects of the reconciliation fight are the voting pattern in the House and the Senate's role as backstop.

The proposed budget cuts were formally sent to Congress on February 18, 1981. Within two weeks, the Senate Budget Committee reported reconciliation instructions to fourteen Senate committees, virtually rubber-stamping the President's proposal; and on April 2, the Senate passed (88–10) a concurrent resolution ordering committees to cut $37 billion from the fiscal 1982 budget. Thus, well before any action by the Democratic House, the Republican Senate had constrained the terms of the debate.

On April 9, the House Budget Committee under Jim Jones (Democrat, Oklahoma) endorsed an alternative budget that scaled back the recommended tax cut and spared many social programs from the knife. Democrat Phil Gramm from Texas and Republican Del Latta from Ohio countered with a substitute more to the President's liking. In terms of the severity of the cuts, Gramm-Latta was the most severe, with the Senate Budget Committee proposal next, and the House Budget Committee proposal least severe.

On May 6, the House overwhelmingly rejected two liberal substitutes to Gramm-Latta. The next day, the House substituted Gramm-Latta for the Budget Committee proposal by a vote of 253–176 and gave it final approval by an even larger margin. Only three Republicans cast any vote against the President on any of the four roll calls, and enough Democrats defected—principally Southern "boll weevils"—to provide the necessary majorities. The Senate approved its version of the budget cuts (78–20) on May 12 with only two Republicans defecting (Weicker of Connecticut and Humphrey of New Hampshire).

Without recounting the details, we note that the story of the 1981 tax cuts, approved one month later, was essentially the same as that of the budget cuts. These impressive legislative victories were achieved because the Senate constrained the House's alternatives and in both bodies Republicans overwhelmingly supported the President. These accomplishments along with the needed infusion of Democratic defections were in turn direct results of the 1980 elections. Despite academic analyses showing that the election was largely a rejection of the Carter administration rather than an endorsement of the conservative agenda, many politicians in both parties perceived it as the latter. For a few months after the elections, the most optimistic Republicans and most fearful Democrats believed that the 1980 elections were only the first step in a realigning sequence that would see the Republicans capture the House and terminate the Democrats' status as the nation's putative majority party. Under such conditions, Republican congressmen were understandably supportive of their party's leader, and even some Democrats viewed the election results as bestowing a certain legitimacy on Reagan administration proposals (Schick 1981). Presidents whose popularity is perceived to have electoral consequences have a stronger hand in dealing with Congress than presidents not so perceived. Thus, as with Johnson in 1964, Reagan's agenda met a better fate than those of presidents like Kennedy and Carter whose victories were narrow.

Moreover, above and beyond the breadth and depth of the presidential party electoral showing, the qualitative fact of control of Congress makes a major difference. A president such as Johnson who comes to office with control of both Houses of Congress will have much greater control of the policy agenda than a president such as Nixon whose party controls neither House. With control of the Senate, Reagan occupied an in-between position that enabled him to keep the Democratic House in a defensive, reactive posture, although it did not ensure the friendly reception Johnson administration proposals received.

The Reagan advantage was not lasting, of course. The President's legislative success reached its zenith with the passage of the reconciliation budget and the tax cuts. The recession that began in late 1981 diminished his popularity, a fact brought home to Representatives and Senators when they touched base with constituents during the Christmas recess. When Congress reconvened in 1982, a number of Republicans began to oppose the President on key issues. The defection of these "gypsy moth" Republicans and some moderate and conservative Democrats who had earlier supported Reagan marked the end of Reagan mastery of Congress. In 1982, the centerpiece of Reagan's state of the union message—a plan to return to the states some forty federal welfare programs—died in Congress.

The 1982 elections scuttled the notion that 1980 had been a realigning election. Although the Republicans retained control of the Senate, the declining economy cost them twenty-six seats in the House and loss of their "philosophical majority." Moreover, the defeated Republicans were supporters of the President rather than gypsy moths. The elections left the President with a House in opposition hands and with congressmen increasingly confident that they could oppose the President without suffering electoral costs. The 1984 elections reinforced this verdict. Despite the President's impressive personal victory, his party gained only twelve House seats.

With narrow control in the Senate, an out-of-control House, and increasingly independent congressmen, the 1983–86 period was one of stalemate. Presidential budgets were pronounced "dead on arrival." The President could not advance his conservative agenda, whereas the Democrats could not roll back defense expenditures and increase support for social programs. Bargaining and compromise replaced the more forceful leadership exhibited in 1981. The story of the 1986 tax reforms highlights the difference between the early and middle Reagan presidency.

In his 1984 state of the union message, President Reagan called for an historic simplification of the tax system. In response, Treasury Secretary

Donald Regan revealed Treasury I in November of 1984. The President's support was lukewarm, however, and in May of 1985 Reagan offered his own plan. Meanwhile, the House Ways and Means Committee drew up an alternative tax reform bill. A rule for this bill was defeated in the House 202–223, with 164 of 178 Republicans voting to reject the rule. Although Reagan was not enthusiastic about this bill, he went to Capitol Hill and appealed to House Republicans to keep the process alive. On December 17, the House reversed itself and sent the bill to the Senate. The President's personal appeal appears to have been less influential than his promise to veto any bill that came to him without substantial change (*Congressional Quarterly Almanac 1985*).

Senate Finance Chair Robert Packwood (Republican, Oregon) substituted his own bill for the House bill and began markup in early 1986. In May, after intense political maneuvering and a major reversal of positions, the Finance Committee unanimously offered a radical bill eliminating myriad deductions and establishing top rates of 27 percent for individuals and 33 percent for corporations. Thus, at this point, there were two different tax plans, both substantially different from the President's. Given its low rates, however, Reagan endorsed the Packwood plan.

In June 1986, the Senate passed the Packwood plan largely unchanged. During July and August, a conference committee met under intense circumstances and hammered out the major differences in the two chambers' bills. During this period, Dan Rostenkowski (Democrat, Illinois) and Packwood were the leading players. Offers passed back and forth with the two chairmen negotiating privately and then taking their tentative deals back to their colleagues for approval. The President's role in these crucial negotiations was minimal.

In late September, the House and Senate approved the conference report, and on October 22, 1986, President Reagan signed the bill into law. Despite the ceremony, however, the President was approving a legislative accomplishment in which he was only one of several important players. In contrast to the 1982 budget fight, his role was limited. To get a bill at all required major compromise not only with House Democrats, but with House and Senate Republicans as well; and in addition to the greater necessity for bargaining and compromise, the President's major contribution was a negative one: the threat to veto any bill outside the bounds of what was acceptable to House Republicans.

Even the 1986 tax fight now looks like a major administration success compared with the presidential-congressional relations of 1987–88. The 1986 elections deprived the Republicans of control of the Senate. This electoral loss, compounded by the President's lame-duck status and the fallout from the Iran-contra scandal, rendered presidential leadership something that existed only in memory. In the 100th Congress, Democrats were able to force reductions in defense spending and even to override presidential vetoes as in the case of the Civil Rights Restoration Act and highway project and sewage treatment spending. In short, the President's final two years saw a loss of control of the policy agenda and a loss of influence over the formation of policies on the agenda.

In recounting the decline of President Reagan's ability to lead Congress, we have emphasized the elections of the 1980s. It is instructive to contrast the electoral fate of Reagan's party with that of Roosevelt's in the 1930s. When FDR took office in 1933, almost a quarter of the work force was unemployed. Conditions improved somewhat by 1934, and in that election the Democrats gained nine seats—the only midterm since the Civil War in which the President's party gained seats. By 1936, unemployment had dropped to about three-quarters of its 1932 level, and per capita income was up by one-third. (The budget deficit had more than doubled but from a small base.) Roosevelt won a smashing victory, and the Democrats gained still more seats in Congress.

When Ronald Reagan became President, unemployment stood at a bit less than 8 percent, whereas the inflation rate was at 13.5 percent. Following the 1981–82 recession, conditions improved markedly. By the 1984 election, unemployment was a hair lower than in 1980, but the inflation rate was only one-third as high as four years previously, and per capita income was up by one-third. On the negative side, the budget deficit had more than doubled from a level already a matter of some concern. In the election, Ronald Reagan was overwhelmingly reelected, but his copartisans in congressional races did not fare nearly so well. Compared with FDR, Reagan had no coattails in 1984 (Jacobson 1985). Why was Roosevelt able to transform personal popularity and economic improvements into solid electoral majorities, whereas Reagan was not? Both were personally popular—in fact, by Gallup's reckoning Reagan's popularity level was slightly higher than FDR's (Gallup Poll 1972). Each could point to significant economic gains during his term of office.

One frequently offered answer is that Americans liked Reagan personally but opposed his policies. Poll data lend some support to this claim, and it may indeed be part of the answer (Fiorina 1988b). In general, however, citizen views on policy issues are weakly held (Converse 1964), and citizens may ratify after the fact what they opposed before hand (Key 1966). Consider the case of Margaret Thatcher's Conservative party in Britain. The Thatcher program is far more conservative than British public opinion, but her government has been returned to office twice while hewing to its right-wing platform (Crewe and Searing 1988). One explanation (beyond the unattractiveness of the opposition) is that citizens view a party's promises in the context of its past performance (Fiorina 1981). In this respect, Reagan looks similar to FDR: the 1984 presidential vote was strongly influenced by economic factors (Kiewiet and Rivers 1985). But the congressional vote was not.

Reagan's popularity and performance did not translate into Republican congressional majorities because of major changes in the pattern of postwar congressional elections. The next section of this chapter describes and discusses these in depth, but by way of introduction we highlight some historical patterns in American national elections.

The extent of the difference between pre- and post-World War II electoral history is not widely recognized. Dwight Eisenhower was reelected president in 1956 without a Republican majority in either House of Congress. This had occurred only *once* before in American history: in 1848 when Zachary Taylor (Whig) narrowly won the presidency because the Free Soil candidate (former President Martin Van Buren) siphoned off Democratic presidential votes while leaving congressional races largely unaffected.[2] An event that occurred once in the first forty presidential elections in our history has occurred four times (1956, 1968, 1972, 1988) in the past nine elections.

Historically, House midterm elections have correctly forecast the victorious party in the next presidential election. Between 1928 and 1944, only twice did the party winning a majority of the House at the midterm election fail to win the next presidential election.[3] Since World War II, eight of ten off-year elections did not presage the presidential results: Democrats won House majorities in 1950, 1954, 1966, 1970, 1978, 1982, and 1986, but the Republicans won the ensuing presidential elections; whereas the Republicans carried the House in 1946, but Truman upset Dewey in 1948.

Thus, there are major differences in the gross features of pre- and postwar American national elections. Franklin Roosevelt was elected in 1932 with Democratic majorities in both Houses of Congress as had been almost invariably the case until then. The Democrats retained these majorities uninterrupted until 1946. Undivided control of national institutions was crucial for the Democratic party's success in legislating the program known as the New Deal. New Deal legislation was passed by partisan majorities, and because the presidential and congressional votes moved together, elections that maintained those majorities were plausibly interpreted as ratifying the New Deal program and providing a mandate for its extension.

The preceding pattern typifies each of the periods in American political history in which significant policy change occurred. The two Republican realignments of the nineteenth century each gave the party fourteen consecutive years of undivided control (1860–74, 1896–1910). The policy shifts associated with these periods were enacted by partisan majorities early in the realignment phases and ratified by electoral victories in subsequent years (Brady 1988).

The crucial difference between Roosevelt and all postwar presidents is that congressional and presidential elections no longer move in tandem. Congressmen now inhabit their own electoral universes. They have less to gain from presidential success and less to fear from presidential failure than they did fifty years ago. Consequently, Democratic presidents cannot take for granted the support of their copartisans; and even more strikingly, popular Republican presidents are denied the sustained institutional control necessary for legislative success. Of course, such control is no guarantee of success—full implementation of the Reagan program might have brought calamity on the country, thereby leaving a negative legacy rather than a weak one. Nevertheless, in the present state of electoral politics, presidents are not given the opportunity to be FDRs.

The Decoupling of Presidential-Congressional Electoral Fates

As noted, divided government is much more common during the contemporary period than it was during earlier times in our political history;[4] moreover, prior to the contemporary period, divided government rarely resulted from a president's failure to carry a majority of the House for his party. Table 13.1 presents one indicator of the extent to which contemporary conditions differ from earlier ones.

At the turn of the century, it was a rarity for a congressional district to register a majority for the presidential candidate of one party and the House candidate of the other. In 1900, for example, only eleven districts did so. The number of such split districts rose in the early twentieth century but remained well below one-fifth of all districts through the New Deal. Since World War II, however, split districts have averaged well over one-quarter of all districts; and post-1964, they have averaged over one-third. Obviously, such split outcomes confuse electoral verdicts: the district has elected a representative of one party, but that same district has voted for the presidential candidate of the opposition. If that presidential candidate is victorious, how much support does the representative owe him? Conversely, if the presidential candidate is defeated, how

TABLE 13.1 Congressional Districts Carried by House
and Presidential Candidates of Different Parties

Year	Percentage
1900	3
1908	7
1916	11
1924	12
1932	14
1940	15
1948	21
1952	19
1956	30
1960	26
1964	33
1968	32
1972	44
1976	29
1980	34
1984	44

Source: Ornstein, Mann, and Malbin (1989).

much independence of his own party's president is prudent? In either case, the electoral verdict is more ambiguous than in districts that support the same party's presidential and congressional candidates.

A great deal of work has gone into attempts to explain the kind of change evident in Table 13.1. In the late nineteenth century, party ties were much stronger than in the twentieth century. Among intellectuals and political elites, the doctrine of party government received a friendlier reception than today (Ranney 1962), and parties structured campaigns and organized the mass public to a much greater degree than in the twentieth century. In addition, ballot forms and voting methods buttressed party regularity (Rusk 1970). Before the adoption of the Australian ballot around the turn of the century, voting was generally semipublic in that voters took their ballots, often color coded, from the parties. Under such conditions, it was more difficult, both physically and psychologically, to split one's ticket.

Progressive era assaults on parties did some damage, but as Table 13.1 suggests, the greater break with the past occurred during the postwar era, especially after 1964. Much more fine-grained research (Alford and Brady 1988) indicates that major changes in House elections occurred from the late 1950s to the mid-1960s. Earlier indications of such changes have already stimulated a huge literature on the decline of competition for congressional seats owing to the increase in the incumbency advantage in House elections. We will not attempt to review this literature here (see Beth 1981–82; 1984); but we will note briefly some of the more important findings.

Incumbents have always fared better than challengers; after all, they are proven winners, and on average they come from districts favorable to their party (Alford and Brady 1988). However, by the 1970s, incumbents' margins could be shown to have increased about 5 percent over their level in the 1950s (Jacobson 1987). Reelection rates have risen almost 4 percent—from about 91 percent over the 1946–64 period to about 95 percent in 1966–86. The 1986 and 1988 elections saw all-time high reelection rates of 98 percent, with only six incumbents losing in each case.

The reasons for the enhanced electoral prospects of congressional incumbents are many, but they can be categorized under the twin headings of the decline of party and the increase in the personal vote. As subjective party affiliations declined, voters became more likely to split their tickets, picking and choosing among the candidates for various offices. However, even among party identifiers, president-House and president-Senate ticket splitting has increased. The reason is that American voters have increasingly come to vote for their representatives as persons and not as the embodiment of political parties. In most of the world, the bulk of the votes cast are not personal; our counterparts in Europe vote largely on the basis of party, social class, religious and ethnic affiliations, with the personal qualities of the candidates much less important than such general factors. Even in the United States, party identification remains the single most important correlate of individual voting decisions. However, over the course of the past generation, an increasing part of the American electorate has come to support congressional candidates on the basis of the personal records, characteristics, and qualities of those candidates. "Vote for the person, not the party." Today's citizens can scarcely imagine any other way to vote.

The qualities people incorporate in their congressional voting decisions are numerous. They appear to give somewhat greater weight to issues than they did thirty years ago; but these are the issue stands of the individual candidates, not the positions of the national party or the performance of the incumbent administration. A generation ago, one could statistically account for the presidential and House vote largely on the basis of the same considerations: party, the state of the economy, the country's position in the world, and so forth. Today, such factors remain important predictors of the presidential vote, but they are less accurate predictors of the House vote (Fiorina 1981, chaps. 2, 8).

Even the individually tailored issue positions of the candidates are not the principal determinants of voting in House elections. The candidates' personal characteristics are extremely important, and voters today are much more likely to evaluate House candidates on the basis of service to constituents and to the larger district than they were a generation ago (Fiorina 1982). Some candidates are able to parlay effective constituency service into a cushion of nonpartisan, nonideological support which enables them to survive in districts not otherwise thought congenial to their party affiliation or ideological leanings. Such representatives are reluctant to take chances, however, and cannot be counted on when the wishes of presidents and constituents seriously diverge. Moreover, most politicians are naturally risk averse, and today's politicians, at least, seem to value their autonomy more than those in earlier eras. Thus, even those who could be elected largely on partisan grounds feel more comfortable with a large personal vote that buffers them from national swings and provides them with a degree of independence in their political careers.

In sum, members who carefully tailor their issue stands to their districts, who emphasize constituency service, and who personally raise large war chests to publicize their positions and services are not good candidates for party regularity and presidential support. They are free agents to a much greater degree than the congressmen of the Roosevelt era or even of the Eisenhower era.

One important consequence of these electoral changes is that modern presidents have shorter coattails than their predecessors. Political commentators remark that Reagan in 1984 (sixteen seats) and Nixon in 1972 (twelve seats) had short coattails, for despite their impressive reelections, few Republican House candidates were carried into office. On the other hand, much was made of Reagan's coattails in 1980 (thirty-three seats) even though they were relatively modest by historical standards: 90 percent of the unindicted House Democratic incumbents who ran in 1980 survived the Reagan landslide.

Presidential coattails have indeed weakened during the modern era, but the picture is more complicated than generally recognized. As Jacobson (1985) notes, popular political commentary usually refers to coattails in terms of congressional seats. Thus, LBJ is said to have had long coattails in 1964, but not Nixon in 1972; and Reagan is said to have had longer coattails in 1980 than in 1984. Academic political scientists, more prone to split hairs, use the concept in a more restricted fashion. We can schematically represent the relationship between presidential vote and House seats as follows:

In contrast to more popular treatments that make a direct jump from presidential vote to House seats, political scientists break down the relationship into the effect of the presidential vote on the House vote (coattails) and the translation of the House vote into House seats (the swing ratio). The distinction is an important one, and changes in both parts of the relationship between presidential vote and House seats have occurred in the modern era.

In the discussion up to now we have been detailing the weakening of the relationship between the presidential and congressional *votes*. With citizens voting on the basis of the personal records and characteristics of the candidates, the vote across different offices is less closely associated than in earlier eras. To be precise, Ferejohn and Calvert (1984) estimate the responsiveness of the House vote to changes in the presidential vote to be 0.95 in the late nineteenth century; that is, when a party's presidential vote increased 1 percent, its House vote would increase nearly the same. After slipping in the Progressive era, the association tightened again to about 0.8 during the New Deal; every percent increase in the vote for Roosevelt was associated with four-fifths of a percent increase in the vote for Democratic House candidates. In the early postwar period, the relationship slipped to under 0.4, and in the post-1964 period it became 0.2–0.3. Thus, Reagan's coattails were approximately one-third as large as Roosevelt's not necessarily because of any failure on his part, but because congressional elections became so much more personalized over the past half-century.

The factors producing the decline in coattails, moreover, also contributed to a decline in the *impact* of such coattails when they occurred. As congressional incumbents expanded their margins, fewer and fewer districts fell into the highly competitive category in which the challenger had a good shot at defeating the incumbent if a swing against the incumbent's party occurred.[5] Thus, if an incumbent had won with 53 percent in the preceding election and the opposing party's president had a 4 percent coattail or if there were a 4 percent reaction against poor economic conditions during one's own administration, the challenging party could win the seat. However, if such marginal incumbents were able to increase their margins by 5 percent to 58 percent, they would be able to ride out such unfavorable coattails or midterm reactions.

The effect of the reduction in the number of marginal districts shows up in the decline of a measure political scientists call the swing ratio. If on average, a 1 percent gain in a party's *congressional* vote leads to a 3 percent gain in a party's seats, the swing ratio is 3. Around-the-world swing ratios in single-member district systems are invariably greater than 1 : 1 and usually fall in the range of 2 : 1–4 : 1. Thus, a swing ratio in excess of 3 during the New Deal period meant that an FDR coattail effect on the order of 3 percent of the vote would yield a Democratic gain in House seats of about 10 percent. In contrast, a swing ratio of 1.4 during the post-1964 period means that a Reagan coattail effect of 3 percent of the vote would yield a Republican gain in House seats of about 4 percent. The electoral machinery did not treat FDR and Reagan equally.[6]

The swing ratio has undergone important changes in the postwar period, especially after 1964. These changes have been detailed elsewhere (Ansolabehere, Brady, and Fiorina 1988), so we will summarize them more briefly here. From a level greater than 3 during the New Deal period (Ferejohn and Calvert 1984), the swing ratio dropped to 2.25 in the early postwar period, then to about 1.4 in the contemporary period. The consequences of this decline are suggested by the hypothetical rerunning of history presented in Table 13.2.

The first column of the table shows the actual number of House seats

TABLE 13.2 Republican Seats in the House

Year	N	N Predicted by 1966–86 Equation	N Predicted by 1946–64 Equation
1966	187	182	223[a]
1968	192	191	238[a]
1970	180	194	166
1972	192	182	223[a]
1974	144	142	157
1976	143	158	185
1978	158	174	191
1980	192	193	241[a]
1982	166	170	203
1984	182	188	233[a]
1986	177	171	206

[a] Predicted Republican majority.

won by the Republicans in the contemporary period. The second column shows the number they are forecast to have won if the relationship between seats and votes that held from 1948–64 had persisted until the present. As shown, under the earlier conditions, the Republicans would have won the House in 1966, 1968, 1972, 1980, and 1984. Such exercises are speculative—they implicitly assume "all else staying the same." Speculative or not, Table 13.2 strongly suggests that the electoral system did not treat Reagan as well as Lyndon Johnson, let alone as well as Roosevelt. As presently constituted, the national election system is clearly less kind to Republican than to Democratic presidents. The Republicans' predicament does not reflect any conscious action or conspiracy on the part of the Democrats. Rather, a number of the changes we have discussed were concentrated in the mid-1960s and were pioneered by Democratic House incumbents. With a heavy majority in the House at that time, the Democratic party achieved an advantage they have not since relinquished.[7]

By combining the two elements of our discussion, we can make an overall comparison of presidential-congressional electoral linkages in the New Deal and Reagan eras:

$$
\begin{array}{c}
\text{New Deal era} = 0.81 \\
\text{Reagan years} \;\; = 0.30 \\
\text{presidential vote} \cdots\cdots\cdots\cdots \rightarrow \;\; \text{House vote} \\
\text{New Deal era} = 3.2 \\
\text{Reagan years} \;\; = 1.4 \\
\text{House seats}
\end{array}
$$

By multiplying the two links, we see that a 1 percent increase in the *presidential* vote during the New Deal era translated into a 2.5 percent gain in House *seats,* whereas a similar increase during the contemporary era corresponds to only a 0.5 percent gain.

Finally, just as congressmen of the president's party no longer have much to gain or fear from the effects of his coattails, they similarly have less to fear from popular dissatisfaction with his performance at midterm time. In recent elections, the effects of national economic conditions and judgments of presidential performance have not had much of a direct effect on the electoral fortunes of congressmen (Ragsdale 1980; Radcliff 1988). With an unpopular and politically weak president, the Democrats lost fifty-six seats and control of the House in the midterm of 1946 but only fifteen seats in 1978. The incentive for congressional Democrats to give the president a hand obviously was greater in the late 1940s. Similarly, with a "charismatic" president presiding over an economic recession, the Republicans lost forty-nine seats in 1958 but only twenty-six in 1982. Other things being equal, the electoral incentive of House Republicans to help Eisenhower was greater than their incentive to help Reagan.

The consequence of the disengagement of presidential and congressional fates is to make congressmen less sensitive to the factors that create national swings, among them presidential performance in its many manifestations. To paraphrase Benjamin Franklin, the electoral linkage between president and Congress formerly gave party members an incentive to "hang together, lest they all hang separately." Now, why should they hang together when they can go their separate ways without penalty?

Throughout the preceding discussion we have concentrated on the relationship between presidential and House elections because the House has historically been the engine of policy change (Brady 1988). Without going into great detail, we simply note that Senate elections too have become less partisan affairs and much more a matter of the records and characteristics of the individual candidates. Issues count for more and constituency service for less than in House contests, especially in highly competitive large-state elections, but we are still referring to individually tailored positions, not associations with presidents and national conditions. Like House contests, Senate contests too have become more individualized and idiosyncratic; senators too realize that their fates depend more on their personal votes and less on the fates of their presidents.

This characterization of Senate elections seemingly conflicts with the results in 1980 and 1986. Republican capture of the Senate in 1980 was a momentous event that fueled the talk of electoral realignment. Similarly, loss of the Senate in 1986 led many to pronounce the end of the Reagan Revolution. Both judgments were greatly exaggerated. With less than 48 percent of the aggregate vote in 1980, Republicans purportedly achieved an historic victory. With more than 49 percent of the aggregate vote in 1986, they purportedly suffered an historic defeat. Senate contests differ wildly in the number of people voting; and unlike House races, most are competitive so that small influences—National Conservative Political Action Committee (NCPAC), Reagan coattails, the weather—can have large consequences. Both in 1980 and 1986 Senate elections were important in shaping the course of presidential-congressional relations, but they do not contradict the argument we have advanced; rather, they stand testimony to the triumph of perception over reality.[8]

Recapitulation

Legacies have both policy and political aspects to them. By driving up the budget deficit Reagan certainly constrained the alternatives open to his successors. By cutting taxes and raising defense spending to new levels, he greatly altered the status quo. Ronald Reagan made a difference: for better or worse, he left a legacy of sorts. Yet a great president leaves an enduring legacy by dealing successfully with national and international problems while in office. This success in turn creates a long-term base of support for his party and his partisan successors in the office; this political legacy preserves and extends the policy legacy (Skowronek 1988).

Sometimes problems are intractable. Perhaps the Iran hostage crisis could have been avoided; but once under way, it is not clear how Carter could have turned it into a foreign policy success. Sometimes policy choices are poor ones, and the president is perceived to have failed: Lyndon Johnson/Vietnam is a possible example. Whether from sheer bad luck or simple bad judgment, presidents can fail.

The potential for effectiveness is enhanced, however, when presidents can guide their policies through the congressional process without destroying their cohesion and/or experiencing delays that exacerbate the problems that the policies are designed to redress. Leadership (or charisma, skill, or whatever) is no guarantee of success, however, as when a strong president implements an unwise policy. Leadership skills combined with good judgment and good fortune are the ingredients of an enduring legacy.

We tend to believe that the contribution of charisma, interpersonal skill, and other personal factors to leadership is overrated. Certainly such things matter. Probably Reagan would have done better in Carter's place and Carter worse in Reagan's; but a dependable following in Congress is worth a great deal, and it depends less on the president's personal skills than it does on a sense of shared fate. We tend to forget that FDR was not such a giant in foresight as in hindsight. Walter Lippmann dismissed candidate Roosevelt as "an amiable man" of no particular consequence, and Oliver Wendell Holmes described him as "second-rate mind, first-rate temperament" (in that order). Good judgment, good luck, and good solid Democratic majorities willing to follow were important ingredients in the Roosevelt legacy.

In the contemporary era, presidents can have good luck and good judgment. They may be highly skilled personally. Yet they are not nearly so likely to have the cooperative congressional majorities usually enjoyed by past presidents. The present situation is particularly acute for Republican presidents who can carry forty-nine states and still lose the House. However, even Democratic presidents are not so well situated as previously. In 1976, Jimmy Carter ran behind 270 of his copartisans in the House; consequently, few of them felt much sense of obligation to him. The conditions that currently prevail in the electoral arena are not conducive to the exercise of leadership, let alone to the development of legacies.

NOTES

1. The following overview of presidential-congressional relations is drawn from various issues of the *Congressional Quarterly Almanac,* supplemented, where noted, by other more specific sources.

2. The Free Soilers ran few congressional candidates. Thus, the Democratic congressional vote was not as affected as the presidential vote.

3. The two exceptions were 1874 and 1878. Actually, inasmuch as Tilden won the popular vote, the 1874 outcome did forecast the *popular* winner of the Hayes-Tilden election.

4. Prior to the postwar era, the only other period in which government was so frequently divided was in 1874–96. During this time, one party controlled both chambers of Congress and the presidency only in 1880–82, 1888–90 (Republican) and 1892–94 (Democratic). To appreciate the uniqueness of this era, recall that it begins with the readmission of the South to the Union and the disputed Hayes-Tilden election and proceeds to three consecutive presidential elections in which the margin of victory was less than 1 percent of the total vote.

5. The classic discussion is Mayhew (1974). During the postwar period, the average proportion of House districts won by less than 55 percent of the vote has declined significantly.

6. Reagan's coattails in 1984 probably were not so weak as popular commentary based on seat gains suggests. Between 1978 and 1980, the Republican House vote increased 3.2 percent compared with a *larger* increase of 3.8 percent between 1982 and 1984. Even considering that the 1982 base was 1.8 percent lower than the 1978 base, these figures suggest that the disappointing Republican seat gain in 1984 owed at least as much to the swing ratio as to a lack of coattails.

7. It should be emphasized that the Republicans have not outpolled the Democrats in the aggregate vote for Congress since 1952. Thus, there is no *prima facie* case that the electoral system is biased against them. What we are saying is that relative to past history, Republican vote gains have not been rewarded with commensurate gains in seats. For a full discussion of bias in the American electoral system see King and Gelman (1989).

8. This point is developed at greater length in Fiorina (1988a).

REFERENCES

Abramson, Paul R., John H. Aldrich, and David W. Rohde. 1982. *Change and Continuity in the 1980 Elections.* Washington, D.C.: Congressional Quarterly Press.

Alford, John, and David W. Brady. 1988. "Partisan and Incumbent Advantage in U.S. House Elections 1846–1986." Working Paper II, Center for the Study of Institutions and Values, Rice University.

Ansolabehere, Stephen, David W. Brady, and Morris P. Fiorina. 1989. "The Marginals Never Vanished?" Research Paper 970, Graduate School of Business, Stanford University.

Beth, Richard S. 1981–82. "Incumbency Advantage and Incumbency Resources: Recent Articles." *Congress and the Presidency* 9: 119–136.

———. 1984. "Recent Research on 'Incumbency Advantage' in House Elections: Part II." *Congress and the Presidency* 11: 211–224.

Bond, Jon R., and Richard Fleisher, *The President in the Legislative Arena.* Chicago: University of Chicago Press, Forthcoming.

Brady, David W. 1988. *Critical Elections and Congressional Policy-Making.* Stanford, Calif.: Stanford University Press.

Burnham, Walter Dean. 1970. *Critical Elections and the Mainsprings of American Politics.* New York: W. W. Norton.

Congressional Quarterly Almanac, 1986. Washington, D.C.: Congressional Quarterly, Inc.

Converse, Philip E. 1964. "The Nature of Belief Systems in Mass Publics." In *Ideology and Discontent,* edited by David E. Apter. New York: Free Press.

Crewe, Ivor, and Donald D. Searing. 1988. "Mrs. Thatcher's Crusade: Conservatism in Britain, 1972–1986." In *The Resurgence of Conservatism in Anglo-American Democracies,* edited by Barry Cooper, Allan Kornberg, and William Mishler. Durham, N.C.: Duke University Press.

Ferejohn, John A., and Randall L. Calvert. 1984. "Presidential Coattails in Historical Perspective," *American Journal of Political Science* 28: 127–46.

Fiorina, Morris P. 1981. *Retrospective Voting in American National Elections.* New Haven, Conn.: Yale University Press.

———. 1982. "Congressmen and Their Constituencies: 1958 and 1978." In *Proceedings of the Thomas P. O'Neill Jr. Symposium on the U.S. Congress,* edited by Dennis Hale. Boston: Eusey Press.

———. 1988a. "The Presidency and Congress." In *The Presidency and the Political System,* 2d ed., edited by Michael Nelson. Washington, D.C.: Congressional Quarterly Press.

———. 1988b. "The Reagan Years: Turning to the Right or Groping for the Middle." In *The Resurgence of Conservatism in Anglo-American Democracies,* edited by Barry Cooper, Allan Kornberg, and William Mishler, 430–460. Durham, N.C.: Duke University Press.

Gallup Poll. 1972. *Public Opinion: 1935–1971.* New York: Random House.

Jacobson, Gary C. 1985. "Politics after a Landslide Without Coattails." In *The Elections of 1984,* edited by Michael Nelson. Washington, D.C.: Congressional Quarterly Press.

————. 1987. "The Marginals Never Vanished." *American Journal of Political Science* 31: 126–41.

Key, V. O. Jr. 1966. *The Responsible Electorate.* New York: Vintage.

Kiewiet, D. Roderick, and Douglas Rivers. 1985. "The Economic Basis of Reagan's Appeal." In *The New Direction in American Politics*, edited by John E. Chubb and Paul Peterson. Washington, D.C.: Brookings Institution.

King, Gary, and Andrew Gelman. 1989. "Systemic Consequences of Incumbency Advantage in U.S. House Elections." Occasional Paper 88-9. Center for American Political Studies, Harvard University.

Mayhew, David R. 1974. "Congressional Elections: The Case of the Vanishing Marginals." *Polity* 6: 295–317.

Ornstein, Norman J., Thomas E. Mann, and Michael J. Malbin. 1989. *Vital Statistics on Congress, 1987–88 Edition.* Washington, D.C.: Congressional Quarterly Press.

Phillips, Kevin P. 1969. *The Emerging Republican Majority.* New Rochelle, N.Y.: Arlington House.

Radcliff, Benjamin. 1988. "Solving a Puzzle: Aggregate Analysis and Economic Voting Revisited." *Journal of Politics* 50: 440–58.

Ragsdale, Lyn. 1980. "The Fiction of Congressional Elections as Presidential Events." *American Politics Quarterly* 8: 375–98.

Ranney, Austin. 1962. *The Doctrine of Responsible Party Government.* Urbana: University of Illinois Press.

Rusk, Jerrold G. 1970. "The Effects of the Australian Ballot Reform on Split Ticket Voting, 1876–1908." *American Political Science Review* 64: 1220–38.

Schick, Allan. 1981. *Reconciliation and the Congressional Budget Process.* Washington, D.C.: American Enterprise Institute.

Skowronek, Stephen. 1988. "Presidential Leadership in Political Time." In *The Presidency and the Political System*, 2d ed., edited by Michael Nelson. Washington, D.C.: Congressional Quarterly Press.

Sundquist, James L. 1983. *Dynamics of the Party System.* Washington, D.C.: Brookings Institution.

14

Meager Patrimony: The Reagan Era and Republican Representation in Congress

GARY C. JACOBSON

When Ronald Reagan relinquished the White House in January 1989 to his chosen Republican successor George Bush, the Democrats remained in firm control of both houses of Congress, bringing into question both the depth and permanence of Reagan's political legacy. After the 1988 elections, Republicans held 175 House seats—five fewer than their postwar average of 180. The dream of a Republican majority, revived when the 1980 elections raised Republican House membership from 159 to 192, the most since Watergate, was once again deferred to the indefinite future. The 1980 election turned out to be the high point; in the five elections with Reagan either heading the ticket or in the White House, Republicans elected an average of 179 representatives, one seat fewer than their postwar mean. For all of its immediate effects on Republican representation in the House, the Reagan era might never have happened.

The Senate's story is different, but with the present chapter only marginally happier for Republicans. They took the Senate in 1980, held onto it through two more elections, then lost it in 1986 when Democrats picked up eight seats despite a healthy economy and widespread popular approval of Reagan's performance.[1] Republicans now hold forty-five Senate seats, one more than their postwar average. They remain within striking distance of a majority—although prospects for 1990 remain slender (Elving 1988)—which was not the case in the two decades preceding the Reagan presidency. Republicans did considerably better in Senate than in House elections during the 1980s, and this requires some explanation; but so does their inability to hold the Senate despite some notable advantages, including Ronald Reagan's high level of popularity on election day 1986.[2]

Democratic control of Congress precludes further progress on Reagan's agenda—building up the military (including the Strategic Defense Initiative—SDI), cutting domestic programs, deregulating the economy, enacting conservative social policies, supporting anti-Marxist guerrillas—and threatens to reverse victories already won. President Bush and his Republican allies will be reduced to fighting rear-guard skirmishes against restoration of Democratic priorities. If, in the end, only budget deficits protect most of Reagan's handiwork, his legislative achievements, although perhaps safe for a time, are unlikely to leave the kind of indelible imprint on the American polity as was left by the New Deal. The Republicans' failure to secure much ground in Congress during the Reagan era thus remains a major threat to the Reagan imprint. It also remains a puzzle. Why have congressional Republicans benefited so little from Reagan's political ascendancy? What does this failure tell us about contemporary electoral politics? These are the questions I shall address in this chapter.

The Republican Opportunity

The first point to establish is that this situation is more than a trivial puzzle with an easy solution. If, after all, Ronald Reagan's electoral triumphs and political victories were strictly personal, then there was no reason to expect other Republicans to have profited from them. Certainly Reagan, with his acknowledged talent for projecting an attractive public persona, has always been more popular than his programs or ideological principles; and we have little evidence that the electorate has grown more conservative over the past decade. On a host of issues, the opposite is true (Fiorina 1988; Miller 1987; Ferguson and Rogers 1985).

Still, it would be a mistake to conclude from this that Reagan's successes were merely personal. In many respects, the Republican party is in much better shape now than it was before 1980. For example, a majority of citizens consider Republicans better able than the Democrats to ensure peace and prosperity. Republicans get higher marks on handling other issues as well, as we shall see. More importantly, an increased proportion of voters now consider themselves Republicans. Whether or not "realignment" is the proper term for what has happened (Fiorina 1988), there are unmistakable signs of a durable shift to the Republican party among party identifiers. It remains the minority party, but it has moved much loser to parity with the Democrats.

Because this point is still controversial, some evidence is in order; it is presented in Table 14.1. The data are taken from three regularly conducted national polls (*New York Times*/CBS News, Gallup, and ABC News/*Washington Post*) and cover the period from January 1981 through February 1988.[3] The dependent variable, the percentage point difference between Democratic and Republican identifiers, is regressed on a dummy variable indicating whether the poll was taken before (0) or after (1) election day 1984, and in all but the first equation in each set, a variable indicating the proportion of respondents who approved of Reagan's performance in the month the poll was taken.

The results are remarkably consistent across the two party identification series and the three presidential approval series. What was a fifteen-point Democratic advantage in party identification is now a five-point advantage. The change was sharp rather than gradual; statistically, the equation works much better with the categorical variable (before or after November 1984) than with a more gradual measure of time (for example, the number of months into the Reagan administration the poll was taken).[4]

Republican support is also highly sensitive to Reagan's standing with the public—or to whatever circumstances affect Reagan's standing with the public—confirming Fiorina's speculation (1988, 436) and, more generally, the susceptibility of party identification to short-term influences.[5] A ten-percentage point difference in the public's level of approval of Reagan's performance makes about a three-percentage point difference in the gap between Democratic and Republican identifiers. The result holds up when measures of approval and party identification are taken from different polls conducted in the same month, so it is not an artifact of correlated errors, a possibility when the independent and dependent variables are measured in the same poll.

Republican fortunes clearly rose and fell with the President's public standing; but independent of Reagan's short-term popularity, Republicans closed about two-thirds of the party identification gap between them and the Democrats during the Reagan presidency. Evidently, the 1984 campaign precipitated a significant and durable increase in Republican strength in the electorate, but this change has yet to register in congressional elections.

Republicans also failed to cash in on major financial and organizational advantages. In recent years, Republican party committees far outstripped their Democratic counterparts in raising and spending money for their congressional candidates. From 1980 through 1986, Republican House and Senate campaign committees raised a total of $418 million

TABLE 14.1 Changes in the Distribution of Partisans during the Reagan Years

Variables	New York Times/CBS News Polls			
	1	2	3	4
Constant	14.1	28.4	30.2	31.2
	(0.9)	(3.5)	(4.5)	(3.8)
After November 1984	−9.3	−7.7	−6.5	−9.0
	(1.3)	(1.1)	(1.3)	(1.1)
Presidential approval				
New York Times/CBS News		−0.27		
		(0.07)		
Gallup			−0.32	
			(0.09)	
Washington Post/ABC News				−0.29
				(0.07)
R^2	0.58	0.71	0.67	0.79
DW	1.21	1.78	1.50	1.45
N	47	44	35	30

Variables	Gallup Polls			
	1	2	3	4
Constant	15.9	35.1	32.9	33.1
	(0.7)	(4.9)	(3.1)	(4.0)
After November 1984	−10.0	−8.0	−8.3	−10.6
	(1.0)	(1.2)	(0.8)	(1.1)
Presidential approval				
New York Times/CBS News		−0.37		
		(0.08)		
Gallup			−0.33	
			(0.05)	
Washington Post/ABC News				−0.29
				(0.07)
R^2	0.66	0.76	0.81	0.78
DW	1.14	1.37	1.59	1.62
N	48	26	48	33

Note: Dependent variable is the percentage of Democratic identifiers minus the percentage of Republican identifiers; in the New York Times/CBS News data, leaners are included as partisans; standard errors are in parentheses. R^2 is the adjusted multiple correlation coefficient, squared; DW is the Durban-Watson Statistic; N is the number of surveys used in the equation.

compared with the Democratic committees' $62 million (Ornstein, Mann, and Malbin 1987, 99–101). The money was used to build technically sophisticated national organizations able to pursue an impressive range of party-building and electoral activities (Jacobson 1989; Herrnson 1988; Sorauf 1988). Among other things, these organizations enabled Republican party officials to distribute funds more efficiently, thereby helping candidates—particularly challengers to incumbents—in close contests in which spending might actually influence the outcome (Jacobson 1985–86). Yet, contrary to expectations—at least my own (Jacobson 1985)—Republicans reaped little net electoral benefit from superior finance and organization. It is noteworthy that most of the Republican senators defeated in 1986 mounted much more lavish campaigns than did their Democratic challengers.

Finally, Republicans could point to six years of steady economic growth, low inflation, rising employment, and improving relations with the Soviet Union, among other things, as evidence of their capacity to govern well. Surely this, too, ought to have helped Republicans running for Congress. The puzzle then is real; why, despite a variety of trends favoring the Republicans, did Democrats easily retain unchallenged control of the House, and why were they able to recapture the Senate?

We face, in fact, a surfeit of potential explanations: the advantages of incumbency, gerrymandering, unfortunate timing, sophisticated ideological balancing by voters, and more. The explanations are not mutually exclusive, of course, and all merit examination. However, I shall argue that the primary explanation for why, at the congressional level, Democrats emerged from the Reagan era in surprisingly good shape lies in a coherent pattern of popular opinions and expectations about parties and institutions which, although raising nearly intractable problems for Democratic presidential candidates, permitted congressional Democrats to hold out, even thrive, against the Republican tide.

Incumbency and Redistricting

A simple, if woefully incomplete, explanation for the Republicans' meager congressional gains is the incumbency advantage. Of course, incumbency cannot account for what happened in Senate elections, in which nine of nineteen incumbent Democrats were defeated in 1980, and seven of nineteen incumbent Republicans lost in 1986. However, it is reasonable to think that the electoral advantages currently enjoyed by House incumbents should dampen any partisan trend there. After all, House incumbents are notoriously successful at winning reelection even in the face of adverse national conditions. More are winning by larger margins now than in the past—their average share of the two-party vote rose from less than 61 percent in the 1950s to more than 65 percent in recent elections—so a reasonable inference is that House incumbents have increasingly insulated themselves against any but the most extreme partisan tide. Thus in the 1980s, House Democrats could ride out a Republican trend that, a couple of decades earlier, would have sent many more of them into enforced retirement.

This inference, however reasonable, is incorrect. At least through the early 1980s, incumbents, even though winning by wider margins when they *won*, were just as likely to *lose* as they had been in the 1950s and 1960s. Wider reelection margins did not make House seats any safer because district electorates had become more volatile, producing larger, more erratic swings from one election to the next. As a consequence, the swing ratio—the rate at which vote shifts are translated into seat shifts— did not change significantly (Jacobson 1987a). The incumbency advantage certainly dampens change but little more now than a generation ago. Republicans were, after all, able to defeat twenty-seven Democratic incumbents in 1980, eight of whom had served nine or more terms in the House, including the majority whip and five committee chairmen. Nor did incumbency protect the twenty-two Republican congressmen defeated in 1982, although Republican resources and organization probably prevented greater losses (Jacobson and Kernell 1983).

Furthermore, the incumbency advantage cannot explain why Republicans did not gain more from open House seats. Even if incumbency slows change, its ability to protect the declining party should erode over time as its members die or retire and their seats are thrown open. In elections from 1980 through 1988, Republicans took 28 percent of the open seats that had been held by Democrats but lost 20 percent of their own open seats to Democrats. Including contests for the new open seats created by redistricting prior to the 1982 election, Republicans gained at most about five House seats, net, through open seat contests during the Reagan era. Since the 1980 election, Republicans have actually suffered a net loss from such contests.

The incumbency advantage is clearly not the only reason Democrats maintain a firm grip on the House; nor can Democratic gerrymandering be blamed for Republican problems. Theoretical analysis and empirical research offer no ground for believing that partisan redistricting prior to 1982 cost Republicans more than a few seats, net, if it cost them any at all (Abramowitz 1983; Born 1985; Cain and Campagna 1987; Oppenheimer 1989). Something more than incumbency or gerrymandering is required to account for Reagan's meager contribution to congressional Republicans.

Timing

Ronald Reagan had a reputation for luck. Imagine the fate of Reaganomics without the collapse of the Organization of Petroleum Exporting Countries (OPEC) or arms control without Gorbachev's ascension to power in the Soviet Union, and it is easy to see why. Yet, if Reagan was lucky, his providence did not rub off on congressional Republicans.

Another explanation for why they did not prosper more during the Reagan years is unfortunate timing. Timing is important because election day opportunities are influenced by decisions made months before the election. Under most conditions, the combination of an attractive well-financed challenger and compelling issues is required to undermine the support an incumbent normally enjoys. Voters do not desert an incumbent without both a good reason and an acceptable alternative (Jacobson 1987b). Thus, a party needs strong challengers to take full advantage of exploitable issues and exploitable issues to take full advantage of strong challengers.

Because potential candidates and campaign contributors behave strategically, this sort of coincidence should be expected. Better (more experienced and ambitious) challengers take the field when national conditions create issues favorable to their candidacy, partly because they know that people who supply campaign money will deem them good investments. The same strategic considerations should produce a crop of inexperienced, poorly funded challengers when a party faces contrary national tides (Jacobson and Kernell 1983).

Only in 1980, however, did Republican candidacies conform to this strategic logic. That year, Republicans fielded a strong contingent of challengers who could take advantage of popular discontent with inflation, Iran, Jimmy Carter, and Democrats in general. Stimulated by 1980 and Reagan's legislative triumphs in 1981, Republicans recruited another strong group of challengers for 1982. However, both the economy and the Reagan's level of popular approval hit bottom around election day, leaving Republicans at a hopeless disadvantage on national issues. Only one Republican challenger was successful (although the threat of strong Republican challenges probably diverted Democratic resources from Democratic challengers, reducing the number of Republican incumbents who were defeated in 1982; see Jacobson 1985–86).

By 1984, the economy had rebounded vigorously, propelling Reagan to a sweeping forty-nine-state victory—nothing wrong with *his* timing (Kiewiet and Rivers 1985); but congressional Republicans did not share this triumph. Part of the reason is that Reagan's issueless "feelgood" campaign gave Republican candidates little rhetorical ammunition (if everything is rosy, why vote for change?). More important was the paucity of strong Republican challengers positioned to exploit the opportunity presented by Reagan's victory and the conditions that fostered it. In part, this was fallout from the disappointing Republican showing in 1982. Republicans had, in effect, wasted some of their best candidates in the futile challenges, and the election results discouraged others by ruling out any imminent Republican takeover of the House. In addition, the dimensions of Reagan's victory were not discernible early in the election year, when final decisions about candidacy are made (Jacobson 1985b).

Republicans also wasted some advantages in 1986. They mounted a very weak set of challenges, only one of which was successful. To be sure, this made strategic sense. An administration's second midterm election is notoriously hard on its party's congressional candidates, and Democrats elected despite Reagan's victory in 1984 would scarcely be easier targets in 1986. Furthermore, Republican resources were obviously going to be focused on maintaining control of the Senate. Nevertheless, the election found the economy still growing nicely and Reagan's performance receiving widespread popular approval; and survey evidence indicates that approval of Reagan and optimism about the economy translated into votes for Republican House candidates—especially when combined with a strong challenge. National conditions made it relatively easy to hold off Democratic challenges (Democrats, too, fielded relatively weak challengers), so Republicans did profit from them. However, a set of Republican challenges like those mounted in 1982 might have increased the profit considerably (Jacobson and Kernell 1990; Jacobson 1988).

Of the four elections with Reagan heading the ticket, only 1980 produced a combination of issues and candidates conducive to Republican success. In 1982, Republicans had the challengers but not the issues. In 1984 and 1986, Republicans had the issues but not the challengers. The dearth of strong Republican candidates poised to take advantage of issues—and the other trends favorable to Republicans, as discussed earlier—is explained partly by strategic choices echoing the experience of 1982 and political folklore about the "six-year itch." This explanation is, I think, incomplete; for reasons that go beyond the immediate strategic environment, Republicans seem to have problems recruiting the kinds of candidates who can win and hold congressional seats under present-day electoral conditions. I will have more to say about this later.

A Rational Electorate?

Voters were, by definition, ultimately responsible for the disjuncture between presidential and congressional election results during the Reagan years. In explanations based on the incumbency advantage or challengers' strategies, their contribution was more or less indirect. An alternative explanation is that Democrats controlled Congress and Republicans the White House because voters explicitly wanted it that way. "There is a strong and sensible desire," according to one version of this argument, "in an era when presidential nominating processes give an advantage to extremists or enthusiasts of both parties, to dividing the control of government, for having Tip O'Neill's or Jim Wright's Democrats there to check and balance Ronald Reagan's Republicans" (Barone and Ujifusa 1987:lxii). Fiorina offers a more formal demonstration of the possibility that "some small but important portion of the electorate is engaging in a kind of sophisticated ticket splitting that permits them to register a preference for a middle course between two parties, neither of which they fully trust to govern" (Fiorina, 1988, 442).

The spatial logic of Fiorina's argument is unimpeachable, but the initial empirical evidence for it is tenuous, and it raises the question of just how many voters are sophisticated enough to engage in calculated ticket splitting based on national policy differences between the parties. There is, however, a different kind of calculated ticket splitting which may be available to a much larger number of voters. Its logic arises from different expectations of presidents and congressmen as well as of Republicans and Democrats and expresses the contradictory preferences of voters themselves.

People want things from government which are mutually exclusive. There is nothing irrational about this; we naturally enjoy the benefits government confers but dislike paying for them. As an old saying has it, "everybody wants to go to heaven, but nobody wants to die." By their nature, budget issues provide the most flagrant examples of contradictory popular demands, but the phenomenon is by no means confined to them. Moreover, the phenomenon is not unique to the 1980s. The important point is that in recent years, the electoral expression of contradictory impulses has yielded Republican presidents and Democratic Congresses.

The evidence for this argument is taken from *New York Times*/CBS

News polls conducted during the Reagan administration and, to a much lesser extent, the 1986 American National Election Study. To avoid swamping the reader with poll results, questions and responses are confined to the Appendix. Citations in the text refer to the survey list and question numbers in the Appendix in which the full questions and responses may be found.

First, consider the federal budget. Public opinion on budget issues is consistently inconsistent. The idea that budgets should be balanced is so ingrained that three-quarters of adult Americans favor a constitutional amendment requiring the federal government to produce one (A1.1). People leave no doubt about how it should be achieved; more than 80 percent want to cut spending, and fewer than 10 percent prefer to raise taxes (A1.2). Even though about half believe that the deficit cannot be reduced without higher taxes, almost two-thirds say they are unwilling to pay more taxes to reduce it (A1.3 and A1.4).

If deficits must be reduced by cutting spending, what should suffer? According to majorities of the public, not health, not education, not social security, not student loans, not aid to farmers, not medicare, not even civil service salaries (A1.5–A1.8). Indeed, more people believe that spending for farmers, the poor, student aid, the unemployed, blacks, social security, the environment, and even space research should be increased than believe it should be cut (A1.9–A1.11). Even though only about 40 percent believe that the war on poverty of the 1960s made things better, 66 percent say that the government should spend money on a similar effort now (A1.12 and A1.13). More people than not are unwilling to see *any* program they deem worthwhile cut to reduce the deficit (A1.14). The only cuts that win majority approval are of defense programs (at least after the enormous buildup of the early 1980s)—most particularly aid to the contras—and Amtrak. A narrow majority is also willing to postpone tax reductions for people earning $50,000 or more (A1.7 and A1.8).

Similarly, contradictory desires appear in other contexts as well. More think business is overregulated than think it is underregulated, but two-thirds agree that "protecting the environment is so important that requirements and standards cannot be too high and continuing environmental improvements must be made regardless of cost" (A2.1 and A2.2). Large majorities also think the government should guarantee employment to all who want to work, medical care for everyone, and day care and after-school care for children (A2.3). Americans clearly dislike intrusive, expensive "big government"; they also clearly appreciate most of the programs that comprise it.

This situation creates a politically significant variation on the classic collective goods problem. Technically, a collective good is one that everyone shares because it cannot, by its nature, be provided exclusively to any individual or subset of individuals: if anyone enjoys the goods, everyone does. The most common political example is national defense, but there are many others. The problem arises because collective goods, by definition, cannot be withheld from people who do not contribute to their production. That makes it economically rational for any individual to avoid, if possible, paying her share—to be, in the jargon, a free rider. Since this is true for every individual, collective goods will not be provided (or, more realistically, will be provided at grossly suboptimal levels) without some institutional arrangement for assuring that the costs will be paid.[6] It makes no sense to contribute to producing a collective good even if the value of the good to you outweighs its cost to you unless you can depend on others to contribute as well; and if logic recommends free riding, there is no reason to expect others to contribute; and so, there is no reason to contribute yourself.

Solving such problems is a central purpose of government to which we grant a monopoly on the legitimate use of coercion so it can, among other things, produce collective goods. It is perfectly rational for an individual to support the creation of an internal revenue service, backed by courts and jails, which taxes him to pay for collective goods because such institutional arrangements guarantee that others will have to pay too and that the collective goods can therefore be purchased. It is also perfectly rational for the same individual to hire the best tax lobbyist and best tax attorney he can afford in order to minimize his own share of the taxes.

An analogous logic applies to contemporary political issues. Majorities plainly, and understandably, desire some broad collective goods: low taxes, a balanced budget, low inflation, less intrusive government, adequate national defense. Aside from defense, all of these goods presumably contribute to economic efficiency, itself a quintessential collective good, and hence to another: economic growth. Just as understandably, majorities prefer to avoid the costs required to achieve them: cuts in government programs and benefits, higher unemployment, greater exposure to market forces, greater environmental risk. These costs are more narrowly focused, and they outweigh the benefits of the broader collective goods to those who have to pay them. People rationally prefer a job to lower inflation, a larger social security check to a smaller deficit. No one has an incentive to sacrifice income to greater economic efficiency or even to risk such a sacrifice if the risk is appreciable.

During the 1980s, the parties took positions that allowed voters to express both sets of preferences at the polls: they could vote for a Republican president committed to the diffuse collective goods of low taxes, economic efficiency, and a strong national defense, and for congressional Democrats who promised to minimize the price they had to pay for these goods. Think of Reagan as the IRS and congressional Democrats as superior tax attorneys, and the logic of this voting strategy becomes clear.

The ground for this sort of ticket splitting is evident in the way the public views the strengths of the two parties. During the 1980s, Republicans were judged better than Democrats at ensuring prosperity, handling inflation, reducing the deficit, protecting American industry against foreign competition, and, since late 1984, keeping us out of war (A3.1a–A3.1f). Democrats were thought better at handling unemployment, protecting social security, dealing with farm problems, and managing the issue of toxic wastes (A3.1g–A3.1m). Democrats were also considered more likely to create a fair budget and tax system (A3.1j and A3.3) and more attentive to groups stuck with the bill for the collective benefits of greater economic efficiency and growth: women, union members, farmers, blacks, and "people like you." Republicans were thought to be more solicitous only of "big business" (A3.1l and A3.2).

Perceived differences between the parties coincide with differences in expectations people have of presidents and members of Congress. Presidents are supposed to pursue broad national interests; uniquely among elected officials, presidents routinely find political profit in conferring diffuse collective benefits at the expense of concentrated particular interests. Members of Congress, in contrast, survive by looking out for the particular because this is what voters want from them. When it comes to congressional representation, most people prefer "delegates" who put district preferences ahead of the national interest to "trustees" who invert these priorities (A4.1); helping people in the district is a more important part of the job than working on national legislation (A4.2). Moreover, most believe that members of Congress *are* more concerned with local than with Washington opinion, overwhelmingly so when specific reference is made to the respondent's own representative (A4.3 and A4.4).

This combination of partisan and institutional expectations strengthens Republican presidential candidates, as Walter Mondale with his gloomy talk of raising taxes and his image as a servant of "special interests" discovered. It also helps congressional Democrats because people want representatives who will protect them from damaging policies regardless of their broader benefits. Voters use different criteria for judging presidential and congressional candidates. Presidential candidates are evaluated according to their views on national issues and their competence in dealing with national problems (A5.1; Kiewiet and Rivers 1985). Congressional candidates are evaluated on their personal character and experience and on their devotion to district services and local issues (A5.2 and A5.3; Jacobson 1987b). Thus, it is not surprising that a majority of voters should have found Ronald Reagan irrelevant to their congressional choice (A5.4).

An interesting consequence of this distinction between presidents and congressmen is that large majorities want Congress, rather than the president, to determine where cuts should be made to balance the budget (A6.1 and A6.2). Survey respondents say they prefer Congress to make the decisions because it is more decentralized, permeable, and responsive to the public than is the White House (A6.2). In other words, Congress has to pay much more attention to the question of who will bear the concentrated costs of producing the diffuse benefits of a balanced budget. People have few illusions about the consequences; a huge majority thinks the five-year timetable for reaching a balanced budget under Gramm-Rudman-Hollings will not be met (A6.4), and most think Congress will be more to blame than the president (A6.3 and A6.4). Still, they want Congress to control the decisions.

Ironically, this might work to the advantage of both a Republican president and a Democratic Congress. The president would get credit for pursuing a balanced budget but is absolved in advance of blame for failing. The blame would fall on Congress, but its members are skilled at avoiding individual responsibility for their collective decisions, and they would profit individually from fighting to protect local interests (Mayhew 1974; Fenno 1978), so no one need suffer real political damage—at least until the next major recession. No wonder the public is skeptical.

Thriving on Disunity

This analysis resonates with a final explanation of why presidential Republicans do so much better than congressional Republicans. Democratic presidential candidates in recent years have suffered from the perception that their party is subservient to a host of special interests including organized labor, racial minorities, feminists, teachers, homosexuals, and other liberal activists (Miller, Hildreth, and Wlezien 1988). They also face the daunting task of trying to build a national coalition out of mutually antagonistic groups: blacks, Jews, working-class whites, southern traditionalists, and affluent college-educated liberals. This is an uphill battle that most recent Democratic presidential candidates have lost.

Democratic congressional candidates, in contrast, are free to assemble local coalitions that may or may not include groups important to the party nationally. They can run as staunch friends of organized labor, civil rights activists, or nuclear freeze proponents when this adds votes, and they can avoid such alliances when it does not. The fragmented decentralized electoral process allows congressional Democrats to turn a severe national problem—diversity and discord—to local advantage. Moreover, they suffer little damage from the charge that Democrats are too solicitous of special interests because members of Congress are *expected* to serve special interests—those of their constituents. The same image that hurts presidential Democrats may, in this way, actually help congressional Democrats.

Conversely, the benefit Republican presidential candidates derive from perceptions that their party is better at promoting economic efficiency and growth, as well as other comprehensive collective goods, may not extend to Republican congressional candidates at all, especially if they can be portrayed as more interested in national issues than in local needs. In general, we would expect Republican Senate candidates to profit more from their party's reputation in this regard than Republican House candidates, if only because states are usually more populous and diverse than congressional districts and so encompass broader interests. This may be one reason that Republicans have been so much more competitive in Senate contests during the Reagan years. Even so, Republican senators first elected on the Reagan ticket in 1980 who seemed more interested in pushing a national ideological agenda than in looking out for the home folks—notably Jeremiah Denton of Alabama and Mack Mattingly of Georgia—were defeated in 1986. Others—like Alphonse D'Amato of New York and Charles Grassley of Iowa—who worked diligently to serve state interests won easy reelection.

These considerations also help to explain why Republicans have found it harder to recruit attractive congressional challengers than might be expected of an ascendant party. The Republicans' dilemma is that the Reaganite view of government clashes with the realities of what it takes to win and hold seats in Congress. For the most part, congressional careers are built on delivering particularized benefits to constituents, not on dismantling, in the name of efficiency, programs that create the benefits. Members are elected to minimize the local cost of producing national collective goods, not to pursue visions of the national interest regardless of local consequences. Thus Republicans sharing Reagan's minimalist conception of government are unlikely to find a congressional career enticing or, once initiated, satisfying. If government is the problem, not the solution, why pursue a career in politics which can only succeed if you are willing to become part of the problem? Those Republicans most strongly attracted to Reagan's priorities are, by that very fact, ill suited to the politics of congressional elections.

The view of government held by most Democrats is, in contrast, far more positive. Their surviving traditions and ideas sanction government assistance to all sorts of groups for all sorts of purposes. Democrats can still believe that government is an honorable calling and that the activities sustaining a congressional career are worthwhile. Democrats thus have far less trouble fielding attractive, experienced challengers comfortable with the demands of contemporary electoral politics, and Democrats elected to the House are less likely to depart voluntarily.[7]

Prospects

Congressional Republicans have good reason to be disappointed by their share of the Reagan legacy, but Reagan himself was scarcely to blame. As long as voters want different, mutually contradictory, things from presidents and members of Congress, congressional Republicans will have a hard time measuring up to presidential Republicans at the polls. It is not merely a question of incumbency, but of *Democratic* incumbency; many of the pursuits that create the incumbency advantage coincide with what voters expect of Democrats. It is not so much that voters balance Democrats in one branch against Republicans in the other to get a government closer to their centrist views, but that majorities prefer a president committed to a set of diffuse collective goods and congressional representatives committed to minimizing what they have to give up to achieve them.

Furthermore, Democratic weaknesses in presidential elections emerge as strengths in congressional elections. An ungainly national coalition lends itself to a wide diversity of state and district coalitions. Poor ideological focus hurts nationally but liberates locally. A reputation for sensitivity to special interests hobbles presidential Democrats; a reputation for sensitivity to local interests is bread and butter to congressional Democrats. Being regarded as the party of the Welfare State has its disadvantages, but it seems to help in attracting talented people to careers in electoral politics.

As firmly rooted as these patterns appear to be, the most likely prospect is for a continued period of divided government. Republicans have every reason to maintain their edge in presidential elections; Democratic hopes lie in Republican mistakes and failures, not in what they offer on their own. House Democrats have figured out how to survive successful Republican administrations; the only serious threat to them would be another failed Democratic administration or a disastrously unpopular presidential ticket.[8] Republicans certainly have some chance of taking back the Senate; in three of the four most recent elections, control of the Senate has hinged on handfuls of votes in pivotal states (Jacobson 1989), and Republican gains in party identification should register more fully in Senate elections (Oppenheimer 1989). However, without an unpopular Democratic administration to provide a focus for their attack, even Republican Senate candidates should have a tough time going one-on-one with the present Democratic incumbents. Ironically, continued Republican control of the White House might actually contribute to continued Democratic control of Congress.

APPENDIX

With one exception (A1.11), all of the questions and results are from the *New York Times*/CBS News national surveys. The polls were conducted by telephone; the typical sample includes about 1,500 respondents. Individual surveys are identified by date; in months with more than one survey, the first is designated "A," the second, "B," and so forth. For all questions, the responses "both," "both equal," "neither," and "depends" were not given as options in the question but were volunteered by the respondent. Dk/na indicates "don't know" or no answer; vol. indicates volunteered.

SURVEY LIST A1   Public Preferences on the Budget

1. Do you favor or oppose a constitutional amendment requiring the federal government to balance its budget?

Response	11/87	5/87B	9/82	1/79[a]	9/78[a]
Favor	75	85	71	73	70
Oppose	14	10	20	16	17
Dk/na	11	6	5	11	13

[a] Different wording.

2. Some people say that the way to reduce the federal budget deficit is to cut back government spending. Others say that the way to do it is to increase taxes. Which solution would you favor: cutting government spending or increasing taxes?

Response	11/85	2/85	2/84
Cut spending	83	81	82
Increase taxes	7	9	8
Both (vol.)	7	6	6
Neither (vol.)	1	2	1
Dk/na	2	2	4

3.   Do you think that in order to reduce the federal budget deficit substantially, it will be necessary to raise taxes?

Response	1/86	10/84B	10/84A	9/84	8/84
Yes	46	43	47	43	52
No	48	47	42	51	38
Dk/na	7	10	11	7	10

4.   In order to reduce the size of the federal budget deficit, would you be willing or not to pay more in federal taxes?

Response	1/88	11/87	1/87	11/85[a]	1/85[a]	1/84[a]	1/83[b]
Willing	36	37	30	36	30	25	38
Not willing	60	60	65	57	66	72	57
Dk/na	4	3	5	7	5	4	5

[a] 10 percent more taxes specified.
[b] Different wording.

5.   In order to reduce the federal budget deficit, are you willing or not willing for the government to provide fewer services, even in areas like health and education?

Response	11/87	9/86[a]
Willing	33	33
Not willing	60	62
Dk/na	6	5

[a] Different wording.

6.   In order to reduce the size of the federal budget deficit would you be willing to have the government reduce scheduled cost-of-living adjustments for people who receive social security?

Response	11/87	1/85	1/83	5/82	3/82
Willing	22	23	42	31	37
Not willing	73	73	53	61	57
Depends, dk	5	3	5	8	6

7. It is expected that if Ronald Reagan's budget for next year is adopted, the federal government could spend as much as $200 billion more than it takes in. To reduce the size of the federal budget deficit, would you be willing or not willing to:

		5/87	
Options	Willing	Not willing	Dk/na
a. Reduce the amount of money available for student loans?	33	60	6
b. Reduce aid to farmers?	27	68	5
c. Reduce proposed spending on military and defense programs?	54	40	6
d. Postpone tax cuts for people earning $50,000 or more?	49	43	7

8. In order to reduce the size of the federal budget deficit, do you think it would be a good idea for the government to spend less on programs to (1) help farmers, (2) medicare, (3) Amtrak, (4) cut salaries of all federal civil service employees or would that be a bad idea?

		1/85		
Response	Farmers	Medicare	Amtrak	Civil Service
Good idea	27	18	50	38
Bad idea	65	77	36	50
Dk/na	8	5	14	12

9. Should federal spending on farm programs be increased, decreased, or kept about the same?

Response	10/87	2/86	2/85[a]
Increased	55	50	36
Decreased	14	12	14
Same	27	30	45
Dk/na	3	8	4

[a] Different wording.

10. Should federal spending on programs for the poor be increased, decreased, or kept about the same?

Response	10/87	1/84
Increased	54	48
Decreased	9	8
Same	34	39
Dk/na	3	4

11. If you had a say in making up the federal budget this year, for which of the following programs would you like to see spending increased and for which would you like to see spending decreased? Should federal spending on _____ be increased, decreased, or kept about the same? (From the 1986 American National Election Study.)

Options	Increased	Decreased	Same	Dk/na
Improving and protecting the environment	48	4	44	4
Aid for college students	39	12	45	4
Social security	63	3	31	2
Food stamps	23	29	40	8
Aid to the contras	8	58	19	15
Assistance to the unemployed	38	13	45	4
Space and scientific research	31	23	41	4
Programs that assist blacks	25	16	52	6

12. There were many government programs created in the 1960s to try to improve the conditions of poor people in this country. Do you think these programs generally made things better, made things worse, or do you think they did not have much impact one way or the other?

Response	1/86	11/84B	11/80	1/78
Made things better	39	41	30	31
Made things worse	18	19	20	14
Not much impact	38	29	42	46
Dk/na	6	12	8	9

13. Whatever you think about those programs of the 1960s, do you think the federal government should spend money now on a similar effort to try to improve the conditions of poor people in this country?

Response	1/86
Should	66
Should not	22
Depends (vol.)	7
Dk/na	4

14. One reason government spending is so high is that everyone fights for the programs they think are worthwhile. Is there a government program that you think is worthwhile that you would be willing to see cut in order to reduce the deficit?

Response	1/85
Yes	31
No	45
Dk/na	24

SURVEY LIST A2   Public Preferences on Government Programs

1. Do you think the federal government regulates business too much these days, does it regulate business too little, or does it impose the right amount of regulation on business?

Response	1/86
Too much	41
Too little	22
Right amount	22
Depends	2
Dk/na	13

2. Do you agree or disagree with the following statement? Protecting the environment is so important that requirements and standards cannot be too high and continuing environmental improvements must be made regardless of cost.

Response	1/86	4/83	9/82	9/81
Agree	66	58	52	45
Disagree	27	34	41	42
Dk/na	7	8	7	13

3. I'd like to know what you think the responsibilities of the federal government are. For each of these items, please tell me if you think this is something the government in Washington, D.C. should or should not be doing.

Areas of Responsibility	11/87 Should	Should not	Dk/na
a. Regulating airline prices and schedules	38	55	7
b. Upholding traditional moral values	53	41	7
c. Seeing to it that everyone has a job who wants a job	71	26	3
d. Guaranteeing medical care for all people	78	19	3
e. Seeing to it that day care and after-school care for children are available	62	35	3
f. Supporting anticommunist forces around the world	52	41	8

SURVEY LIST A3   Public Evaluations of the Parties' Ability to Handle Problems

1.   Regardless of how you usually vote, do you think the Republican party or the Democratic party:

Problem	Rep.	Dem.	Both	Neither	Dk
a. Is more likely to keep us out of war?					
9/86[a]	40	31	4	6	18
12/85	38	30	5	10	17
10/84A[a]	37	34	3	6	20
1/84[b]	32	38	3	6	20
6/83[b]	28	39	4	10	19
10/82[b]	33	34	7	8	18
9/82[b]	35	39	3	5	17
5/82[b]	29	41	5	8	18
4/81[b]	29	37	2	13	19
b. Is more likely to make sure the country is prosperous?					
9/86[a]	45	35	5	4	12
c. Is better able to ensure a strong economy?					
10/84A[a]	54	27	2	4	13
d. Is better able to handle inflation?					
12/85	50	26	3	7	15
6/83[b]	41	32	4	6	17
10/82[b]	46	32	3	6	13
9/82[b]	38	33	3	10	15
5/82[b]	35	34	3	10	18
4/81[b]	45	17		24	14
e. Is more likely to reduce the federal budget deficit?					
12/85	45	28	4	10	14
6/85[c]	45	25		13	17
10/84A	43	30	1	10	16
5/82[c]	46	28	3	7	16
f. Is better able to protect American industry against foreign competition?					
9/86[a]	37	35	3	8	18
4/86	44	28	4	5	19
12/85[c]	45	24	6	6	20
6/83	38	32	4	5	21

g. Is better able to handle unemployment?

9/86[a]	37	40	3	6	13
12/85	36	40	3	7	14
10/84A[a]	44	37	2	3	14
6/83[b]	30	48	3	6	12
10/82[a]	30	52	3	4	12
5/82[b]	23	51	3	7	17
4/81[b]	36	31	4	11	18

h. Is better at keeping the social security system healthy?

9/86[a]	33	46	5	7	10
10/84A[c]	24	54	5	3	13

i. Is likely to make the right decisions about social security?

10/82[a]	30	49	4	4	14
9/82[b]	27	54	3	4	12
5/82[b]	27	52	3	4	12

j. Is more likely to create a budget that is fair to all people?

12/85	32	40	5	7	16
10/82[b]	35	45	3	6	12
9/82[b]	32	50	2	5	11
5/82[b]	28	46	4	7	16

k. Would do a better job of solving the problems faced by American farmers?

9/86[a]	23	52	2	6	17
2/86[c]	17	42	6	7	28
12/85	18	54	5	10	14

l. Cares about the needs and problems of people like yourself?

9/86[a]	26	52	6	4	11
4/86[c]	34	44	6	7	10
12/85[c]	31	42	6	11	10
10/84[ac]	36	46	4	3	11
5/82[c]	28	51	4	6	11

m. Is better at handling the problem of toxic waste?

9/86[a]	24	33	6	14	23

[a] Probable voters.
[b] Registered voters.
[c] Alternate wording.

2. Who do you think cares more about the needs and problems of _____: the Republican party or the Democratic party?

12/85

Group	Rep.	Dem.	Both	Neither	Dk/na
Big business	66	17	5	2	11
Women	22	48	7	6	17
Union members	17	63	3	2	15
Farmers	18	54	5	10	14
Blacks	16	57	8	5	15
People like you	31	42	6	11	10

3. Who do you think is more concerned about seeing that the tax system is fair: the Republicans in Congress or the Democrats in Congress?

Response	*6/85*
Republicans	35
Democrats	40
Both	7
Neither	4
No opinion	14

SURVEY LIST A4　Congressional Role Expectations

1. If a member of Congress thinks a bill is in the best interest of the country, but a majority of the people he or she represents are against it, should the member of Congress vote for the bill or vote against it?

Response	*5/87B*
For	34
Against	59
Depends	3
Dk/na	4

2. What do you think is a more important way for a Congressman to spend his time: helping people in his district who have problems with the government, or working in Congress on bills of national interest?

Response	*9/78*
Helping people in his district	48
Working on national bills	28
Both	21
Dk/na	3

3. Would you say that most members of Congress are more concerned about what people in Washington, D.C. think or more concerned about what people in the districts they represent think? (Probable voters only.)

Response	*10/86*
People in Washington, D.C.	38
People in districts	49
Both	4
Neither	1
Dk/na	8

4. What about the member of the House of Representatives from your district? Is that representative more concerned about what people in Washington, D.C. think or more concerned about what people in your district think?

Response	*10/86*
People in Washington, D.C.	20
People in district	64
Both	3
Neither	1
Dk/na	11

SURVEY LIST A5   Criteria for Voting in Presidential and Congressional Elections

1. Some people choose among presidential candidates by picking the one closest to them on important issues. Some other people choose the one who has the personal characteristics—like integrity or leadership—they want most in a president. Which is more important when *you* choose: issues or personal characteristics?

Response	*10/87*
Issues	54
Personal characteristics	34
Both	8
Neither	1
Dk/na	3

2. Sometimes people decide to vote for a candidate for the U.S. House of Representatives because of national issues. Sometimes it's because of local or state issues. Sometimes it's because of the candidate's political party. And sometimes it's because of the candidate's character or experience. This year, what will make the biggest difference in how you vote—a national issue, a local or state issue, the candidate's political party, or the candidate's character or experience? (Probable voters only.)

Response	10/86	9/86	4/86[a]
National	22	20	30
State and local	25	23	20
Party	6	9	1
Character/experience	40	41	37
Other/dk/na	7	7	11

[a] Alternate wording.

3. Would you be more likely to vote for a candidate for the U.S. House who is more interested in helping people in your district who have a problem with the government or for a candidate who is more interested in working in Congress on bills of *national* interest? (Probable voters only.)

Response	9/86	10/82
District	47	54
National	40	36
Both	8	5
Dk/na	4	5

4. Do you think of your vote for Congress this fall as a vote for Ronald Reagan or as a vote against Ronald Reagan or isn't Ronald Reagan much of a factor in your vote? (Probable voters only.)

Response	10/86	9/86	10/82
For Reagan	26	26	23
Against Reagan	12	16	21
Reagan not a factor	55	51	51
Dk/na	7	7	5

SURVEY LIST A6   Institutional Responsibility for the Budget

1. Last year, the President and Congress agreed to a law requiring the federal budget to be balanced within the next five years. Who do you think would make better decisions about what to do to reduce the federal deficit: Ronald Reagan or Congress?

Response	1/86
Reagan	29
Congress	59
Both equal	4
Neither	2
Dk/na	6

2. Who *should* have the most say about what cuts should be made to balance the budget—the President or Congress?

Response	11/85
President	20
Congress	71
Both equal	4
Dk/na	5

What is the main reason you feel that way? (Those answering "Congress.")

Response	11/85
More people have input	26
Power not concentrated in one person	10
Representativeness, for the people	16
Other	13

3. In your opinion, whose responsibility for balancing the budget is greater: the President's or that of Congress?

Response	1/82
President	23
Congress	63
Both equal	9
Dk/na	5

4. Do you think the budget will be balanced within five years?

Response	1/86
Yes	15
No	77
Dk/na	8

If not, whose fault will that be, the President's or Congress?

Response	1/86
President	15
Congress	35
Both	20
Dk/na	7

NOTES

1. Real disposable income had risen by 4.2 percent over the year preceding the election; in the last Gallup Poll before the election, 63 percent approved of Reagan's performance; both figures are substantially higher than average, particularly for an administration's second midterm.

2. Fortunately for Republicans, revelations of the administration's dealings with Iran and the contras came after the election.

3. None of the surveys covers all 86 months of this period; observations include only those months in which the party identification and presidential approval questions were asked; hence the number of observations varies between and across survey organizations.

4. It also suffers from fewer problems of serial correlation. The Durban-Watson statistics are not strictly appropriate to these equations, for the period between surveys is variable; but they do suggest that some serial correlation is present in the first equation in each set. This does not bias the parameters, but it does exaggerate their precision. The results change little when corrected for autocorrelation using the Cochrane-Orcutt procedure; the Democratic advantage in party identifiers drops 8.3 percentage points (from 13.4 to 5.1) in the *New York Times*/CBS equation and 9.2 percentage points (from 15.6 to 6.4) in the Gallup equation. The Durban-Watson statistics for the other equations indicate either no serial correlation or fall into the ambiguous range; in the latter case, correcting for autocorrelation changes the parameters by no more than 5 percent in any case.

5. For a longer and more fully specified time-series model that makes the same point, see MacKuen, Erikson, and Stimson (1988).

6. Except under very restricted—and politically rare—circumstances (Olson 1965; Hardin 1982).

7. In the four elections following the Republican sweep of 1980, 13 percent of the House Democrats were challenged by Republicans who had previously held some office, whereas 23 percent of the House Republicans faced experienced Democratic challengers. Moreover, 8.5 percent of the Republican incumbents voluntarily gave up their House seats, compared with 5.5 percent of the Democratic incumbents (and a larger proportion of the Democratic departures were to run for higher office). Despite their much smaller share, Republicans voluntarily relinquished more House seats than did Democrats. These differences are statistically significant at $p < 0.05$.

8. Republicans look hopefully to the next reapportionment as they did ten years ago, but the analysis offered here suggests that they are in for another disappointment.

REFERENCES

Abramowitz, Alan I. 1983. "Partisan Redistricting and the 1982 Congressional Elections." *Journal of Politics* 45: 767–70.

Barone, Michael, and Grant Ujifusa. 1987. *The Almanac of American Politics 1988.* Washington, D.C.: National Journal.

Born, Richard. 1985. "Partisan Intentions and Election Day Realities in the Congressional Redistricting Process." *American Political Science Review* 79: 305–19.

Cain, Bruce E., and Janet C. Campagna. 1987. "Predicting Partisan Redistricting Disputes." *Legislative Studies Quarterly* 12: 265–74.

Elving, Ronald D. 1988. "Democrats Tighten Senate Hold by One Seat." *Congressional Quarterly Weekly Report* 46 (November 12): 3249–52.

Fenno, Richard F., Jr. 1978. *Home Style: House Members in Their Districts.* Boston: Little, Brown.

Ferguson, Thomas, and Joel Rogers. 1985. "The Myth of America's Turn to the Right." *The Atlantic* 257 (April): 43–53.

Fiorina, Morris P. 1988. "The Reagan Years: Turning to the Right or Groping toward the Middle." In *The Resurgence of Conservatism in Anglo-American Democracies,* edited by Barry Cooper, Allan Kornberg, and William Mishler. Durham, N.C.: Duke University Press.

Hardin, Russell. 1982. *Collective Action.* Baltimore: The Johns Hopkins University Press.

Herrnson, Paul S. 1988. *Political Parties and Congressional Elections: Party Campaigning in the 1980s.* Cambridge, Mass.: Harvard University Press.

Jacobson, Gary C. 1985a. "The Republican Advantage in Campaign Finance." In *The New Direction in American Politics,* edited by John E. Chubb and Paul E. Peterson. Washington, D.C.: Brookings Institution.

———. 1985b. "Congress: Politics after a Landslide Without Coattails." In *The Elections of 1984,* edited by Michael Nelson. Washington, D.C.: Congressional Quarterly Press.

———. 1985–86. "Party Organization and Campaign Resources in 1982." *Political Science Quarterly* 100: 603–25.

———. 1987a. "The Marginals Never Vanished: Incumbency and Competition in Elections to the U.S. House of Representatives, 1952–1982." *American Journal of Political Science* 31: 126–41.

———. 1987b. *The Politics of Congressional Elections,* 2d ed. Boston: Little, Brown.

———. 1988. "The Effects of Campaign Spending on Voting Intentions: New Evidence from a Panel Study of the 1986 House Elections." Paper delivered at the annual meeting of the Midwest Political Science Association, Chicago, 14–16 April.

———. 1989. "Parties and PACs in Congressional Elections." In *Congress Reconsidered,* 4th ed., edited by Lawrence C. Dodd and Bruce I. Oppenheimer. Washington, D.C.: Congressional Quarterly Press.

Jacobson, Gary C., and Samuel Kernell. 1983. *Strategy and Choice in Congressional Elections,* 2d ed. New Haven, Conn.: Yale University Press.

———. 1990. "National Forces in the 1986 Congressional Elections." *Legislative Studies Quarterly.* Forthcoming.

Kiewiet, D. Roderick, and Douglas Rivers. 1985. "The Economic Basis of Reagan's Appeal." In *The New Direction in American Politics,* edited by John E. Chubb and Paul E. Peterson. Washington, D.C.: Brookings Institution.

MacKuen, Michael, Robert Erikson, and James A. Stimson. 1988. "Macro Party Identification: A Preliminary Analysis." Paper delivered at the annual meeting of the Midwest Political Science Association, Chicago, 14–16 April.

Mayhew, David R. 1974. *Congress: The Electoral Connection.* New Haven, Conn.: Yale University Press.

Miller, Arthur H., Anne Hildreth, and Christopher Wlezien. 1988. "Social Group Dynamics of Political Evaluations." Paper delivered at the annual meeting of the Midwest Political Science Association, Chicago, 14–16 April.

Miller, Warren E. 1987. "The Election of 1984 and the Future of American Politics." In *Elections in America*, edited by Kay Lehman Schlozman. Boston: Allen & Unwin, Inc.

Olson, Mancur. 1965. *The Logic of Collective Action*. Cambridge, Mass.: Harvard University Press.

Oppenheimer, Bruce I. 1989. "Split Party Control of Congress, 1981–86: Exploring Electoral and Apportionment Explanations." *American Journal of Political Science*, forthcoming.

Ornstein, Norman J., Thomas E. Mann, and Michael J. Malbin. 1987. *Vital Statistics on Congress, 1987–1988*. Washington, D.C.: Congressional Quarterly Press.

Sorauf, Frank J. 1988. *Money in American Elections*. Glenview, Ill.: Scott, Foresman.

Postscript

15

Looking Back: Meanings and Puzzles

RICHARD E. NEUSTADT

This volume has invited us to look back on the Reagan years and to think about the changes this Republican administration has had upon foreign policy, economic and fiscal policy, institutional development, and presidential-congressional relations. These changes constitute what we can call, for better or for worse, "the Reagan legacy," a phrase some critics have already invoked. Instead of going over the elements of that legacy again—after all, our contributors have done their work well—I propose that we pause and muse a bit about the term legacy. What does it mean for our consideration of the Reagan years.

There are at least three ways to understand "legacy," and all three senses of the word have been used in this volume. One is successes and failures as understood by the conventional wisdom at the end of a presidential administration. Second is opportunities and constraints facing a succeeding presidency directly as the product of this presidency. Third is retrospect—a retrospective view in the sense of place in history. Let me start with the third understanding, move back to the second, and finally offer three puzzles for future commentators on the Reagan years.

I would like to look at retrospective assessment by quoting a number of sages—various kinds of sages including political scientists and former presidents. To begin with, Clinton Rossiter used to say that the greatness of a president as judged by historians will depend on the greatness of the times in which he lives; and since Ronald Reagan did not live amid world war, civil war, depression, the founding of the republic, or its dissolution, the likelihood is that he will have to stand *at best* in the second rank. It is possible that if the evolution of Soviet-American relations now takes a turn that the historians regard as watershed in quality, then he may come close to greatness; but I am making no such prediction. The best he can hope for possibly is to stand with Teddy Roosevelt, and it may be no accident that he has chosen TR's biographer to do his own.

My second sage is the historian, Arthur Schlesinger, Jr., who used to say that a president's reputation in history depends in large part on how interesting he is to successive waves of historians. In this respect, I think, Ronald Reagan will do almost as well as Franklin Roosevelt and very much better than Harry Truman or poor Mr. Carter (who will get substantially less interest than he deserves from successive generations of historians). So we will be hearing about Mr. Reagan—he will not disappear because the historians will continue to rewrite each other's histories of him.

To quote Rossiter again, a president's reputation, his standing historically, will depend in large part on that of his predecessor and his successor and how lucky or unlucky he is in his choice of both. Mr. Reagan had Mr. Carter before him and has Mr. Bush after him. I can make no prediction of the next four years, but I would say that Mr. Reagan's prospects are reasonably good.

Mr. Eisenhower (another sage, you see) is quoted as having said, "No man should be president after the age of seventy." As the historians go over and over the Reagan record, this aphorism will come in for intensive discussion and testing, and it will undoubtedly affect the retrospect.

Mr. Truman himself said, after he left office (he thus became a sort of sage by definition), "That wasn't Truman's foreign policy! That was Stalin's foreign policy! I never could have got a thing through the 80th Congress if it hadn't been for Stalin." This is certainly a useful reminder of how much of Mr. Reagan's future reputation and his retrospective reputation will rest on others than himself and on events outside himself, not least perhaps, on the Soviet Union—and also on our economy.

Fred Greenstein, assuredly a sage, commented to me, "It helps a lot for presidents to depart from the scene at the right psychological moment." We do not yet know exactly how that's going to come out for Mr. Reagan, although it is worth watching. Fred had in mind Franklin Roosevelt dying before the end of World War II instead of after the reconversion troubles a year later, for example. Think also of Abraham Lincoln who passed from the scene at precisely the right dramatic moment. Then taking it a little beyond the death question—suppose Adolf Hitler's generals had persuaded him to postpone his war for three years. Franklin Roosevelt would have left office in 1941 and be generally judged then and now an unsuccessful president: the man who could not end the depression and who could not solve unemployment. In retrospective judgments, the externals matter; so does timing.

Bob Pastor, another sage by definition (being like me, a former White House aide), postulates deeply unfortunate effects from Mr. Reagan's economic policy—effects that will be identified as haunting our future and for which Reagan will be blamed. I must say, however, that in some respects I think this matter is subject to Fred Greenstein's observation, slightly stretched to what Henry Kissinger used to call in another connection "a decent interval." I do not know how long immediate, untoward, publicly visible effects of the deficit have to hold off before they will be blamed by historians and historically on *others* than Mr. Reagan.

Implicit in our discussions is a great deal of underlying disagreement about what Reagan's legacy will come to mean in retrospect. I daresay that that is inevitable in these circumstances. The sages explain it all to you: we disagreed more than we cared to say, and we will all be reinterpreting our disagreements as long as we continue to write.

There is another way to look at "legacy"—the second way I mentioned—in opportunities and constraints that immediately affect the successor president. Here, a good deal has been said, mostly by indirection, in this volume. Let me try to sharpen some of it up.

Unless the economy softens markedly in the near future, Mr. Reagan leaves, in terms of imagery, a pretty big screen for Mr. Bush to fill. The image includes Reagan, the chief of state, almost always striking the right note. The image includes Reagan as tough tactician in congressional relations during 1981, of which much has been written in this book. The media report presidential-congressional relations as a spectator sport, and the White House understood that fact in the Reagan administration. They may not have understood substance, but they surely understood *that*.

Along with concrete images, passed on as an inheritance, are concrete actions. In Ronald Reagan's time, for instance, there have been some White House staffing innovations that Mr. Bush might like or hate, may choose to follow or not, but that he would be very ill advised not to consider. Let me just list those innovations. First is the personnel selection system that gave the White House more potential control over department heads and associates than any previous White House has held. The control may not have been exercised, but it was there. Second are relations with the media. In the age of satellite transmission and minicameras, an extraordinary piece of work was done in the first term and continuing into the second whereby natural needs and dependences of the television medium and of television reporters—by now a dominant group in the White House press corps—were consistently turned to White House account. For the first time, the President's personal schedule and his congressional relations were tightly tied to photo opportunities and other aspects of his media relations. The President was literally "produced" as never before; he had never been orchestrated before in the same way. There is no great mystery about this, it could easily be studied, and any new president could decide whether or not he wished to adopt the same techniques.

Further, the White House Staff was carefully—although not ostensibly—divided into a two-level operation with a tight choke point between the top level and the second level (a choke point in the human form of Richard Darman and Craig Fuller, taken together). The second level, along with Cabinet members, was kept rather consistently subordinate to the six or eight top-level assistants who, as a practical matter, conducted much of the presidency. Future presidents will have to take a look at that. The consistency has not often been seen before, nor the choke point.

Then there are some carryovers of policy. This volume's contributions have referred often to the budget deficit, but nothing about the relatively imminent arrival of social security surpluses created by the social security reform of 1983—which, from about 1993 or so through the third decade of the next century will be enormous—will virtually wipe out the deficit, reducing it to thoroughly manageable proportions as a share of gross national product. Nobody is going to be talking about the budget deficit in five years time unless laws are substantially changed. That is an "old" problem. In terms of the social security reform, one part of the legacy of Reagan's years is an enormous opportunity for *new* controversies over how best to use the surpluses. By present law, these have to be invested in government bonds. Do we want alternative investments? Do we want them directed to capital needs to infrastructure rather than to general revenue, hence deficit reduction? How do we best use these huge sums so as to prepare the economy for the burden our workers will have to bear when the baby-boom generation retires? Here is an extraordinary interesting set of issues and hardly anyone has even noticed it yet! The budget deficit conveys a glaring risk in the short run; but the opportunity perhaps is also there, created by those coming surpluses.

Another opportunity of the same sort, perhaps a little paradoxical— a chance to change the subject, alter context—is found in unreadiness of the armed forces, starved for material in order to provide funds for big-ticket items. Future presidents will have the chance to retrieve from Mr.

Reagan the defense issue, the strength-through-defense issue by stressing readiness. It is an option, it is an opportunity, it is expensive, it will reduce the degree to which defense outlays can be cut; but it gives any future administration a new set of issues to stress and emphasize—a set different from Reagan's but equally "strong."

Then there's a mélange of things abroad, created by current policy, which may convey opportunities. Alternatively, they may point to mine fields. They certainly constitute legacies of some sort, whether in Central America, on the West Bank, in the Persian Gulf, in Panama, or at Geneva and Vienna.

Nowhere here is what Mr. Truman inherited from Mr. Roosevelt. Aside from a negative on taxes, there is no twenty-one point program, no economic bill of rights, nothing of a long-term programmatic character on the domestic side, to which a next Republican administration (and the one after that) is going to feel bound in detail; nothing like that. Still, these short-run programmatic opportunities and risks are surely part of Reagan's legacy; and it seems to me they got rather short shrift from us in this book.

Finally, Reagan's legacy includes some puzzles for political scientists. The first is familiar to you: puzzles about Mr. Reagan's operating style. The Iran-contra affair has brought into question Reagan's management style. Had it not been for that affair—or for the likelihood that something else would go awry sooner or later—we would now be hip-deep in panegyrics to the clean-desk management style, and we would have been unable to get clear of the mythology thus created for a very long time—if ever. There are risks in the way Mr. Reagan chose to "manage" and in the style of his operation of the presidency. They showed themselves in that one instance; other instances will emerge with his memoirs and papers. A mystery remains, a puzzle of considerable importance, at least to one as interested as I in presidents within the presidency. Whatever else Mr. Reagan showed himself to be, he certainly demonstrated politically shrewd instincts about public sentiment in this country and about when to change the scene in public relations—this on a number of occasions both in his governorship and the presidency. Remember "redeploying" the Marines to sea in 1983! How then, does a man uninterested in detail but generally with such sharp fingertips—how then does he come to the White House and fail to notice what the "plumbers" proved in Mr. Nixon's time? Namely, the White House, as a national shrine, is no place for covert operations since these subject the presidency to the kind of strain in public sentiment no president should want to put upon it for its *own* sake, let alone *his!*

How is it that such a lesson rang no bell in this man's mind? What does that say of governors, of people outside Washington, who enter its community for the first time as president?

The second puzzle is a matter of charisma. Charisma is a misused term, if one turns to Max Weber for its original full definition. Yet it has been misused so long that we accept it in its contemporary usage as having to do with a current of affection and inspiration flowing from the masses to the leader and felt by the leader for the masses—and felt by the masses to be felt by him—a feeling that *he* cares for *us,* which prompts the response that *we* care for *him.* This is inherently mysterious. Many of our presidents have not had this quality; but in a television age, those who do not have it are likely to run far greater risks than formerly. Mr. Reagan, in some way or fashion, had it, or a great deal of it. We need to try to understand how much, and why.

Just as a starter, let me offer you a couple of clues. I have asked myself why, in 1984, the *New York Times—even* the *New York Times—*ceased putting quotation marks around the nickname "Gipper" as applied to Ronald Reagan. I hypothesize that this was the long-term result of an assassination attempt that failed in the third month of his presidency, a moment the country watched in fascination. On that occasion Reagan's gallantry was tantamount to nature imitating art. Real life imitated the movies. Thereby, I suggest, the movies—first and foremost his—were virtually incorporated into reality. That having happened, those quotation marks have nowhere to go but off! So they did! Seriously, we need to understand much more about that process than I have seen anyone attempt to give us up until now.

Also—here is another clue—we need to understand what it means that Mr. Reagan voted five times for Franklin Roosevelt (the fifth time was in 1948), that he was a founding member of "Americans for Democratic Action," that what has been called his "populism" is a direct and natural feeling of good "New Deal" Democrats—working-class and middle-class—in the 1930s and 40s. I myself do not believe that charisma as experienced by Reagan is conceivable, nor is the Reagan phenomenon conceivable if one ignores the fact that he is a Republican who had been a believing Democrat as late as the Truman years.

One final puzzle needs to be explored. We were told by Gary Jacobson in his chapter that Republicans had great difficulty attracting candidates for Congress and that Democrats were knee-deep in them. That probably is so, but my anecdotal evidence rebuts it. From where I sit, back East, young people seem to have been mightily attracted to politics in Mr. Reagan's wake, and it is not because they took the lesson of his antigovernmental rhetoric. It is because they caught the body English of his old Democratic enjoyment of government. Among my former students, at this moment, there are at least a dozen young Republicans fanning out to their home districts to run for office. Indeed, the former student who most recently got to Congress also is Republican, from Iowa. He is too old to have been drawn to politics initially by Reagan, but he profited from the legitimation Reagan gave the acting profession, running his campaign off residuals from *Love Boat!* Is he, or are my younger students, narrowly ideological antigovernmental Republicans, eager for office as such? Not at all. These are youngsters much like many of their Democratic counterparts, who turned Republican as matters of family background, evolution, or convenience, or necessity in their own parts of the country, and whose liking for government in the concrete is pervasive, whatever they may say or feel about it in the abstract. Reagan is the only president the younger of them have experienced as adults—and they draw from him a zest for politics quite unlike that associated with Republicanism, at least since Teddy Roosevelt. How can that be—and why? Reagan assuredly is part of the answer.

So in all three of those respects, the political scientists among us have more work to do, these puzzles among others to resolve, or at least tackle. On that note, not a bad one, I am happy to conclude.

Index

Designed by Martha Farlow

Composed by The Composing Room of Michigan, Inc., in Rotation and Glypha display

Printed by R. R. Donnelley and Sons, Inc., on 50-lb. S. D. Warren's Cream White Sebago